Breaking Blue

The Themes, Thesis, and Colors of *Breaking Bad*

By Pearson Moore

Breaking Blue

The Themes, Thesis, and Colors of *Breaking Bad*

Covering all five seasons of Breaking Bad

By Pearson Moore

Featuring illustrations by
Martin Woutisseth
and
Michael Rainey

Breaking Blue
The Themes, Thesis, and Colors of *Breaking Bad*

Cover concept and design by Pearson Moore
Cover photograph copyright © Pearson Moore 2012
Cover titles and layout by Ludwig Design, Inc.
Periodic table illustration copyright © Pearson Moore 2013
Yellow nitrile gloves courtesy of I.S.A. Corporation, Salem, Oregon

Printed by Inukshuk Press

ISBN: 978-0-61-596030-2

To Jerome

Semper Fi

Table of the Elements

1 H 1.01							2 He 4.00
3 Li 6.94	4 Be 9.01	5 B 10.81	6 C 12.01	7 N 14.01	8 O 16.00	9 F 19.00	10 Ne 20.18
11 Na 22.99	12 Mg 24.31	13 Al 26.58	14 Si 28.09	15 P 30.97	16 S 32.07	17 Cl 35.45	18 Ar 39.95
19 K 39.10	20 Ca 40.08	31 Ga 69.72	32 Ge 72.61	33 As 74.92	34 Se 78.96	35 Br 79.50	36 Kr 83.80
37 Rb 85.47	38 Sr 87.62	49 In 114.82	50 Sn 118.71	51 Sb 121.76	52 Te 127.60	53 I 126.90	54 Xe 131.29

Table of Contents

Introduction to Breaking Blue

Breaking Bad Splash
Copyright 2012 Martin Woutisseth, used with permission

Marie is dressed in black.

Your eyes grow big and you lean in closer to the television screen. Marie never wears black. Something's up. *Something important is about to happen.*

Indeed. Marie, the character who always wears purple, who smothers her poor husband Hank in a house filled wall-to-wall with violet and lavender, never wears black.

Something very important is going to occur in the next few seconds. You pause the action, do an online search. "Aha!" You jab at the screen and turn to your friend, also a *Breaking Bad* fan. "Black means violence."

Your online source catalogs the many times Hank or a bad guy wears black, always accompanied by pistols or rifles or submachine guns drawn and ready. The fan site congratulates itself for recognizing good guys wear black too, but only when something nasty is going to happen.

You have goose bumps now, thrilled at the prospect of Marie Schrader wreaking havoc, pulling out a sidearm to show the bad guys who's boss. You and your friend sit down again. Your hand trembling, you jab the PLAY button on the remote.

Marie walks into the building. She summons the person she's looking for. They go to an office and talk. There is no yelling. No drama. They just talk.

"What?" Your friend turns to you, visibly upset. "I thought you said black means violence? Where is Marie's gun? What's going on here?"

Mystified, you stare at the screen and watch as two people have an orderly discussion. No guns. No threats. Definitely not the smallest bit of violence going on anywhere.

You consulted the online fan site because you know *Breaking Bad* uses color symbolism and you were hoping to extract more meaning from the scene. You were right to suspect that Marie's black blouse and slacks were significant. In fact, even though the fan site couldn't provide a useful and consistent meaning for Black, Marie's purposeful and very unusual color change clarifies the meaning of specific elements of the conversation, helping you put the scene into context and make better sense of the scenes that follow.

Now if you only knew what Black meant!

I believe this book can help.

Over the last two years I have spent 1200 hours analyzing the themes and color symbolism of *Breaking Bad*. I have put together a scheme that delivers a consistent understanding of the entire five seasons, from the mad gas mask ride in the RV to the final overhead shot of the makeshift laboratory. This book makes sense of motifs I have found explained nowhere else. An important example is Hank's mineral collection. My color-based analysis of the show's themes explains Hank's Season Four obsession with 'rocks' and shows how it symbolizes his character's major objectives. In fact, the central color themes of the show can be understood through Hank's minerals. I have sought out a clear explanation of Hank's hobby at dozens of websites, but not a single blogger has provided a satisfactory rationale for the DEA agent's fascination with rocks. I explain Hank's off-hours diversion in a way that sheds light on his approach to reeling in his arch-nemesis: Heisenberg.

This book will explain *exactly* why Marie was wearing black, and what it means to both characters in the pivotal scene in Season Five. By the time we arrive at that discussion, I will be able to mention the association briefly in passing because that's all you will need to understand. You will already have been fully grounded in the significance of the color and why it was particularly meaningful in Marie's case from our analysis of other scenes and from our understanding of Marie's personality. As you will learn, Black in *Breaking Bad* never means 'violence'.

Using this book as a guide, you will gain a deeper appreciation of *Breaking Bad*. My intention is to stimulate your own thinking about the show and to provide my view of what it all means, one color, one motif, and one theme at a time.

Getting It Right

"Wait a minute, Pearson," one of you says. "I read *Breaking White*, your introduction to *Breaking Bad*."

"I hope you enjoyed it."

"I did. It was fascinating! But you got it all wrong. After I read your book I watched an interview with Vince Gilligan. He said the color white means 'bland'. But you said something completely different in *Breaking White*. You got it wrong!"

"I appreciate your opinion. I stand on what I wrote."

Before your wide-open jaw makes you lose your balance, grab a chair and let's talk about Vince Gilligan's vision of the show he created.

I am not demonstrating audacity or disrespect when I say my understanding of *Breaking Bad* has as much merit as Vince Gilligan's. My comprehension of the show is not nearly as profound or as meaningful as his. He created it, he knows the characters, situations, symbolism, and themes better than anyone on this planet. But if you asked him, I think he would tell you it is *your* responsibility to make sense of it. He is not obliged to explain anything, and he probably won't.

My understanding of the meaning of white in *Breaking Bad* differs from Vince Gilligan's. Not only that, with utmost respect, I completely reject his understanding of the color. That probably sounds audacious or even maybe a bit arrogant, but that is not my intention, and I don't believe audacity figures into this at all. If it is true that each of us in our own way must make sense of a work of art, it follows that we are going to use different thought processes and pull on different bits of our own experience to serve as template or foundation for the conceptual structure we apply to a piece of art.

Breaking Bad is art, with intentionally embedded symbolism, metaphor, allusion, allegory, and all manner of recurring and interlocking motifs and themes. If I am honest with you, true to myself, and respectful of the *Breaking Bad* team's hard work, I will build my understanding in a consistent manner. I will resist the urge to take a liter of Vince Gilligan, a pinch of Aaron Paul, a half cup of Michelle MacLaren, and two drops of Adam Bernstein, mix it all up and pretend it's mine. If I did anything like that I would end up with a meaningless, aimless mish-mash that would help no one gain a better understanding of the show.

Imagine a conversation between two writers on the show, Simon Symbolist and Collin Colorist:

"White always means purity," Simon says. "When you see a character wearing a white blouse it means she's being true to herself, she's showing her character's purity."

"Wow." Collin sucks in his breath. "I never saw it that way. I always thought white meant being simple-minded, like a buffoon. You know: Walter White, out there in the desert, gun pointing out at no one in particular, wearing nothing but his white underwear. He was like a circus clown—and the white underwear symbolized that."

Everyone on the cast and crew will have at least a slightly different take on the meaning of *Breaking Bad*. In some cases, you will find writers or directors diametrically opposed in their explanations of a color motif or character motivation. That is normal, it's honest, and it's also one of the factors making it more difficult for ordinary viewers like you and me to bring light to the rich complexity of the show.

By now you ought to realize I make no claims that this analysis 'gets it right'. In fact, I am biased to believe that there is no such thing as a 'right' way of looking at *Breaking Bad*, or any other piece of art for that matter. A few fans of my first novel, *Cartier's Ring*, told me the story is a romance. Now, my first thought was to say it is absolutely not a romance. I didn't write the novel that way, it was never my intention to create an enduring love interest for the protagonist, and I studiously avoided elements of the romance genre. But my opinion doesn't matter. A few people see *Cartier's Ring* as a romance and that's the reality of it for them. My understanding carries no more merit than theirs.

As you continue reading you will see historical examples of art analysis and criticism, one of which was portrayed in *Breaking Bad* itself: a discussion of Georgia O'Keeffe's 'vagina' paintings. As you will learn, our independent analysis of art is something *Breaking Bad* upholds as a virtue. You will appreciate at least two profound reasons supporting the contention that your interpretation of *Breaking Bad* carries just as much weight as Vince Gilligan's or anyone else's.

LOST Humanity, published in 2011

11

But why read *this* interpretation of *Breaking Bad?* What makes this book special? In the end, only you can answer that question. But there is historical precedent for the belief that this book might be useful to you. My weekly blogs on the ABC television series *Lost* were read by hundreds of thousands of fans worldwide. They were translated into French, Spanish, Polish, and Russian—not by me, but by fans. I was bombarded with emails and Facebook messages demanding that I collect my essays into a book, and that's what I did. *LOST Humanity* quickly became a bestseller. Within a couple of months, the ebook version had outsold every other ebook on *Lost; LOST Humanity* remains the #1 bestselling ebook ever published about the series, and paperback sales are steady even four years after the show ended its run. There's no guarantee, then, but there's a better than even chance that you will find this volume useful to your appreciation of *Breaking Bad.*

Epiphanies in Shards and Smoke

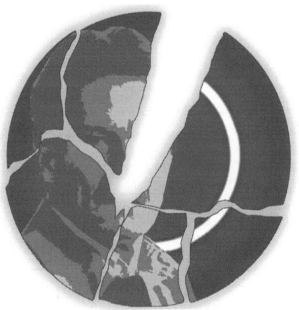

"The Yellow Plate"
Copyright Michael Rainey 2012, used with permission

"The universe is trying to tell me something."

We will hear similar words only a few times in the five-year run of the series. They will be uttered at odd moments, given breath by dejected characters, entering our awareness not so much through our senses as through the central core of our consciousness.

Breaking Bad is morality play on a scale rarely attempted. The primal sense that the Universe has structure and priority and value will come to the fore at unpredictable moments during the show. For me, one of those eerie moments was at the table in Jesse Pinkman's kitchen, when Walter White focused all of his intellect and emotion on the broken shards of a yellow ceramic plate. A utensil which no longer served its purpose, discarded as worthless trash, suddenly carried such value as to become the most meaningful item in Walter's world. He would see in the jagged, ill-fitting pieces a set of instructions calling upon him to make a crucial decision about the priorities he would apply to his life.

Many such "aha" moments occur in the series. Some will experience the smoke from Hank Schrader's Cuban cigar as an epiphany. Others will see in Gustavo Fring's pressed yellow button-down service shirt an electrifying statement of the unyielding tension holding the characters in their places, forcing them into confrontation, demanding an irrevocable exercise of volition. We sense in these scenes a plan, an objective—some force of nature that compels us to take a stand based on precepts we accept.

Some of us will construct from the yellow shards of broken ceramic a set of precepts incongruent with the unyielding tension and final destiny of the universe. Walter White, we will come to realize, is one of those whose arrangement of fragmented pieces will bring him into fundamental opposition with that destiny. But he is not the only one who will manufacture untenable hierarchies of misplaced value. During the course of *Breaking Bad* many characters—even some we initially believe to have a sound philosophy of life—will render decisions unacceptable to society, to the laws of the State of New Mexico, or to their relationships with family and friends.

Breaking It Down

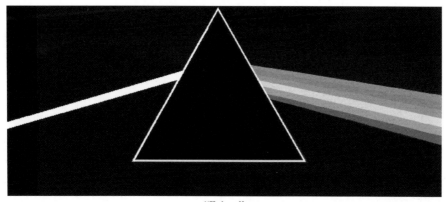

"Prism"
Pearson Moore 2012

13

To 'Break Bad' means 'to go wild, get crazy, let loose, forget all your cares … have a great time, break out of your mold.' It can also mean "To challenge convention, defy authority … to skirt the edge of the law." (Urban Dictionary, 2006-2011). When I say 'Breaking Blue', though, I am using the word 'breaking' in a different sense, more along the lines of an intense, open-ended discussion. To 'break a story,' for instance, means to brainstorm the plot and structure of a novel, play, or movie. The phrase is used by writers to describe the process of taking a basic concept or bare-bones plot and turning it into an interesting, dramatic, conflict-drenched story. In a sense we are 'breaking down' *Breaking Bad*, but we are doing it with the intention of rebuilding the story, 'breaking the story' so that we can understand it according to the terms we apply.

'Breaking Blue' refers to an intense process through which we examine, discuss, and debate the symbolic, dramatic, and plot-related significance of Blue and all of the other important colors in the *Breaking Bad* Universe. We engage in this close discussion neither as writers nor as viewers. I consider that an unengaged observer or viewer lacks the emotional connection and intellectual immersion necessary to understand *Breaking Bad* at multiple levels. Only those who go to the next level, who become **viewer-participants**, who become part of the story, are able to appreciate *Breaking Bad* to the fullest extent possible.

I contend that Blue is the visual statement of *Breaking Bad*'s thesis; 'Breaking Blue', then, refers to an attempt to dig into and understand the core of *Breaking Bad* philosophy, themes, and symbols.

We Are All Criminals

Breaking Bad appeals at many levels. The show not only incorporates heavy symbolism at every turn, but it turns symbols upside down and inside out, it approaches metaphor within metaphor. Good guys do bad things that result in unexpected boons to peripheral players. Bad guys sometimes do good things for entirely unselfish reasons. Legality, morality, motivation and virtue are juxtaposed and mixed and melded into situations that force us to re-examine our own values, to re-think our priorities.

Consider, for example, this truth: Everyone reading these words is a criminal. Yes, **you**, not the person sitting next to you. You are a criminal who has made choices that endanger women and men. You have put children at risk. You regularly court the possibility of severe fines and penalties, and jail time. If you are lucky your criminality will not result in suffering or bloodshed. But these destructive actions do eventually result in misery and horrible, grisly deaths. Yet you persist in your criminal behavior. You justify it. You embrace it.

Breaking Bad never addresses the fact that 99% of drivers in the United States exceed the speed limit by an average of seven miles per hour, as I did in the paragraph above. But it confronts other equally sobering truths about the way we choose to live our lives, and does so in an unapologetic, in-your-face manner that ought to repulse, but only attracts.

Breaking Bad is enormously entertaining, masterfully conceived and executed serialized storytelling of the highest order. I am not alone in considering it one of the best series on television, but I have special reasons for considering it so.

For one thing, I am a chemist. I've taught high school chemistry. Not only that, but my deepest area of expertise is in crystallization, and my broadest region of expertise includes the efficient extraction and purification of high-value chemicals from biological sources. I have been doing this type of work since the mid-1970s. If I were interested in manufacturing methamphetamine, I have the expertise to create a product every bit as pure as Walter White's. If I wished, I could isolate deadly ricin or any other highly toxic material, and I could quickly and easily create delivery systems for efficient ingestion. I know how to poison people and how to turn a dead body into unrecognizable glop. I am about the same age as Walter White, with similar background and pre-Heisenberg credentials.

I appreciate *Breaking Bad*, then, as a technical 'insider', and this close knowledge of the scientific side of the show has resulted mostly in my admiration. *Breaking Bad* takes no shortcuts, makes no excuses, and adheres in most ways to an intellectually authentic vision of science as it is actually done. That is not to say that everything portrayed on the show is scientifically or technically correct. In particular, as you might have guessed, you should definitely not try to cook methamphetamine according to the *Breaking Bad* formula. You'll only create a mess.

My fluency in the technical aspects of the production only contributes to my awareness and enjoyment of the artistic aspects of the show. Chemistry is developed into the primary metaphor for Walter White's descent into moral depravity, but chemistry and science themselves are never sullied.

Consequences, Change, Conflict

What is the nature of the *Breaking Bad* universe? Does consequence follow action inevitably in always-predictable fashion? Does an outcome depend on the inputs to the situation, with the calculus of retribution tied to so many variables that we cannot foresee the effect our actions will have in the world? Or is the world constructed in some other way, with constraints of cause and effect we have not imagined in our daily decisions and debates?

We will experience over five seasons innumerable instances of consequences. We will spy on characters as they devise simple plans, well engineered to account for every contingency, thought out to the smallest detail and possibility, that will nevertheless fail through unintended, under-appreciated, or unconsidered complications.

"If there's a larger lesson to 'Breaking Bad,' it's that actions have consequences." (Vince Gilligan, New York Times interview, 10 July 2011) Often the outcome is unforeseen, despite the best-laid plans, and the result is black comedy of the most stinging and delicious and hilarious nature. Occasionally a well-considered action results in intentional or unpredicted anguish, misery, and death. Judgment will, at times, literally rain down from the heavens. "I feel some sort of need for biblical atonement, or justice, or something," Gilligan said. "I like to believe there is some comeuppance, that karma kicks in at some point, even if it takes years or decades to happen." (Vince Gilligan, New York Times interview, 10 July 2011)

We need not authorize moral *carte blanche*, for any character. "Journalists … will say to me, 'How are we supposed to like [Walter]?' And I say, 'Are you supposed to? Where's the rule that says you're supposed to follow some edict?' All the rules are broken, you can go anywhere." (Bryan Cranston, interview on hypable.com, 18 October 2012) We don't have to dance around our feelings about characters, equip them with excuses or alibis, or try to rationalize any of their actions. "Vince Gilligan … believes his main character…meth dealer Walter White, should go straight to hell." (Martin Miller, Los Angeles Times, 1 September 2012) Each of us has license, then, to think anything our consciences tell us we should feel about each character.

The extreme circumstances imposed by radical change and pursuit of extraordinary personal gain will bring about unusual, morally challenging events and create strange bedfellows. This is demonstrated in many of the close relationships between main characters, the most obvious being Walter White's complicated ties to his DEA brother-in-law, Hank Schrader. But irony and topsy-turvy ethics will play out in almost every relationship and are intentionally built into the conflict-ridden fabric of the show.

In particular, *Breaking Bad* achieves something rarely portrayed on television or in cinema: credible family relationships. For reasons I will discuss later in this book, families are usually the first aspect of reality excised from any fictional characterization of human life. *Breaking Bad*, though, relishes the situational, emotional, psychological, and storytelling complexity imposed by the realistic demands of family interaction. As a writer and storyteller myself, I appreciate this insistence on the unabashed confrontation of messy, real-life scenarios. Neither hero nor villain operates in a vacuum in *Breaking Bad*. Family is not only important, but it is the center of every major event of the series. "La familia es todo," as one character will say. This kind of storytelling is rare, not because it is in any way irrelevant, but because it requires the most expert implementation of the storytelling arts. Quite simply, most authors are not up to the mind-numbing rigors of realistic storytelling focusing on multiple players with conflicting and ongoing agendas. In *Breaking Bad* we are witnesses and privileged participants in the rarest of cinematic creations.

How To Use This Book

My objective in this book is to pose questions and to stimulate thought. I will discuss ideas I believe relevant to the *enjoyment* of *Breaking Bad*. There are no truths in these pages. I do not possess insider knowledge regarding Vince Gilligan's intentions, Anna Gunn's artistic interpretations, or scholarly positions on *Breaking Bad* concepts or symbols. I hope you will consider every statement in this book as a starting point for your own contemplation of the television series. You are not obliged to believe as I do. You are not required to construct arguments as I have, or to prioritize ideas and enumerate symbolic interactions as I do. In fact, I hope many of you disagree. Without diversity of opinion and insight there is no basis for discussion. Art is meant to be discussed, weighed, considered, and re-evaluated.

Period 1	1 H 1.01							2 He 4.00
Period 2	3 Li 6.94	4 Be 9.01	5 B 10.81	6 C 12.01	7 N 14.01	8 O 16.00	9 F 19.00	10 Ne 20.18
Period 3	11 Na 22.99	12 Mg 24.31	13 Al 26.58	14 Si 28.09	15 P 30.97	16 S 32.07	17 Cl 35.45	18 Ar 39.95
Period 4	19 K 39.10	20 Ca 40.08	31 Ga 69.72	32 Ge 72.61	33 As 74.92	34 Se 78.96	35 Br 79.50	36 Kr 83.80
Period 5	37 Rb 85.47	38 Sr 87.62	49 In 114.82	50 Sn 118.71	51 Sb 121.76	52 Te 127.60	53 I 126.90	54 Xe 131.29

Periodic Table of the Elements for *Breaking Blue*
Excluding the Transition Elements
Pearson Moore 2012, PD

Breaking Blue is arranged according to the elements of the periodic table. Scientists and those readers familiar with the periodic table of the elements will observe that the *Breaking Blue* table excludes the transition elements. This is because in the *Breaking Blue* scheme each period of the periodic table corresponds to one season of *Breaking Bad*. Since each season (except the first) will have no more than eight chapters, we won't need the transition elements.

The table format may seem a bit odd, but there is precedent. Dmitri Mendeleev's second periodic table in 1871 used a similar scheme.

Mendeleev's Periodic Table of 1871

	I R_2O	II RO	III R_2O_3	IV RH_4 RO_2	V RH_3 $R_2O.$	VI RH_2 RO_3	VII RH $R_2O.$	VIII RO_4
1	H 1							
2	Li 7	Be 9.4	B 11	C 12	N 14	O 16	F 19	
3	Na 23	Mg 24	Al 27.3	Si 28	P 31	S 32	Cl 35.5	
4	K 39	Ca 40	? 44	Ti 48	V 51	Cr 52	Mn 55	Fe, Co, Ni, Cu 56, 59, 59, 63
5	Cu 63	Zn 65	? 68	? 72	As 75	Se 78	Br 80	
6	Rb 85	Sr 87	? Yt 88	Zr 90	Nb 94	Mo 96	? 100	Ru, Rh. Pd, Ag 104, 104, 106, 108
7	Ag 108	Cd 112	In 113	Sn 118	Sb 122	Te 125	I 127	
8	Cs 133	Ba 137	? Di 138	? Ce 140	?	?	?	?, ?, ?, ?
9	?	?	?	?	?	?	?	
10	?	?	? Er 178	?? La 180	Ta 182	W 184	?	Os, Ir, Pt, Au 195, 197, 198, 199
11	Au 199	Hg 200	Tl 204	Pb 207	Bi 208	?	?	
12	?	?	?	Th 231	?	U 240	?	

Periodic Table of the Elements
Dmitri Mendeleev, 1871

You will gain the most from the discussion in *Breaking Blue* if you watch a full season of the show before reading the corresponding period in the book. The first prologue ("Walter") discusses mostly the first episode, but the second prologue ("White") refers to important scenes as late as Episode 1.05. By the time you reach Chapter H you will see references to events as late as Episode 1.07. Similarly, in

Chapter Li (the first chapter in Period Two) you should expect to find discussion of events as late as the end of Season Two. I mention a few events from third season in Chapter Ne, but the real analysis of Season Three begins in Period Three with Chapter Na.

Careful readers will note that the first chapter after the second prologue is Chapter H (for hydrogen, the first element), but this entry is not followed by Chapter He, which is the next element in the period table. Instead, Chapter H is followed by Chapter D.

There is no Element D in any periodic table of the elements, but I have used sound scientific reasoning to include this chapter immediately following Chapter H. The rationale takes into account concepts critical to our discussion of *Breaking Bad*. To understand my thinking you will need to read the book. I invite you now to begin the adventure of *Breaking Blue*.

"Walter White"
Copyright Michael Rainey 2012, used with permission

Prologue I

Mr. Chips becomes Scarface.

In almost every interview he has granted, this is the phrase Vince Gilligan has employed to describe the character arc, and the primary focus, of *Breaking Bad*. An ordinary fellow, a doting father and beloved high school teacher, is transformed before our eyes into the most despicable and vicious of criminals, a modern-day embodiment of evil.

If these four words accurately described the totality of *Breaking Bad* we would have no reason to marvel at the thoughts and emotions effervescing in our minds. There are aspects of *Breaking Bad* that go beyond the raw dramatic power of the scenes, the tour-de-force acting by talented actors, and the extraordinary voyage into the heart of the despicable and the damned. The most important elements of *Breaking Bad* are those that evade our immediate perception, that lurk in the background of our conscious selves, that burst forth not as logical assessments of character or plot, but as emotional revelations of primal identity.

At some point in the series we are repulsed by Walter White. We hold out hope for his redemption, for an episode or a season or three seasons. But at some point, the hope and charity and good will in our hearts are displaced by pragmatism—or heartfelt demands for tempered justice or untempered retribution. Some composers and artists beg that we withhold judgment. There are no such entreaties from the creators of *Breaking Bad*. Vince Gilligan "believes his main character, high school chemistry teacher turned meth dealer Walter White, should go straight to hell." (Martin Miller, Los Angeles Times, 1 Sep 2012) We are given *carte blanche* to act as judge and jury in approving or condemning the actions and essential core of the characters in *Breaking Bad*.

But if this were our only means of interacting with the characters, nothing would distinguish Walter White and Tuco Salamanca and Gustavo Fring from the cardboard cut-out characters in the boring-as-hell procedural dramas that are a blight on 21ˢᵗ century television. *Breaking Bad* is not a 60-episode-long whodunit. It is not even a whydunit. Discerning the motivations of Walter White is integral to the enjoyment of the show, but personal rationale is not the central question of the series.

The primal center of *Breaking Bad* is not Walter White, but our personal reaction to him. At some point in the series, all of us will become united in our disgust and absolute contempt for Walter White. But the most interesting aspect of the drama is that we will arrive at this point in different ways, with unique sets of unconscious circumstances and considerations weighing on our conscious decision to consign him to the dark folds of our scorn and disdain.

The brilliance of Vince Gilligan's creation, though, is not that it arouses our righteous indignation, or that it stirs in us a sense of justice or a desire to see karma run its course. If this were the only objective, we could satisfy the urge with any courtroom drama or testosterone-filled action-adventure movie of the 1980s.

Every one of us will paint a different portrait of Walter White. The colors and lines and features we use to paint this portrait depend not so much on the facets of the character on the screen, and not to any particular isolated notion we have regarding a facet of his personality. More than anything, our personal and widely varying concepts of good and evil, humanity and integrity, and identity as responsible human beings will have direct bearing on our assessment of Walter. But these aspects of thought and disposition are not evoked in series or in a vacuum. Rather, *Breaking Bad* forces simultaneous consideration of several distinct but inter-connected thoughts and emotions. The grandeur of *Breaking Bad* is found in the **multiplicity** of ways it forces personal connection with us, the audience-participants.

That *Breaking Bad* creates multi-dimensional characters and a fascinating fictional world places it among the better dramas of 21ˢᵗ century television. That the series accomplishes all this and also drives our emotions and compels our unreserved intellectual and personal participation places the show at the pinnacle of artistic creation. Some of the most discerning and hard-to-please television and pop culture critics consider *Breaking Bad* the most meaningful series ever to have appeared on television. It achieves this distinction because it appeals to us in rare and profound ways.

The focal point of our enchantment is the character we will love to hate: Walter Hartwell White. If we are to arrive at a deeper appreciation of our feelings and thoughts about this man, we will have to devote some time to understanding his origins, his motivations, and the personal and social constructions that define him as a unique individual. I believe that in order to do this properly we are going to have to move beyond the four-word description of his character arc. In fact, I believe we are going to have to discard the notion that a complete or even adequate portrait of Walter White begins with a consideration of Mr. Chips. Two other characters from 1930s literature are essential to our understanding of Walter White, and if we truly wish to unveil the man's complexity, I believe we need to reach back all the way to mid-19ᵗʰ century New York City, to a chill night in October, 1858, when a frail, sickly child was delivered into the world. But let us begin with a closer look at Walter White.

Walter Hartwell White

I am not going to catalog here every one of the characteristics of Walter White. My objective in this first of two prologue essays is to identify what we might call the "origins" of Walter White—those aspects of his character that informed his lifestyle and life choices prior to his decision to break bad. Facets of his identity that move beyond his character arc and impinge on plot trajectory, such as Walter's vocation of chemistry teacher and the deeper meaning of his surname, are important enough that they will receive their own essays and will not be developed here. In the case of Walter's last name, for instance, the word 'White' is not merely a surname, but also a color that in itself is an important motif in the story.

Man Suppressed

The script for the second scene of the pilot episode specified that Walter was dressed in tans and browns—colors intentionally chosen for their blandness, such that he would blend into the browns, pastel greens, and beiges of the dining room and kitchen. Bryan Cranston grew a moustache and thinned it out so it looked like a "dead caterpillar." Cranston's intention was to make Walter White appear as "impotent" as possible.

Walter White is man emasculated. He is less than he should be, less than he could be, held captive by and subordinate to forces we cannot know with certainty. Rather than "wearing the pants" and leading the family as father, he has become the subordinate parent, neither the head of the family nor even an equal partner to his hard-charging wife, Skyler. The importance of this point to the story is impressed on us in the second scene after the opening flash-forward in the pilot episode.

Skyler: [Placing in front of Walter a plate of eggs and artificial bacon] Happy birthday!
Walter: [Disappointed or surprised] Look at that.
Skyler: *That* is veggie bacon, believe it or not. Zero cholesterol and you won't even taste the difference. What time do you think you'll be home?
Walter: Same time.
Skyler: I don't want 'em dicking you around tonight. You get paid 'til five, you work 'til five, no later.

In the space of just 32 seconds we learn from this dialog one of the most important truths about Walter White: he is ruled by his wife. She decides what he will have for breakfast, and she even decides whether he will enjoy it or not. She decides how long he will work and precisely when he will return home. If there is a problem at work, she, not Walter, lays down the law.

More importantly, though, we learn that Skyler is not the only person pushing Walter around. We understand from the context of Skyler's words that Walter's employers at the car wash have been habitually "dicking him around," a phrase rich with meaning, especially in the stifling atmosphere of the Whites' breakfast table on the morning of Walter's 50th birthday.

As important as these first few seconds are to our assessment of Walter, the events of the next minute are even more important, for it is in this crucial moment that we learn Walter could choose to behave in a very different way.

Skyler: [To Junior] You're late … again.

Junior: There was no hot water, *again*.

Skyler: I have an easy fix for that: You wake up early and then you get to be the first person in the shower.

Junior: I have an idea: Buy a new hot water heater. How's that idea, for the millionth, millionth time.

"Flynn"
Copyright Martin Woutisseth 2011, used with permission

Junior is behaving as a normal, slightly rebellious teenager, but more important to our analysis of Walter White, he is demonstrating the possibility of standing up to Skyler and her dictates. This brief interaction demonstrates that Walter does not have to acquiesce. He could assert himself and his needs and desires if he wished. For some reason or set of reasons, though, he has chosen to cave.

Junior: [Examining the artificial bacon] What *the hell* is this?
Skyler: [Expressing parental disapproval] Hey!
Walter: Veggie bacon. We're watching our cholesterol … I guess.
Junior: Not me. I want real bacon, not this fake crap.
Skyler: Too bad. Eat it.
Junior: Phew. This smells like Band-Aids.
Skyler: Eat. It.
Junior: [Makes a face at Skyler]
Skyler: [Makes a face back]
Junior: [Looks away and sighs, disgusted with his mother but finally accepting her authority]

Bacon was not an arbitrary choice in this scene. Bacon carries symbolic significance with devastating importance to Walter's standing as father, husband, and provider.

First of all, notice again that Junior is pushing back against Skyler's rules. In fact, he asserts that his desire is more important than her fiat: "Not me. I want real bacon, not this fake crap." The contrast with Walter's nearly unspoken acquiescence to the presence of artificial food on his plate is striking. But because the food under discussion is bacon, Junior is symbolically doing much more than underscoring Walter's status as emasculated lackey to his wife.

A provider is one who "brings home the bacon." We are to understand that in his rejection of "fake crap" Junior is not speaking only for himself, but for masculine propriety in general. He was forcefully directing our attention to the incongruity—to the subversion of masculine prerogative—exemplified by a *woman's* decision to replace real bacon (symbolically, the value that a man brings to his family) with artificial bacon. Symbolically, Skyler was asserting that Walter was not the provider for their family.

A real man works hard, and by the sweat of his brow, brings home the bacon. He brings home not only the resources that provide the necessities of life, but the spice of life, the little extra things that make family life pleasurable. One of those extras is bacon.

Vince Gilligan grew up in Richmond, Virginia. While hogs are not a major livestock item on Virginia farms, they are plentiful just across the border in North Carolina. In fact, North Carolina is the second largest producer of hogs after Iowa, and the residents of Virginia are major consumers of North Carolina pork. I am not privy to Vince Gilligan's home life as a child, but I know that he and his closest friends would have been quite familiar with pork as an essential component of Virginia culture. As

Azrael, a Jewish resident of the Southern United States noted, "Sorry guys, as much as I love ya, I'm going to have to be a lapsed Jew. A breakfast without bacon is like a day without air down here in Dixie." (Contributor Azrael, found at http://littlegreenfootballs.com/article/6425_Love_Letter_from_London/comments/, April 30, 2003) Or as Glenn from Dallas noted, "A breakfast without bacon is like kissing your sister: It's just not right." (Glenn/Dallas, http://dallasdigestforum.com/, 26 June 2010.)

Hogs and Pigs Inventory 2002

1 Dot = 15,000 hogs and pigs.
U.S. total is 64,405,103 hogs and pigs.
[Source: U.S. Department of Agriculture, Economic Research Service,
based on data from National Agricultural Statistics Service.]

I point out these cultural facts about bacon because while I don't know the cultural status of bacon in Albuquerque, I am somewhat conversant with Southern tradition, and I know the culture of Dixie had significant bearing on Vince Gilligan's early life. I don't know that Gilligan consciously chose bacon as the focal point of the first two minutes of *Breaking Bad*, but the symbolic import of this common breakfast food seems not only obvious, but a natural extrapolation from Gilligan's personal experience.

The fact that Skyler could trump a man's real bacon and substitute for it a woman's artificial bacon means that Walter was not truly a provider. He was not truly a man. He was not truly a father. When Junior used words considered inappropriate, it was Skyler, not Walter, who called him on his unseemly language. As Bogdan Wolynetz, Walter's boss, would later say, it is Skyler, not Walter, who "wears the pants" in the White family.

Just as the choice of bacon as focal point in the breakfast scene was not accidental or arbitrary, so too the placement of "dicking around" in Skyler's ultimatum was not the result of unexamined fiat. "Dicking around" in the immediate context of Skyler's instructions meant to mistreat, to play with someone, to force someone to do things they do not wish to do. However, in the greater context of the breakfast scene, we are not out of line if we connect the verb 'to dick' to the noun 'dick,' which is the most common slang term for penis. Approached from this point of view, we could understand that when Skyler said Walter should not allow his employers to continue "dicking [him] around" she meant Walter (who is not a real man because he does not bring home the bacon) should not allow himself to be pushed around by real men (who aggressively dicked him around). Or to the crux of the harsh symbolic significance of Skyler's words, Walter, who symbolically lacks a dick should not allow himself to be pushed around by real men who have dicks.

It's a Cruel World After All

We are given a few well-placed indications that something more than Walter's decision to live in impotence may be at play in this drama. At 18:42 in the pilot episode Walter acknowledges the condition that is causing his coughing fits and physical weakness: Inoperable Stage 3A lung cancer. "Best case scenario, with chemo, I'll live maybe another couple of years." Immediately following the scene in the doctor's office Skyler confronts him with another encroachment of the cruel world into their middle class reality.

Skyler: Did you use the Mastercard last month? Ah, $15.88 at Staples?
Walter: Um … oh, we needed printer paper.
Skyler: Walt, the Mastercard's the one we *don't* use.
Walter: Okay.
Skyler: So, how was your day?
Walter: [Having just received news he will soon die] Oh, well, you know … I don't know … it was … fine. [smiles]

Walter may be the victim of forces over which he has no control. Even though he is not a smoker, and it is unlikely that exposure to chemicals impinged on his health, nevertheless he has contracted a rare, aggressive case of nonsmoker lung cancer. In addition, even though Walter does not seem to have spent extravagantly (his choice of a Pontiac Aztek is probably meant not only as a sign of poor taste, but also as an indication of obsessive frugality), he owns at least one credit card that is causing some degree of financial distress for the family.

I don't want to downplay the importance of cruel fate or undeserved destiny to the greater story of *Breaking Bad*, but I wish to defer a discussion of social forces and "acts of God" to later chapters in this book. Fate has not been kind to Walter White, but rather than attempting an analysis of forces beyond human control, I want to concentrate on Walter's reaction to his diagnosis and the place he occupies in the world.

The Rape of Kitty Dukakis

Walter's reaction to his diagnosis is not only unusual, it is unsettling. He has just been told that he has inoperable cancer. If he agrees to the most aggressive treatment regime possible he might live another two years. Even if he does live, though, he will be barely conscious for most of that time. Through unending cycles of chemotherapy, radiation, nausea, weakness, vomiting, hair loss, susceptibility to sudden infection, he will hardly be living a life anyone would consider normal or even tolerable. He will have to subject himself to unending misery to eek out a few months of suffering before he finally succumbs. He should be angry, or sad, or desperate, or at the end of his ability to process intellectually. Instead, he sits calmly, absorbs the news with about as much emotion as we might expect from someone who has just heard the weather report for a land far away.

Governor Michael Dukakis
Copyright 1988 Hal O'Brien, CC-SA 3.0

There is precedent for such a stunning lack of emotional response. During the 1988 presidential campaign, the Democratic Party nominee, Michael Dukakis, was seen by many as a wooden, emotionally detached man not fit to govern. In the first debate of the campaign, Bernard Shaw, then the CNN prime time news anchor, articulated one of the most famous questions ever put to a presidential candidate:

Bernard Shaw: Governor, if Kitty Dukakis [Gov. Dukakis' wife] were raped and murdered, would you favor an irrevocable death penalty for the killer?

Gov. Dukakis: No, I don't, Bernard, and I think you know I've opposed the death penalty during all of my life … ah … I don't see any evidence that it's a deterrent and I think there are better and more effective ways to deal with violent crime. We've done so in my own state and it's one of the reasons why we have had the biggest drop in crime in any industrial state in America …

It is a common belief that people listen not so much for what is said but the way in which it is said. This was certainly true of popular reaction to Governor Dukakis' response to the rape question. The question itself should have struck him as offensive, unfair, and not worthy of dignified response. He should have been shocked that anyone would pose such a question. Instead, he responded with less emotion than one would expect from the HAL 9000. No one wanted a robot sitting in the Oval Office; Dukakis' wooden, insensitive, *inhuman* response to this question is cited as one of the main reasons for his defeat in November, 1988.

I am going to return in later essays to a deeper discussion of Walter's lack of emotion. But Walter's disconcerting emotional detachment is only one of the unsettling features of this passage in the pilot episode. We also have to grapple with his decision to withhold vital information from the person presumably closer to him than anyone else in the world: his wife, Skyler White.

The Separation of Church and State

We see from the very beginning of *Breaking Bad* that Walter White maintains an impenetrable wall not only around his emotions but around any feature of his life he might consider personal. At this early point in the series I serve no one by providing my take on Walter's psychological state and the underlying scientific reasons for his strange, inhuman behavior. But we can discuss the ramifications of his withdrawal.

First, we need to understand that Walter's decision to withhold from Skyler his diagnosis of terminal cancer was not a choice many married couples would consider to fall in the range of personal discretion. Walter was morally obliged to inform his wife of his condition because her legal, financial, and emotional wellbeing would be irrevocably affected by his slow death due to disease. It is precisely in situations such as these that a married person ceases to have personal autonomy. The marriage contract Walter voluntarily signed sixteen or seventeen years ago stipulated exactly this concession of freedom as a condition of married life.

Walter will insist throughout the remainder of the series on the justifiable beneficence of maintaining a rigid wall of separation between his personal, criminal endeavors and his public, family life. It will become the White family's "separation of church and state."

Regardless of the psychological determinants of his mental state, Walter somehow has the ability to rationalize the withholding of personal information, even when he is under moral or ethical obligation to share his knowledge. This ability has immediate bearing on the story, especially regarding his decision to keep his illegal activities secret from everyone. Vince Gilligan is not the first writer to develop a protagonist with the ability to live in a world he holds secret from everyone around him. Several of Walter's character traits are found in earlier works of fiction. I feel our understanding of Walter will benefit from a brief examination of three of these literary predecessors, all of them drawn from the interwar period of the 1930s.

Mr. Chips

Goodbye Mr. Chips is a 1934 novel by James Hilton, perhaps best known for his story of Shangri La in the novel *Lost Horizon*. Probably few people, though, can identify the protagonist of Lost Horizon, Hugh Conway, while the name 'Mr. Chips' has so permeated modern culture that most everyone can recite the essential facets of the fictional man's character.

Charles Edward Chipping, Mr. Chips, was a failure in the classroom until he met the person who changed his entire outlook on life, Katherine Bridges. Katherine instilled in Mr. Chips a sense of humor and fundamentally converted him from the hapless stick-in-the-mud he had been. Thanks to Katherine, Mr. Chips was able to relate to his students in ways no other teacher could.

Goodbye Mr. Chips is not so much the portrait of a teacher as it is the examination of an extraordinarily empathetic human being. His greatest demonstrations of level-headed compassion and charm occur not in the classroom, but in ordinary life. He is depicted as possessing not only empathy, but a courage of heart unique in his world, conditioned not by culture or society, but by the dictates of fundamental humanity. In one of the most moving passages of the novel, Mr. Chips publicly recites the names of fallen alumni of Brookfield who had only recently died in the First World War. To the astonishment of almost everyone present, he includes in his recitation the name of a former German colleague who had died fighting in the Kaiser's army.

We see already that Mr. Chips' life moved in quite a different direction from the route pursued by Walter White. But the influences on Mr. Chips were very different, too. The foremost influence in his life, his wife Katherine, allowed him to become more of a man than he had been prior to her interventions. This positive effect is exactly the opposite of Skyler's influence on Walter's life. We also see in the life of Mr. Chips no "separation of church and state" between his personal and public behavior. Mr. Chips is an open book, not a top-secret vault.

It is for these and related reasons that I believe we need to move beyond Charles Chipping to more completely appreciate Walter White. I believe two other 1930s characters, from works by philosophically opposed authors, must be considered if we have any hope of understanding the true origins of Walter White.

The Secret Life of Walter Mitty

The Secret Life of Walter Mitty, a 1939 novel by James Thurber, is probably more familiar in its later incarnation as a Danny Kaye movie of the same name, released in 1947. The name Walter Mitty is synonymous with the idea of an incapable person who daydreams of himself in heroic roles, or an individual who tries to pass himself off as someone he is not.

In Thurber's novel, Walter Mitty has five daydreams while driving his wife into town to go shopping and have her hair done at the beauty salon. He dreams of being a Navy pilot, a brilliant surgeon, a conniving assassin, a Royal Air Force pilot volunteering for a suicide mission, and finally that same pilot standing before a firing squad.

Like Walter White, Walter Mitty is married to a domineering wife who imposes her will on her husband with the expectation that he will accept her dictates without question. Like the later Walter, Thurber's protagonist erects a firm, thick wall between public life with his wife and the private world of his daydreams.

Walter Mitty is much closer in character and behavior to Walter White than the more frequently invoked Mr. Chips. In fact, it seems to me unlikely that Vince Gilligan created the character of Walter White without direct reference to Walter Mitty.

Danny Kaye in *The Secret Life of Walter Mitty*
Unknown artist, publicity trailer, 1947, PD

We recognize two important differences immediately. The first is that Walter Mitty's flights of fancy contain none of the darkness associated with Walter White's embrace of criminal and immoral activity. Walter Mitty inhabits his secret world not as a criminal but as a hero whose exploits would be celebrated by everyone. Walter White's secret activities, on the other hand, would serve as just cause for imprisonment or execution.

Second, Walter Mitty's life is unexceptional—we might even say boring. Walter White's life is about as far from boring as one could imagine. Doomed to die in a year or two, a surprise baby on the way, and no resources to pay for any of the treatment regimes he might undergo, Walter White would love to have even one boring option. Instead, any choice he could reasonably make is fraught with uncertainty, pain, and death.

There is a 1930s fictional character who flirted with danger and death, whose range of life choices never included boring options, and whose story exuded only darkness and psychological pain. I believe *The Short Happy Life of Francis Macomber* is the most natural starting point for a contemplation of the origins of Walter White.

Ernest Hemingway's Francis Macomber

Ernest Hemingway considered himself among the "Lost Generation" (la génération perdue)—those of the age who had fought in the First World War, who bore the weight of the world on their shoulders without receiving their due. The world of Ernest Hemingway and Gertrude Stein abided neither by rhyme nor reason, and the human inability to contend with fickle nature is on full display in their literary style, called modernism.

Ernest Hemingway, Paris, 1924, Unknown photographer, 1924, PD

In Hemingway's short story, "The Short Happy Life of Francis Macomber," the titular protagonist is outwardly strong but inside fully a coward, similar in many ways to Walter White. He struggles with nature, in the form of the wild beasts of Africa, and fails to win the early battles. He collects a lion trophy only because of the intervention of his guide, Robert Wilson. Bagging the lion is the proof of manhood, and just as Walter White failed to "bring home the bacon," Francis Macomber failed to get the lion. Francis, like Walter, is being "dicked around," especially by Wilson, the guide, who is sleeping with Francis' wife. Like Skyler, Francis' wife, Margot, rules over him and prevents the full expression of his masculine nature. Margot seems almost a force of nature herself, which for Hemingway means she must inevitably win any confrontation involving Francis.

The climax of the story has Francis finally standing his ground against a charging buffalo, shooting at it even as it comes within range of goring him. But just as he is about to enjoy the crown of full manhood, his wife, from the distant car, shoots—presumably at the buffalo—and the bullet pierces Francis' skull. Francis dies on the spot.

Francis could never win, of course, because modernism denied tidy and happy outcomes.

These modernist ideas are important to our consideration of *Breaking Bad*. At some point we need to pose the question of accountability. Is Walter White alone to blame for his decision to break bad, or do we need to take into account social forces and "acts of God"? Hemingway would have us place the blame on nature itself, and the individual human being's twisted relationship with the world. Even when Francis Macomber finally found courage inside his bones, he was denied the victory to which he was entitled. Could it be that Walter White is likewise doomed, that even if he acted courageously the forces of cruel and primal nature would break and destroy him?

I will not offer my own response to this fundamental question—not yet, anyway. I do not hesitate out of deference to your sensibilities as viewer-participant, but rather out of my bias as a novelist. I believe we do a disservice to Vince Gilligan and his writing team, and ultimately therefore to ourselves, if we attempt to force *Breaking Bad* into the narrow confines of one literary style or another. I believe any attempt to categorize *Breaking Bad* as an example of existing thought systems is convenient but ultimately short-sighted and illegitimate. Convenient, because it sure is easy to treat a television show as a paint-by-numbers endeavor that fits into pre-existing literary templates. Illegitimate, because the driving force behind *Breaking Bad* cannot be the will to demonstrate the superiority of a thought system. *Breaking Bad* must stand on its own internal merits, and not be forced to stoop to someone else's way of interpreting Walter White.

What I do offer here is an alternative way of looking at the relationship between nature and humans, using precisely the same imagery invoked by Hemingway. The intention is to show that Hemingway's vision is not uniquely valid. We have license to apply any interpretive pattern we favor.

A Bull Moose's Victory

Ernest Hemingway knew of at least one man who had never run from a charging buffalo, or even a ferocious lion. Theodore Roosevelt was a man's man and a hero to every boy born between 1885 and 1910. The courageous colonel who had created the Rough Riders and led the charge on San Juan Hill (for which he was posthumously awarded the Congressional Medal of Honor), the take-no-prisoners President of the United States who "spoke softly but carried a big stick," the diplomat who won the Nobel Peace Prize, and the naturalist and big game hunter who always bagged his prey, Theodore Roosevelt proved himself time and again equal to any challenge.

What's more, Theodore Roosevelt was a self-made man, at every level of his being. Born underweight and frail, TR was diagnosed early with severe asthma. He was so weak doctors advised that he be kept at home and not allowed to mingle with other children. He should be given at least a fighting chance of making it through childhood, though most believed he would die before his teenage years.

As soon as Roosevelt could think, he forced himself into a strict and exhausting routine of physical exercise. "Make your own body," he told himself, and through an unyielding regime of vigorous exercise and outdoor living, he transformed himself from dying invalid to arguably the most robust man of his generation. He climbed mountains, hiked in rain and snow, and generally confronted any obstacle with zeal.

Roosevelt's robust physique was not the stuff of fanciful tales, but hard reality. On October 14, 1912, Roosevelt was campaigning in Milwaukee, Wisconsin. Exiting his car to enter the arena where he was to speak, he was confronted by John Schrank, who fired his revolver at point plank range into Roosevelt's chest. The Bull Moose refused medical treatment. He went into Milwaukee Auditorium and gave a speech lasting 80 minutes. He did finally agree to medical treatment after the speech, but he didn't want the doctors fishing around in his chest. The bullet was never extracted from his body. He got a good night's sleep and continued campaigning the next day. Surviving a shot that would have killed most men, he suffered not much more than a momentary inconvenience to his campaign schedule.

Theodore Roosevelt
African Game Trails, 1910

Modernist Envy?

We know that Ernest Hemingway compared himself to Roosevelt, and found himself lacking. This is the biting poem Hemingway wrote shortly after TR's death in 1919:

Roosevelt
Workingmen believed
He busted trusts,
And put his picture in their windows.
"What he'd have done in France!" They said.
Perhaps he would—He could have died

Perhaps,
Though generals rarely die except in bed,
As he did finally.
And all the legends that he started in his life
Live on and prosper,
Unhampered now by his existence.

The final thought of the poem is clear: Roosevelt's legend was always bigger than the lesser reality of the man, and now that he was dead his legend would (unjustly) grow larger.

All of this is just so much sour grapes. If anything, the legend could never portray the full reality of Roosevelt, the man's man. But Hemingway was intent on proving the man false. When he planned his big game hunting trip in Africa—following the same trails Roosevelt had blazed 23 years before—he hired Philip Percival, the very same man who had guided Roosevelt.

Philip Percival was the template for Hemingway's fictional foil, Robert Wilson. But who was the template for Francis Macomber?

Hemingway was a hunter. He surely realized, though, even after a few days of tracking big game, that he was no Theodore Roosevelt. Perhaps he unfairly painted himself as the cowardly Francis Macomber. Roosevelt, after all, had never had to struggle with the bottle, as Hemingway did all his adult life. Roosevelt may have grown up under an excessively cautious mother, as Hemingway had, but Roosevelt's mother never dressed Theodore in girl's dresses, as Ernest's mother had.

Ernest Hemingway was a man of his time, but he was not a modern only because that was the artistic route to follow at the time. He was a modern in outlook because of his own upbringing and his very personal acquaintance with inner shortcomings and the failure to achieve the level of manhood he so desperately sought.

I think it is difficult not to see Hemingway as an unfortunate slave to unhappy destiny. But I think it is equally difficult to see Roosevelt as anything other than a self-made man who conquered every difficulty nature threw in his path.

The question we must ask ourselves is simple: Is Walter White more like Theodore Roosevelt, or more like Ernest Hemingway, or has he blazed an entirely new trail?

Gandhi spinning
Birla House, Mumbai, 1942
Unknown photographer, PD

Mohandas Gandhi On Homespun Cloth (called 'Khadi' in India)

If we have the 'khadi spirit' in us, we would surround ourselves with simplicity in every walk of life. The 'khadi spirit' means illimitable patience ... The 'khadi spirit' means also an equally illimitable faith … illimitable faith in truth and non-violence ultimately conquering every obstacle in our way. The 'khadi spirit' means fellow-feeling with every human being on earth. It means a complete renunciation of everything that is likely to harm our fellow creatures, and if we but cultivate that spirit amongst the millions of our countrymen, what a land this India of ours would be!

—Mohandas K. Gandhi, *Young India*, 22 September 1927

Prologue II

The color white can mean many things. For the Mahatma Gandhi, white was a potent political symbol which he wielded to great effect against his philosophical adversaries, the colonial authorities of Great Britain.

The image of Walter White wearing only a green shirt and "tighty-whitey" jockey underwear in the New Mexico desert is burned into our memories. We have the feeling that the white jockey briefs are meant to convey greater significance than that of a simple undergarment, but what is that significance?

Colors are strong motifs throughout *Breaking Bad*. They carry raw symbolic power intended to mold our thinking about characters and their actions. As with most motifs in *Breaking Bad*, however, the correspondence between symbol and the idea it expresses is never static. Good guys wear both black and white, and every color in between. Bad guys are as likely to wear pink and yellow as they are to vest themselves in blue or black. How do we discern symbolic meaning when the symbols themselves are constantly changing?

Many have attempted a color analysis of *Breaking Bad*. "Red is the color of violence," we are told by one self-appointed expert. "Pink is the color of death," another proclaims, after she views the final episode of Season Two. With all due respect to these wannabe authorities, I disagree with their assessment. If red always represents violence in *Breaking Bad*, when we see Junior wearing bright red boxer underwear are we to believe that he is a seething bundle of rage, just waiting for the opportunity to kill the next person who insults him?

The connection between colors and the ideas they represent is fluid, varying from situation to situation and from one character to another. Over the course of five years we will see Walter White wearing clothing of just about every hue and shade imaginable. Nevertheless, it is possible to discern certain dominant trends and such is my intention in this chapter.

The Gandhian Example

The Mahatma's Satyagraha Salt March in 1930 had as its final result the production of pure white salt, a symbol of India's determination to gain political and economic freedom from British overlords.

Great Father Gandhi on the Satyagraha Salt March
Unknown photographer, March, 1930, PD

Salt had political and economic significance at the time because Indians were legally bound to pay a salt tax to the British Empire. By walking to the sea with the intention of making salt and then using it without paying the tax, Gandhiji was breaking British colonial law.

We could certainly understand white salt to symbolize the purity of Indian aspirations toward independent statehood. My impression, after studying the saint's march, his declarations during that march, and independence movement activity around that time, is that salt was more than anything a symbol of Indian unity. In essence, salt became the Great Father's way of proclaiming that India was already a state, already independent at heart, and it remained only for the less-than-observant British to recognize the fact of Indian independence.

As important as salt was, though, I have to believe Gandhi's most effective political weapon was probably the homespun cloth (khadi) he made himself, spinning yarn on wheels he built, transforming the yarns into cloth he weaved on hand-made looms. He famously wore a single white covering, often referred to as a "loincloth" (though the garment covered him from navel to knee). Winston Churchill detested Gandhi, referring to him as a "half-naked fakir."

The symbolic essence of the Mahatma's "loincloth" becomes obvious after only a brief acquaintance with the saint's writing on the subject. In the Richard

38

Attenborough film biography, the Mahatma is depicted at a resistance rally, encouraging the hundreds of thousands listening to him to burn their British-made garments:

> English factories make the cloth–that makes our poverty. All those who wish to make the English see, bring me the cloth from Manchester and Leeds that you wear tonight, and we will light a fire that will be seen in Delhi–and London! And if, like me, you are left with only one piece of homespun–wear it with dignity!

I don't know that the final statement, "If, like me, you are left with only one piece of homespun—wear it with dignity" is an authentic quote, but in the end it doesn't matter. The words accurately convey Gandhi's thought about Indian-made cloth. Homespun, or 'khadi,' was again a symbol of Indian unity, but it also became a Gandhian symbol of Indian and human dignity. One could not feel dignified wearing clothing that enslaved its wearer, but one would feel the complete liberating weight of dignity in consciously deciding to wear garments made by friend and neighbor.

Walter's Essence

The Indian saint's loincloth and the meth manufacturer's jockey underwear are both white, both undergarments, both representative of something essential to the person.

Jesse: Those [Pointing to Walter's jockey underwear as Walter removes his green shirt] Wow. Those … ah … you're keepin' those on, right?
Walter [Turning to face Jesse, stares at him for a moment, sighs] Come on. [Enters the RV]

Walter won't take off the white jockey shorts. He seems disgusted that Jesse would even ask the question. But the question appears valid to us as viewer-participants, too. It is hard to imagine a less dignified image than that of a high school teacher in the New Mexico desert, stripping to his underwear so he can manufacture crystalline methamphetamine. The image is so incongruous, in fact, that we find ourselves laughing. *Breaking Bad* is categorized as "black comedy," after all, and this highly memorable scene is one of the first of hundreds that will have us chuckling or even rolling on the floor.

We can be certain that the "tighty-whiteys" do not represent Walter's dignity. He lost any semblance of dignity when he removed his shirt and slacks. He did not seem at all concerned about modesty. It is not difficult for me to imagine Walter White going skinny dipping with Skyler or perhaps even with college buddies. I really doubt that simple modesty played any role in his decision to retain the jockey shorts. The reality of cable television and its legal limitations might normally apply in our thinking, but only moments before in the pilot episode we were witness to a topless woman whose breasts were blurred out by editors. If it had been important that Walter remove his underwear, we can be sure the editors would have blurred out his nudity—or not.

We will see at least two scenes later in the series in which Walter's naked backside appears without any editorial blurring.

But Walter kept his underwear on throughout the remainder of the episode. The decision was conscious, and the imagery was intended to carry bold, symbolic significance. The white jockey underwear was intended to represent to us an essential aspect of Walter's character—something he would not surrender, even if he gave up his dignity and every shred of any other human quality we might believe him to possess. The white underwear, then, is symbolic of something Walter will not give up, no matter the situation or the personal cost to him.

What is the one essential aspect of Walter White's character that he refuses to give up?

Purity as Metaphor

We see intentionally chosen white garments in several situations throughout the series. In Season One, this choice is most evident in the meth manufacturing sequences. Both Walter and Jesse are depicted wearing white Tyvek clean room garments. This costume decision by the *Breaking Bad* production team is interesting for a number of reasons.

Seagate's Clean Room
Copyright 2008 Robert Scoble, CC-SA 2.0

First, garments of the type Walter and Jesse wear during meth synthesis are typically required only in the final stages of manufacture. Yet we see both characters wearing the suits during the entire synthesis routine. An amateur meth manufacturer would use any clothing he liked, but the idea here is that Walter White is no amateur meth manufacturer. He is applying fundamental chemical principles and top-flight technical expertise to the manufacture of high-purity drug product rivaling the quality of anything available through FDA-approved pharmaceutical processes.

The reality as I have experienced it is a bit different than what is portrayed onscreen. I have worked in the major types of pharmaceutical manufacture as consulting scientist or co-creator of processes. In the synthetic processes I have developed the full splash suits we see Walter and Jesse wearing are usually not specified until the penultimate and final steps of a process. The PPE (personal protective equipment) used in the early steps of a process would be determined by the safety concerns posed by the chemicals and the limitations of the manufacturing equipment. It is unlikely, indeed, that a pharmaceutical process would require hours-long respirator ("gas mask") usage; any such requirement would likely be due to the inadequacy of the manufacturing process. But I have collaborated in creating FDA-approved processes that require workers to wear respirators for the full eight or twelve hour shift, too, due to extraordinary process requirements that could not be relieved by practical manufacturing system upgrades.

The safety concerns in the penultimate and final steps of the process are superseded by product integrity concerns. Full Tyvek "space suits" are *de rigueur* even in final operations in which there is practically zero safety concern for the workers. The intention in the penultimate and final operations is to prevent even the slightest contamination of product, and the most likely source of contamination, by far, is the workers themselves. In early steps of the process a simple hairnet to keep hair out of the product may suffice, but in the final step the workers will wear a hairnet underneath the hood, and the entire face may be covered, not for worker protection, but to keep hair and even the smallest particle of dry skin out of the product.

My first impression on viewing these scenes, as a pharmaceutical chemist, is **overkill**. Walter and Jesse are wearing the wrong type of PPE at the wrong time. My first impression, as a hack writer with authority-level expertise in pharmaceutical process development, is that the clothing has been chosen not to demonstrate fidelity with pharmaceutical manufacturing norms, but to make a symbolic or metaphorical statement.

I am very comfortable coming to this conclusion regarding the rationale for putting Jesse and Walter in white Tyvek in Seasons One and Two. First of all, Vince Gilligan hired top-rate industry experts to advise him on the nitty-gritty technical details of pharmaceutical and methamphetamine manufacture. Second, a very intentional change in laboratory garment color was made later in the series for symbolic reasons. Third, as a writer, I know something about "how the sausage is made," and the tasty sausage we enjoy as viewer-participants is often delivered with heavy doses of flavor-enriched symbolism and metaphor, even if delivering that symbolism means we have to depart a bit from realism.

The cover of *Breaking Blue* provides an example of a storyteller's concession to symbolism. If I had wished to deliver a realistic portrayal of a pharmaceutical manufacturer holding a handful of blue methamphetamine I would have depicted a hand covered with a blue or purple 3-mil nitrile glove. These are the gloves used in industry, and they are the gloves faithfully portrayed in *Breaking Bad*. But I had to accomplish several artistic goals. The blue meth had to stand out as the focal point of the image, and that was virtually impossible if the glove holding the meth was also blue. Using instead a yellow nitrile glove (which was a major research undertaking—*I found only one manufacturer of yellow nitrile gloves in the world!*) made sense, because the yellow glove would also help me with a second objective, which was to emphasize the symbolic importance of the color yellow in *Breaking Bad*.

But I had two even greater objectives. Bringing attention to the blue meth as focal point was paramount because the final goal of this book is to reveal the symbolic importance and meaning of the color blue in *Breaking Bad*. Finally, the gloved hand, held in precisely the same way as the hand holding the two stones on the cover of *LOST Humanity* (my first book on the television series *Lost*), would project imagery I have been associating with my pen name, Pearson Moore. When readers see a hand held out this way on a book cover, I want them to think, "Oh, a Pearson Moore book."

Purity as Revelation of Self

"The Transfiguration"
Carl Heinrich Bloch, circa 1880

Many impressions pop through our heads when we see these men in their white clean room chemical suits: Professionalism, technical prowess, scientific excellence, manufacturing integrity—but probably the first thing that comes to mind is ***purity***.

Walter White's methamphetamine is beyond compare in quality and physiological effect because it is absolutely pure.

Jesse: This is glass grade … I mean you got … Jesus, you got crystals in here two inches three inches long. [Turning to Walter] This is pure glass.
Walter: [nods]
Jesse: You're a damn artist. This is art, Mr White.

Jesse says this in the pilot episode, when Walter is "cooking" in white jockey underwear and black apron. It is only in later episode that we see Walter in the full white Tyvek suit. Gilligan has thrown plenty of red herrings onto the path toward an understanding of the color white. "White is the color of vanilla, of blandness," he said during an interview in early 2011 (Interview by Mike Flaherty, Vulture.com, 16 May 2011). Walter frequently appears dressed only in his jockey underwear to serve as biting humor. In the introduction to Episode 1.04, for instance, Hank describes the unusual expertise of some new players in the meth market:

> Now, we don't know who they are or where they come from, but they possess an extremely high skill set. Personally, I'm thinkin' Albuquerque might just have a new kingpin.

As Hank is talking, the visual switches to Walter, dressed only in his white jockey shorts, brushing his teeth. How could someone so 'vanilla,' so *bland*, be "a new kingpin"? The idea is preposterous, and the juxtaposition of Hank's speech extoling the "high skill set" with Walter brushing his teeth in his underwear is high cinematic art.

But we know the color white does not mean 'bland,' and we know the virtue associated with Walter's jockey underwear is not "an extremely high skill set" in meth making. The metaphorical purity of Walter is not defined by his mastery of chemistry. "Actually it's just basic chemistry," Walter says in the pilot episode in response to Jesse's praise. "But thank you, Jesse, I'm glad it's acceptable."

If white does not mean 'bland' and it does not mean "extremely high skill set," what does it mean?

The Unbearable Grayness of Being

We receive another red herring (ah … *white* herring?) in Episode 1.05, "Gray Matter." Badger is dressed almost entirely in white. He juggles glass bottles in the RV, stuffs Cheetos up his nose, and generally behaves in a manner unbecoming. So is white perhaps the color of buffoonery? Wouldn't all of Walter's early appearances in white jockey underwear fit perfectly as symbolic representations of a competent man who has turned himself into a clown?

The image of Badger dressed in white, behaving as an undisciplined jester, ought to fit, but it does not. Jesse and Badger are, after all, best friends. We could easily imagine Jesse, a day or a week before meeting Walter White 'professionally,' behaving in the same childish manner as Badger. But something has changed inside Jesse.

"Wow," Badger says, in awe of Jesse's knowledge of chemical glassware, "you really know your shit." Jesse smiles and shrugs. "It's just basic chemistry," he says, parroting the words Walter used only days before. So the fact is, it's not "just basic chemistry." That Walter made meth of incomparable quality and Jesse knows (or *thinks* he knows) the proper technical terms for various types of glassware is not inconsequential. It is fundamental to Walter, and fundamental to Jesse.

White and black make gray. This is the basis for the multi-billion-dollar company Walter, Elliott, and Gretchen started some 20 years before. Walter's last name is White, Elliott's last name is Schwartz, which is German for *Black*. Thus, when they formed their company, the three founders (Walter White, *his* girlfriend Gretchen, and his friend Elliott Schwartz) named their entrepreneurial creation Gray Matter Technologies.

How do I know Gretchen was Walter's girlfriend (or possibly fiancée)? Look at the way they interact with each other in the introduction to Episode 1.03. Walter and Gretchen are not acquaintances. The way he touches her while they're talking, the close proximity of their bodies, the way they look at each other—they are more than friends.

Why would he give her up, to his best friend, no less? Why would he give up his share in the company, a company he founded with his own sweat through extraordinary technical abilities that led him to become "Contributor to Research Awarded the Nobel Prize"?—a company now worth billions of dollars? What could be worth so much to Walter White that he would forego a life of pampered luxury, a salary of millions of dollars per year? Why would he decide, in essence, that White could not be mixed with anything else, that he would not surrender White to become Gray?

At Elliott's birthday party (1.05) Skyler revealed Walter's diagnosis of terminal cancer. Elliott first offered Walter a job, "Yes, kind of like some fig leaf, you know, some face-saving bullshit that allowed me to generously accept his charity."

Skyler: Okay, what did you say? Walt?
Walter: What do you think I said?
Skyler: Why? Walt!

Walter did not respond to Skyler's question. We got our answer, though, moments later in the New Mexico desert, from Walter's protégé, Jesse Pinkman.

Purity and Prejudice

Jesse has spent a day and a half in the RV trying to synthesize meth meeting his new standards. He picks up a nearly perfect crystal with tweezers. His friend, Badger, marvels at the product.

Badger: You are a genius, bro. This [stuff] is unreal. When I get back I'm gonna burn that dollar bill … 'cause we're gonna make some mad dough!
Jesse: [Examining the crystal] It's not right. [He's upset]
Badger: What do you mean it's not right?
Jesse: It's … cloudy. It's not supposed to be cloudy, okay, that last time it was glass.

Badger: So what? Cloudy, not cloudy? It looks good enough to me!"

Jesse: [nods, sighs] "Good enough." [He picks up the tray of meth, goes out the door]

Badger: Yo! What are you doing?

Jesse: [walks eight steps away from the RV, throws the trayful of meth into the air.]

Badger: AGH!! Are you out of your mind? I totally would have smoked that!

Jesse: Look, it's not for you, it's for our customers. They're going to demand a certain standard.

Badger: WHAT?! What? What are you? WHAT?!

Jesse: We'll just do it again, until we get it right.

Jesse's customers are "going to demand a certain standard." The statement would have made more sense to Badger if Jesse had formed the words in Sanskrit, or Swahili. Badger was probably more discriminating that any of Jesse's potential customers. He had held a job and he was occasionally able to speak in full sentences that could be deciphered into some semblance of Standard English. But Jesse's words constituted the most insufferably obtuse declaration Badger had ever heard.

Jesse's customers have no 'standards.' As he will say later, in Episode 3.10, "We make poison for people who don't care." Even those among us who have never tried Jesse's product understand the appropriateness of Badger's response to Jesse's rationale for throwing out perfectly good product. Jesse's action would be stunning to any reasonable observer. We know there is absolutely no connection between the quality of Jesse's product and his customers' 'standards.'

It took Vince Gilligan five episodes to define the meaning of the single garment Walter White would never surrender. In the end, it was the character who is the moral center of the series who spelled it out for us:

Alright, look at it this way, okay. It's the bottom of the ninth, bases are loaded, you're up. But you got a bum arm, alright? There's no frickin' way you're gonna hit a homer, okay? So you can either let the *pinch hitter* take the bat, or you can hold onto your pride and lose the game. Get what I'm sayin'?

No one in the room understands Hank's baseball analogy—except us. The 'pinch hitter', the guy who will step in for Walter, is Elliott Schwartz. Hank means to say Walter doesn't have the financial resources to win against cancer, so he should allow Elliott Schwartz to pay for his treatment.

You got your pride, man. I get it. Okay, I get it. But if Daddy Warbucks wants to chip in, man, I'm with your old lady on this one. I say take the money and run, man.

All things considered, with Walter's responsibilities as father, husband, and high school chemistry teacher, his priorities are out of line, Hank is saying. Pride is important. But pride is not the most important element in a well-lived life.

Hank discovered the essential core of Walter, the aspect of his brother in law's inner self that he will not surrender, never compromise (never allow White to be compromised into Gray), never remove from his person even when he has given up everything else that others may consider essential to life as a fully expressed human being.

White, in Breaking Bad, is symbolic of PRIDE.

This may not be true for other characters, but it is true for Walter White. Pride is so important to Walter that he was willing to give up his girlfriend, give up his company, give up the opportunity to enjoy a life on Easy Street—and now, two decades later, he is willing to give up his very life rather than surrender his pride.

Walter didn't remove his white jockey shorts during that first day of cooking because it symbolized the core value motivating every choice he has ever made in his life.

Some will say he is entitled. Give me liberty or give me death. Live free or die. Didn't Walter's ancestors fight a war with Great Britain over these very ideas? Isn't pride the greatest of virtues which a fully alive human being might jealously guard in daily life, as a matter of principle, as possibly the supreme expression of human life?

Jesse: Tell me why you're doing this, seriously.
Walter: Why do you do it?
Jesse: Money, mainly.
Walter: There you go. [Walks away]
Jesse: Naw. Come on, man. Some straight like you, giant stick up his ass, all of a sudden age—what? Sixty? He's just gonna break bad?
Walter: I'm fifty.
Jesse: It's weird, is all, okay. It doesn't compute. Listen, if you've gone crazy or something, I mean, if you've gone crazy—or depressed—I'm just sayin' that's something I need to know about, okay? I mean, that affects me.
Walter: I am awake.

Indeed. Walter is awake, maybe for the first time in his life. Even if he did end up surrendering his pride in little ways after he gave up Gray Matter, he will never do so again. Not even in little ways. Walter White is fully awake. He will wield his pride as the most lethal weapon ever depicted on a television series. Eventually all of his philosophical adversaries will fall to the power of his symbolic weapon—unless, of course, there is in the *Breaking Bad* universe a symbolic virtue of greater power than pride. Is there, after all, a more important element in a well-lived life?

¹₁Higit School
Chemistry Teacher

"Michael Faraday's Christmas Lecture"
Alexander Blaikley, circa 1856

"The chemistry must be respected."

Walter White might have uttered this declaration anytime during Season One, but the words did not actually depart his lips until Season Three (3.05). *Breaking Bad* certainly "respects the chemistry" both literally and figuratively. The show has elevated chemistry to become the metaphorical backbone of the show, and accomplished this without requiring any knowledge of chemistry on the part of viewer-participants.

'Chemistry' and 'Teacher' are essential themes in *Breaking Bad*, and we will frequently return to these ideas in later chapters. Walter's formal classroom lectures are placed low on his daily priority list, but he is methodical and conscientious in his approach to mentoring Jesse, and their teacher-student relationship will only grow in importance in coming seasons.

If chemistry acts as the storyteller's center, and if the student-teacher relationship is the concept that places characters in proper relation to each other, the idea of 'high school' is foundational to Walter's character and the decision he makes to break bad. Understanding the connection between Walter's vocation and the trigger events and conditions is important to our deeper enjoyment of *Breaking Bad*.

I will touch on all three concepts (chemistry, teacher, high school) in this essay, with particular emphasis on chemistry. I will address chemistry as a technical discipline, to be sure (I am a professional chemist, after all!), but I will devote the bulk of this chapter to an examination of chemistry's importance to Walter's personal life and the manner in which he prioritizes his thoughts, actions, and time.

Chemistry 101: Observation

Walter White's first chemistry lesson (1.01) was not much different from the first lesson many of us received in high school.

Chemistry—it is the study of … what? Anyone?
Chemistry is—well, technically, chemistry is the study of matter. But I prefer to see it as the study of change. Now just think about this. Electrons, they change their energy levels. Molecules: molecules change their bonds. Elements: they combine and change into compounds. Well, that's all of life, right?

Envisioning chemistry as the study of change is the natural bias of *Breaking Bad*. Walter White, after all, must eventually be transformed from Mr. Chips (or Walter Mitty or Francis Macomber) into Scarface. But designating chemistry as the study of change makes sense from a practical, technical point of view, too. My first chemistry teacher, Frederick P. Buechler, impressed this point upon our class by giving each student a candle and a box of matches for our first lesson. "Record your observations about these two objects, but be sure you record only observations, not conclusions." Now, you wouldn't think that the observation of a candle flame could be all that interesting, but you'd be wrong.

Mr. Buechler: Stand up and tell the class your observations about the two objects.
Student: When we lit the wick, the candle started burning.
Mr. Buechler: You 'lit the wick'? How?
Student: With the match.
Mr. Buechler: [Takes an unlit match from the box, touches it to the candle wick. Nothing happens] Like that?
Student: [Laughing] No, the match was lit.

Mr. Buechler: 'Lit'?

Student: I mean the match was burning.

Mr. Buechler: What does 'burning' mean?

Student: [Confers with another student, faces front, smiling] It was oxidizing.

Mr. Buechler: Oh ho! Oxidizing. Do you mean the cellulose of the match was reacting with molecular oxygen from the atmosphere, leading to the sustained generation of light energy and the production of carbon dioxide and water through oxidation?

Student: [Frowning, perplexed] Yeah, I guess.

Mr. Buechler: No, sorry. Those are conclusions, not observations. Now, if you had told me you struck the match head on the side of the box, you **saw** flames, you **heard** a sizzling noise, you **smelled** a sulphurous odor, you **felt** heat from the flame—**those** are observations.

"Sherlock Holmes"
D. H. Friston, 1887

49

The two hours Mr. Buechler devoted to the study of a candle were the most important two hours of my career as a chemist. Good chemists, Mr. Buechler taught us, are first of all good observers. As chemists, though, we have a natural bias in terms of wishing to observe, record, and make sense of *changes* in matter, just as Walter White told us in his first lesson. A red liquid in a bottle and a blue liquid in a bottle are somewhat interesting, and we can characterize the physical properties of these two liquids, but in doing so we could be physicists or even psychologists, not necessarily chemists. But if we start with a red liquid in a bottle, do something to it (turn it upside down, heat it, pass it through sand, add a few crystals of something, or shake it—or whatever) and the color changes to blue, we are much more interested because change is what we enjoy observing (studying) as chemists.

Observation is important to us as viewer-participants, too. The extent to which we make observations, rather than injecting our conclusions (personal biases) into what we see and hear transpire on the screen, determines our ability to gather enough information to make sense of the show. At some point we will have to render judgment—we will have to make conclusions—but the longer we can make observations rather than formulate conclusions, the more we will become aware of important contributing factors to our analysis.

Thus, in the previous chapter I could have just started the essay by saying "The color white in *Breaking Bad* symbolizes pride," but in so doing I would have biased your analysis of data. You would have been searching for ways that a particular scene indicated pride, rather than considering the placement and interaction of elements within a scene and the full range of possible meanings. By delaying the statement until the end of the chapter, I invited you to make wide-ranging observations and come to your own conclusions. Quite likely you decided that the color white means something else—the comic unsuitability of a character's mindset in a given situation, perhaps, or the fundamental aspect of the character's inner self, or some other idea entirely. Any of those are fine, and I hope as you read these essays you will consider the ideas I bring to the fore as mere examples of ways to consider the show's deeper meaning. My analysis is not "right" or "better" than anyone else's examination of *Breaking Bad*.

The Meaning of Life

Walter White concluded his first chemistry lecture with a thought that will resonate throughout the five years of *Breaking Bad*. We know the words are important because they appear in the very first episode. Walter is addressing us directly:

[Chemistry] is all of life, right? It's the constant, it's the cycle, it's solution, dissolution, just over and over and over. It is growth, then decay, then transformation. It is fascinating, really.

So that there would be no confusion in our minds regarding the significance of Walter's statement, he made his understanding of the meaning of life clear in Episode 1.03, when his then-girlfriend, Gretchen, recited the molar quantities of each element making up the human body and Walter recorded them on the blackboard.

"Chemist Comedy, Mixed with a Bit of Island Humor"
Pearson Moore 2012

It was an interesting exercise in many ways. We think of life as being carbon-based, but as Gretchen's analysis showed, the human body contains far more hydrogen and oxygen atoms than it does carbon atoms. This, of course, is because humans are primarily composed of water, as Walter noted in passing ("Oxygen 26 [percent]—there you have your water"). Carbon makes up only nine percent of the human body, on a molar (number of atoms) basis.

The happy couple continued their analysis all the way through the trace elements, "down where the magic happens."

Walter: So, the whole thing adds up to 99.888042%. We are
                 0.111958 percent shy.
Gretchen: Supposedly that's everything.
Walter: Yeah?
Gretchen: Uh-huh.
Walter: I don't know. I just … I just … just seems like
                 something's missing, doesn't it? There's got to be more to a human
                 being than that.

Episode 1.03 advanced the plot in significant ways, but it also reached into Walter to reveal one of the most important facts about his belief system. All of this was accomplished in the context of an extended meditation on the meaning of human life. It was in this episode that Walter had to decide whether to kill Krazy-8 or allow him to go free.

Walter's academic discussion with Gretchen regarding the nature of human life was juxtaposed with the nausea-inducing scene in which Jesse and Walter mopped, sponged, and squeegeed the liquid remains of Emilio Koyama into the toilet. Perhaps there was more to human life than hydrogen, oxygen, carbon, nitrogen, phosphorus, calcium, and sodium, but these are precisely the materials we saw Walter dump into the toilet. The repulsive scene made clear that nothing more than simple chemical compounds form the human body. The juxtaposition made clear the deeper truth that something much greater was at stake.

Walter wanted to believe there's more. "[It] just seems like something's missing, doesn't it?" His academic struggles took on life-and-death significance as he looked into the eyes of Krazy-8 and sought a reason to keep the young man alive. He agonized over the pros and cons of ending the life of his prisoner. Maybe to his surprise, he discovered several good reasons to spare Krazy-8's life. Among the many reasons Walter recorded on the Let Him Live side of the ledger:

It's the moral thing to do.
Judeo/Christian principles
You are not a murderer.
Sanctity of life—
Won't be able to live with yourself
Post-traumatic stress
Murder is wrong

The single entry on the Kill Him side of the ledger was striking and persuasive:

He'll kill your entire family if you let him go.

"Osiris Judging the Human Heart"
Unknown artist, the Papyrus of Hunefer, circa 1375 B.C.

The cold calculus associated with this analysis seemed clear: Walter was obliged to kill Krazy-8.

The conclusion must have been clear to Walter, too, even if the thought of what he had to do was unthinkably disgusting. That he hesitated meant he was considering other possibilities. Perhaps he contemplated the possibility that human life cannot be quantified, that there is more to life than chemistry. He brought up moral concerns, after all, but what did these concerns really mean to him?

I think Walter was truly struggling with the morality of his decision. I believe in some way, perhaps unconsciously, he was attaching more than chemical significance to the human life he contemplated snuffing out.

But I believe in the end he appealed to the scientific part of his mind to render the final verdict on Krazy-8's fate. The scientist would ask about the validity of conclusions. Perhaps, Walter might have thought, his conclusion was based on inadequate observation. Had his incomplete understanding of criminal life led him to jump to conclusions about what Krazy-8 would do to his family?

So Walter gathered more data. The fascinating aspect of his slow walk down to the basement is that his subconscious feeling that there was a spiritual value to human life was probably much stronger than the relatively feeble sense that he had inadequate information to render an informed decision. His conscience was weighing more heavily on his heart than his scientific self was weighing on his intellect, but he must have taken some degree of comfort in believing that he was merely gathering data for a particularly important experiment.

What he found in the course of his data collection is that Krazy-8 had a heart. He had a family, he cultivated wide-ranging interests, and he'd even studied at university. He was the son of a respected member of the community. He was well spoken, well studied, and calm in his bearing. Even if Walter had no hard data, everything about Krazy-8's civilized discourse and reasoned disposition appealed directly to Walter's moral sense. Walter decided the non-scientific evidence of the heart could not be denied. With a sense of resignation, then, and perhaps a good measure of relief, he returned upstairs to retrieve the key that would give Krazy-8 his freedom.

I think this was a critical point for Walter White. Possibly for the first time in his life he was allowing feeling, intuition, and conscience to guide a major life choice—in this case the decision to let Krazy-8 go free. If he had not thought to retrieve the broken ceramic plate from the trash, his life might have turned out quite differently. He might have made ethics the first consideration in any future decision. He might have been a happier man.

But Walter scooped up the pieces of the plate and put them together, and in that moment the full weight and unwavering constancy of the universe came crashing into his conscious awareness. Krazy-8 would, indeed, kill Walter's entire family.

The Universe

Walter had been willing to suspend and subsume to human compassion every scientific and logical lesson he had learned in his life. He had consented to surrender his intellect to his heart. Now, with the cold scientific evidence before him, in the brutal dishonesty of the missing shard, Walter's scientific training was vindicated, his worst fears confirmed. The Universe, Walter concluded, was communicating to him what his intellect had been telling him all along: You cannot trust Krazy-8. If you allow the psychopath to go free he will kill your entire family.

With Walter, I had the overwhelming sense in this scene that some unalterable aspect of life was intruding into Walter's interaction with the young meth distributor. But I think my perception of the unyielding nature of the Universe differed significantly from Walter's. I did not understand Walter's destiny to have been determined at that moment, but rather three days earlier, when he had made the decision to break bad. It was that earlier decision that forced Walter into the unpleasant Catch-22 predicament of choosing between his family's life and Krazy-8's life.

Even at that moment, though, staring at the broken pieces of ceramic plate on Jesse's kitchen table, Walter had more than two options. He could have gone to the police with his story. He could have fled with his family. He could have gone into business with Krazy-8, as he later did with Tuco.

I believe we need to understand the significance of this moment to Walter. He believed the Universe was confirming what he had believed all along: Human science and logic are the final judges of human value. As we learned in Episode 1.03, Walter had believed this all his life:

Walter: Just … doesn't it seem like something is missing?
Gretchen: What about the soul?
Walter: [Turns to look at Gretchen, laughs, walks toward her]   The soul? [Brings his face to within three inches of hers]   There's nothing but chemistry here.

The body language of Walter's last words to Gretchen in the university classroom indicated the double entendre: Chemistry referred to the material reality of the human body but also to the sexual attraction between Walter and Gretchen. More importantly, though, it confirmed any lack of spiritual sentiment in Walter's outlook. The human body was composed of chemical elements and sexual feeling, nothing more.

But juxtaposition was again used to tell us that the question was not settled in Walter's mind. As he sat in his car thinking on those words uttered 20 or more years in the past, he must have been wondering what had caused him to give up Gretchen. He was at a disadvantage here, in that he had to factor in the complexities of his relationship with the woman before and after their human body discussion in the empty classroom. Thanks to selective editing, we viewer-participants suffer no such limitations. The guiding force of Walter's life, his deference to the law of logic, was the aspect of his character that drove him away from Gretchen. She, in her open-minded appeal to Walter's spiritual essence, was willing to forgive his lack of spiritual self-knowledge. Walter, on the other hand, had to leave her, because he could not subscribe to any notion of spirituality. The fact that Walter was portrayed sitting in his car, meditating on the long-ago incident in the university classroom, can only mean that even though Walter doesn't realize it himself, he still is, in some sense, a spiritual being and not the collection of chemical elements and compounds he has believed all his life.

We will hear of this unseen character, The Universe, at critical moments in the next several seasons. For now, we may believe that chemistry stands outside of or subordinate to the overwhelming features of the unseen character. The genius of Vince Gilligan, though, is that he is going to bring chemistry back into the fold before the end of this series. All of it will make sense, even if now we must struggle with so many plot threads and character traits and trends and developments that we find ourselves confused. The descent of Walter White is clear. The reasons for his descent, and the symbolism attached to his fall, seem shrouded in dense mystery.

Some will say that Walter is a disciple of particular philosophical positions. Walter is a materialist, we are told. The problem with statements like this is that they give short shrift to scenes such as the one at the end of Episode 1.03, depicting Walter in a decidedly non-materialist contemplative state of mind. But the greater problem with the willy-nilly application of inadequate generalizations is that they are going to fall short of the full truth. By the end of the series it will not be pride or materialism *per se* that leads to the downfall of Walter White.

Walter's blindness to the full reality of human life and his determination to surrender his heart to his intellect prevented him from understanding what the Universe was telling him in the broken plate. We need to be better scientists than Walter. We need to refuse to ascribe his behavior to paradigms and theories and other black-and-white academic categories, because all of them will prove inadequate. Let us resolve to be good scientists. Let us observe and not arrive at hasty conclusions. Let's allow Walter to be Walter—or Heisenberg—and see where he takes us.

Science Teacher

"The chemistry must be respected."

"Bill Nye the Science Guy"
U.S. Dept. of Education, #ThankATeacher, 2012, PD

The words are spoken from a position of authority and they constitute excellent advice from chemistry teacher to pupil or protégé. Walter told Jesse to put Emilio's body into a polyethylene container. Jesse used ordinary logic to figure out that a solid porcelain bathtub must be superior in all ways to a flimsy blue plastic container. If hydrofluoric acid could "chemically disincorporate" a human body, what would it do to a thin plastic bin from a department store?

We witnessed the result of Jesse's 'logic' when the bathtub and floor underneath gave way to the inexorable corrosive power of hydrofluoric acid—used for over a century to etch glass, steel, ceramic, and yes, porcelain.

As an aside, for any would-be disincorporators out there, hydrofluoric acid is likely to violently incapacitate, render unconscious, cause permanent acute injury, and ultimately kill anyone attempting to use it in this manner. It is very unlikely to render and disincorporate any mammalian body—at least in the way depicted on the television show. There are cheap, effective, 100 percent chemical means of turning dead bodies into untraceable masses of gelatinized goop, but *Breaking Bad* isn't divulging that information, and I'm not, either. Likewise with the production of methamphetamine. If you pay close attention in the later episodes you will be able to discern a formula for the synthesis of methamphetamine. Good luck trying to apply it, though. You will end up with a useless mess if you attempt to duplicate Walter's Blue Sky formula.

A chemical reaction that *Breaking Bad* doesn't intentionally misrepresent is the thermite reaction:

$$Fe_2O_3 + 2\,Al \rightarrow 2\,Fe + Al_2O_3$$

The reaction unleashes torrents of light, heat, and sputtering, splattering gobs of molten, 4570 °F liquid metal, exactly as portrayed in the methylamine robbery sequence. In fact, the sputtering and splattering can be more severe than depicted, even with small amounts of thermite, and there's no way to stop the reaction. Water is worse than useless in a thermite fire, because spraying it on the burning material will only spread it around. Even sand would just turn into molten rock in the presence of thermite. There is a humorous video on Youtube in which a British television version of Mythbusters attempts to put out a thermite fire with liquid nitrogen, which will put out most any fire—but not a thermite reaction. The only thing accomplished by dousing with liquid nitrogen was to spread the red-hot liquid metal into a huge radius around the container.

Walter teaches this and many other lessons useful to practitioners of the illicit arts. As we saw in Episode 1.05, Jesse was a faithful journeyman, even rejecting good product because it did not rise to his mentor's uncompromising standards.

High School Teacher

The ineffectual, disrespected, underpaid and under-appreciated high school teacher is a common caricature in modern culture, and it is at times a largely accurate portrait. Walter White had to be someone ready to break bad; making him an underpaid high school chemistry teacher working a second job was a credible way of achieving this storytelling goal.

Teaching does not have to carry the negative connotations we have chosen to assign to it in our culture. My experience of teaching was very different from Walter White's, even though I taught at precisely the same grade level, following an almost identical syllabus, to teens the same age as those in Walter's class. The difference was culture. Whenever I entered the classroom the students stood at attention and addressed me not even by my surname, but only as "Sir" (actually "Monsieur," since we were in a French-speaking country). If any of my students were in town sitting with friends when I walked by, they would stand and face me out of respect for my position as a "professeur des sciences physiques." Those of my colleagues who were native West Africans were shown perhaps even greater respect, since their students knew that these women and men had overcome extreme adversity to become professeurs. But regardless of our ethnicity or origin, we were respected, even revered, because of our decision to apply our technical expertise to the teaching of children.

There is no longer any such reverence of teachers in Western cultures. We need to keep this cultural fact in mind as we explore Walter's life and decisions. We should also factor in the sad fact that he was obliged to take a second job just to make ends meet, and that his health insurance was inadequate to the financial challenge of providing suitable cancer treatment. *Breaking Bad* is calling our attention to the deplorable, truly inexcusable fact that healthcare in the United States is sub-par, far lower than the quality one can expect in any other developed country in the world. Upholding the virtue of capitalism in the realm of healthcare is arguably the most important factor in the diminished economic capacity of the country.

I leave it to viewer-participants to decide the importance of cultural and socio-economic factors in Walter's proclamation that he is "awake"—that is, that he has made a free decision, unencumbered by any cultural, social, or familial consideration, to break bad. Is he truly free, or is he slave to forces beyond his control?

One factor we must include in our calculus is the fact that he is a teacher by choice. He could have remained an entrepreneur, but he made a personal decision to withdraw from the company he co-founded. He knew teachers are paid less than scientists in other professions. Though I served as a chemistry and physics teacher in the Peace Corps in Togo, West Africa, when I returned to the United States I didn't even consider a career in teaching. I got into industry as quickly as I could, established myself as a researcher, and worked my way up the technical ladder to the highest scientific rungs. In the last few years I have consistently earned three or four times the salary I would have been paid as an experienced teacher. Walter understood the disparity in compensation as well as I do, but he chose to teach.

Chemistry as Metaphor

"Respect the chemistry." Chemistry is more than a technical discipline. When Walter utters those three words, in Season Three, he is instructing us. But since we know 'chemistry' refers to something greater than subject matter in a lecture hall, we know we are being told to respect something of far greater importance. I have a sense of this greater entity after taking in four and a half seasons of the series, but it is my own personal impression. At this early point in the series—only five or six episodes in—I don't want to paint a full picture. Instead, I want to invite you to look around on your own. When chemistry is invoked as a focal point in an episode, what is really being said?

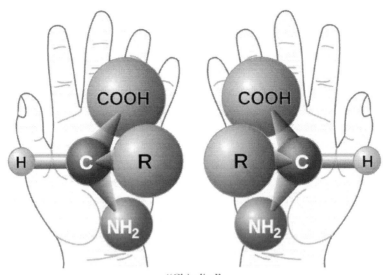

"Chirality"
National Aeronautics and Space Administration, 2011, PD

For instance, in Episode 1.02, Walter explains the idea of chirality. It's a bit advanced for the second day of 11th grade chemistry, but Walter has simplified quite a bit.

> Chiral—from the Greek word *hand* [χὲρι]. Now the concept here being that just as your left hand and your right hand are mirror images of one another … identical and yet opposite—well, so too, organic compounds can exist as mirror image forms of one another all the way down to the molecular level.

> Although they may look the same, they don't always behave the same. For instance, thalidomide. The right-handed isomer of the drug thalidomide is a perfectly fine, good medicine to give to a pregnant woman to prevent morning sickness. But make the mistake of giving that same pregnant woman the left-handed isomer … and her child will be born with horrible birth defects.

> Mirror images. Active, inactive. Good, bad.

Pursuing chemistry as metaphor, we know the stereoisomers under discussion here are not thalidomide, but the far more dangerous substance known as Walter White—who before the end of Season One will be known as the truly lethal entity, Heisenberg.

But what does 'chirality' mean in reference to Walter? Is he one isomer or the other, or a dangerous, misleading mixture of both the right-handed (good, moral) and left-handed (bad or 'sinister', immoral) stereoisomers? In *Breaking Bad*, has he turned from some right-handed, good side of his nature toward a pre-existing left-handed side of his personality, or did he create the Heisenberg persona from whole cloth, entirely from scratch? Did 'chirality' predestine him to criminality? Does 'chirality' mean that he has a *choice* of right-handed responsibility and left-handed criminality? Does 'chirality' mean he needed to consciously activate (decide "I am awake") the bad side of his nature?

I believe *Breaking Bad* offers us a few responses to the question. We have several examples, after all, and not just Walter White. We are already acquainted with Jesse's drug trafficking, Marie Schrader's kleptomania (1.03) and Hank Schrader's predilection for illicit Cuban cigars (1.07). Soon enough we will learn of Skyler's sins. But we will also have to include important extenuating factors into our analysis; by the end of Season Two many of us may wish to adjust our definitions of 'chirality'.

One of the most important factors we must consider is the effect of family. Over the first four seasons of *Breaking Bad* we are going to become familiar with not fewer than four families, some of them extending into three or four generations. As we will see, every bond of husband to wife, mother to son, sister to sister, has greater bearing on individual actions than even a desire to remain chirally pure (or enantiomerically contaminated!). Walter needs to tell us to "respect the chemistry," but we require no such instruction regarding our families. A father will sacrifice anything, or commit any deed, for daughter or son. We will look at family bonds in the next chapter.

The White Family Residence
Copyright 2011 Martin Woutisseth, used with permission

Chapter D

Devoted Family Man

"La familia es todo." Hector Salamanca ("Tio") says this in Episode 3.07, but the rule applies equally well throughout *Breaking Bad*. Family is everything, and nothing anyone does can change that rule. As we will see in coming seasons, the law is so unbending that even greatest necessity cannot dislodge this fundamental principle from its position at the pinnacle of every character's list of priorities. We will see good guys perform unthinkable deeds in the name of family, and we will see bad guys heroically sacrifice all for sons and daughters. Family is the great equalizer, the one value that trumps ethics, morality, good grooming, and causes the most selfish person to surrender everything without a moment's hesitation.

The absolute, inviolate nature of this truth will be pounded into our conscious awareness in powerful, dramatic ways over the next four seasons. The rule will certainly become a major touchstone and a dramatic turning point at the end of Season Five. The most complete understanding of *Breaking Bad* philosophy, then, requires that we become well acquainted with the full significance of family to the show's fictional world.

Literary Periodicity

Each season of *Breaking Bad* corresponds to a period in the periodic table of the elements, or chapters, in this book. So, Season One is given Period One, spanning hydrogen to helium, Season Two is given Period Two, from lithium to neon, and so on. Some of you have already started looking for a chemical element with the symbol 'D' and have come up empty-handed. "I thought this guy was a chemist. Doesn't he know there's no element with atomic symbol D?" Well, yes, I am a chemist, and depending on the chemist you consult with, there either is or isn't a chemical element designated by the symbol "D.". In strictly formal terms there is no element called "D," but many chemists apply the symbol D to a common isotope of hydrogen, called deuterium. Deuterium is nothing more than elemental hydrogen with a neutron in the nucleus (ordinary hydrogen has no neutrons—it is the only chemical element bearing this structural distinction). Even those who are not trained in physics or chemistry will have heard of the substance called 'heavy water'. Heavy water is D_2O, deuterium oxide, composed of two atoms of deuterium ('heavy hydrogen', if you will) and one atom of oxygen.

By considering the periodic table in a way foreign even to some chemists, I am symbolically stating that we need to look at *Breaking Bad* in more than traditional, tried and true ways. We may even need to move beyond our ordinary comfort zones if we truly wish to enrich our understanding of the series.

It is certainly true that many facets of *Breaking Bad* characters must be studied if we have any hope of making sense of Walter White's descent into criminality. It is not enough to say that Walter is driven by pride, or that every one of his shortcomings and failures derives of a materialist mindset. This may be true for the cardboard characters offered up in procedural television and shoot-'em-up movies, but any such interpretation of character motivation in *Breaking Bad* will fall far short of the truth. You cannot watch the first two episodes of *Breaking Bad* and then skip to Episode 5.08 and seriously believe that you will absorb a complete, balanced and well-informed appreciation of everything that takes place.

You can do this very easily in police procedurals. Watch *Law and Order*, Episode 1.03, then advance to Episode 12.22. Do you have any difficulty understanding any part of the episode twelve *years* into the series? Didn't think so. In fact, you could speak with a fan of the show who had watched every episode from the first 12 seasons. She could confirm that you picked up on all of the important developments in the episode.

Breaking Bad is a serial drama but certain themes, such as family, come up at regular intervals. Attaching my discussion of the show to the periodic table of the elements makes a great deal of sense, symbolically, because I will return to the same or similar topics throughout my analysis of later seasons. Heisenberg, in particular, is assigned an important position at the far-right group in the table, called the Noble Gases. I will explain some of the symbolic significance of this in Chapter He.

A Father's Heart

My name's Walter Hartwell White. I live at 308 Negra Arroyo Lane, Albuquerque, New Mexico. To all law enforcement authorities, this is not an admission of guilt. I am speaking to my family now. Skyler, you are the love of my life, I hope you know that. Walter Jr., you're my big man. There are … there are going to be some things … things that you'll come to learn about me in the next few days. I just want you to know that no … no matter how it may look, I only had you in my heart. Good-bye.

"There are going to be some things…"—like a dead body, tens of thousands of dollars in cash, and a complete roving methamphetamine laboratory set up in an RV. Oh, and your father was arrested in his underwear forty miles out in the desert. Some things.

Perhaps even then, in the very first minute of *Breaking Bad*, Walter could not have expected his family's forgiveness or even their understanding, but he could probably count on their love. Early in the series Walter Jr. decides that he has his own identity and he begins to go by the name of Flynn. But as soon as it becomes apparent that Skyler is disrespecting his father, Flynn reverts to Walter Jr. Regardless of anything Walter may have done, his son loves him and will stand by him. Even late in the series we witness acts by Walter, Skyler, and Walter Jr. that could only be attributed to familial love.

Tabula Rasa

Most television and movie heroes are single, divorced, or widowed. If a husband or wife is present, he or she is more often than not entirely absent whenever dramatic actions take place. Captain Kirk roamed the galaxy unattached except for the obligatory single-episode fling with an old flame. President Bartlet was married, it's true, but we never saw Abby in the situation room. When Flight 815 (*Lost*) crashed in 2004 there were 72 survivors (I'm counting the dog, Vincent), but only two married couples among them. Perhaps the married couples were preferentially killed on impact? Or maybe married people hardly ever fly together?

Having written scenes involving married couples, I think I understand why we rarely see television dramas involving married protagonists: Marriage makes for difficult writing. It's much easier to have a head-strong protagonist with a single agenda than to take the time to write in all the complications associated with married life. An unattached hero can come and go as she pleases without ever having to talk with hubby or find a broom closet big enough to store the kids while she goes out to save the city (or the country, or the galaxy).

That is to say, marriage is inconvenient to drama. Drama is governed by rules of economy. Only those characters that contribute to the dramatic action can be included in a scene. If spouse and children do not contribute to the drama, they cannot be present. An interesting corollary to the Rule of Economy is Chekhov's Gun, which states if a gun appears on stage in Act One we need to see it used at some critical point later in the play. *Breaking Bad* has made frequent use of this rule throughout the last five years, although only once with an actual gun.

Tabula Rasa, empty slate, is often used in drama to simplify the situation, essentially to force the main players to concentrate on the problem at hand without facing the distractions of real life. Nothing that happened before the stage is set is allowed to complicate the drama. More often than not this is done at the beginning of the novel, with a contrivance of setting: In a lifeboat after the ship was sunk ("Lifeboat"), locked in a jury room upon conclusion of the trial ("Twelve Angry Men"), in the antechamber to heaven ("Steambath"), or in a deserted location after a plane crash ("The Grey," *Lost*).

"Light and Dark"
Copyright 2011 Pearson Moore

Lost is a special case. Portraying almost exclusively unattached, single individuals, *Lost* began with a plane crash (setting *tabula rasa*) on a deserted island (setting *tabula rasa* II) invisible and inaccessible to the outside world (amplification of setting *tabula rasa* II), compounded by literal *tabula rasa*:

Kate: I want to tell you what I did - why he was after me.
Jack: I don't want to know. It doesn't matter, Kate, who we were - what we did before this, before the crash. It doesn't really... three days ago we all died. We should all be able to start over.
(*Lost*, Episode 1.03, "Tabula Rasa")

If *Lost* had relied on these three *tabula rasa* crutches throughout the first season it is unlikely that the series would have been approved for a second season. Probably it would have been forgotten long ago ("Oh, yeah, *Lost*—wasn't that the *Gilligan's Island* remake? Plane crash instead of getting lost at sea?"). One of the things that Lost began to do immediately was to show the futility of *tabula rasa*. About 30% of the show consisted of detailed flashbacks which demonstrated the inexorable trajectory of destiny in the lives of every major character, and many of the minor characters. The Island had ruled their lives long before the crash of Flight 815 and continued to determine their fate for the remainder of the series. By twisting many storytelling conventions into convoluted pretzels, Lost became the groundbreaking television series of the 21st century to which all other dramas of merit are inevitably compared.

Tabula rasa, then, is an over-simplification, a storytelling fantasy that allows the novelist (or playwright or showrunner) to remove the complicating aspects of reality that are normally thought to interfere with economic storytelling. This fantasy reached its high point, I think, in the 1976 soft-erotic film *Laure* (called *Emmanuelle Forever* in the United States). The movie was a kind of erotic treasure hunt, with the ultimate goal of discovering the Mara Tribe in the Philippines. The Mara practiced an annual ritual in which certain members of the tribe were allowed to forget their past, including past relationships. No more husband or wife or children, no responsibilities—a complete and literal *tabula rasa* that would allow the sexually liberated to live their unattached, hedonistic lives. It was the most logical concluding argument of the sexual revolution.

Family and Responsibility

A reasonable extrapolation of memory erasure is self-annihilation. If members of the Mara Tribe can forget all past relationships—all responsibilities—the result may initially appear to be freedom for the individual undergoing erasure of memory, but it would mean lack of care for young children, leading to their abandonment or to their attachment to foster parents. Wholesale severing of relationship and abandoning of responsibility would inevitably lead to social disintegration, chaos, and death. Hedonism presents the tantalizing illusion of freedom, but it is actually the surest form of slavery.

"Peasant Family"
Le Nain Brothers, circa 1640

The idea that true freedom begins with responsibility seems to be the hidden thesis underlying *Breaking Bad*'s unusual emphasis on family. *Breaking Bad* rejects *tabula rasa*, insisting on the realistic portrayal of complicated family relationships, not only within the nuclear unit, but including the further complications of extended family.

We are told in the very first minute of the series that family considerations will weigh heavily on Walter's decisions—in fact, his family is more important to him than just about any other aspect of his life. We know this because rather than hiding or plotting an escape or devising an excuse, Walter's first thought is to provide a video apology to his family. This is a crucial dramatic revelation of Walter's inner self and an indication of the direction of future decision points in the series. Far from pushing family to the periphery, *Breaking Bad* will insist on bringing Skyler, Junior, and (later) Holly to center stage. Every major character is attached to family and not an artificially independent agent. Even Walter's antagonists have family, and some of them have important extended family, too, whose relationships are detailed onscreen.

In Season One we are introduced to two antagonists: Hank Schrader and Tuco Salamanca. Hank is not only married, but he is wed to Skyler's sister, Marie, making him Walter's brother-in-law. Tuco Salamanca seems initially to fall into the standard loner bad guy role, but before the end the first season we learn that Tuco also has an important relative, Tio Hector (the old man in the wheelchair). The unusual emphasis on family ought to serve as a clue regarding the significance of Hector Salamanca. He's not just some colorful background to Tuco's antics; Hector will prove critical to events throughout Seasons Two, Three, and Four.

Later in the series we will meet an antagonist to Walter who appears to have no familial connections, but for the very reason that he seems disconnected he will immediately raise our suspicions about him. Eventually we will learn of a connection, a man the antagonist insists is family, but the nature of the antagonist's 'family' will only serve to raise even more suspicions about him. But this antagonist, like every other major character, will base his actions first of all on family considerations.

Jesse and Jake

Jesse seems at first to be the outlier in *Breaking Bad*'s story of conflicted families. He has no wife, no children, and not even a girlfriend (unless we count the well-endowed woman who throws his clothes out the second-story window in the pilot episode).

I am going to say something here that may well be at odds with the opinion of most viewers of the complete five-season series: ***Jesse's family connections are deeper and more important than those of any other character in the series***. I can build a logical case for this assertion, but my position probably ought to be considered to occupy the realm of opinion rather than carrying any objective validity. The argument I intend to make throughout Breaking Blue will depend on this statement.

Many important events involving Walter's sidekick in later seasons will alter viewer-participant evaluation of Jesse's significance to the story. However, since my original impression of Jesse and Jake has remained unperturbed since Season One, I do not feel any scruples in relaying my opinion about him early in the first period of our 'periodic' examination of the series.

"Two Boys in a Landscape"
(A young boy and his protective older brother)
Herman MijnertDonker, circa 1652

Jake seems to be everything that Jesse is not. An academic achiever of unusual distinction, Jacob Pinkman has received awards and honors not only in his extracurricular coursework ("Most Distinguished Mathlete"), but also in sports and in citizenship ("Environmental Consciousness Award"). As if that were not enough, he plays the piccolo and has full command of the English language.

But it turns out that Jacob and Jesse are alike in two important ways. The marijuana cigarette that Jesse's parents consider the final straw is not Jesse's but Jake's. Ironically, the joint becomes Adam Pinkman's rationale for kicking Jesse out of their house. Jesse and Jacob share an interest in illicit drugs, and this fact causes Jesse an additional degree of discomfort after being evicted.

Jake: Thanks for not telling on me. Think I could have it back?
Jesse: [Grinding the pot into the sidewalk under his shoe] It's skunk weed anyway.

The most obvious conclusion we might draw from this interaction is that Jesse disapproves of his younger brother's forays into "gateway drugs." Or perhaps he's upset that Jacob's experimentation with pot is the unjust cause of his eviction. Or, less likely but still consistent with the scenario, Jesse thinks "skunk weed" is beneath the dignity of his accomplished and talented brother.

I want to offer an opinion for your consideration. We could argue that Jesse is upset with his parents because they are kicking him out, and angry with Jake for the essentially unrelated reason that his younger brother is experimenting with drugs. That is, we might come away from this scene believing that many things are on Jesse's mind, that several facts related to his family are causing discomfort in his personal life.

I believe a reasonable and possibly stronger alternative take-home idea is that Jesse is experiencing a single source of pain in the scenes involving his brother, and that that pain is the same in the first scene as in the final one: Jesse is sad that he and his brother are both estranged from their parents.

Pay close attention to the scene in Jake's room in Episode 1.04. Jake is absorbed in homework on his computer rather than engaging with his older brother. But there is an element of this scene that will immediately raise the concerns of every parent taking in the proceedings: Jake is on the computer, in his room, and *the door is closed*. Responsible parents—parents who engage with their children—do not allow young children to access the Internet without constant supervision. I am not commenting on Adam Pinkman's parenting skills. Rather, I am simply pointing out that the closed bedroom door and the computer in a child's room could be considered signs of unnecessary distance between parents and son.

The only portrait we have of Jacob Pinkman is that of a child withdrawn, disengaged, essentially on his own and alienated—estranged—from his parents. Thus the boy's marijuana usage is not a one-off deviation by an otherwise level-headed young man. It is the natural outcome of child-parent remoteness seen in the unsupervised computer and the closed bedroom door.

I believe it is this mode of alienated existence that is the second way in which Jesse and Jake are alike. Jesse is old enough to feel pain for his younger brother, pain for Jake's distance from their parents. Pain, because he knows Jake is ignorant of the damage his estrangement from his parents will wreak in his young life. I believe the greatest pain in Jesse's life is his alienation from his mother and father. If we look at the Pinkman home scenes in this way, in which Jesse's pain is the result of familial alienation, the dynamic becomes simple, easy to understand, but more important to our comprehension of the greater series, this view is consistent with the thesis of family's centrality to *Breaking Bad*'s message.

Skyler and Walter

Regardless of the placement of alienation in the prioritization table of *Breaking Bad* themes, we must consider the role of Walter's secret life and its effect on those closest to him. Walter tells us in his Scene One confession that family is paramount to him, and the first member of his family he mentions on the video is his wife, Skyler.

I believe it is essential to keep in mind that Walter's emotional withdrawal from Skyler did not begin with his illicit drug activity. It didn't even begin with his diagnosis of lung cancer. In fact, we are led to believe that emotional distance has been a feature of their marriage, on both sides, for many years.

After Walter has been humiliated by Skyler and Hank—and at his 50th birthday party, no less—Skyler gives him a late-night birthday present in bed: a hand job while she focuses on her eBay transactions. While she stares at the screen and masturbates him with one hand under the covers, they discuss such romantic and erotic topics as the car wash, driving to Los Alamos to see the Mars rover photographs, and painting the house. Just as Walter seems to respond to her half-hearted, essentially peripheral ministrations, Skyler's eyes grow big and she seems excited. "Yes! Fifty-six!" she shouts. Her excitement has nothing to do with Walter; the cause of her joyous … ah … ejaculation (sorry, I couldn't resist) is not Walter's physical state, but her unexpected victory on eBay. Her small revenue-generating initiatives mean more to her than a few brief moments of intimacy with her husband. In fact, the scene indicates her emotions are devoid of any sense of intimacy.

The series of scenes in which Walter learns of his cancer and short moments later divulges not the slightest hint of health problems to Skyler is confirmation that neither of them is in a position of emotional intimacy or even emotional honesty with each other.

All of this happens prior to Walter's decision to break bad. Walter's transition from Walter Bland to Walter Mitty (his dreams of wealth when he sees Hank's drug bust on television) to Heisenberg is facilitated by the fact that he has not been emotionally or factually accountable to his wife or to anyone else for a long, long time.

We should acknowledge two possible, perhaps likely, consequences of his emotional detachment from Skyler.

First, Walter has been existing in an emotional desert for a long and unhealthy period of time. It is difficult to image even a strong individual being able to exist indefinitely under such conditions without actively seeking some positive change.

Second, as we continue to witness events that may be considered triggers for Walter's decision to break bad, commit murder, or perform other criminal deeds, I think we need to keep in mind the chronological precedence of Walter's emotional distance from Skyler. It is entirely possible that later events could be the result of factors other than Walter's lack of emotional connection. Recall the "chemistry" between Walter and Gretchen in Episode 1.03, for example. We are led to believe that at least for a time Walter enjoyed an emotionally close relationship with Gretchen, but at the same time he held views that did not include the possibility of a spiritual dimension to human life. Thus, his emotional withdrawal later in life, with Skyler, may be the major factor in his turn to illicit drugs, or it may be only one of several decisive influences. Yet another possibility is that the emotional distance evident in Episode 1.01 is itself the result of some earlier occurrence or state of being. I will discuss trigger conditions and events at greater length in Chapter T.

Walter and Jesse

Walter White and Jesse Pinkman have a strained relationship but we know Jesse is the protégé to *Mr. White*, the exalted mentor. Jesse will continue to address Walter as Mr. White throughout the five seasons, even as they experience the majority of the show's most frightening and game-changing events side by side. Walter will never be Jesse's equal, but always his superior.

Admiral McCain and Commander McCain
Vice Admiral John S. McCain, Sr., with his son, Cmdr. John S. McCain, Jr.
U.S. Navy, 2 September 1945, PD

We might expect just such an asymmetrical relationship, strictly on the basis of the age differential or the stunning disparity in technical expertise. But theirs is not a loose or distant student-teacher affiliation. Due to the fact that they cannot discuss the nature of their illicit activities with anyone else, they will naturally develop the intimate kind of rapport associated with only the closest of mentor-protégé relationships. It seems reasonable that any such close proximity and the sharing of information only between themselves could lead to something more like a liaison or a family bond.

In light of *Breaking Bad*'s strong emphasis on the importance of family, the slow evolution of a father-son relationship—perhaps even an emotional bond—between Walter and Jesses seems possible or even likely. I imagine Walter's emotional distance from his wife and son and Jesse's (possible) feeling of alienation from his father may tend to enhance the potential for an emotional, family-like bond between the two men.

The importance of these possibilities, in my mind, is not so much the proliferation of quasi-familial relations between people not related by blood, but rather the establishment of a kind of conceptual topography or matrix of different ways of thinking about family, friendship, relationship, responsibility, and the inter-related topics and themes that flow directly from those ideas.

If it is true that family relationships are the basis of emotional or spiritual freedom in the *Breaking Bad* universe, could Walter become Jesse's spiritual salvation, or vice versa? Could Jesse supply Walter with emotional riches sufficient to propel him out of whatever psychological malfunction or deficit of the soul that allowed him to actively pursue a life of crime? If family is the source of true happiness in *Breaking Bad*, could it be that family is the only means of true conversion?

We have been led to believe that all of these considerations will become moot in the case of Walter. Mr. Chips must become Scarface, after all. Perhaps an endgame conversion of the soul is possible for Walter, but even if it is not, possibly other players in the saga will benefit from the influence or intervention of family or friend. As we will see in coming seasons, Walter is not the only character who will wade neck-deep into the chemical sewer he has built. Characters we now consider innocent will succumb to raw temptation, while others who seem beyond redemption will begin to show signs of potential healing and growth.

Regardless of the details, we can be sure of one constant in the world of *Breaking Bad*: La familia es todo. It is as constant and regular as the periodic (repeating) motion of a pendulum—or the periodic resurfacing of themes in every season of a most fascinating television program.

Chapter T

³₁**T**rigger
Conditions
& Events

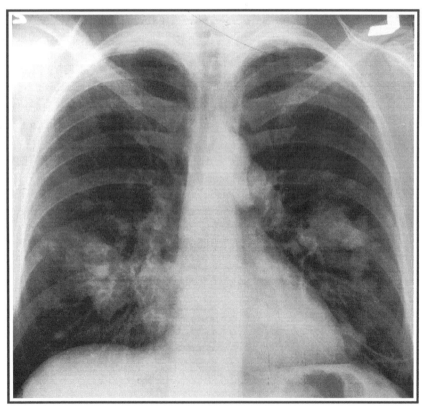

X-Ray Evidence of Advanced Lung Cancer
National Cancer Institute 2009, PD

Tritium is an unstable isotope of hydrogen. It has a short half-life, and it decays not into hydrogen, but into helium, an element with properties very different from those it started with. Hydrogen is always ready to form bonds with other elements. Hydrogen, for example, burns in the presence of oxygen to form water. Helium, though, is a loner. It never combines with oxygen, or any other element for that matter.

From our anthropomorphic point of view for the purposes of this book, we could say helium is too proud to create bonds with other elements. In our 'periodic' scheme in this book, Hydrogen refers to high school teacher Walter White, while Helium refers to the proud loner, Heisenberg. Continuing our chemistry analogy, Tritium is the state Walter occupies at the critical decision point between Walter White, chemistry teacher, and Heisenberg, notorious drug lord. Our study of tritium focuses on the trigger conditions and events that lead Walter to the knife-edge decision between the ordinary life of teacher and devoted father, and the extraordinary life of a criminal übermensch.

Pre-Existing Condition

We learned in the first breakfast scene of Walter's pre-existing condition. Not lung cancer or shortness of breath. Not fainting spells or cough. Walter's pre-existing condition was lack of manliness. He allowed his wife and son and everyone else to walk all over him. Rather than bringing home the bacon, he ended up working a second job, only to be given the task of cleaning and shining the sports car belonging to the same student who had insulted and disrespected him in chemistry class. "Oh my God," the boy's girlfriend squealed into her mobile phone, "you would not believe who's cleaning Ted's car!"

Walter escaped the degrading insults at the car wash only to experience them heaped up and flowing over in his own home at his surprise birthday party.

"Glock 22," Hank says, pulling out his quite substantial sidearm. "That's my daily carry…. You forget the 9-mil, alright. I've seen one of those bounce off a windshield one time. When you gotta bring a gun, baby, you gotta bring enough gun. Forty Cal."

When Hank hands the unloaded gun to Junior, Walt, in his feeble voice, tries to note his disapproval, but Junior and Hank are so absorbed they don't pay attention to the emasculated entity whose birthday party they're celebrating.

Junior hands Walter the weapon but he doesn't even want to touch it. He finally takes it and seems surprised.

Walter: [Hefting the Glock] It's just heavy.
Hank: That's why they hire men! [Motioning to Walter, grinning] Hey, it's not gonna bite you, alright. [Turning to his DEA friends] Looks like Keith Richards with a glass of warm milk, eh?
[DEA guys laugh]

Weight Gain Advertisement
Unknown artist, circa 1920

When Hank offers a toast the only positive compliment he can think of is that Walter's "heart is in the right place." Then he grabs Walter's beer and shouts "Na zdrowi!" [Polish: To your health] Before Walter can say anything, Hank blurts out, "Hey, turn to Channel Three!" For the next three minutes we see Hank Schrader, local DEA hero, being interviewed on KCAV television regarding his latest meth lab bust.

It is Walter's party, but he has to endure disgrace piled on top of contempt, everyone laughs at him, and he isn't allowed to toast his own health. In a final insult, Hank steals away any attention Walter may have had and focuses everyone on himself, the man's man who carries a real weapon and busts bad guys and drug dealers.

What occurs next is telling. Walter is off by himself, far away from the television, until the news reporter begins to talk about the money Hank seized. The video shows what must be hundreds of thousands of dollars in thick, tight rolls. Walter walks toward the group and stares at the screen.

Walter: Hank, how much money is that?
Hank: Ah, it's about 700 grand. Pretty good haul.
Walter: Wow. That's unusual isn't it, that kind of cash?
Hank: It's not the most we ever took. It's easy money—'til we catch you!

Walter is all but drooling in response to the sight on the television screen. This is probably not the typical response of a citizen viewing video of a drug seizure; no one else gathered around the television appears to share Walter's fascination with the visuals. The important aspect of this scene to me, as I attempt to identify a rationale for Walter's later decisions, is that the celebration of Hank's success, and the revelation of Walter's lust for easy money, occurs a full day before Walter learns of his medical condition.

Resignation or Resolve

I hope no one reading this book ever has to hear the words Walter's doctor directed at him: that he had inoperable Stage Three lung cancer and he was not likely to live. I am among those who have had to sit on Walter's side of the desk to hear a prognosis no one should ever have to confront.

In late 1995 my wife was diagnosed with Stage IIIA breast cancer. The prognosis was only marginally better than Walter White's: The oncology team gave my wife a 50% chance of living another five years.

Fight or flight? Confront the cancer head-on and beat it, or run away and wait for death to come?

"Thumbs Up"
Pfc. Shawn Williams, seriously injured by an IED, gives the Thumbs Up sign
Kandahar Province, Afghanistan
Lt. J. G. Haraz Ghanbari, U.S. Navy, 17 June 2011, PD

I suppose there are people who crumble, who decide to throw in the towel at the first mention of a terminal diagnosis. I don't suppose my wife and I are alone, though, in the kind of reaction we had. We made arrangements for treatment, for babysitters so I could continue working. We researched doctors, treatment plans, advanced surgeries, innovative imaging options. I cooked the meals, washed the dishes, took care of the kids, did the laundry, did the shopping, took care of my wife, talked with her doctors and surgeons and technicians every day, drover her to and from treatments and surgeries, **and** worked 40 hours every week in the laboratory. A schedule, I suppose, that most working women are used to.

The bottom line is that neither Kim nor I ever thought of giving up, even when the X-rays, MRIs, and sonograms were discouraging at best, even when treatments showed no sign of reducing the cancer. We just kept on fighting, working hard, keeping our spirits up. Even when things looked their worst, we smiled, kept our chins high, gave the thumbs up. This didn't go on for days or weeks. We didn't have to keep up this extraordinary effort and mind-numbing, wearying discipline for months. We did it for two and a half *years*. We never crumbled. We never stopped.

Why did Walter cave? Why did he initially choose not to fight?

The situation my wife and I faced was different from Walter's in two important respects. First, my medical insurance back in 1995 would cover most of the tests and treatment, and second, the times and my verbal skills were such that I was willing—eager—to fight for every test and round of treatment my wife would need.

But times, as they say, have changed. By any account, healthcare in the United States is no longer what it was in 1995. Health insurance costs more and delivers less than in any other developed country in the world.

Poverty and Death or Bankruptcy and Death

George Stroumboulopoulos
Copyright 2007 Robin Wong, CC-SA 3.0

In 2004 the popular Canadian television host and commentator George Stroumboulopoulos ("Strombo") took on the task of advocating for his hero Tommy Douglas to be chosen as the Greatest Canadian. Tommy Douglas could claim dozens of important social and cultural advances during a political career that spanned over fifty years, not just for his home province of Saskatchewan, but for all of Canada. Tommy is the Father of Canadian Medicare. If you get sick in Canada, the last thing you have to worry about is how you're going to pay. It's taken care of for you. It's called universal healthcare.

Strombo would probably agree that of the ten advocates, he had the easiest case to make. But excellent showman that he is, Strombo didn't take any chances. He chose as his visual one of the small concrete boundary markers defining the border between the United States and Canada, and there he made his final pitch.

This is what it all boils down to: The 49th parallel. It's the dividing line between our way, and their way. And did you know, that on that side [pointing to the United States] every thirty seconds someone declares bankruptcy because of medical bills. What I'm saying is Americans go broke—being sick. And I just can't tell you how glad I am we don't live that way. That's all thanks to Tommy.

In Tommy Douglas' words:

I think that medical care is so important that it ought not have a price tag on it. I think that we have come to the place where medical care, like education, ought to be available to every citizen, irrespective of their financial state.

Tommy Douglas won the competition. For the last ten years he has been known as "The Greatest Canadian," and it's because he created Canadian universal healthcare that he is honored with a title no one else can claim.

In most countries, the choices Walter faced would include a shorter, more aggressive treatment, or less aggressive treatment aimed at allowing him to continue working while therapies continued. Death would not be an option. In the United States, unless he could call upon almost limitless reserves of cash, his choices were abject poverty followed by death, or bankruptcy followed by death.

My wife lived past the five year mark. In fact, she is in better health than most women her age. Almost every day she says she is thankful that cancer struck 18 years ago and not now. If either of us were to receive today a diagnosis similar to the one Kim heard in the mid-1990s, our paltry health insurance would ensure our death, regardless of our willingness or eagerness to fight.

Why did Walter cave?

Surely we have to consider his psychological state, but I think we can also look to his training as a scientist and his logical, realistic outlook. Given the less than adequate coverage provided by his health insurance, he must have known that fighting the cancer was futile. Even if he sold everything he owned, at some point early in

Pearson Moore

treatment he would have exhausted his financial resources, and treatments would come to an end. He would die, regardless of any amount of fighting he did.

Social and Personal Accountability

There is no single rationale for Walter's decision to break bad. We could place some degree of blame for Walter's financial predicament on the barbaric socio-economic system of the United States. The self-destructive tax structure favoring the wealthy, the glaring lack of adequate healthcare for U.S. citizens, and regressive, neo-feudal social structures are destroying what was once a great country. To believe that the monstrous conditions of the United States, in which children and the poor are simply allowed to die, are blameless in this matter constitutes a strong element of fantasy thinking.

"The Mad Scientist"
Bela Lugosi as the Mad Scientist in *The Devil Bat*
Unknown photographer, Producers Releasing Corp., 1940, PD

For the sake of clarity let us go to an extreme view of the situation. Let us posit that the U.S. healthcare system is barbaric. Let us agree that a system that rewards powerful plutocrats who siphon off money for corporate and personal gain rather than allowing for adequate medical treatment would be considered not only less than civilized, but actually criminal and sinful in any other developed culture.

Even if we grant all of this, though, we are left with the fact that Walter decided to manufacture methamphetamine to earn enough money to leave his family a nest egg after his death. This question, I believe, must be considered apart from any condition of social depravity.

I am well compensated in my position as Principal Scientist to a thriving pharmaceutical company. I have enjoyed several decades of financial ease. Even so, there have been times, especially early in my life, when I had barely the resources to feed and house myself. I have suffered prolonged periods in which I was one paycheck away from homelessness. But I enjoyed then the same unusual, highly specialized knowledge and skillset that has made me useful to companies throughout North America. In particular, I certainly have Walter White's level of expertise, and in exactly those areas that would make it easy for me to manufacture the highest quality methamphetamine. In addition, I have rare skills given short shrift in *Breaking Bad*. Isolate ricin from *Ricinus communis*? It's not all that difficult.

My deepest expertise is in crystallization, but the area of expertise in which I am most useful is the extraction and purification of high-value chemicals from biological matrices—from plants, animals, fermentation broths, and marine sources. I could, if I were so inclined, help companies isolate botulinum neurotoxins or even more deadly poisons. I could lead efforts to weaponize the material. But I don't. I could sell my expertise to companies of questionable repute. But I don't.

There have been opportunities. There are always opportunities. One of the most interesting of these involved the isolation of a particularly high-value material from soybeans in the early 1990s. The work was highly confidential. Out of the blue one day I received an invitation to interview with one of the world's largest private companies. I was not looking for a job at the time, my name was not in circulation. Somehow this company's agents had found me, but it went much deeper than that. I refused to miss a day of work. Fine, fine, they said, we'll interview you on Saturday. They flew me across the continent on a Friday red-eye to their world headquarters, gave me a very nice hotel suite. On Saturday I found the interview consisted of a brief tour of the world class facilities (very impressive!)—with emphasis on a lab devoted to soybean studies. And then I was asked to give my presentation. I handed the company's Executive Vice President a list of five topics I would not discuss, four of which were bogus subjects, the fifth was the soybean research. I began my presentation, but I was interrupted less than fifteen minutes into it. "Tell us about your soybean work," the Director of R&D said. I politely declined. The questions persisted, and it became clear from the gist of their very forceful inquiries that they knew exactly what I was working on. All they wanted to know was how I was doing it, and how I was able to do it at a much lower cost than they could. I declined to respond to their questions. During their impolite, unethical barrage I finally sat down. "I'm done with my presentation," I told them. I thanked them for their time, gathered my things, and called a taxi. I stomped the vile dust off my feet before getting into the taxi.

It was the most egregious instance of attempted industrial espionage I witnessed in my career. The criminals with whom I had shared a conference room represented a company that every few years is found guilty of price rigging or other illegal behavior. They are routinely slapped with fines in the hundreds of millions of dollars which they pay with essentially zero effect on their bottom line. It was clear to me, sitting in the toxic, ethically noxious environment of that research building, that these individuals were used to getting what they wanted, regardless of the damage they caused to other companies.

The point of this story is not to paint me as some kind of paragon of morality. The fact is, most of you reading these words would behave in precisely the same manner, given the temptations that Walter or I have faced in our professional careers. The greater point I wish to make is that any of us, put into a situation in which we are given the opportunity to make fantastic amounts of money through illicit channels, will instead choose to do what is right, even if this means unusual suffering for ourselves and our families. We would do this regardless of the social accountability weighed against our civilization for any of its moral shortcomings.

Wouldn't Walter behave in the same manner? Even though the enormous piles of cash he saw in the video record of Hank's meth bust were attractive, wouldn't he have chosen the high road rather than descending to ethical depravity for the sake of personal gain?

Given a broad range of circumstances we could consider adequate to social health, I don't believe there's any question: Walter would have done the right thing. The problem is that the circumstances Walter inhabited failed to coincide with normalcy. Something about his experience drove him to consider the production of addictive poison simply to realize a financial windfall. I don't think there can be any question regarding the role of his cancer prognosis as the singular and final trigger event. I am concerned with the trigger conditions, the factors that so warped his mental state that he was able to succumb to animal lusts.

Strength and Weakness

In painting our portrait of the pre-Heisenberg Walter White we will become misled if we do not include the bold and vivid strokes that capture his unusual brilliance. Walter White, at one time in his career, had the potential to achieve limitless wealth, power, and influence. He could have been on the cover of *Scientific American* or *Time*, right next to Elliott Schwartz. We know he harbors the same extraordinary abilities he proved in his creation of Gray Matter Technologies—his skillset has neither deteriorated nor become obsolete, as we learned at Elliott's party. Even now, decades after his seminal contributions to crystallography and positron emission spectrometry, he could easily and quickly become an influential leader in imaging technology, solid state chemistry, or any number of cutting edge disciplines. Instead, he has chosen to withdraw, to hide his talents under a basket.

It is because of this dramatic choice, among other facts of Walter White's background, that I believe we are being asked to consider Walter's decision to break bad as entirely his own, as a meditation on personal rather than social forces. Walter White is not a victim of the times, a victim of circumstance, a victim of anything. *Breaking Bad* is not social commentary, but morality play. Blame society if you will for Walter's unfair financial burden. Blame fate for giving him cancer. Blame Gretchen and Skyler for their inability or unwillingness to engage sexually and intimately. But in the end, I feel, we must limit accountability for the decision to break bad to Walter alone.

Near the end of Skyler's "intervention" we learn an essential facet of Walter's mindset.

Walter: What I want—what I need—is a choice.
Skyler: What does that mean?
Walter: Sometimes I feel like I never actually make any of my own choices, I mean. My entire life—it just seems like I never had a say—about any of it.

He knows he is no ordinary man. He is a Samson of the laboratory, a rare, clear-thinking researcher who can push beyond the shortsightedness of current science, a gifted thinker with the kind of intellectual resources and innate curiosity that drive discovery and creation of technological benefits for all humankind. He knows this because he knows his brainchild, Gray Matter, is thriving and delivering what had only been a dream and a promise back in the early years.

In his mind, though, he is the victim. He is Samson shorn of hair, reduced to intellectual infirmity by the forces arrayed against him. "I never actually make any of my own choices," he said, and the fundamental choice forced upon him was Gray Matter. Gretchen was his Delilah, probing him for weakness, finding it, and forcing him to choose, backing him into a corner so only a single course of action remained. Poor unappreciated, unloved, unrecognized Walter.

Gray, of course, is metaphor. Gray is collaboration, give and take, sharing. It is the concept of contributing to an entity greater than self, greater than White or Black (or Schwartz). It is the willingness to give of oneself, to surrender oneself to such an extent that some attractive facet is lost, becomes inextricably mixed into something else. The purity of White is lost in the collaboration with Schwartz to form Gray. "Molecules: Molecules change their bonds. Elements: They *combine* and change into compounds. Well, that's all of life, right?" Yes, that is pretty much all of life—to give of oneself to form something greater.

We could blame his parents. Or his teachers. Or the neighborhood he grew up in. At some point, though, a man becomes accountable, even if that man was repeatedly a victim in his youth. If he is a human being, if he shares in the necessary qualities we associate with civilized, moral life, he will take a stand against propagating the same injustices that plagued him in years past. Perhaps in some cases this stand requires unusual moral fortitude, but it is society's firm demand nevertheless.

I wonder if Walter ever broke bad. I wonder if his constitution was such that he was not only receptive to the assertion of his tighty-whitey pride, but that the way his brain was wired, the way his soul was configured, somehow determined that he would never combine with anyone to "change into compounds," that he would never surrender any part of himself to create a more enduring, more meaningful entity. Maybe Walter White was always Heisenberg.

"Heisenberg"
Copyright 2011 Martin Woutisseth
Used with permission

Chapter He

He^{2}isenberg

A Google search for Heisenberg + "*Breaking Bad*" returns seven hundred thousand web pages. Tens of thousands of artists have painted, drawn, sculpted, and otherwise rendered Heisenberg's image in hundreds of media types, from oil paints and watercolors on canvas to ink pen on Styrofoam, from papier-mâché to bronze, and every conceivable medium in between. Heisenberg is one of television's most fascinating fictional creations, ranking with Mr. Spock (*Star Trek*), Kramer (*Seinfeld*), Locke (*Lost*), and J. R. Ewing (*Dallas*).

Heisenberg's appeal must be due in large measure to the unusual, expressive range of Bryan Cranston's face and the stunning costuming choice of dark jacket, dark glasses, and black felt pork pie hat. But the enduring nature of Heisenberg's artistic appeal must derive of his standing as one of television's most memorable anti-heroes. He attracts because he disgusts.

There is more to our attraction than loving him, or loving to hate him. We see in Heisenberg the potential of anyone to break bad. A responsible father, a high school teacher—an ordinary guy—can become the most abhorrent sociopath. Even those who base their actions on solid and pure motivations, those who are in every way "awake," may descend into a way of life that independent observers would label immoral, unethical, or criminal.

But there is much more to Heisenberg. The majority of the next four seasons will become an extended meditation on the full meaning of this character's philosophy of life, motivations, thought patterns and behaviors. He will change in ways we could not have expected, and we will have to adjust and adapt our assumptions about the relation of character traits we assume are common to the human condition. We will be surprised to learn that the connections are different than those we thought we could rely upon.

We begin our discussion with this idea: Cancer did not create Heisenberg. In fact, Heisenberg did not originate with any negative concept, event, or condition. His genesis was in *Breaking Bad*'s most consistently positive theme: Family created Heisenberg.

Call to Manhood

"David" by Michelangelo, circa 1504
Photograph copyright 2005 Rico Heil, GNU-FDL 1.2

"I am awake."

Walter's diagnosis of terminal cancer gave him a reason to engage. His life to that point had been nothing more than demoralized, painful survival at the uninvolved, uncommitted, disengaged periphery of life. Now he had a reason to live. More important to his fundamental identity, though, he had a mechanism for asserting his manhood.

Skyler, Hank, Marie, and even Walter's own son, had all laughed and poked fun at him, abused and disrespected him, and in general considered him not a true father or husband. Because family is central to *Breaking Bad*, Walter's inability to provide, to fulfill the minimum expectations of a family, meant that he was not truly a man. Now Walter knew he would die, but he realized he could leave his family an enduring legacy.

The money he made through the sale of methamphetamine would keep his family housed, clothed, and fed for years, and would even pay for their unborn baby's college. Whenever his family thought of him, even decades after his death, their first thought would be, "Dad provided. He was the perfect father and husband. He was everything a man should be." Walter's legacy would become the unassailable proof of his manhood. How many men could die in the knowledge that their families would think them extraordinary, noble exemplars of masculine fortitude and self-sacrifice?

Walter in Season One did not express a desire to live. He acquiesced to Skyler's "intervention" and agreed to treatment only because this was her wish, not because he truly wanted to endure the rigors of treatment only to face certain death after such a prolonged period of suffering.

Walter "woke up," became vitally engaged in life, not because he was anxious to please Skyler or hope against hope that he could find some way to survive terminal cancer. He woke up because he wished to leave a legacy. We wanted people to think "I wish I could be a real man, like the great and noble Walter White, who spared nothing and sacrificed all for his family."

I don't want to claim at this early point that I have a full grasp of Walter's true motivations. Even after two viewings of each episode of *Breaking Bad* I don't think I can claim to have such clear insight into Walter White's being. I think it is possible that we are not meant to have any such insight. Are we supposed to know how "chirality" applies to Walter White? I believe the concept is something to consider as an ongoing question and not a position upon which we must build a rational, syllogistic argument.

I would like to suggest that we may look at Walter's desire to leave his family a nest egg in at least four ways.

Four Winds of Change

East Wind: Creativity, Balance, Confidence

First, Walter's move to break bad may have been only the most obvious sign of a radical re-engagement with life, catalyzed by a terminal diagnosis of cancer. In the past he and Skyler had enjoyed no more intimacy than a handjob while she monitored sales on eBay and he talked about painting the house. But now all that would change. Walter's new enthusiasm for life would bring zest to their love life, he would become engrossed in his son's interests, and every day would be approached as a new adventure and yet another opportunity to fully participate in every aspect of his family's life. Maybe for the first time in his life he would enjoy and project the kind of balance and confidence that are the cherished benefits of a life in order.

North Wind: Courage, Energy, Knowledge

Second, Walter's decision to break bad may have been informed by multiple underlying motivations, conditions, and events. Let us recall that Walter seemed to have no firm concept of the spiritual nature of human reality. If *Breaking Bad* is an examination of motives and desires and ways of thinking, perhaps we ought to consider Walter's materialist outlook as a kind of blinder that prevented him from seeing and following routes to fatherhood and husbandhood. Walter could not be the kind of father and husband others might have liked because he lacked the philosophical, psychological, and emotional resources required in these types of relationships. However, he still wished to be a father and husband, and in leaving a financial legacy to his family he was at least demonstrating his good intentions. Perhaps part of becoming "awake" was a sudden self-awareness, not only of his biological mortality, but also of the limitations of character that impinged on his abilities as father and husband. If he achieved this level of self-awareness it is difficult to imagine this new knowledge would not affect his decisions and actions. Taking positive steps on behalf of his family, in the face of personal limitations, would demonstrate a rare species of courage that would only strengthen his legacy and reputation.

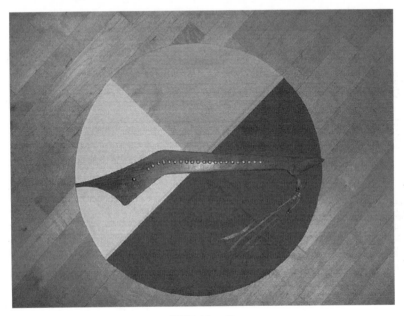

"Okichitaw"
Four Directions: East, South, North, West
Photograph by Flmgnra, 2008, PD

South Wind: Success, Focus, Strength

Third, consider the jockey underwear as a guiding image in our examination of possibilities. Walter was proud. Hank understood Walter's decision to forego cancer treatment as a manifestation of pride, and I believe we are justified in considering his mindset in this light. Maybe Walter White was not only psychologically incapable of choosing to serve his family (due to a materialistic understanding of life or due to any other factor we might like to draw from his backstory) but he was philosophically opposed to the interactions inherent in family life. He was proud, therefore aloof, separate, distinct.

Walter was proud. He could not participate in Gray Matter because Gray (White mixed with Black or Schwartz) meant giving up White, surrendering himself to a greater entity. This surrender of self is the very essence of family life, and especially for parents. Being a father means surrendering, sacrificing self for the good of children and spouse. Because Walter was proud, he could never be a true parent, he would never enjoy real intimacy with his wife. His legacy, on the other hand, was an obtainable goal because it did not require of him any surrender to a family-style Gray Matter enterprise. All he had to do to achieve a positive reputation that would outlive him was to give the appearance of having been a loving, engaged parent. A financial nest egg would provide a tangible proof of his strength as a father, his success as a husband.

West Wind: Choice, Challenge, Proof

Finally, a central principle of *Breaking Bad* is change. Chemistry—metaphorically our meditation on Walter White—is "the study of change." If we accept change as a primary element of this journey, Walter White will necessarily exist in a different philosophical and psychological state at the beginning than he will at the end of the adventure. It seems likely that anything as important as the factor determining Walter's decision to break bad would be one most subject to change.

But what kinds of change should we be looking for? One way of changing could be an instantaneous break. He was proud in Episode 3.05, but all of a sudden in Episode 3.06 he was humble. A second mode of change would be gradual movement along a continuum. He started from a materialistic point of view, but possibly over the course of several seasons he will gradually become grounded in spiritual understanding and practice. He will move from agnostic high school teacher to church-going gangster.

I think there's another way of looking at this, and it involves the frequent touchstone of chirality. We don't know with any certainty what chirality is supposed to mean, as I have already mentioned in earlier essays. In the same way, we don't know what "change" is supposed to entail in Walter's life, but one of the possible routes of change, it seems to me, is personal volition. Maybe all of the negative and positive character attributes determining Walter's outlook and behavior at the end of the final season were already present at the beginning of the first season. Perhaps change, as we experience it over the course of *Breaking Bad*, will focus mostly on Walter White's decision to unleash character traits that were earlier suppressed or neglected. Challenges over the next seasons will result in the growing importance of personal choice.

Heisenberg: Family Man

The decision to break bad is not connected to the choice to become Heisenberg.

Consider an angry and determined man who has made a sudden change in life and is now resolved to act against his enemies and pursue his interests. He acquires innovative weapons, confronts those who stand in his way, kills his enemies, and enjoys the spoils of his aggression.

This could be a description of Heisenberg, but it could just as easily be a description of a kind-hearted man whose company we appreciate, whose presence in the neighborhood is not only positive, but reassuring to everyone. The man we speak of is a federal law enforcement agent, and we are glad to hear that when he confronts armed criminals he is firm, stands his ground, and if they do not yield, he disarms or even kills them. Those who oppose Hank Schrader in the meth labs see him as an angry, ominous, unyielding presence. Rightfully so, and bully for Hank.

"Migrant Father with His Young Son"
Unknown photographer, Environmental Protection Agency, 1972, PD

In the last chapter we considered some of the events and conditions that led to Walter's decision to break bad. In this chapter we've looked at the influence of family concerns, and especially Walter's image of himself as husband and father, but none of this explains the decision to adopt the Heisenberg persona. Walter was in the RV, happily making meth several days before he decided to call himself Heisenberg.

We understand change is going to be important throughout this amazing voyage, and we saw two 180-degree changes that precipitated Walter's adoption of the Heisenberg posture.

The first course reversal was dramatically portrayed in the introduction to Episode 1.06. Walter's verbal pledge of "No more bloodshed, no violence" was juxtaposed with flash-forward visuals of a bloodied and angry Walter leaving Tuco's bunker, money bag in hand, walking past the burning, smoking, shattered fragments of the drug lord's bombed-out lair. Events early in the episode led Walter to abandon his pledge of violence-free drug manufacture.

The dramatic turning point occurred in the hospital room where Walter experienced first-hand the outcome of Jesse's attempted drug negotiation with Tuco.

Pain and Suffering

"Tuco Salamanca"
Copyright Martin Woutisseth 2011, used with permission

"Yo," Skinny Pete said, "I didn't catch your name."

Walter looked sick as he sat down in the chair next to Jesse's hospital bed, across the room from Skinny Pete. He didn't respond to Skinny's inquiry.

I think it is possible to believe that Walter wasn't prepared at that moment to offer his real name or an alias. More likely, I think, is the possibility that Walter was psychologically overcome and unable to process anything in his mind beyond the nearly fatal pummeling Jesse had received at the hands of Tuco.

Walter glanced one final time at Jesse. He seemed more nauseated than angry. Contextually, we are to understand Walter's feelings were not induced by the cancer treatments, but by Jesse's critical condition. "Tell me about this Tuco," Walter told Skinny Pete. "Tell me everything about him."

The next morning, Junior greeted "Bad-ass dad," who arrived at the breakfast table sporting a freshly-shaved head. Skyler's response was discomfort, to the point of almost crying. What Skyler saw as a sign of her husband's frailty and mortality, her son preferred to interpret as evidence of strength and depth of character.

Later in the day, when Walter confronted Tuco, he wore only the jacket and the shaved head, no dark glasses or pork pie hat.

"What's your name," Tuco asked.

"Heisenberg."

Walter didn't need the hat, but several other critical elements were required. The cancer, of course, which forced the bald head. But the projection of a persona was far more important, as we learned at breakfast earlier that day. Walter's baldness had to be understood as an outward sign of his inner resolve and extraordinary strength. Mercury fulminate was the crown that placed Heisenberg above Tuco in the "bad-ass" category. It was the proof that Heisenberg could be crazier and more deadly than even the unpredictable and dangerous Tuco Salamanca, but that was not the character trait that propelled him to a position of superiority over Tuco. Drug lords get into pissing matches on a regular basis, but in the end it is not guns that win wars, it is charisma. Wars are won by the sustained commitment of soldiers willing to risk their lives. Soldiers will commit to the highest order of risk only if their leader is someone they can believe in, a person they can trust to overcome the enemy.

The mercury fulminate was important, then, not so much because of its lethal force—its ability to pop eardrums and blow out windows—but because it was the crystalline icon in a grand deception successfully leveled against Tuco. Heisenberg could play meaner and tougher than anyone else in the game, but he was to be feared because he could outsmart everyone else. Tuco was unpredictable but stupid. Heisenberg was unpredictable but crafty, imaginative, eerily intelligent. His piercing eyes spoke of a mental resourcefulness that outstripped the petty bounds of "street smarts."

Piled on top of all this was crystal-pure audacity.

Tuco: "It's your meeting. Why don't you start talking and tell me what you want.
Walter: Fifty thousand dollars.
Tuco: [Laughing] Oh, man … [Laughing] Fifty Gs! How you figure that?

Walter: Thirty five for the pound of meth you stole, and another fifteen for my partner's pain and suffering.

He could have demanded anything. Fifteen thousand dollars for finding a new partner who wasn't beaten up and essentially useless, for instance. Fifteen thousand dollars so Walter could set up his own business without Jesse.

The question I asked myself during this episode began with the introduction. "The chemistry is my realm," Walter told Jesse. "Out there on the street, you deal with that." Jesse's responsibility was the selling side of the business, the part of the operation presumably beyond Walter's skill level. "This operation is you and me." For five episodes we were led to understand that Walter's inexperience in the drug trade would prevent him from interacting in a competent manner with distributors and kingpins. Walter *needed* Jesse because of the two of them only Jesse knew how to sell. This division of expertise was the single fact responsible for their unlikely partnership.

Episode 1.06 changed all the partnership parameters and forced us to scramble for a new understanding of Jesse's relationship with Walter. Heisenberg's commanding performance demonstrated in convincing manner that he possessed both the gumption and ability to deal with the most difficult and unstable personalities in the business. In fact, where Jesse had failed, Heisenberg succeeded.

Walter didn't need Jesse.

The Real Heisenberg

I believe the nature of the relationship between Walter and Jesse is the sublime question posed at the end of Season One. We know Jesse is an equal member in the partnership. But if he no longer offers business acumen that Walter lacks, what is his value to the partnership? This is not a rhetorical question. I do not argue here that Jesse really had no value, that his value has evaporated, that he is now expendable. Any such conclusion or inference would be incorrect and would not address the reality of the philosophical difficulty posed by the last one and a quarter episodes of the first season. Even stripped of his business contribution, Jesse is critical to the partnership.

It seems to me obvious that Jesse's profound value is found not in the realm of business, but in personal areas. Something about Jesse is necessary to Walter/Heisenberg's psychological or emotional wellbeing. But that statement does not even begin to address the question. The crux of the problem is that we now have two characters whose needs must be understood: Walter and Heisenberg. This is not rhetorical, either. The extent to which Heisenberg is real and differs in substantive ways from Walter White I believe to be critical to the complete understanding of *Breaking Bad*.

Is Heisenberg only a blustering façade that has no real connection to anyone or anything, other than to serve as vehicle for Walter's desires? Or is there a depth to Walter's creation that may eclipse the surrendering, incompetent, impotent, emasculated Walter White?

In *The Strange Case of Dr. Jekyll and Mr. Hyde*, Dr. Jekyll's body became inhabited by two diametrically opposed personalities: the original Dr. Jekyll and the diabolical, lusting, murderous Mr. Hyde. Mr. Hyde eventually asserted such control that by the end of the novella Dr. Jekyll was forced to resign. Dr. Jekyll wrote:

> Will Hyde die upon the scaffold? or will he find courage to release himself at the last moment? God knows; I am careless; this is my true hour of death, and what is to follow concerns another than myself. Here then, as I lay down the pen and proceed to seal up my confession, I bring the life of that unhappy Henry Jekyll to an end.

Will Heisenberg, likewise, crowd out Walter and claim everything that was once Walter's as his own? Or will Heisenberg come out only at Walter's beck and call? Will Heisenberg become more real than Walter, or will he remain nothing more than a posture for business, a feared but fictional persona in the drug world?

As I stated above, the decision to break bad was not connected to the choice to become Heisenberg. I believe Walter became Heisenberg at a specific moment in Episode Six. It was not in his confrontation with Tuco. By then he had already chosen his persona. It was not before he entered Jesse's hospital room.

"Yo, I didn't catch your name."

It was when Walter sat down next to Jesse, feeling Jesse's pain, becoming nauseated by the young man's suffering, that Walter formulated his silent response to Skinny Pete's question. "My name is Heisenberg," he told himself.

Walter became Heisenberg in direct response to Jesse's pain.

Walter White could use science to overcome his empathy for Krazy-8; Heisenberg had no such ability, since Heisenberg was guided not by science, but by desire. Walter White, materialistic scientist, could live life in a psychological bubble, disconnected from family and friends, estranged from wife and son. Heisenberg, desire-driven drug mastermind, enjoyed no capacity for emotional withdrawal. He had to achieve human intimacy, as we saw in the opening scenes of Episode 1.07. Skyler was not making love with Walter in the Aztek outside the high school building; Heisenberg was raping her.

Skyler: Where did that come from? Why was it so good?
Walter: Because it was illegal.

It was illegal because it was not Walter, it was Heisenberg. If you doubt that Heisenberg was the one in the car, if you doubt that he was raping Skyler, hold your doubts until Season Two, Episode One, Scene Five, and we will discuss the question again.

Heisenberg could force sexual intimacy on Skyler a few times perhaps before she realized she was not being groped and compromised and penetrated by Walter, but by some other man. But he could achieve only distant connection with anyone else. For instance, he could dance around the question of the illicit pleasure of Hank's Cuban cigars, but he could never come out and say, "I make the best meth in all of New Mexico. I can't tell you what a pleasure it is to be the absolute best at something." He could never have intimacy or even true friendship with Hank.

Most painful to Walter, though, must have been the fact that he could never have real father-son intimacy with Walter Junior. This must have caused greater anguish than any kind of emotional estrangement from Skyler.

Junior, after all, exhibited all the signs of having real love for his father, and confidence in his masculinity. "Bad-ass dad" was a compliment, an assertion that his father was strong. Skyler, on the other hand, had to express nonverbal alarm at Walter's frail appearance, with his newly shaved head, because in her mind Walter had always been feeble, emasculated, not a true husband.

But Walter could never bring Junior into the meth lab. "I make the purest methamphetamine in all of the Southwestern United States. Aren't you proud of me, Son?" Junior could never be proud of such an accomplishment, and therefore Walter could never share with his own son the greatest single achievement of his life—the singular proof of the value and virtue contained in the pride he felt for himself.

Jesse, on the other hand, was already a protégé, already demanding of his work the same high quality he saw in Walter's careful technique and scientific artistry.

Heisenberg is more a family man than Walter White. Walter could shrug his shoulders and leave his wife and son. Heisenberg, on the other hand, desperately needed Skyler and Junior. He could force himself on Skyler—at least in Episode 1.06. But he could not force himself to be any more of a father to Junior, could not allow Junior into emotional intimacy, because that close sphere was illegal, toxic to a teenage boy, antithetical to the father-son relationship.

With no way to achieve a close father-son bond with Junior, Heisenberg looked around for other sources of intimacy. And there he sat, in a hospital room, a few floor tiles away from a young man not five years older than his biological son.

"I am Heisenberg" is synonymous with the statement never uttered in Season One, but built into the foundation of the edifice we know as *Breaking Bad*: "I am Jesse's father."

Chapter Li

"Tuco Salamanca's Home"
Copyright Martin Woutisseth 2011, used with permission

The prosecutor, his face contorted in righteous indignation, jumps to his feet, pointing an accusing finger. "He's lying, Your Honor!"

A gasp jolts the courtroom. The judge, normally sober and calm, is so struck by the accused's contempt for justice that he turns angry eyes toward the scoundrel. We the viewers are no less indignant. We saw him commit the crime in the opening minutes of the program. We know he is guilty. We know his lies serve only to deceive, to convince us he is something he is not.

Breaking Bad is founded on lies. Walter's lies were of the type we have witnessed millions of times in thousands of procedural crime dramas on television and in the movies.

But if deceptive and conspiratorial falsehoods were the only species of lies on *Breaking Bad* the series would not have risen to the rarefied heights of critical artistic recognition. There were no courtroom scenes in *Breaking Bad*. When we were allowed glimpses into the criminal justice system, we saw process failures, self-serving lawyers, and the triumph of wrong over right. If we did not witness the traditional, well-worn procedural rules of justice, should we be surprised that *Breaking Bad* refused to exploit the trite and boring cause-and-effect relationship of criminal deception?

Breaking Bad is founded on lies, but it is the *nature* of those lies, their unintended and unforeseen consequences, and the way they affect characters that give this series its biting edge and imbue its plotline with deep authenticity. Perhaps the show's greatest achievement is that it served up lies we did not see and forced us to deal with consequences no less striking than those experienced by the characters. In fact, by the end of the series we realized we had become victims of an unusual but necessary deception, but the falsehood was nothing less than *Breaking Bad*'s greatest dramatic achievement.

Truth or Consequences

First Lady Nancy Reagan
Official White House Photograph, 1987, PD

"Just Say No."

Getting involved in illicit drug manufacture is immoral and illegal. That's it. There are no other consequences. If you sell or purchase drugs all it means is that you're a bad person.

95

I imagine even Nancy Reagan would have argued that involvement in illicit drugs has the potential for consequences beyond those to the user. The connection between drug use and crime was well established by the time the former first lady began her anti-drug crusade in the mid-1980s. We may disagree about the root cause of drug-induced crime, but no one of reasonable mind could argue that the allure of illicit drugs and the cost of maintaining a drug habit do not lead to crime, violence, and suffering.

One of my favorite scenes occurred in Episode 1.07, when Walter and Hank relaxed by the backyard pool. Glasses of scotch in hand, Hank lit up a perfectly wrapped stogie.

Walt: Cuban. Huh.
Hank: I did a little favor for a FBI guy.
Walt: Now, I was under the impression that these were illegal.
Hank: [Laughs] Yeah, well, sometimes forbidden fruit tastes the sweetest.

I laughed the first time I watched the scene, reminded of Chevy Chase's bit about the 'Mattress Police' in the 1985 comedy "Fletch."

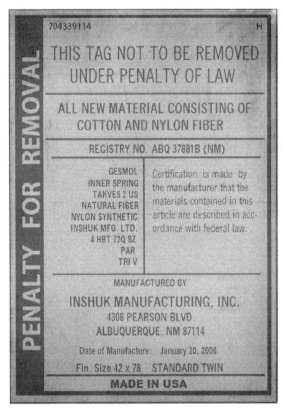

"Mattress Tag"
Copyright 2013 Pearson Moore

But as I discovered in researching this book, the importation, sale, and enjoyment of Cuban cigars is a serious matter under United States law. The penalties are severe. In 2002, Richard Connors, an attorney in Skokie, Illinois, was sentenced to 37 months in prison for bringing a few Cuban cigars into the country. (Abovethelaw.com, 15 August 2012, accessed on 8 October 2013.) The 1996 Helms-Burton Law actually *increases* the penalties for importation of Cuban cigars (Cigaraficionado.com, November 1997, accessed on 8 October 2013), and Customs regulations (31 CFR Part 515) allowing individuals to declare up to $100 worth of Cuban goods (including cigars) were rescinded in 2004. (www.treasury.gov, Cuban Cigar Update, 9/30/2004) If you try to bring even a single Cuban cigar across the border you may find yourself handcuffed and sent off to federal prison.

Hank had no reason to fear jail time or fines. Enforcement of statute on Cuban goods is irregular at best, and dependent on jurisdiction. If the local 'FBI guy' was handing out illegal contraband to his friends in law enforcement, even a complaint to the nearest FBI office about Hank's stash of Havana stogies would have been pointless.

The scene was not intended to portray Hank's ability to skirt the law. The point of his guilt-free enjoyment of a fine smoke was that *Breaking Bad* is not an examination of the legality of Walter's methamphetamine operation. To underscore that truth, the two brothers-in-law continued their philosophical discussion.

Walt: It's funny, isn't it? How we draw that line?
Hank: Yup. What line is that?
Walt: What's legal, what's illegal. Cuban cigars, alcohol. You know, if we were drinking this in 1930 we'd be breaking the law. Who knows what will be legal next year.
Hank: You mean like pot?
Walt: Yeah, like pot. Or whatever.
....
Hank: Friggin' meth used to be legal. Used to sell it over every counter and every pharmacy across America.

Walter and Hank sat outside where anyone in the world could see them, imbibing a powerful, mind-altering drug (alcohol) and smoking illegal contraband (Cuban cigars) that could have resulted in a $60,000 fine and three years in federal prison. Yet *Breaking Bad* would have us think no less of Hank. In fact, he may be the only hero in the series.

The implication of this poolside exchange is that *Breaking Bad* isn't about legality or even about drugs *per se*. It's about choices, lies, and consequences.

How Green Was My Deception

Webster tells us a lie is "a false statement made with deliberate intent to deceive." But the dictionary doesn't stop with that first definition, and neither does *Breaking Bad*. If we wish to understand deception in its many forms, we must recognize those objects or events "intended or serving to convey a false impression," for those are lies, too, no less than a false verbal statement. In fact, I hold this manner of deception more important on *Breaking Bad* than the spoken variety.

The first episode of the second season contained a powerful scene that communicated much about the characters and the direction *Breaking Bad* will take. After Walter witnessed Tuco pummel a man to death he came home to find Skyler, her face covered in green avocado therapeutic face mask. He cried into her shoulder and began lifting her bath robe. He was trying to initiate sex, and Skyler would not have it.

"Enough. Hold up. Stop it. STOP IT!"

After Skyler pulled away and straightened her robe, Walter went to the backyard and wept. After a few minutes (or hours) she went outside to chastise Walter:

"I know you're scared, but you can't take it out on me."

Skyler was telling Walter that she knew his attempt at having sexual intercourse did not begin with a desire to make love with his wife. His desire to conquer her was, in that moment, a result of events unrelated to Skyler. That is, Walter was trying to use her as a means of reducing fear or anxiety or other emotions he was experiencing, none of which had anything to do with Skyler. Physical love is the expression of spiritual and emotional bonds between two lovers. The action Walter tried to take, though, was not based on spiritual or emotional bonds. In fact, what Walter was attempting was nothing short of rape.

That is, Walter's attempt at sex was a lie. He wished Skyler to believe in that moment that he was attracted to her, that he wished to physically share those emotional and spiritual attributes that guided their marriage. But it was a deception. The emotion weighing on his mind was the senseless murder of Tuco's lieutenant, not his psychic investment in and appreciation of Skyler as his lover.

Now the aspect of this scene I found most compelling was Skyler's intuition. I doubt anyone reading these words considers a woman with green goop smeared all over her face to be in any way attractive or sexy. Skyler would have known that. Walter began the interaction by crying on her shoulder, not by expressing his love. But the actions that followed were simply not consonant with Walter's character. He was not himself. The way he was touching her was not the way a caring man touched his lover. She sensed something was wrong. She knew Walter's actions were intended to deceive so that he could gain control over her to satisfy his own selfish whims.

Even if she incorrectly attributed Walter's actions to his fear of cancer and not to some other major event in his life, she nevertheless understood Walter's gropings as a lie. I believe this to be the critical truth of the scene. Skyler understood Walter as no one else could.

A Rainbow of Deceptions

Placing Skyler in an avocado face mask was no accident. The green color of her mask, no less than her blue underwear, carried heavy symbolic meaning. The color of clothing, objects, and background bears enormous significance in *Breaking Bad*, as I will argue throughout this book. One of the most obvious examples of color symbolism is the character of always-lavender Marie Schrader and her Purple Palace.

At first glance, Marie's kleptomania is understood as a quaint comparison to Walter's far greater crimes. I believe we gain the most in our interpretation of Marie by thinking of her shoplifting sprees as a type of deception. I look at Marie's kleptomania as falsehood on three levels or 'energy shells': She lied to those from whom she stole, she lied to herself, and she lied to the world around her. To use *Breaking Bad* terminology, she lied to the Universe. The distinctions between the three levels are important primarily because Marie, in my opinion, is not merely a humorous sidelight but in fact she holds the key to puzzling out the true significance of Walter's crime. To understand the Purple Princess is to understand Heisenberg.

The shoe store scene in Episode 1.03 reveals important facets of Marie's deception-based illness.

"Excuse me, Ma'am. Ma'am." The shop clerk interrupted her cell phone conversation with her boyfriend long enough to address Marie. "You need to be wearing footies before you try those on."

Marie, insulted and annoyed, said, "I'm extremely clean."

"Yeah, well, I'd really appreciate it." She glared at Marie for a moment, then clicked her cell phone back on. "Hey, sorry about that," she said, apologizing to her beau for the inconvenience.

A good manager would have taken the clerk aside for reprimand, retraining, or termination. Marie was a customer—the person who determined the company's future. Without customers the company would fold, but the clerk was treating Marie as an inconvenience, as a person unworthy of her time, an unwelcome interruption to her cell phone call.

We know Marie's theft of the purple shoes was no mere tit-for-tat by a disgruntled customer, as we learned when she stole an expensive child's tiara (Episode 1.07). More than that, Marie didn't keep the tiara for herself, but offered it as a gift to Skyler's as yet unborn baby girl.

If we wondered about Marie's penchant for shoplifting on behalf of friends and family, her mental state became clearer in Episode 2.01, when Hank revealed that Marie was in therapy for kleptomania. She was seeing a therapist named 'Dave'. Just as the shoe store clerk considered Marie a distasteful inconvenience, Marie hated her sessions with Dave. The implication is that Marie did not understand her compulsion as anything that required intervention or adjustment. In her mind, she was not stealing.

There is a lot more to Marie's state of mind, most of which can be understood through the symbolic nature of the color purple. Unfortunately, we don't get another opportunity to study her kleptomania until Season Four. I'm not going to wait that long to discuss the color purple; those familiar with the periodic table will probably guess that I'll address purple next period (next season) in Chapter P. They would be correct!

I will begin my discussion of color in Chapter C. I won't go into much detail on purple, since this is a primary *Breaking Bad* color. Though purple seems straightforward in meaning, its significance is far deeper than a simple "Marie thinks she's a princess so she wears royal purple." Analyzing purple, then, would kind of be like analyzing the answer before considering the question. Rather than putting the cart before the horse, I will dig deeper into the meaning of white, black, and gray. I feel certain attitudes toward color may detract from our ability to understand Vince Gilligan's symbol-laden world, and for this reason I am going to concentrate the discussion on the secondary color green and the primary color red. My hope is that this treatment will allow viewers a deeper appreciation of the primary color yellow which will become important later in Season Two and critical to a deeper understanding of Season Three. Yellow and blue are the two power colors of *Breaking Bad*.

The Curve of Binding Dramatic Energy

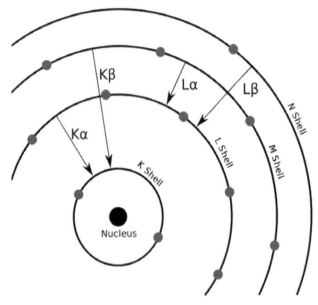

"Atomic Shells"
Copyright 2008 Henrik Midtiby, CC-SA 3.0

As I mentioned above in "A Rainbow of Deceptions," I prefer to look at Marie's problem with kleptomania as a 'shell' of lies. I'm using the word shell in the scientific sense of an atomic energy level or electron level around an atom. The idea I'm trying to convey is that of a lie wrapped around a deeper lie that itself is wrapped around an even deeper lie, akin to the layers of an onion or the energy shells of an atom. Others have referred to Marie's and Walter's deceptions as a 'house of cards' waiting for the right moment to fall. I believe the shell or onion analogy is more useful to our understanding.

If Walter built a 'house of cards' it turned out to be quite a resilient little structure, standing up to nearly every challenge over the course of two years of his life (or six seasons of the show). The image of a house of cards conveys the idea that virtually any random event could cause the precarious hovel to collapse, but this proved not to be the case. The image of an onion, on the other hand, communicates the notion of solid and orderly structure, as well as the concept of greater and lesser components.

There are many ways to look at the structured layers. We might begin with the idea of chiasm.

Chiasm in LOST 1.05, Act 4, Scene 5

Analysis by Pearson Moore, June 2010

A. 45.01 to 45.07 Water, Leadership. Jack: I'm no leader.

B. 45.08   Locke changes subject:
                     Why are you here, Jack?

C.   45.08 to 45.10   Jack: I'm crazy. Locke: Jack not crazy.

D.   45.13 to 45.14   Jack chases the White Rabbit.

E.   45.14 to 45.15 The chase has no reason.

F.   45.17   The Rabbit is not real.

G.   45.19 to 45.21   Jack: The Rabbit is hallucination.

H.   45.22a   The Island is not magic, but real.

I. CHIASTIC CENTER 45.22b **The Island is different. Special.**

H'.   45.22c   The Island is not scary, but real.
                              (we all feel it.)

G'.   45.22d   Locke: Rabbit is hallucination.

F'.   45.22e   What if Rabbit is real?

E'.   45.22e   Locke: Jack's chasing the Rabbit.

D'.   45.22e   The chase has a reason.

C'.   45.23 to 45.25   Jack: Rabbit is impossible. (Jack crazy)
                          Locke: Rabbit possible. (Jack not crazy)

B'. 45.26   Locke changes subject:
                      Island is beautiful.

A'. 45.27 to 45.32   Water, Leadership.
                      Locke: Jack is not (yet) a leader.

Chiasm in "White Rabbit" (*Lost*, Episode 1.05)
Copyright Pearson Moore 2010

One of the reasons Locke's 'Island' speech in *Lost* Episode 1.05 ("White Rabbit") was so memorable was its chiastic, layer-within-layer onion structure. The central idea of Locke's speech was, "This place is different. Special." The statement became emphatic because of its placement within mirrored layers of lesser proclamations.

The analysis of *Breaking Bad* poses as many difficulties as the process of breaking (understanding) *Lost*. I believe that by layering the various elements of *Breaking Bad* we can more easily elucidate the primary themes and theses.

In searching for conceptual helps we might consider deep-background sources. "I feel some sort of need for biblical atonement, or justice, or something," Vince Gilligan said of *Breaking Bad*. (*New York Times Magazine*, 7/10/2011) In the *Fresh Air* interview of Gilligan, he said this about retribution:

> I can stand the thought that there's no heaven. But I don't know
> that I can stand the thought that there's no hell, because, you

know, where is Hitler then? You know, where is Pol Pot? There's got to be some kind of a payback. (*Fresh Air*, 9/19/2011)

Though Vince Gilligan considers himself agnostic on the question of God, he makes broad appeal to biblical thought in *Breaking Bad*. I find a passage from the wisdom literature of Hebrew scripture particularly useful in understanding the series. King Solomon's list of sins (Pr. 6:16-19) provides a chiastic hierarchy of crimes that seems to fit well the structure of Walter White's story.

Solomon's Seven Sins (Proverbs 6:16-19)

1.	Proud eyes
2.		Lying tongue
3.			Shedding innocent blood
4.				**Wicked plots**
5.			Running toward evil
6.		Lying witness
7.	Sowing discord

We looked at Walter's pride in our analysis of the first season. We'll take a closer look in Chapter C. For now it's enough to note that the seven sins outlined in Chapter Six of Proverbs establish a kind of layered cascade. Not everyone who exhibits pride in her accomplishments succumbs to the temptation of lying about herself, but lying is a natural outcome of pride, and constitutes a deeper transgression than simple pride. Deeper still is the crime of shedding innocent blood. In terms familiar to many readers, pride might often be considered a 'venial' sin, while lying could be considered either 'venial' or 'mortal', depending on circumstances, but the shedding of innocent blood is always, without question, a 'mortal' sin.

The importance of Solomon's ranking of sins to viewer-participants of *Breaking Bad* is that the construction of 'Wicked Plots' is considered the worst of crimes against Deity and humanity—worse than the shedding of innocent blood or a propensity for ('running toward') evil.

I will not define the crimes I consider 'Wicked Plots', nor will I even claim that Walter White builds anything that could be considered 'Wicked'. I leave that for viewer-participants to decide. But the beauty of Solomon's concept of layered crimes is the notion that there may be sins greater than even the murder of innocents. An essential corollary question to the Mr. Chips to Scarface narrative is that of the unforgivable sin. Is there a point at which Walter White commits crimes of such magnitude that there is no possibility of rehabilitation? Will *Breaking Bad* reach a time when Walter White simply cannot be forgiven? It is a fascinating question that warrants consideration throughout the progression of the series.

Chapter Be

Beetle
Francis de Laporte de Castelnau, 1856

"Peekaboo" (Episode 2.06) opens with a point-of-view shot looking up at Jesse from pavement level. He's smoking, waiting, and pleasantly distracted by something we find out is a beetle. He bends down, offers the insect his hand, and it crawls over his fingers. Jesse smiles, gently releases the beetle, and Skinny Pete strides toward him. Pete looks down in disgust, squashes the insect with his shoe and says, "Damn, bitch."

The entire sequence takes 37 seconds but, occurring as it does in the opening scene, the event is intended to shock and at the same time convey important information. It is not a throw-away moment. In fact, it's not difficult to assign four levels of symbolic significance.

In the immediate context of Jesse's mission to 'bring God' to Spooge and his girlfriend, Pete's message to Jesse is simple: "Get real, man. You're gonna threaten two druggies with death. If you're looking out for bugs you're head's in the wrong place." The sequence illustrates the fact that Jesse is out of touch with his killer side. Moments later, just before entering Spooge's rat-infested lair, he practices his "Pay up, Bitch" speech, trying to convince himself that he's ready for the confrontation. He is not, of course, and his lack of killer instinct causes the encounter to go disastrously wrong for him. The first message of the sequence, then, is that Jesse is far outside his comfort zone. As Krazy-8 told Walter (Episode 1.03), "Trust me, this line of work doesn't suit you." Jesse's just not cut out to be a killer.

The beetle is a powerless innocent, too, and I doubt anyone would argue with the common contention that the beetle is symbolic of the nameless Young Boy in the care of Spooge and his girlfriend, likely the girlfriend's child. Jesse risks his own safety to ensure the boy's welfare, just as he risked Pete's disapproval in his gentle manner with the insect.

But we might also see in the beetle a broader indication of Jesse's deep empathy for children. We've already observed that he cares for his younger brother, Jake. Beginning in Season Three we will see him become a caring father figure for Brock Cantillo, a young boy crucial to the overall plot. At his very core, Jesse loves children.

The Metamorphosis

The appearance of the beetle might have served as nothing more than a shocking introduction to Episode 2.06 and a harbinger of Jesse's empathy for the young boy if not for constant recurrence of the insect theme throughout the series. If we include the spider imagery of Season Five, *Breaking Bad* contains at least 11 high-profile references to insects:

2.03	"Bit By a Dead Bee"
2.06	"Peekaboo" (beetle image)
3.10	"Fly" (fly motif)
4.09	"Bug" (insect image)
5.04	Fly poster (fly motif)
5.05	"Dead Freight" (spider motif)
5.06	"Buyout" (spider motif)
5.08	"Gliding Over All" (fly motif)
5.11	"Confessions" (spider motif)
5.14	"Ozymandias" (the 'dung beetle' sequence)

I said there were 11 insect references but I listed only ten above. There is an 11th reference, and it is the one I wish to discuss in this chapter. Possibly the key reference occurs in Episode 3.09, titled "Kafkaesque." Franz Kafka's most famous work by far is *The Metamorphosis*, a novel long associated in most readers' minds with the image of a detestable insect.

Die Verwandlung, original cover illustration, 1916

Those who have read the novel in English will not be surprised to see an insect featured on the front cover.

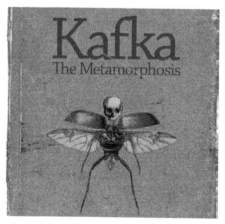

An English language cover of *The Metamorphosis* circa 1920

Many essayists have already commented that the beetle image in Episode 2.06 and the reference to Kafka in Episode 3.09 go together like sauerkraut and schnitzel. I am willing to believe there is a connection, but if so, my guess is it's more like sauerkraut and streusel. Just try eating both of those in the same meal!

Several peculiarities of *The Metamorphosis* (German title *Die Verwandlung*) are important to this discussion. In particular, I believe Kafka's manipulation of the German language is essential to our understanding of the way Vince Gilligan & Co. applied Kafkaesque imagery throughout the series.

Here is a typical English language translation of the first sentence of *The Metamorphosis*:

> As Gregor Samsa awoke one morning from uneasy dreams he
> found himself transformed in his bed into a gigantic insect.

There are multiple problems with this translation, probably chief among them the fact that Kafka never wrote the word 'insect'. Here is the opening sentence of *Die Verwandlung* as Kafka wrote it:

> Als Gregor Samsa eines Morgens aus unruhigen Träumener
> wachte, fand er sich in seinem Bett zu einem ungeheuren
> Ungeziefer verwandelt.

The critical word is the noun, *Ungeziefer,* which my Langenscheidt dictionary renders as *vermin*, not insect. If we trace the word back to Kafka's time and place, the intended meaning was probably something closer to 'unclean animal'. Placing the word 'insect' in the English translation of the sentence can be justified on the basis of local usage, but we need to consider Kafka's personal history, too. *Ungeziefer,* in Kafka's time, could mean vermin in the same way we might say 'bug' in English. But it could mean 'unclean animal', too, and there are reasons to believe he intended to at least plant this idea in readers' imaginations, even if his greater intention was somewhat different.

Franz Kafka was Jewish. He grew up in Prague, then part of the Austro-Hungarian Empire. Most importantly to our discussion, Franz was the grandson of Jakob Kafka, a Jewish Shochet (ritual slaughterer). At least in his childhood, then, Kafka was likely to have associated the word *Ungeziefer* with the idea of a ritually unclean animal, not with the concept of an insect. Thus, a more nuanced and probably better translation, in the sense of maintaining the intention of the original author, might come closer to David Wyllie's outstanding rendition:

> One morning, when Gregor Samsa woke from troubled dreams,
> he found himself transformed in his bed into a horrible vermin.

Take a moment to look at the first edition cover. We see a distressed man in a bathrobe, taut hands covering his face. The door behind him is open, but so engulfed is he in overwhelming angst that he is oblivious. The open door might indicate escape or deliverance, but the man is too caught up in the emotion of the moment and remains a prisoner to the great roiling tempests seething inside him.

There's no insect anywhere to be seen, and this was no accident. In instructions to the publisher, Kafka said, "An insect is not to be drawn. It is not even to be seen from a distance."

The important aspect of Gregor Samsa's transformation is not the physical result but the psychic/psychological result. This is why **Kafka insisted on a cover that depicted deep angst in an otherwise normal human being**. Samsa was disgusted with himself. That was the essential message.

Real fans of *Breaking Bad* will wish to read *The Metamorphosis*. We are at a distinct disadvantage if we don't read German, but even native Germans fluent in their mother tongue need to read carefully. *Die Verwandlung* is not meant to be smooth sailing, for its deepest meanings are symbolic and its language was **intentionally** vague and esoteric.

Franz Kafka was unusually well educated. He certainly knew standard German (*Hochdeutsch*), but he purposefully composed *Die Verwandlung* in highly vernacular Czech- and Yiddish-influenced German. On top of all that, Kafka intentionally employed ambiguous phrasing, imagery, and expressions to obfuscate rather than clarify. Why he chose to do this I believe is at the heart of his literary style and points to a major theme in *Breaking Bad*.

Kafkaesque

Franz Kafka knew that real understanding is not academic. If I appreciate the truth of something it is because I have absorbed that truth into my soul. Anything less than this is less than fully true because it lacks vitality. If I can take it or leave it, if Gregor Samsa's struggle occurs only at arm's length at the periphery of my detached interest, there's no intensity, there's nothing in his struggle that carries any meaning for me. On the other hand, if I have emotional connection with Samsa, his struggle becomes my struggle, and any truth he holds dear takes up residence in my heart.

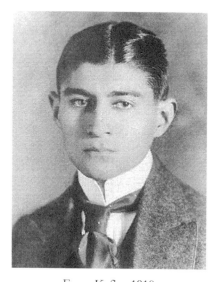

Franz Kafka, 1910

107

Kafka used disorientation, vagueness, and a sense of unease or helplessness to magnify the bureaucratic senselessness of life. The adjective 'Kafkaesque' is thrown around all too easily, and I believe that is the significance of the title of the 9th episode of Season Three. Jesse's therapy session focuses on the meaning of the word.

Jesse: One day pretty much bleeds into the next. Been workin' a lot…It's in a laundromat, it's totally corporate…It's like rigid, all kinds of red tape. My boss is a dick. The owner's a super dick…the place is full of dead-eyed douche bags, the hours suck, and nobody knows what's going on, so…
Leader: Sounds kind of Kafkaesque.
Jesse: Yeah, totally Kafkaesque. Majorly.

Those who have seen the first nine episodes of Season Three can appreciate the irony of Jesse's words. The situation he describes would find resonance with anyone who's worked in a corporate environment. But for a situation to be Kafkaesque means we *don't* understand, we *don't* empathize because we can't figure it out. When the Leader says, "Sounds Kafkaesque," his words are laughable because what Jesse has described is *not* Kafkaesque at all. The irony of it, though, is that Jesse's real situation—the one he keeps hidden from the group—is entirely Kafkaesque. His very presence at a drug rehabilitation/support group while he is working 14 hour days to churn out the region's supply of methamphetamine is definitely Kafkaesque.

Kafkaesque does not necessarily have to mean brooding and angst-ridden emotion in the face of structural meaninglessness, as Saul Goodman demonstrated later in the episode.

Saul: You know you need to launder your money, right?
Jesse: I ain't buyin' no damn nail salon, so just forget it.
Saul: Well, you want to stay out of jail, don't ya?…'Cause I got three little letters for you: IRS. If they can get Capone, they can get you…Oh, who's this? The Tax Man, and he's looking at you. What does he see? He sees a young fella with a big fancy house, unlimited cash supply, and no job. Now what is the conclusion that the Tax Man makes?
Jesse: I'm a drug dealer.
Saul: [Makes loud buzzer noise] Wrong! Million times worse: You're a tax cheat. What do they do? They take every penny and you go in the can for felony tax evasion.

Saul's words should be meaningless. Unfortunately, though, and very ironically, his words are 100 percent correct. The senseless, Kafkaesque hierarchy of laws in the United States means a criminal is more likely to face charges of tax evasion than incarceration for murder. The underlying ironic truth—that the United States is more interested in tax collection than in the apprehension of dangerous of criminals—is most certainly Kafkaesque.

The restaurant scene near the end of the episode mirrors Saul's nail salon appeal. Both are hilarious. Jesse, commiserating with Skinny Pete and Badger says,

"What's the point of bein' an outlaw when you got responsibilities?...I gotta pay taxes now? What the hell's up with that? That's messed up, yo. That's Kafkaesque."

The serious side of Kafka's jumbled vision is the interior aspect of it all: angst, self-loathing, fear, a sense of helplessness. I believe these are the realities that Vince Gilligan and the writers are pointing to in their evocation of insect imagery throughout *Breaking Bad*. Episode 3.09, "Kafkaesque," looks at the outside, superficial, humorous aspects of a structured world that lacks true cohesion. The very next episode, 3.10, titled "Fly," is considered by many to be the finest episode in the entire series. I have to believe it is Episode 3.10's unflinching examination of Walter's inner struggle that elevates the episode far above even the normally outstanding episodes of *Breaking Bad*.

So we sit in front of the screen, watching an insect crawl over Jesse's fingers. Should we feel amusement, or benign interest, as Jesse did? Or should we instead feel revulsion, even hatred, as Skinny Pete did? I cannot say, and I believe *Breaking Bad* does not tell us. Regardless of any feelings we may have about the beetle, though, my recommendation is to give the insect your full attention. Think about it, in as many ways as your consciousness allows. For in the insect motif, in our revulsion and disgust and angst, may possibly lie the key to our understanding of the most powerful series written for television.

Chapter B

B^5eau Jest

"Saul Goodman"
Copyright Martin Woutisseth, used with permission

Breaking Bad, I have often said in my online essays, is not social commentary. It is morality play, writ large. But the show is not above using the ironies and counter-intuitive aspects of society to tell its story. It paints a picture of the criminal underworld as Kafkaesque but it also draws upon cultural and legal structures to magnify the moral dilemmas faced by Walter and those he pulls into his conspiracies.

Saul Goodman is one of the series' most interesting creations. Not really Jewish (his real surname is McGill, not Goodman; we never learn his real first name), he's not really a lawyer either, as his law degree is from the "University of American Samoa" (there is no such institution). Nevertheless in most cases throughout the series he remains true to the legal demands of his adopted profession. That Saul usually operates within the law, even when his actions often appear immoral, is yet another irony of the *Breaking Bad* world. Saul Goodman is *Breaking Bad*'s beau jest to the legal profession.

I have to admit ignorance of the legal system. My formal training is in science and linguistics, not law. But my sister is a paralegal, and though I have no personal understanding of the system of justice, I have always found it fascinating.

Necessity in Adversity

Defense Attorney Clarence Darrow, circa 1918

How can a defense attorney represent a client she knows to be guilty of a crime? The simple answer is that she must do so. In fact, she is legally and ethically *required* to do so.

The fact that a defense attorney must use every bit of legally-permissible ingenuity at her disposal to help her client is a direct outcome of the constitutionally-enshrined insistence that an accused individual is innocent until proven guilty by a jury of his peers. The jury determines guilt or innocence based on evidence presented by adversaries, usually the defense attorney and the prosecuting attorney. As the accused is presumed innocent, the legal system is not permitted to require his testimony. By proxy, the system is equally prohibited from requiring the defense attorney's testimony. In the United States, the prohibition against compelling the accused's testimony is further safeguarded in the Fifth Amendment to the Constitution.

Legally, then, the question of whether the accused or the defense attorney knows of the defendant's guilt is moot. It is irrelevant to the legal system because justice is a matter of evidence presented and not dependent on how the accused feels about himself or his relation to society.

Even if the attorney's client admits he committed the offense with which he is charged, he may be guilty of no crime. He may be lying to his attorney. He may have been coerced into committing the act. He may be guilty of a far lesser crime than the one for which he is being prosecuted. There may be compelling, legally-defensible reasons for his action. In the end, it's not the defense attorney's business to determine guilt or innocence. Her single charge is to present evidence of innocence in as compelling a manner as she can without circumventing the law.

For the most part, this is precisely what Saul Goodman, Esquire, did for his clients Walter White and Jesse Pinkman.

Ethical Used Car Salesman

Emil B. Toman, Salesman
1928, placed in PD 2009

We first meet Saul Goodman in the second scene of Episode 2.08 ("Better Call Saul"). Using cheesy sets, cheap graphics, and bad actors, Saul's television commercial sets him up as a sleazy, unethical character that anyone with half a brain would know to avoid. When we next see him, he's sitting opposite Badger in a jailhouse interview room pulling up papers from his briefcase about Brandon Mayhew's arrest for public masturbation. Somehow Saul mixed up names or case histories because Brandon was not arrested for a trivial misdemeanor but for felony narcotics possession and sale. He would be doing real time in the Big House unless he could find unusually competent legal representation. Based on our introduction to Saul and his inability to even keep cases straight, he should have seemed a most unlikely candidate for representing one of Heisenberg's street dealers.

But the next scene provided the critical information about Saul's suitability as legal representative to any of Walter's goons. We saw him walking down the hallway of the Albuquerque Police Station, speaking loudly into his Bluetooth earpiece. We've experienced this sequence before, in Episode 1.04, in the person of businessman 'Ken', owner of the sports car with the 'KenWins' license plate. Saul Goodman is nothing less than a carbon copy of the swaggering, inconsiderate, me-first entrepreneur who has no interest in others' welfare even when they're his clients, as we observed in his jail cell interaction with Badger.

We know from the events of Episode 1.04 that Walter hates people like Ken and Saul. The irony is that Walter had to engage Saul as legal representative if he wished to continue his illegal methamphetamine business and not end up in prison himself. To avoid personal loss he had to further compromise his own ethics. In forcing Walter to deal with Saul, to 'shake hands with the Devil', we see concrete examples of several *Breaking Bad* themes, including the stripping away of ethics, unforeseeable consequences, and irony.

Saul is the bottom of the barrel in terms of personal attorneys. As I noted above, he's not really an attorney at all. Walter had to engage him because he had no other choice. Despite his Heisenberg bravado and inflated sense of self, Walter was almost broke. After his cancer treatment costs and the DEA's seizure of Jesse's $67,920 (Episode 2.03), the most Walter could afford to pay was a few thousand dollars for Saul's help and $80,000 for Jimmy Kilkelly's performance as Heisenberg.

Some viewers of Episode 2.08 will come away from the nighttime trench scene thinking Saul was exercising professional formality in requesting that Walter and Jesse each pay him a dollar to establish 'attorney/client privilege'. Others may look at the scene and believe Saul was merely trying to distract them from what he took to be their real intention: to kill him. After all, money does not have to change hands for a defense attorney to legally and ethically work for a client. Any attorney at any time can work without payment, simply out of the goodness of her heart. It's called *pro bono* work, and many lawyers regularly give a large percentage of their time to this type of charitable assistance.

After watching the entire series twice, I'm inclined to place myself in the 'Professional Formality' camp regarding Saul's request for payment to establish attorney/client privilege. I understand he was trying to save his own skin, and disorienting Walter and Jesse with a seemingly off-the-wall request was a good way to do it. I understand he didn't need the money to officially and legally represent them as their attorney. In American law, though, there is an additional, complicating concept of 'Consideration'. Consideration is a tangible good or service one person gives in exchange for a second person's service or action on the first person's behalf. In many legal situations Consideration renders a contract legally enforceable. Consideration is the legal glue that binds parties to a contract.

In the trench scene, for instance, imagine that Saul tells the two hooded men he will represent them but he does not insist on an exchange of money. All of a sudden the police show up and Saul rats on them, disclosing every illegality he can recall having seen or heard. Without Consideration, all Walter and Jesse can claim is that a spoken contract existed and Saul was violating that contract. But with the exchange of money their claim of broken contract would carry greater legal standing. They could sue Saul for breach of contract, and they'd probably win. Perhaps Saul's trench-side testimony might even have to be thrown out of criminal court.

But how does this relate to an 'Ethical Used Car Salesman'?

Beau Geste

Kepi Blanc Soldiers of the Légion Étrangère
Tech. Sgt. H. H. Deffner, U.S. Army, 1992, PD

Lawyers and politicians are often considered the least ethical of all people, routinely lumped together with used car salesmen and prostitutes in the public's estimation. Many consider that leaders in the legal and political fields, having been accorded personal stature and public trust, have an obligation to act on behalf of society. When these leaders act out of selfish desire, they betray that trust.

I believe in the nighttime scene at the trench, Jesse's gun to his head, Saul was demonstrating an ethical continuity of character. Recall the earlier scene in the car outside Saul's office. Walter expressed to Jesse his disgust with Saul's behavior. "He won't take a bribe," Walter said, shaking his head in disbelief.

No. Saul would not take a bribe. The fact was beyond belief to Walter. After all, Saul dressed like a circus clown and he would represent anyone—for a price. How unethical was *that*? As we've already discussed, there is nothing unethical about representing criminals. It's not only ethical under the American system of law, in cases

114

involving a contract it can be legally binding and necessary for an attorney to do everything she can on behalf of a client.

Saul is not perfect. But Walter is less perfect than Saul. The mistake Walter made, and the error we should try to avoid, is looking at Saul as we would a used car salesman or prostitute. He was neither of those, and in critical scenes I think he may have been far more than an attorney in a clown suit. He will come to be used as comic relief in an otherwise deadly-serious drama series, but I feel in some situations he may serve a dual purpose, to include solid ethical grounding for Walter's moral compass.

Foreign Legion Adventures
Unknown artist, circa 1930, PD

At critical moments in the future, I see Saul as having offered Walter a *beau geste*—a kind and noble gesture based on good intentions but meaningless in execution and result. Saul, to my mind, might be compared to a mercenary soldier, such as a newly-minted Kepi Blanc in the Légion Étrangère (French Foreign Legion).

Even today, the Légion Étrangère is full of 'thieves, scoundrels, and blackguards', but they constitute a determined, courageous, and *honorable* fighting force: a real-world irony. The final irony in *Breaking Bad* is not that Walter had to condescend to hire Saul. The far greater and more enduring irony is that Saul, in the end, will have demonstrated greater honor and morality than Walter, or indeed most of the players in this tale of greed and death and depravity.

Chapter C

Color

Lyndon Johnson, President, and Ronald Reagan, Actor
Official White House photograph circa 1967, PD
Publicity still from "Law and Order," 1953, PD

Good guys always wear white, bad guys always wear black. While the old adage may be true in politics and movies (or is it horseshoes and hand grenades?), it's not always true in real life, and it's never true in *Breaking Bad*.

I will not argue with those who claim Lyndon Johnson's heroic service in the United States Navy, where he was awarded the silver star for bravery, and his visionary leadership as President of the United States and architect of the Great Society mark him as one of the real 'good guys' of the 20th century. He was every bit the American hero. But the color white has quite different connotations in *Breaking Bad*. In like manner, some political leaders mislead and wreak havoc and can be considered real 'black hats'—forces of evil in the world. But the color black in *Breaking Bad* denotes neither evil nor even necessarily a 'bad guy'. If we wish to understand the series, we must move beyond the symbolic color associations we've acquired during our lives and look at color in a completely new way.

Color Theory in *Breaking Bad*

The meaning of color in *Breaking Bad* is not fixed. If we see Walter wearing cyan the significance is far different than seeing Skyler vested in aquamarine. The symbolic nature of color changes from one season to another, even from one dramatic event to another.

In some sense, then, trying to figure out the color symbolism is like trying to hit a constantly moving target. We may throw up our hands at the complicated, ever-changing, multi-layered nature of color symbols, letting loose in angry vitriol against Vince Gilligan and his writers. Was there any method to their madness? Perhaps they chose bold colors on a whim. Maybe they were only pretending to associate color with meaning, hoping to be seen as greater artists than they were.

Yet we look at the names: White, Pinkman, Skyler, Schwartz (German for Black). We hear the characters themselves explain that Gray Matter Technologies was the symbolic combination of White and Schwartz into a single company with a single vision for generating science-based goods and services. There are scenes in *Breaking Bad* that virtually demand interpretation based on color, a fact we recognize even in our frustration over the complicated symbolism.

I believe Gilligan & Co. had a system, even as it changed from character to character and scene to scene. It may be helpful to consider color in almost geometric terms, looking at the height, depth, and breadth of a particular color in its association to thematic ideas of the show.

Color Height

Some colors are higher, or more important than others. The color that first pops into my mind in this regard is Marie Schrader Purple. She virtually owns the color throughout the entire five seasons. Other colors are lower, or less important and more humble. Probably the first colors we think of in this regard are white or beige.

The color purple has long been associated with royalty, and I believe this is part of the symbolism Vince Gilligan attached to Marie's single-hue wardrobe. Purple is Marie's personal statement and not a symbolic representation of her true self. She thinks herself a princess, or a queen, and she demands that others treat her in a manner befitting her exalted status.

White is a lowly hue, the prideful color that becomes the silly-looking undergarment protecting Walter's dignity as a man.

Black is a high color. It is natural, I suppose, to think of 'dark' or evil intentions when we see Heisenberg at the junkyard dressed in dark pork pie hat, dark glasses and black jacket. Black, we might decide, means evil.

Fair enough. Our understanding of *Breaking Bad* may profit from such an association. But what do we say of Hank and his lieutenants, dressed in black as they prepare to storm the lair of an illegal drug manufacturer? Is Hank 'evil' in that moment?

We could change tack at that point and claim that black means *violence*. I did say that color symbolism changes from scene to scene, after all. When a DEA team knocks down the door to a house they are certainly not evil, but no one is going to argue that their actions are not violent. Fair enough.

The problem, of course, is that other colors—red, for instance—are likewise associated with violence. We could claim that sometimes black means violence and other times red means violence. And…ah…maybe if a guy's wearing red *and* black he's really, really violent. Yeah, that's it! That must be what Vince Gilligan was trying to say…

No.

That's not it.

It's at this point I believe we are better served by relinquishing our attachment to worn-out color associations and trying to see color with new eyes. When I look at Heisenberg in his black pork pie hat I see a man who has made a purposeful, conscious decision to project an aura of confident ruthlessness. Most of all, I see a man committed to a mission.

Black means irreversible commitment. Hank, dressed in SWAT-team black, is irreversibly committed to breaking down the druggie's door. Heisenberg, dressed in black, is irreversibly committed to carrying out the drug deal. If we see a character dressed in black, she's on a mission. Many were confused in Episode 4.03 ("Open House") when Marie wore a black jacket rather than Marie Schrader™ purple. She was still Queen Marie, but the black shell encasing Her Worship meant she wasn't visiting open houses for fun and games. She was on a mission: the acquisition of properties that were rightfully hers. Like the spoon, for instance—and the picture frame.

Black is a high color, more important than white or beige. The other frequently-used high colors are purple and blue. As I've probably already said, blue is the highest color in the *Breaking Bad* Universe, and I will discuss its deep significance to the series in later chapters.

I see red as a medium color meaning unchanneled, chaotic, youthful anger. Two hues closely associated with red—yellow and orange—are lower colors. I do not mean to say that yellow and orange are less interesting. In fact, yellow and orange carry some of the most fascinating conceptual associations of the show. It is not difficult to assign three levels of meaning to yellow and orange, with deeper and more significant symbolism arising later in the series. I will begin to discuss orange in Chapter O.

At least for Season Two, I've found it useful to think of yellow in terms of its normal associations: Danger, Warning, Caution. The neon yellow sheets on Jesse's bed virtually scream out "Danger!"

One of the confusing aspects of the lower colors is that their associations are fluid. They can carry one symbolic connotation in an early scene and an entirely different significance in a later scene. We can make sense of this seemingly nonsensical arrangement if we take into consideration other dramatic properties of *Breaking Bad* color.

Color Breadth

Many of you were interested in the color themes of *Breaking Bad* long before you made the decision to purchase this volume. A good number of you are disappointed or shaking your head in disgust. "Pearson missed the point. White doesn't mean 'pride'. It means 'blandness'. Vince Gilligan said so himself." Indeed. Here is the original quote, from the series creator's interview with Vulture in 2011:

> [The name] "Walter White" appealed to me because of the alliterative sound of it and because it's strangely bland, yet sticks in your head nonetheless — you know, white is the color of vanilla, of blandness. (Vince Gilligan, interview with Vulture.com, 5/16/2011)

This is not the only instance in which Gilligan discussed the significance of color. I've read dozens of his interviews. I've read Bryan Cranston's and Aaron Paul's statements and musings on the subject. I wouldn't think of contradicting the artist who created the series. I doubt Vince Gilligan will ever read these words, but if he does, my guess is that he would agree with this simple assessment: The colors of *Breaking Bad* indicate more than a single idea. I'm not going to request Gilligan's endorsement, though. Instead, I'm going to call upon two authorities you may never have heard of: Anna Marly and Alexander Alexandrov. It could be argued that these two artists' manipulation of symbols saved France and Russia in the darkest hour of their countries' existence, when fascism threatened the world. It can also be argued that it was precisely this application of symbolism that Vince Gilligan used as a template to bring substance and depth to *Breaking Bad*.

The Multidimensionality of Color Symbolism

Few movies have driven me to tears. I have thick skin and I'm not as sensitive to the plight of others as I ought to be. But when Victor Laszlo stands at the top of the stairs of Rick's Café Americain and tries to countenance the loud singing of arrogant Nazis, extolling in verse the superiority of the Aryan Vaterland, then rushes down the stairs to the orchestra and commands, "Play La Marseillaise. Play it," the next two minutes always bring tears to my eyes.

The music stirs the emotions, without question, but Michael Curtiz used the French National Anthem to make a bold statement that could not be confined to patriotic sentiment. By drowning out the fascists and their racist singing, Curtiz was asserting the eventual defeat of Nazi Germany. He was proclaiming the fact that good always ascends over evil. But he was doing even more than this. The Marseillaise scene paralleled the final statement of the movie, when we hear the first ten notes of the anthem in the background while Captain Louis Renault in the foreground throws the bottle of Vichy water into the trash, kicks it away, and grimaces. Just as La Marseillaise unifies everyone into Liberté, Égalité, Fraternité, so too Renault's rejection of Nazi occupation is "the beginning of a beautiful friendship" with Rick.

But the symbolic importance doesn't stop there. The patrons of the restaurant grudgingly put up with the Nazis, but only because the Aryan racists exerted military and political control over Casablanca and most of Morocco. With the playing of La Marseillaise their true allegiance came to the fore. They were and would always be French, guided by principles of Liberté, not cowed by Nazi thugs. While they seemed to accept Nazism, when Victor Laszlo summoned their true feelings they could not but stand and join in the great anthem of all free people. Their true nature was not far from the surface, boiling and seething, but more than that, too. We know because Renault didn't tell his subordinates to arrest Rick for killing Strasser. "Round up the usual suspects," he said. The word 'usual' was telling: Renault had been working for a long time, behind the scenes, sabotaging Nazi interests.

Michael Curtiz grounded "Casablanca" in La Marseillaise, but in making the anthem the central unifying symbol of French resistance and resolve he brought a new dimension to the great hymn, to the point that 70 years later a strong, culturally necessary bond exists between movie and anthem.

Alexander Alexandrov, circa 1940
Official Soviet Portrait, PD

The struggle against Nazi aggression was fought on several fronts. Millions of Russians died as the Germans invaded and swallowed up the entire western side of the country. One and a half million Russians died of starvation when the Nazis blockaded Leningrad for three solid years. The Russians felt they were in a struggle with the Devil himself, and they were losing. Konstantin Simonov's brilliant 1941 poem "Wait for Me" (Жди меня) lifted spirits for many years, but in 1944 Alexander Alexandrov delivered the fatal artistic blow that became Mother Russia's great rallying battle cry.

120

It's not the words of the Soviet National Anthem that are important. It's the thunderous, crashing, unstoppable melody, the ineffable musical expression of Russian identity that finally drove the Nazis out of Russia. The words are different now, after the defeat of Communism in the Second Russian Revolution in 1991, but the melody is the same.

The relevance to *Breaking Bad* is that there are ideas too grand for words. There are concepts that can only be expressed in music or painting or color. A word must usually be taken as symbolic of a single idea. The color white, or the painting of a man in a boat rowing away from his family, can mean many things and the meaning can change over time. La Marseillaise means more at the end of Casablanca than in the restaurant scene. The Russian National Anthem once proclaimed the greatness of Communism but now it simply states the undying nature of the Slavic spirit.

Symbolic breadth can be expressed in any number of ways. Sometimes, again, color or music delivers a more succinct message than words convey. Anna Marly's great hymn, "Le Chant des Partisans," is a stirring call to the cause of Free France during World War II, urging French citizens to kill the invaders, free the prisoners, promising "Friend, if you fall, another will depart the shadows to take your place." But it is not just a call to arms. The final and most important element of the song is the ending, in which the music and the refrain slowly recede into the background and finally disappear entirely. The message of undeterred resolve, of emotion boiling and seething below the surface, ready at any moment to depart the shadows, is powerfully conveyed in the slow recession of music and voice. "Le Chant des Partisans" is both a call to action and a statement of French identity and resolve. If you haven't heard this stirring song, you haven't truly lived. Of the pre-1960s versions I like Germaine Sablon's interpretation the most, but nothing can beat the more recent inspired renditions by Les Stentors, many of which are available on Youtube.

If song can signal multiple ideas simultaneously, color symbolism is equally free to render complementary or even competing or conflicting concepts. So white in *Breaking Bad* can at the same time mean 'blandness' but also 'pride'.

Color Depth

In Episode 1.05 ("Gray Matter") Badger's white apparel does not convey the notion of blandness. It certainly does not project the concept of pride. In these scenes inside the RV Badger is the undignified counterweight to Jesse's single-minded pursuit of glass-grade meth. Jesse is sober, mature, and focused. Badger is reckless, childish, and undisciplined, and the color of his clothing reflects all of those attributes. The color does not carry 'profound' meaning, but the symbolic value is richer than it was in the pilot episode, when an equally childish and reckless Walter White stripped down to his 'tighty-whitey' underwear.

While the symbolic breadth of the color white increased in Episode 1.05, the meaning took on deeper tones as well. From the perspective of the fifth episode we can look back at the series premiere and see Walter dressed in the Emperor's new clothes.

Sacrificing his dignity, the white underwear was as bland as his surname, but also symbolized a kind of undignified pride as well as recklessness and lack of maturity.

In Episode 2.11 we saw Gus Fring for the first time. I don't imagine I will surprise many viewers by saying this is not the last time we will see him. Gus will become one of the most important characters in the series, and one of the more memorable characters in modern television. When we first saw him he blended in with the other workers at Los Pollos Hermanos. In his blue button-down shirt he was virtually indistinguishable from his subordinates. But later in the episode, when Walter returned to the restaurant, Gus was vested in a brilliant yellow shirt. His clothing was no less intense than the yellow sheets on Jesse's bed. Danger. Caution.

I believe for the purposes of Season Two we could look at Gus' shirt and consider the color a warning, that Gus was a dangerous man and Walter would have done well to avoid him. But I don't think the symbolism has traction in later seasons. The meaning of the color yellow will change in the future. Yellow will take on greater depth.

Did the writers of *Breaking Bad* intend to change color values as they proceeded through the series? I believe the answer is found in a striking change of laboratory attire. In Season Three a deliberate decision was made to retire the off-white bunny suits of Season One and replace them with gleaming yellow Hazmat suits. In a show that normally took pains to portray events in a plausible and authentic manner the Hazmat suits were obviously placed for their symbolic value. I've worked in pharmaceutical R&D for over 35 years. Not once have I seen day-to-day laboratory work performed in bright yellow splash suits. White, gray, blue, green—absolutely. But never yellow.

My take on the evolution of color symbolism was that the writers grew in their appreciation of the potential for conveying meaning through color. In the early seasons color symbolism was largely conventional. I am convinced that the heavily symbolic nature of some colors, such as orange and blue, was intentional, even from the very beginning. The meaning of lesser colors, like yellow, probably grew over time.

Color depth can be appreciated in the connections between colors. The unfocused anger of red might be seen as the final result of the cautionary warning of yellow, for instance. Purple and blue, close cousins on the color wheel (and in the Roy G. Biv rainbow), are high 'power' colors in *Breaking Bad*. We know that *Breaking Bad* colors carry meaning in relation to each other from the example of Gray Matter. White is blandness, pride, immaturity, lack of dignity, and purity of self-expression, but it is also the opposite of black. White and black mixed together make gray, and we know gray symbolizes compromise and willingness to work together. As we proceed through the final three seasons we will begin to understand color relations between yellow and red that are no less profound than those between white and black, and they're entirely unrelated to 'danger'.

We might consider depth in terms of concentric layers. A vest or jacket could be understood as a temporary, superficial, or projected attribute. For instance, we could understand Heisenberg's black jacket as a kind of task uniform he removes when he has completed the mission. Hank's black SWAT vest could be seen in the same way; when the raid is completed he removes the vest and he's back to good ol' Orange Hank, done with raids for the day. In a more conventional sense we might think of Walter's black jacket as projecting an aura of toughness, but underneath he's still milquetoast-beige Walter White.

Underwear might be considered a character's identity statement. If we strip away vest or jacket and shirt or blouse we are left with the single garment protecting or defining the character. Walter wore white. Junior's drawers were red (he did show anger from time to time), and, most interestingly, Skyler's panties were blue. I'll have more to say about her blue underwear later on.

A shirt could be thought of as representing the daily and changing attributes of the character. If Walter wears green we know he feels a sense of unfulfilled desire or greed. If he's wearing beige he's either fading into the background or trying to do so. If he's wearing purple it means that, like Marie, he's grasping for a regal bearing that is not for him to possess.

Property and Pretense

In fact, Walter cannot wear purple any more than Marie can. Marie thinks herself a princess. She believes she is so far above others that anything in her realm—even property claimed by her subjects—is rightfully hers. So she seizes the color purple, makes it her own, just as she takes anything she desires from any retail store or private home.

But just as Marie has no right to shoplift objects that do not belong to her, she has no right to wear purple. She's shoplifting the color, too, because it can never belong to her. Marie's obsession with royal purple is a reflection of Walter's obsession with regal power. Personal power of the kind Walter seeks is not available to anyone in the *Breaking Bad* Universe. It's that karma thing that Vince Gilligan speaks of. The high colors—Purple, Blue, and in some sense Black—are out of bounds for characters. If they try to wear these colors they are breaking the rules of the Universe.

The curious exception to the No High Colors rule is Skyler. Perhaps a few viewers will intuit the underlying reason for her ability to apparently disobey the rule. By the beginning of the fifth season I imagine most viewers will have figured it out. For now it's something to keep in the back of our minds as we consider some of the more accessible color qualities.

When Skyler confronted Marie about the stolen tiara we were never told whether Marie understood that she had committed a crime. I tend to think Marie's regal mindset was more than superficial, that something at the very core of her being told her she was an Überfrau for whom rules of conformity did not apply. But I also get the sense that at some deeper level she understood that at least a part of her kleptomania was wrong. Perhaps she recognized others' needs or rights, for instance. At the very least we know that Skyler's confrontation made her feel uneasy.

The most likely source of confrontational angst was the recognition that Marie was lying to herself. The Princess Marie charade was proving to be a costly routine that threatened her closest relationships, and she knew it.

Whether or not Marie understood her kleptomania as an illness we know purple was not a color she could claim as her own—the color did not accurately reflect the true nature of her being.

In an important sense I feel white is likewise a falsehood for Walter. The white underwear represents pride, conveying a feeling that one is set apart from others, similar to the arrogance projected by Marie's regal purple. But the 'tighty-whitey' underwear demonstrates an undignified and *undeserved* pride. In the desert cook scenes and the more recent bathroom scenes he was dressed in the Emperor's new clothes, but we laugh not because he's nearly naked but rather because in his vulnerable everyman nakedness he is no Emperor. The writers and director made this clear in the introduction to Episode 1.04, when Hank told his subordinates, "We got new players in town…They possess an extremely high skill set." The camera then cut to Walter in his white underwear, brushing his teeth in the bathroom. "Personally," Hank said as we watched Walter frothing white toothpaste, "I'm thinking Albuquerque might just have a new kingpin."

Even the most closely-held personal attributes, represented in underwear color, could be understood not as inherent properties of the person, but as projections of unmerited identity. But because they're worn as underwear, these badges of personal identification are the properties most valued by the characters. Skyler didn't want to surrender her blue underwear in Episode 2.01. Anyone attempting to take away Walter's pride would experience whatever degree of wrath he could muster at the moment. In the first season Walter's pride forced him to angrily quit the car wash. Toward the end of Season Two he called his son's 'Save Walter White' website 'cyber-begging'. "I *earned* that money. Me," Walter told Saul, speaking of his drug revenue and his refusal to have any of it laundered through the site.

If purple, blue, white, and black are 'off limits' are there any colors that can signify an *inherent* property of characters and not a personal choice? Yes, I believe there are a few. One of them, I feel, is orange, as I will explain a couple of chapters from now.

I've put together a 'Color Interpretation' card on the next page, arranged in reverse 'rainbow' order, beginning with the 'high colors' Black and Purple. I do not claim to possess infallible insight into the true meaning of *Breaking Bad*, so I have included a column for your own assignments of symbolism. I have left blank spaces for colors that will be discussed in later periods of the book. Some colors include multiple shades, such as 'Red-orange' and 'S-bräu' (Schraderbräu) orange. I've also left blank spaces under some colors to allow for multiple assignments. The low colors Yellow, Orange, and Green can all be interpreted in many ways and the table reflects that.

Color Interpretation in *Breaking Bad*

Color	Shade	Allowed	Moore Interpretation	My Interpretation
Black		Yes/No	Decisive commitment On a mission Dark intentions	
Purple		No	Royalty Übermensch	
Blue		No		
Green	Dark	No	Unfulfilled desire Greed	
	Light	Yes	Envy, Greed	
Yellow		Yes	Warning, Danger	
Orange	Light	Yes		
	S-bräu	Yes	Purposeful pleasure	
	Neon	Yes		
	Rust	Yes		
	Reddish	No		
Red		No	Unfocused anger Youthful anger	
Pink		Yes		
Beige		Yes	Conformity Neutrality	
White		Yes/No	Pride Blandness Conformity Lack of dignity Lack of discipline Childishness	

Chapter N

egro y Azul

"An Absinthe of Light"
Spacepleb, 2009, CC-SA 2.0

Reality—and the way it is perceived and manipulated—is one of the most fascinating aspects of *Breaking Bad*. At times a character will seem oblivious to a clear threat. At other times he will succeed in pushing events to conform to unreasonable, near-impossible expectations. More often than not, though, conflicting personal agendas and the complexities of the Universe will conspire to force undesirable outcomes.

Perhaps it should have been obvious to Walter that petty dealers did not arbitrarily deem a territory 'off limits'. Why would drug distributors voluntarily reduce their potential profits? He should have known that otherwise undisciplined entrepreneurs bent on maximizing personal gain would not have curtailed profit capabilities unless a greater outside force had been imposed on them. "Respect the chemistry," Walter was wont to say. He would have accomplished more for his personal safety if he had instead repeated the mantra Respect The Cartel.

An Ordinary Greed

"There's no need to over-analyze this, Pearson," some of you are saying. "Walter's greed made him blind to anything other than his own desires." He wasn't like us because ordinary people don't just get up one day and decide to manufacture and distribute illicit drugs. Walter's species of greed was different than the average Jill or Joe's selfishness.

I think there may be some wisdom in that belief, but I would like to invite debate. I contend we can identify multiple causes for Walter's selective blindness and in looking at the multi-layered nature of his greed we will gain a foothold for understanding future events and the way Walter decides to confront them. In fact, I'd like to present for your consideration a bold proposition: Walter's greed was no different than the kind any of us displays in day-to-day living.

Greed does not require selfish intent or even arrogant self interest. In fact, greed can find full expression in the most humble of hearts.

Walter's attitude toward Albuquerque drug territories may have had a basis in motivations and facts unrelated to greed, and I believe we benefit from an examination of these factors. If this pivotal episode of the second season were nothing more than a brief study of a diseased mind we would not need to do this. We could simply shrug our shoulders, resigned to the mysterious fact that there are evil people in the world. But that is not what *Breaking Bad* is about. "Negro y Azul" is one of the more chilling episodes of the series because it speaks to the truth that even if we are Mr. or Ms. Chips, every one of us carries the potential to become Scarface. Worse, the transformation can occur without our knowledge or consent.

In considering the Albuquerque drug market, Walter brought to bear assumptions he had learned over the decades. Even though he had taught high school chemistry for many years, he had once been a scientist-entrepreneur, and he made a point of studying Gray Matter's innovations and successes every week. He was no longer a part of the business world, but he was tuned into it. One of the undeniable laws of business is that if you have a superior product people will prefer it over an inferior product. Gray Matter was doing so well because it offered new, superior ways to achieve important objectives. In the same way, Walter's blue meth was so far superior to anything else available it would corner the Albuquerque market. The best competing product was 50 or 60 percent pure. Walter's 99.1% material delivered potent effect, an unearthly high no one had experienced before, and fully twice the punch of anything his competitors could deliver. Since illicit drugs constituted a completely free market, Walter's far superior product would become the only version of meth sold in the city. Even if he raised his price a little, the small cost differential would not deter customers because the high purity ensured a mind-blowing reaction.

If only Walter's analysis were correct, his business model might have made sense. His model ignored vitally important facts, of course. But his analysis was not based only on ignorance. Far greater character flaws were in play.

Scope Creep

"No one has a good Alzheimer's drug," the Vice President of Business Development says. "We see a potential for exploitation." He takes his seat and now it's my turn to stand in front of the 16 most powerful vice presidents and directors at my company. I've been doing background library research for the last ten months and believe I've identified a technically feasible route to a new pharmaceutical that can delay disease onset and enhance quality of life. With my superior's blessing, I withhold information indicating a small potential for disease reversal. Some weeks later I'm given the green light. I assemble two three-member teams: an extraction/purification group and a synthesis crew. In six months we hope to have a synthetic analog of the naturally occurring alkaloid that showed interesting biological response.

"Pearson," my boss says to me a few days later, "Dave in marketing is interested in enhanced memory effects."

Uh-oh. I know what's coming.

"That's not part of project scope," I say, but I know my protests are futile. Dave is Executive Vice President of Marketing. He always gets his way.

"It's important," my boss insists. "John's on board."

Well, that's the end of that. John is the new CEO. Fat chance an Associate Director like me is going to dissuade a new chief executive bent on making a name for himself.

"See what you can do," my boss says, and hurries away before I can say anything.

'What I can do' turns out to be the creation of a new set of artificial membranes geared toward the evaluation of alkaloid effect on the conformation of a certain class of proteins known to affect memory retention. The work occupies two members of my purification team for over four months.

Even as I move into aggressive double-time mode, working 15 and 16 hour days, I know there's not much chance we'll meet deadline, now that we have twice as much work to do. When the day of the dreaded meeting arrives, I stand in front of the 16 most powerful individuals at my company.

"We have identified a methoxy analog that shows some promise. Response was 17 percent higher than the parent alkaloid, six percent higher in the memory retention membrane models."

"What?" Dave can barely withhold his disgust. "All you can show is a 17% improvement? How many analogs did you look at?"

"We created 635 derivatives."

Dave groans. "Six plates." He shakes his head. "We gave you six months. All you could deliver was a plate a month."

Well, no, I delivered a memory retention model that had never existed and all of the research that went into building it. But I can't tell Dave that. Not when he was the one responsible for doubling my workload without adding any additional staff to the project.

~~~~~

Dave's actions are not unusual. In fact, the expectation that a team can expand its workload without having to work any longer or harder has a name: Scope Creep. Rare indeed is the industrial or commercial project that is not bogged down with ideas, initiatives, and labor-consuming tasks that were not part of the workload when the project was chartered. Scope Creep is the major cause of timeline extension, cost overruns, unpaid overtime, and frayed nerves and emotions.

Dave is not greedy. He's not selfish. In fact, he's more down to earth and caring than many of the people I work with. His idea was that memory enhancement was so closely allied to the slowing of Alzheimer's disease progression that a few side studies wouldn't cost much in terms of time or resources, but the benefit to the company would be enormous. He was just trying to do the right thing.

In the end, though, Dave's initiative had an extremely negative effect on the entire company. From an outsider's point of view we might judge Dave and say his actions were selfish or greedy. But since I know Dave, I've seen his compassion for people throughout the company and in his personal life, too, I'm not much inclined to consider him to have been motivated by greed. What I do know is that, as brilliant as he may be in the realm of marketing, he has virtually no understanding of the intricacies of chemistry, biochemistry, and pharmacodynamics. He certainly had no basis for knowing that his innocent suggestion (accompanied by firm expectation) would result in an additional 3600 hours of work for my teams.

I believe we can look at Walter in the same way. He was not necessarily greedy in seeing opportunity for expansion of operations in Albuquerque. But in terms of evaluating the real cost of expansion, he was no less ignorant than Dave.

Walter's problem in this episode was not greed. In fact, I believe we could posit that he was not adding to or increasing the severity of any sins he may already have committed. The problem was not sin. It was ignorance of cause and effect. In industry such ignorance most often leads to Scope Creep. In Walter White's world, this variety of ignorance was likely to have a more profound effect.

Even Los Cuates de Sinaloa told us this was the case. Heisenberg was already dead, they said in harmonized voices. He was so ignorant of the ramifications of over-reaching and moving onto others' turf—stepping on the Cartel's toes—that he didn't know he was living on borrowed time.

Deceptions Dark, Symbolisms Weak

"You are a blowfish," Walter tells Jesse. He's just an ordinary fish in the sea, a fish like any other, but when he puffs himself up people believe he's bigger than he is. "He crushed a man's skull under an ATM machine," they say, whispering in fear and admiration. "Yeah," Jesse says, entranced, caught up in the undeniable power of the image. "I am a blowfish."

It doesn't matter that Jesse didn't crush the man's skull. It certainly doesn't matter that Jesse probably doesn't have what it takes to kill anyone in this manner. The only part of the story that has ongoing relevance to Walter, Jesse, and their great blue initiative is the perception of Jesse's deadly invincibility.

There are two fatal flaws in Walter's blowfish metaphor. I will discuss one of the problems in this section. The second and far deeper difficulty requires a discussion of other symbolic elements of the episode, and I will take on that challenge in the two sections following this one.

Deception is important to the plot of *Breaking Bad* but at its heart the series is a statement about self-deception. The fantasy that Jesse was a 'Blowfish' allowed Walter to manipulate the behavior of the drug-buying underworld to suit his schemes. He had to encourage people to believe in the fantasy, as he did at the Los Alamos museum, but for the myth to have enduring effect Jesse had to buy into it, too. Jesse had to allow himself to be deceived into believing and knowing in his heart of hearts that he was a blowfish.

When I heard Walter tell Jesse he was a Blowfish, I saw in my mind's eye a similar attempt at coercive self-deception from the 1993 masterpiece "Schindler's List." Oskar Schindler, desperate to curtail Amon Goeth's arbitrary bloodbaths, gets the Nazi drunk and then plants in his mind an idea about the nature of power.

Schindler:	They fear us because we have the power to kill arbitrarily. A man commits a crime, he should know better. We have him killed and we feel pretty good about it. Or we kill him ourselves and we feel even better. That's not power, though: That's justice. That's different than power. Power is when we have every justification to kill, and we don't.
Goeth:	You think that's power?
Schindler:	That's what the Emperor said. A man stole something, he's brought before the Emperor, he throws himself down on the ground, he begs for mercy. He *knows* he's going to die. And the Emperor pardons him. He's a worthless man. He lets him go.
Goeth:	I think you *are* drunk.
Schindler:	That is *power*, Amon. That is power.

Schindler is portrayed as planting in this inhuman monster's mind the idea that he is a wise and benevolent Emperor, in contrast to the 'worthless man'. He has absolute power, which can only be expressed in mercy and forgiveness. To do anything less is to become the 'worthless man'.

Schindler's attempt to dissuade Goeth from evil tyranny was laudable, and the movie showed the attempt successfully play out in Goeth's life—for a morning and an afternoon, when he went back to killing any of the prison inmates he felt like shooting.

The effort aimed at changing Goeth's behavior had to fail. The objective could be achieved only if Goeth bought into his status as a powerful and benevolent emperor, a kindly Germanic god who would pardon sins great and small. But this could not happen for three reasons. First, it was not true self-deception, since Schindler was the initial aggrandizing catalyst, not Goeth himself. But second, and most importantly, Goeth was not benevolent. He was a sick, inhuman demon, and nothing Oskar Schindler suggested or tried to plant in the man's rotten psyche could change that fact. To understand the third reason for Schindler's failure, we need to look at a successful case of self-deception.

Black and Blue

'Negro y Azul' is Spanish for 'Black and Blue'. At first glance the title could be considered the description of a challenge or fight and its outcome. Los Cuates de Sinaloa sang of the Mexican Cartel 'losing respect' because of Heisenberg's new drug and their understandable interest in neutralizing this latest challenge to their control of the New Mexico drug market. 'Black and Blue', for the last 120 years or so, anyway, has meant 'covered in bruises as from a fight'. Get ready, the song seemed to say, for an epic battle is looming.

Appreciating *Breaking Bad*'s penchant for visual symbolism, we seek clues in the music video's imagery. At one point the musicians sing of 'the drug colored blue' as an image of several pound bags of blue meth appears on the screen. Blue, then, seems to refer to the blue meth, and by extension, Heisenberg himself. The reference to 'black' is a bit more difficult, but at a critical moment members of the Cartel move from right to left in black silhouette. In the visual language of the cinema, movement from right to left is 'against the grain' and meant to draw attention. It is more often than not the dynamic used to portray the villain or antagonist. Thus, we might understand the song to signal a fight between the Cartel and Heisenberg.

But the Ballad of Heisenberg doesn't seem to be about struggle. By asserting control of 'Duke' (the local name for Albuquerque, taken from the city's original patron, the 8th Duke of Alburquerque, Francisco Fernandez de la Cueva, Viceroy of New Spain in the 1650s; the extra 'r' in the Viceroy's title is correct, not a typo!), Heisenberg was claiming for himself territory that had been in Cartel hands for a long time. The song wasn't about a fight to control the city's drug trade. The idea that resonates through the piece is simple: Heisenberg is an ignorant fool who will soon be dead.

Know Thy Enemy

"If you know your enemy as yourself, you will fight without danger in many battles."

So said the cocky, self-assured El Paso DEA agent in response to Hank's question about the large bust of Jesús Malverde occupying his desk. The Spanish-speaking Anglos in the El Paso office spent a good deal of time laughing at the newest culturally ignorant Gringo the Albuquerque office had sent them. Hank was an English-only fish out of water in the West Texas office. By the end of the episode no one was laughing, and most of the agents who thought they knew their enemy, able to 'fight without danger', were dead.

Taking a closer look at the music video that began the episode, we saw several images of a Mexican man dressed in a brilliant white shirt, the buttons flanked by matching black breast pockets. Every time he appeared we saw him raise his hands to the sky, as if in supplication to his gods. The image of a dark-haired man in white shirt with black pockets, usually wearing a black bandana around his neck, is an instantly recognizable icon to tens of millions of Mexicans: Jesús Malverde, the patron saint of Mexican drug lords.

The strange cult of Malverde began over a century ago with the mythical killing of a local Mexican bandit, Jesús Malverde. A legend grew up around this figure, forming him into a kind of Mexican Robin Hood who stole from the rich and redistributed his captured money to the impoverished residents of Sinaloa.

In the last 30 years or so the drug lords of this western state and surrounding provinces turned Malverde into a positive symbol of Mexican drug dealers. The imagery and mythology tell Mexicans that drug lords, cast in the mold of Jesús Malverde, are bandits unjustly hounded by the police. After all, the drug dealers are just selling the Gringos north of the border the drugs they want—and would obtain from other sources anyway—but they're also bringing in desperately needed money and in this way they're lifting up the poor. There's no sin in the drug lords' actions, because the Norteamericanos will purchase the drugs regardless of anything the poor Mexicans do. By tapping into Gringo desire for illicit drugs, the Mexican drug dealers are able to bring hard cash and merciful relief to the lives of millions.

It's a potent myth, and it works fabulously.

A major reason for the success of this mythological fantasy derives of its positive nature. There's no 'blowfish' here. There is no fabled entity of invincible might that will crush your skull under an ATM should you not live up to the blowfish's expectations. There's only a friendly, benevolent bandit, eager to serve you and suffer unjustly for you. More than anything, the kindly drug lords represented by Jesús Malverde just want to give you money so you can survive and maybe even enjoy life a little.

Best of all, no one has to fall into self-deception because there is no Jesús Malverde—at least there was never a bandit who suffered and stole on behalf of the poor of Sinaloa in the way this mythological figure did. Jesús Malverde is so perfect, in fact, that no one even has to compare him to a 'worthless man', as Oskar Schindler attempted to do in building up Gothe's image of himself.

The legend of Jesús Malverde is the perfect self-deception because it allows millions of Mexicans to think of themselves and drug lords as something they are not and can never be. The myth makes combating Mexican drug traffic virtually impossible. Who can fight against a saint of the poor, a modern-day Robin Hood?

The fantasy of Jesús Malverde shows why Walter's effort to portray Jesse as a 'Blowfish' was doomed to fail. Even if he could persuade Jesse of the fable that he was a ruthless killer, tyrants always fall because people cannot long endure living in a state of fear. Walter should have made Jesse into the mythical Candyman of Albuquerque, or the Willy Wonka of the West, or the Wizard of Duke, or whatever. Virtually any positive image would work as long as it elevated Jesse to the rarefied status of benevolent saint. Saints live forever, after all, even in death, and people revere them.

Lessons from the Ballad

"Negro y Azul" is representative of the delightful complexity of this show. We take from the episode lessons that should have become Walter's primer for advanced studies in illicit drug distribution. Instead, he blundered forward, unjustifiably confident that brilliance, ingenuity, and knowledge of logic and science were sufficient prologue to any problem he could face. Pride was not his only flaw—the far deadlier sin was arrogance, the conviction that he did not need to learn from bad decisions and unforeseen outcomes. It was arrogance that caused his ignorance, and ignorance in turn that put a target on his back.

We learned from this episode not to accept statements—whether factual or symbolic—at face value. 'Black and Blue' might mean 'beaten until bruised', but it might refer to Walter's blue meth and his black pork pie hat. It could indicate a deadly competition between the Mexican Cartel (Black) and the ignorant, arrogant Gringo, Walter (Blue, representing his superior meth product.). If you accept the arguments of Chapter C (Color), you are aware of yet other ways of considering the episode's symbolism. For instance, if Blue is a 'forbidden' color, its symbolic importance in the episode is magnified. I will discuss color-based templates for this episode in later chapters.

The best-laid plans fail. Murphy was an optimist, as anyone who has ever been charged with shepherding an industrial process from concept to commercialization knows very well. So it was in this episode that 'Jesse Jackson' failed as soon as a passing biker praised Jesse by his true surname. Ironically, the praise was for the imaginary, legendary Jesse, not the real Jesse. That which is false reveals that which is true—a sweet, twisted irony of a type we see play out in almost every episode.

If the seeds of Heisenberg always existed in the soul of Walter White, it is equally true that the imperfections of which those seeds were made could be found in plentiful supply at the heart of Walter's character. He was always full of pride and arrogance. One of the important lessons of this episode was the almost unbelievable depth of Walter's ignorance, made all the worse and untenable by his snobbish dismissal of truths that did not comport with the logical patterns of his superior intellect. He could have learned so much from every failure. He could have recognized and accepted his ignorance. In humility he could have adjusted his scientific mind to the complex verities of the real world. He could have had a fighting chance for life. Instead, his conceit brings him closer to sudden and painful death.

Hank Schrader
Copyright 2011 Martin Woutisseth, used with permission

Chapter O

Orange

If anyone is to take down Heisenberg, chances are that person is Henry "Hank" Schrader. In Season One and in the early episodes of Season Two we saw him deployed as a comic character, much appreciated in a show that develops serious subject matter. But under the bubbly, courageous, go-get-'em exterior, we see a somber, conflicted, sometimes worried man confronting his own fears and limitations. The complete range of that emotional and psychological depth is conveyed in a single color—Hank's color—which is nothing less than the strongest, most important hue on the *Breaking Bad* palette: Orange. If we are to understand Heisenberg we must gain sure knowledge of black and blue. But if we are to appreciate the full message of *Breaking Bad* we must have intimate knowledge of the color worn by the series' greatest hero. This chapter is about the protagonist of *Breaking Bad*, Hank Schrader, and the color that expresses his full identity, orange.

Authority

Orange is an 'allowed' color, as opposed to blue, which is 'forbidden'. I have made this statement in earlier chapters but so far I have not supported it. In the second season we learned the distinction, apparent in the color's use by two different characters.

We know well by now that color expresses a character's identity, true nature, or personality. The nature of the expression varies from one character to another, so that Marie, for instance, consciously chooses purple to express her chosen identity as royalty, while white is a more or less unconscious depiction of Walter's pride.

Orange is the visual expression of Hank's personality. We know that one aspect of his personality can be described in reference to his chosen vocation of law enforcement officer. Hank enforces the law. If orange accurately expresses Hank's identity, we would do well to look for color associations with the idea of law enforcement.

It's important to take care in our definitions and avoid common generalizations or concepts. Some commentators have said orange means 'judgment' but I believe this is incorrect. If we think of Hank as 'judge' I believe we are being led astray and we will not get to the heart of his character.

The key to our understanding of the foundational symbolic meaning of orange is found in Episode 2.08, "Better Call Saul." In the final scene of the episode, Walter is at his desk, grading the test paper of Matt Feight. At the top of the paper Walter writes, in bold red marker, "40. NOT EVEN CLOSE." The critical aspect of this scene is the color of Walter's shirt: dark orange, almost rust. Hank Schrader orange. DEA orange.

The thing is, Walter *never* wears orange. That's a bit of an over-simplification, of course, but of the hundreds of shirts we will see him wear over the course of five seasons, he dons an orange one perhaps four or five times. We know, then, that this strange adoption of orange, virtually unseen in Walter's narrow color palette, carries enormous significance. We look at the bold red pen comment, "Not even close," and perhaps feel pity for poor Matt Feight. We might even imagine the distraught boy muttering to himself, "Who appointed Mr. White judge and executioner over me?"

No one appointed Walter White 'judge and executioner', but he *was* appointed, and that fact is important. Walter White was *appointed* by the State of New Mexico as a teacher. In the same way, the United States Federal Government *appointed* Hank Schrader as an agent of the Drug Enforcement Agency. *Both Walter and Hank, in their official, professional roles, exercise prerogative given to them by a higher power.* In Walter's case, he applies the prerogatives of a teacher; Hank exerts the prerogatives of an officer of the law.

When they exercise the prerogatives of their appointed areas, both Walter and Hank are exerting *authority*. In each case that authority is legitimate and allowed because it is bestowed by a higher authority (the State of New Mexico or the United States of America). Orange, then—the dark, somber, almost rust-colored orange preferred by Hank—is the color of legitimate, conferred authority.

Hank doesn't always wear dark, brooding orange, but it is his true color. He wore it in Episode 1.04 as he outlined 'Operations Icebreaker' to his subordinates. He wore DEA Orange when he took aim and put a bullet between Tuco Salamanca's eyes. (Episode 2.02) He'll wear the same color during some of the most important events of the series.

He was wearing a subdued, almost beige-like orange in Episode 2.05 when his boss called him a 'great white shark' and promoted him to Albuquerque Liaison for the Tristate Border Interdiction Task Force. Hank had a fancy new title and probably a small pay raise, too. He should have been on top of the world. Instead, at the end of the scene, we saw him go into the elevator and lose control of himself.

If we wish to understand why, we need to go to Hank's man cave and spend a few minutes making some really good homebrew.

Schraderbräu

In the early episodes of Season Two we began to see another side of Hank. Especially after he killed Tuco Salamanca, during Hank's private moments we saw an upset, vacillating man losing control of his emotions and his life. The two sides of Hank were forcefully juxtaposed in Episode 2.05, "Breakage."

As Hank mumbled the lyrics to a 1970s Löwenbräu commercial he filled bottles and torqued down on a manual bottlecapper to seal each one. Marie opened the garage door, disgusted at what she saw. Hank was playing hookey. He told his wife he was just taking a day off, but we know better. He couldn't face a day in the office. He couldn't risk losing control in front of his co-workers as he did in the elevator. So Marie left, unsatisfied by Hank's excuses, and the garage door closed. As soon as it did, Hank bore down on the bottle-capper with enough force to break down a door, shattered the bottle, and cut himself. He was out of control. We see the proof in his bleeding hand, in his distraught face, but most of all in his *clothing*.

Hank's outer Teddy Roosevelt was expressed in the happy, bright orange Hawaiian shirt on the Schraderbräu label. Hank's inner Hamlet, on the other hand, was expressed in the washed-out, grayish orange swirls of the shirt he wore in the man cave scene. We barely detect the orange pattern in the otherwise dark gray and black shirt.

Interestingly, both Hank's man cave shirt and the Schraderbräu shirt have wild patterns, highly unusual in the conservative, solid-colors-only world of *Breaking Bad*.

Craziness Gradient

Only two major characters are allowed to wear tops as wild as Hank's Schraderbräu shirt: His wife, Marie Schrader, and Jesse Pinkman. I will discuss Marie in Chapter P. Jesse wears yellows, reds, and black, but his shirts are often adorned with fire-breathing dragons, skulls, bright swirls, or other bold or wild decorations. If ever we see Walter, Skyler, or Gustavo wearing anything other than a solid color, the pattern is small, discrete, repeating, and invariably boring and conservative. The most frequently used patterned shirts on these characters employ a bland range of hues: beige, dull yellow, light green, washed-out brown, and so on.

One other major character is allowed to depart from solids and conservative plaids and stripes: Walter Junior. But Junior's shirts are not anything we could call 'wild'. There are no dragons or stylized guns, no flamboyant skulls or marijuana leaves. Junior occasionally wears bold—though usually pastel—stripes and plaids.

As with Hank's man cave shirt, Jesse's wild shirts indicate disorder, lack of control, and severe inner conflict. Junior's bold stripes indicate normal teenage vacillations and angst but nothing nearly as severe as the titanic forces at play inside Jesse's soul. In later seasons we will hear Junior give voice to some of the most sensible statements of the series. Conflicted as he may be, Junior has a good head on his shoulders.

The key feature of both the Schraderbräu shirt and the man cave shirt is that both are out of control. Neither one expresses Hank's true, inner self, which is legitimate, conferred, self-confident authority.

In Season Two Hank has lost his self-confidence. As the season progresses we see him fall into panic attacks and fits of anger, doubt, and fear. Why?

Breathtaking Revelation

By the end of Episode 2.05, we understand the nature of Hank's inner struggle. Hank throws Tuco's grill into the river because the device is not for him to possess. His friends thought he would enjoy a 'trophy', much as a hunter might mount a deer head on his wall. But Hank was no hunter. He was neither executioner nor judge, and in recognizing that truth he had to give up anything that symbolized such a claim.

Unfortunately, even if Hank knew he was no executioner, he didn't know that he could claim orange for his own. He still didn't know that he carried legitimate authority, and that such power did not mark him as judge, executioner, or claimant of powers or authorities that were not his to exert.

Notice during the promotion scene Hank is wearing washed-out orange and his boss is wearing solid blue. It's a light blue shirt, 'understated', we might say, and perhaps on the edge of acceptability in the *Breaking Bad* Universe. My feeling is the color choice was intentional, because at the end of the scene we are given a breathtaking revelation into the meaning of color and the deeper significance of the themes.

Hank leaves the office, gets into the elevator, the door closes, and he enjoys a few precious seconds of composure before his world falls apart. Suddenly he's grabbing the walls of the elevator, hyperventilating, struggling beyond strength and reason not to fall into a quivering puddle on the floor of the elevator. He's losing control of himself.

The elevator was painted for the show. There's no question in my mind, because the importance of Hank's breakdown had to be made absolutely clear. To do this, the writers emphatically stated that the elevator Hank stepped into had to be bold, bright, oppressively *blue*. Hank, in that moment of sheer spiritual terror, was surrounded on all sides, up and down and all around, by the most powerful color in the Universe: Pure, unopposable *blue*.

I'm not going to say yet what I believe the color blue means. I think Hank's experience of uncontrollable terror tells us more than any words I might use to express theories of theme or color. If we absorb this scene into our psyche we know without having to be told that *Breaking Bad* is telling us the color has profound meaning, unmatched by any other color or theme or idea expressed in the series.

Hank is fearful of blue. He cowers in its presence. Why? What is the nature of the color's power over Hank, and indeed, over every character on the show?

I leave you to wonder, to ponder. I believe there are probably dozens of valid interpretations of the elevator scene and the exact symbolic nature of the color blue in *Breaking Bad*. We will see many powerful instances of the color's use over the next three seasons, and from time to time I will point out scenes or events I feel illustrate the meaning of this greatest of *Breaking Bad* colors.

Chapter F

F⁹amily

"Familienidylle"
Aimé Pez, 1839

I spend somewhere around one to two dozen hours analyzing, researching, and finally writing about each episode of *Breaking Bad*. My work on companion volumes for *Lost* and *Game of Thrones* proceeds in exactly the same way. One ought to expect unusual insight as the natural outcome of such allocation of time and effort, I suppose. The greatest sense I have, though, is not any kind of rare vision or knowledge as much as it is an awareness of awe and sober appreciation for the television series I am privileged to enjoy with you.

A truly great artistic creation breaks new ground. It forces us to consider novel ideas, or it approaches old ideas from such unexpected angles that we are left shocked, confused, or unable to process using our own limited understanding. Great drama communicates striking, fresh ideas about the human condition, often centered around the nature of human interaction. In *Lost*, for example, we faced the new idea of a Constant, and a type of relationship I dubbed the 'Strange Attractor Pair', using the language of scientific chaos theory. I believe *Breaking Bad* achieves an even higher order of novelty by expanding on and increasing the complexity of one of the world's oldest and most central relational concepts: Family.

The Basic Concept

Father Knows Best, Cast Photo, 1960, PD

Breaking Bad is the most compelling family drama I have experienced. I watched nearly every episode of *Father Knows Best* in reruns and I never missed an installment of *The Waltons* during the 1970s. I have to confess I haven't seen an episode of *Malcolm in the Middle*, though I'll probably take a look now that I've come to appreciate Bryan Cranston's formidable talent, demonstrated in *From the Earth to the Moon*, "Saving Private Ryan," "Argo," and other films.

Father Knows Best was light comedy but it offered memorable characters with distinctive personalities. *The Waltons* took the notion of family to a higher level, depicting the emotional and spiritual connections between John-Boy, his parents, and his siblings. It went further than comedies like *That Girl*, or *Leave It to Beaver*, though, in dramatizing the bonds between John-Boy and his extended family, including both paternal grandparents.

But even The *Waltons*, praiseworthy as it may be in terms of dramatic and historical value, was based on conventional notions of familial relation. We have the firm sense that John and Olivia were instrumental in working the rich cultural soil that nurtured John-Boy's ambitions and abilities as a writer. The Walton family was a crucible, then, but it was John-Boy who wove family experience and connections into a solid foundation for his later career.

The Waltons, Cast photo, 1972, PD

Breaking Bad at first glance seems to share little or nothing with *The Waltons*. It's hard to imagine that anyone in Walter's family, even unintentionally, could have set him on the path toward illicit drug manufacture. We seek cause-and-effect connections, but there are none to be found. *The Waltons* boiled down to Strong Family Connections→ Well-Balanced Young Man. While Walter was distant from his wife even before the series began (as evidenced by the first three episodes of the first season), we have a pretty good sense by now that emotional estrangement was not a trigger event for Walter's decision to make illegal drugs.

We could argue a positive connection between Walter's family and the meth business. After all, Walter told Jesse and anyone else who would listen that everything he did was for his family. Jesse could even quote the exact amount of money Walter said he needed: 737 thousand dollars. But now, at the end of Season Two, we know 737 referred to an ill-fated airplane, not to Walter's annuity fund. Similarly, Walter's descent into depravity had nothing to with his family, but was entirely the result of his self-deception and misguided desires.

Family in *Breaking Bad* is neither cause nor effect, it is *condition*. Family is not a secondary plot thread, it *is* the plot. In a way I've never seen attempted before, family is the completion and perfection of the protagonist. Family is Walter White's identity.

Essential Identity

Sarah Bernhardt as Hamlet, circa 1885

One of my favorite moments in cinema occurs during the opening of the 1999 film "Galaxy Quest," a parodic homage to the original *Star Trek* series. Alexander Dane is a great Shakespearean actor. He is tired of playing the Spock-like 'Dr. Lazarus' and refuses to appear before a gathering of thousands of fans. The star of the series, Jason Nesmith, tries to talk Dane into walking on stage, but the actor is intransigent—until Nesmith invokes a truth Dane cannot deny:

Nesmith: You *will* go out there.
Dane: I won't, and nothing you say will make me.
Nesmith: The show must go on.
Dane: [pauses, cringing] Damn you. Damn you. [Striding toward the stage] I won't say that stupid line one more time.

It is Dane's identity as actor that forces him to take the stage, even though he detests every minute. Identity cannot be denied.

Dr. Lazarus' 'stupid line' is the element of "Galaxy Quest" that elevates the movie from simple parody to poetic homage of *Star Trek* values. When he's forced to say "By Grabthar's hammer," he cuts every word with disdain verging on disgust. But later, when an adoring Thermian (symbolically representing *Star Trek* fans) dies in Dane's arms, he realizes his identity is deeper than that of a mere actor. "By Grabthar's hammer, by the sons of Warvan," he says to the dying man, "you shall be avenged." Now every word of the pretentious statement has profound meaning. He is no longer Alexander Dane, actor, but Dr. Lazarus, exemplar of humanity.

Dane's transformation parallels that of Leonard Nimoy, who played Mr. Spock in *Star Trek* TOS. Nimoy's first autobiography, *I Am Not Spock*, was a discussion of the differences between himself and the iconic character he brought to life. Though he never disowned, or even distanced himself from, his *Star Trek* character, he fully embraced the identity in his second autobiography, *I Am Spock*, published 20 years later in 1995.

Both Mr. Spock and Dr. Lazarus are only superficially aliens. Their true *raison d'être* is to serve as ironic attestation of a great truth: The nobility of our humanity is not confined to our identity as *Homo sapiens*. Our true essence is something greater than anything coded into our DNA. It overcomes every obstacle and defeats every evil. Humanity is the essential attribute of every thinking creature—even a pointy-eared Vulcan. As Captain Kirk said at the end of "Star Trek III" during Spock's funeral, "Of my friend I can only say this: Of all the souls I have encountered in my travels, his was the most...human."

The greatness of *Star Trek* comes down to the insistence that our identity as human beings is grounded in a nobility that cannot be dissolved or even reduced. The genius of *Breaking Bad* is its relentless expansion on the notion of identity; the show makes the concept of family central to the development of Walter's personality. As we will see, the series is uncompromising in its assertion that Walter's true self cannot be separated from his identity as spouse, father, and brother-in-law.

Relation and Identity

One of the great speeches about fatherhood occurs in the third season of *Breaking Bad*. Walter is conflicted over actions he's taken. His boss, Gustavo Fring, sets him straight.

Walter: I made a series of very bad decisions, and I cannot make another one.
Gus: Why did you make these decisions?
Walter: For the good of my family.
Gus: Then they weren't bad decisions.
What does a man do, Walter? A man *provides* for his family.
Walter: This *cost* me my family.
Gus: When you have children, you always have family. They will always be your priority, your responsibility, and a man...a man *provides*.
[Pauses for effect]
And he does it, even when he's not appreciated, or respected, or even

loved. He simply bears up and he does it…*because he's a man.*

Gustavo's words are hard and uncompromising, delivered with such conviction and force as to exclude timid assertion or cowardly rejection. There is no counter-argument to be made because there is no argument here. There is only truth.

The power of these words!

"Self Portrait, With Father"
Dick Ket, 1938, PD

Consider the way Gus makes his point, but consider most of all the words he chooses. He is not illustrating his point. He is not pleading or cajoling or even making an argument as such. He is carving out of elemental matter the necessary identity of man as father, but more than that: His words define man as man, as the essential confluence of identity and character that admits of no further reduction. A man provides, because that is what he does, because he's a man.

Gus studiously ignores the word father and consciously substitutes the more powerful, foundational concept of *man*. Not once does he say 'father', but he intentionally repeats the word *man*, fully five times. He's not allowing Walter to ignore the identity or place a conditional or contingent or fleeting alternative. He is a man, therefore he must provide.

A man provides for his family. It is a statement of identity, a fundamental relation describing the very fabric of the universe. One could imagine Walter trying to wiggle his way out of the conundrum. "I never wanted to be a father," he might say under his breath. "I could get a divorce, I could disown Junior, I could flee the country"—as if any of these choices would somehow negate the truth of his fundamental identity as a man. Even if he succeeded in liberating himself from any of the legal or cultural or social expectations of fatherhood, it remains uncontestably true that he is a man. Even if society says he is not required to provide because he is not legally a father, he nevertheless must provide because he is a man, because a man provides.

The undeniable truth that Walter is a man at once establishes a set of irrefutable corollaries. Walter is son to a father, son to a mother, infant brought forth from a community that allowed mother and father to conceive, gestate, and give birth. Gustavo's assertion of the word **man** over any other is tantamount to demanding Walter's affirmation of unchanging identity. Regardless of circumstance—whether he is husband and father or bachelor and childless—he is a man and he will therefore provide. If he chooses to neglect Skyler or Junior, he is choosing not to provide, therefore he is choosing not to be a man.

The significance of Gustavo's words is that any such refusal of responsibility is impossible, not because to do so infringes on moral imperative, but because such a cowardly retreat constitutes a self-contradictory assertion, an invalid statement about the nature of the universe. A man is that biological-social-physical-spiritual entity which provides, and there's no way to get around it.

Family and Identity

If Walter does not acknowledge and act on and order his life according to the indisputable truth of his relation to Skyler, Junior, and Holly, he is denying that which cannot be denied. In a sense that transcends and overcomes our tendency to insist on the unconnected nature of autonomous individuality, Walter cannot be described or understood independent of his connections to wife, son, and daughter. While lesser philosophies and second-rate television series insist on considering an artificial and impossible construct—the aloof and unconnected individual—*Breaking Bad* takes pains to identify and describe a real flesh-and-blood human being in all his inter-connected complexity.

A man is defined by relation. I am my father's son. I am my daughter's father. Walter White is his father's son. Walter White is Junior's father. Whether Walter White is high school chemistry teacher and citizen or ruthless drug lord and murderer—or all of these—he is first of all son, husband, and father. He may choose to give up teaching or quit the drug business, but he cannot choose to surrender his identity—that is, he cannot choose to reject or ignore the relations that define his identity as an inter-connected person.

Here, then, is the unique and powerful genius of *Breaking Bad*: This thought-provoking drama delivers the most complex, fascinating, and complete character sketch we are ever likely to see in fiction: Walter White, husband and father.

Chapter Ne

Necrology

"Jane Margolis"
Copyright 2011 Martin Woutisseth, used with permission

Walter crossed a line in Episode 2.12. Many—possibly most—fans consider the death of Jane Margolis the pivotal moment when Walter White made the transition from victim to victimizer. The point is worthy of debate but it seems to me the prevailing sentiment has validity not only from an emotional standpoint, but from the main characters' point of view. This moment in Jesse's bedroom will haunt Walter for years to come, affecting his dreams, his thoughts, and his plans. In coming seasons Walter will reflect on a bewildering cascade of crimes and transgressions, but the importance of this most noxious sin of omission will never fade.

Jane's death was the most recent in a long series of murders but just the third direct result of Walter's crimes. In fact, Heisenberg has really just begun his spree of death and destruction. By the end of the series he will be credited with 198 murders, accounting for 69 percent of deaths portrayed on the show. In the face of so much carnage, why is the death of Jane Margolis such an important watershed event?

Logic Versus Necessity

The murder of Emilio Koyama was the price of admission into the world of crime and illicit monetary gain. When Emilio recognized Walter as a participant in the DEA raid he assumed Walter was a federal agent. Walter delayed his execution by offering to synthesize meth. When he mixed red phosphorus with water to form deadly phosphine gas he was acting in self defense. Emilio's death became Walter's first warning that illegal actions carry enormous cost, but more importantly it constituted the first proof that Heisenberg's logical mind will never account for all contingencies. Murphy's Law prevails, and Heisenberg's constant refrain that "This will never happen again" because he's figured out every possible problem in advance can already be understood as a fatal flaw in his character. No mind, no computer, no system of thought is sufficient to create, explore, and address every possible failure scenario attached to a particular action. If ever we hear Walter proclaim a plan to be bulletproof, that it cannot fail, that it will not result in injury or death, we can be sure of its failure and we will know to look for gruesome casualties.

The *Breaking Bad* Universe does not unfold or behave according to Heisenberg's plan. Walter can dream and outline and theorize and cogitate all he likes, but he will never design a fail-proof event. Walter proposes but the Universe disposes. (Homo proponit, sed deus disponit.)

Complicity and Necessity

The Yellow Plate (Episode 1.03) was the symbol of inevitable complicity. With the missing shard, the Universe forced Walter to become accomplice to the death of Krazy-8 or the death of himself and his family. It was the symbol of disastrous consequence inevitably devolving from a bad decision. While Walter had choices, not one of the paths available to him led to a positive outcome. Death was the only possible result of going bad.

"The Fall of Man"
Hendrik Goltzi, 1616

We see the Forbidden Fruit as a choice posed by the serpent, but the Yellow Plate offers us a new way of thinking about personal autonomy. I want to propose that we consider the Tree of the Knowledge of Good and Evil just another element in the Garden of Eden. Adam and Eve cannot fly like birds, they cannot swim like fish, they cannot burrow like moles, and they cannot eat of the Tree of Knowledge of Good and Evil. The injunction against eating the fruit of one tree could be seen as nothing more than a common-sense law, just another edict of nature like the laws of gravity or the laws of aerodynamics. If Eve jumped off a cliff in the belief that she could flap her arms and fly, the result would be a hard landing and probably death. If Adam ate of the fruit of the forbidden tree, the outcome could only be as determined by the Author of the Universe. We could certainly ascribe a moral dimension to the decision to jump off a cliff, but we could equally consider the result as simply conforming to the structure of the Universe. Adam and Eve enjoyed complete and unrestrained volition, but every action they undertook would proceed according to the common-sense natural laws of the Universe.

We don't need to impose a moral understanding to see that jumping off a cliff could result in only one outcome. In like manner, we can look at the Yellow Plate as expressing etiological necessity, not as a choice between two evils.

Adam and Eve were completely free, but even in their freedom they were forced to adhere to the laws of nature. Freedom forced them into a necessary complicity with natural law. The Yellow Plate forced Walter into a necessary complicity

148

with the laws that governed the manufacture and distribution of methamphetamine. The wages of meth is death.

Pandora's Progress

"Pandora's Box"
Frederick S. Church, circa 1890

Pandora's Box does not indicate a mechanical universe, though. In saying that death is the natural outcome of jumping off a cliff and expulsion from the Garden is the natural result of eating forbidden fruit we are not positing the necessary progression or cascade of events from a single decision. Even if we believe freedom has little or no significance in the context of the Yellow Plate, nevertheless Walter enjoys complete freedom constrained only by natural law.

It's difficult to keep this truth in mind, especially in light of the frequent occurrence of death over the course of Season Two. More than that, many of the deaths have been the result of what appear to be non sequiturs. Tuco killed No-Doze without justification or logical cause of any kind. Gonzo died in a weird, improbable accident. A grocery store clerk was murdered so Spooge could steal an ATM, and then Spooge himself was murdered, his head crushed under the machine because his girlfriend didn't want to hear his taunts. Tortuga was murdered and his head impaled on a tortoise shell and a DEA agent died when he touched the booby-trapped tortoise. The arbitrariness of death in this second season seemed only to affirm that Pandora's

Box was open to the world, with every manner of illogical, random evil loosed on humanity.

Again, we can assign a moral context: Pandora must have had sinister intentions since her action resulted in the unleashing of evil on the world. But I don't think the Greeks intended for us to look at Pandora as an evil person. I believe they saw a progression from curiosity to unexpected and adverse consequences. If this is true, it may be helpful in our consideration of the necrology of Season Two if we ponder non-moralistic interpretations of events.

For one thing, we don't need to understand *apparent* randomness as indicating absence of causality. If we keep in mind that death is the natural and sometimes only permissible result of certain actions or conditions, and if we surrender to the notion of a Universe with its own agenda, understanding cause and effect to have their origin in a kind of metalogic, there's no need to ascribe second season deaths to random evil. We could take the position that the deaths are the inevitable outcome of natural law, that the Universe—to borrow an idea from Eloise Hawking—is undergoing 'course correction'.

"Pandora and Epimetheus"
Arthur Rackham, circa 1910

We think of death as 'bad'; we consider that only 'negative' outcomes can follow illicit actions, but there is ample room to consider wide-ranging interpretation free of moralisms. If Edith Keeler lives, great evil is unleashed on the world. On the other hand, her death will bring about a great boon. (*Star Trek* TOS, Episode 1.28) The death of Edith Keeler is predicated on the undoing of an event that must be understood as inherently good. If she lives, she succeeds in convincing President Roosevelt to delay entry into World War II. Everyone in her world understands this delay to be a good thing, but the cascade of events descending from that decision includes Nazi Germany's development of the atomic bomb. There may be any number of moral consequences accruing from nuclear power in Nazi hands, but in the *Star Trek* universe the most important outcome is scientific: Humanity will never discover the warp drive, and interstellar space travel will be impossible.

Neither does it follow that death must always be the outcome of a particular sequence of events. The Pandora myth says that after evil has been unleashed on the innocent world a single bright entity remains: Hope.

I'm making an effort to consider the necrology of Season Two from non-obvious mythological points of view because I believe a direct examination of the facts around Jane's death does not allow for the richer understanding the writers intended. If we just break out the black and white paint set, smear black paint on Walter and sprinkle white paint on Jane, we do a disservice to the series and to ourselves. We have an inkling that Jane is not innocent, but neither is Walter entirely corrupt. If he were completely beyond hope he would not have cried when he saw Jane vomiting. He would not experience the soul-wrenching doubts and pains and angst of the next three seasons. But these traumas are indeed a part of Walter's arc, and therefore we need to look at Jane's death on as many different levels as we can.

Innocence and Corruption

Hush, little baby, don't say a word,
Mama's gonna buy you a mockingbird.

. . .

And if that dog named Rover won't bark,
Mama's gonna buy you a horse and cart.

And if that horse and cart fall down,
You'll still be the sweetest little baby in town.

Sunrise, sunset. Walter carries a little girl, an innocent baby in his arms. "Lay her on her side," Walter warns, "in case she throws up."

A chance meeting at a bar has him seated next to a man, Donald Margolis, the father of a girl—a girl he once carried, an innocent baby in his arms.

"Is this the little girl I carried?" Donald asks. She's 27 years old. "I don't remember growing older," Donald complains. "When did she get to be a beauty? Wasn't it yesterday when she was small?"

Sunrise, sunset.

I quote a Russian Jew in 1905 marveling at the strange rhythms and continuities of life, a father's ruminations on the Book of Ecclesiastes.

One generation goes and another comes,
But the world constant flows, its rhythm drums.
The sun rises high and the sun goes down nigh.
…
What has been, so it will be spun;
What has been done, that will be done.
Nothing is new under the sun.

Sunrise, sunset. It's the law as writ in the first chapter of Ecclesiastes. One daughter is this day born, another daughter is this day dead.

Zero Mostel as Tevye
"Fiddler on the Roof"
Publicity Photo, Graphic House, New York, 1964, PD

There is nothing new under the sun. Innocence falls to corruption, baby girls become young women, and fathers can only watch. First they keep vigil, then they cry in their distant lookout, but never despair of their watchful guard.

"Family," Donald says. "You can't give up on them, never. What else is there?"

Perhaps others can see that the innocent baby becomes the corrupt young woman, but this is a truth ever hidden from a father's view. A man does not know these things because it is not within his conscious awareness. A man can be son, husband, or father, or all of these, but he can only observe and witness and understand those truths that relate to father, wife, or child. A man's father is blameless, a wife is adored, a child is loved, and all are provided for. "When you have children, you always have family. They will always be your priority, your responsibility, and a man…a man *provides*."

By definition, a man provides. In the same way, a man knows his daughter to be innocent. "You can't give up on them, never," because they are always blameless. In Walter's mind, Holly will always be vested in pink—the color of innocence—even when she is old and gray and others have felt her pettiness and scorn and selfishness. She will always be perfect in Walter's mind. So too for Donald Margolis: In his mind, Jane will always be perfect—innocent in every way.

Walter had a 'nephew', he told Donald. That's when the wise father of the 27-year-old girl, unaccountably and impossibly stained by the corruption of illicit drugs, nodded and enunciated the truth Walter already knew: You can't give up on them. Even when you're not appreciated, or respected, or loved—even when they slam a door in your face.

Walter's 'nephew' surely didn't appreciate his imposition of an after-the-fact rule regarding the distribution of his drug money. But it took Jane to recognize the immorality—the corruption—of Walter's refusal to give Jesse "what's coming to him," the just fruits of his meth lab labors.

But Jesse would have none of it. Jane's demand that Walter hand over the money didn't take into account the full reality of Jesse's place in the world.

"He's my partner," Jesse whined.

"*I'm* your partner," Jane said, correcting him.

I loved that little bit of linguistic jousting, pitting a traditional definition of partner—a principal in a joint business venture—against a very new definition—a husband, wife, spouse, or lover. But the linguistic twisting of words occurred in the broader context of a symbolic twisting of relation. While Jesse thought of Walter as a business partner, Walter considered Jesse his 'nephew', or actually a son, as I claimed a few chapters back. The symbolism relays the truth: Jesse is no business partner. He's much more than that.

We know Jesse is family. We had only a vague sense of this until the last two episodes of Season Two, but now the connection is certain, carved into the color scheme that is at the core of *Breaking Bad* symbolism. Holly wears pink for the same reason that the singed teddy bear was pink: Pink is the color of innocent childhood. Jesse is Pinkman: Innocent Child-Man. More importantly, he is **Child** in the same way that Walter is **Man**. Just as 'man' means far more than any assignment of sex chromosomes, 'child' in *Breaking Bad* has little or nothing to do with chronological age. The word 'man' establishes a relationship between that person and the significant others in his family. 'Child' establishes the same types of relationships, but in a subordinate role.

Walter as Man-Father must provide for, mentor, and watch over the Child-Son Jesse. This is why, as soon as Donald reminded Walter "You can't give up on them, never," he left the bar and immediately headed toward Jesse's apartment. "Hush little baby," don't worry or cry, because Man-Father will take care of all Child-Son's needs. That is what a man does, and that is what Walter did—or set out to do—in returning to Jesse's apartment. We cannot but act as mockingbirds, we cannot but imitate what our mothers and fathers before us have done, because this is what a man does.

Corruption and Loathing in Albuquerque

I completed this chapter several weeks ago. In the meantime I continued with my bedtime reading, which for the last few months has focused on key events leading up to the American Revolutionary War. As I uncovered historical connections—some of them quite radical—that I had never understood before, I began to see the final episodes of Season Two in a new light. I started out several weeks ago with the narrow goal of writing down a few thoughts on the loss of innocence but, like Hunter Thompson on his famous trip to Las Vegas, I discovered a far more important quest along the way.

Graffiti image of Hunter S. Thompson
Thierry Ehrmann, 2009, CC-SA 2.0

The pivotal factor turned out to be the dual usage of the word 'Partner'. The fact that a single word could represent two gradations of similar concepts, both denoting association or relation, set me thinking about the inter-twined themes of corruption and innocence. I finally realized a third important element—association—was central to the final episodes of the second season.

Jane, an outsider to the central Walter-Jesse relationship, saw in Walter a greed-induced corruption where Jesse saw justifiable contingencies of purpose. Walter, an outsider to the central Donald-Jane relationship, saw in Jane a drug-induced corruption where Donald saw historical contingencies of blame. Jesse understood Walter as a man driven by logical connections, Donald understood Jane as an innocent whose life had been corrupted by others like Jesse. Walter was not greedy in any sense and Jane was not defiled or corrupt in any way. In blood relation there is no possible way to see corruption. Only in distant association, in a superficial or peripheral involvement, can any of the players assign blame or understand another's actions to be the result of a corrupted soul. Familiarity breeds love, not contempt. Intimacy is the mother of unconditional acceptance.

Everything was fine and in its place and as it should be until that fateful night when the *non-random*, purpose-filled *Breaking Bad* Universe brought two commiserating fathers together to share hard-won insights over cold beers. Donald's words made Walter realize he was Jesse's father. When Walter broke into Jesse's apartment—for the second time—he found his partner in bed with his lover. He looked at the heroin needle, looked at Jane, and felt deep loathing for her and the abyss into which she had drawn his son. She was corrupt, and an evil, corrupting influence on Jesse.

Two important realizations coalesced in those strange and horrible minutes when three people occupied yellow sheets. First, we understood Jesse and Walter were, in fact, more than mere business partners. Partner in the modern sense indicates an intimacy closer than friendship, and for these two men that partnership was expressed in a Father-Son bond. Second, Walter had an epiphany that would haunt him for the rest of his life.

He loathed her, hated her, because he could, because he was distant and uninvolved. He looked at her in disgust—until she began vomiting into the air.

In that split second everything changed. She was no longer the greatest mistake Jesse had made. "Lay her on her side, in case she throws up," Walter had instructed only hours before. Now here was a daughter flat on her back, subject to death by asphyxiation on her own vomit. A daughter—Jesse's partner—Jesse's equal—and *therefore Walter's daughter.*

Familiarity breeds acceptance. Intimacy is the mother of unconditional love. The most intimate moment in life is the instant of death, and in this horrible moment Walter realized his son's lover was not corrupt, she was innocent.

Innocent. She was an innocent, a daughter—*his* daughter—and he drew back, held his breath, loosed his tears—and watched her die. This is the central episode in *Breaking Bad*, containing the pivotal scene of the series, because it is in this moment that Walter White sacrifices that which cannot be sacrificed: Innocence.

When Bad Things Happen to Pink People

Walter's choice of attire 36 minutes into the final episode of Season Two ought to have shocked even those viewers not tuned into the color symbolism of the show. Walter appeared in the doctor's office wearing the brightest pink sweater I have ever seen. In fact, looking at John Larue's catalog of Walter White's clothing colors over all five seasons, I find nothing to match the brilliant intensity of this pink sweater.

The decision to vest Walter White in neon pink was a thunderous announcement, the importance of which was so great that the conventions of artistic subtlety were abandoned. The all-consuming question doesn't even need to be stated.

I have watched the final ten minutes of Episode 2.13 eight times, the great question guiding my frame-by-frame analysis. The sweater, so shocking in its incongruity, never fit into any of the scenes. I tried to understand the bold pink color as a statement of Walter's status as innocent victim of lung cancer, but the association didn't work, regardless of my efforts to force the sweater into the doctors' message of reprieve from inevitable death.

The sweater's significance became clearer in the next scene, in the Whites' bedroom when Skyler was packing.

Walter said Gretchen and Elliott paid for his cancer treatment. He had no other source of income. He went to his mother so he could tell her face-to-face of his diagnosis. He wore pink because he's an innocent victim. But then Skyler unleashed the litany:

> You have a second cell phone.
> Gretchen and Elliott didn't give you a dime.
> The cancer treatment—over a hundred thousand dollars—is paid up.
> You never went to your mother's.
> Your mother *doesn't even know* you have cancer.

It's not that Walter has created one big lie hidden by lots of smaller lies. The reason Skyler could not fathom his deception until now is that virtually every word exiting Walter's lips has been a lie.

We know the lies hide crimes of almost unimaginable magnitude. But many of us have the sense that Walter's most horrible transgression was the sin of omission in Jesse's bedroom. The awful irony, though, is that he committed no crime. Is a bystander guilty if he does not offer assistance to an injured or dying woman? Does statute require citizens to exercise medical expertise in emergency situations?

The ironic, Kafkaesque, inhuman reality is that even if a dozen helpless witnesses saw Walter withhold assistance from Jane, he could not be prosecuted for her death. If an officer decided to arrest Walter and bring him to trial, any attorney licensed in New Mexico could gain his freedom with practically zero effort.

As we know from Hank's predilection for Cuban cigars, *Breaking Bad* is not an examination of legality or illegality. It's important to understand that Walter's culpability is not tied to this or that federal or state law. There is no law stating that an adult son must inform his mother of his medical condition, yet of the many sins contained in Skyler's bedroom litany, probably the most important and least forgivable crime was the fact that Walter didn't tell his mother of his diagnosis.

This second sin of omission is not about deception or distortion, it's about the state of Walter's inner self. Lying to Skyler, paying off his medical debts through illicit means, and maintaining a sense of pride in not relying on others have become so important to Walter that his relationship with his own mother has become meaningless. So too, his relationship with Skyler. Lying to her has gained such importance that deception is the only basis for their connection to each other.

The pink sweater was an angry visual assertion of dissonance, a declaration that something of consequence was out of kilter. If Skyler's litany had been the final statement of the season, we might have understood the pink sweater as the visible sign of the rupture of their marriage. But Walter continued wearing the sweater, in the backyard, next to the pool, when he heard a great explosion and looked into the sky.

The sweater *had* to be brilliant neon pink. It had to be completely incongruous because it indicated a fundamental rupture, not between Walter and Skyler, but between Walter and the Universe. The very sky was torn asunder. No prosecutor or magistrate would ever hold him accountable. But the burden of 167 innocents— represented by the pink teddy bear—came to rest on Walter's shoulders.

I do not share the feeling that Jane's death was Walter's most important turning point. I believe a particular event in Season Five constitutes the moment in which he sealed his fate. But the gravity of her death, indicated by the overhead tear in the fabric of the Universe and the loss of so many lives, will remain a critical point of reference for the balance of the series.

"Santa Muerte"
Copyright Martin Woutisseth, used with permission

A Na ranjado

Spanish is my second language. My seventh grade Spanish teacher, one of the first Peace Corps Volunteers, created something of a stir when he began teaching not Castellano but the language spoken in the New World, in Mexico. For six years I studied not only the language but the culture, history, literature, and customs of Mexico. I read *Lluvia Roja* and *El Laberinto de la Soledad*. I knew to say 'Bueno' not 'Hola' when answering the telephone. I could recite the Aztec origins of the eagle, snake, and cactus symbols and their connections to Quetzalcoatl and Tenochtitlan. Over a period of six years I became fluent in the language and conversant in the culture. But in all that time I never, ever heard of Santa Muerte.

I remember getting off the bus a mile or so from the Basílica de Santa María de Guadalupe in Mexico City. I could have taken a bus all the way to the doors of the Basílica, of course, but I had been told I would not appreciate the deeper significance of this greatest of Marian shrines unless I walked the final mile. I was struck immediately by the calm determination of a handful of people, hands clasped before them in an attitude of prayer, on their knees, advancing one knee at a time over the concrete sidewalk. Many of them, I knew, would spend hours on their unprotected knees, rubbing the skin off, leaving a trail of blood behind them as they inched their way toward the Basílica to pray.

As I came closer to the shrine the great plaza surrounding the ancient church (this was long before the construction of the new basílica) was filled with dozens, perhaps hundreds of devout Mexicans, on their knees, some of them crying, some of them in pain, all of them resolute and undeterred. The penitential crawl to the Basílica and the grace it conferred outweighed any injury to body or soul.

The experience of all this was shocking to a teenage boy growing up in the Midwest. I had read about Mexican piety, had heard our teachers explain it, but witnessing with my own eyes, hearing with my own ears meant it inhabited the same reality I did, that the truth of it could not be denied. It was a truth beyond faith or reason. It was proof of Franz Werfel's paraphrase of Thomas Aquinas, "For those who believe, no explanation is necessary; for those who do not believe, no explanation is possible," the words that began *The Song of Bernadette*.

We can scoff, those of us lacking faith, but as Aquinas said, no amount of explanation will convince our jaded intellects. Perhaps, though, we tell ourselves, as real as the piety may be, it is for show, nothing more than a public demonstration of personal virtue. Maybe so. I was an impressionable teenager, after all, not a full adult wise in the excesses and deceptions of the world. But I had later experiences of plainly dressed women and men prostrating themselves before an altar, of quiet contemplatives and intercessors who lost themselves in hours-long prayer for the benefit of others. Were these people likewise caught up in artificial remonstrance of personal faith?

El Mundo al Revés

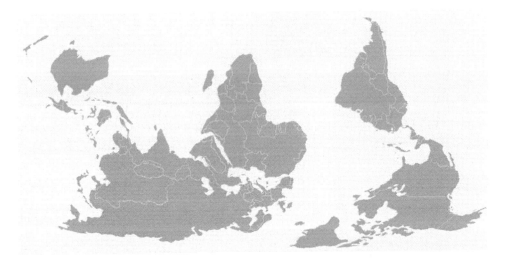

The question of authenticity weighs heavily, for the first scene of the first episode of the third season confronts us with an unearthly depiction of extreme piety. At first, seeing only a handful of poor men scraping the ground, we understand it as the unexamined devotion of superstitious peasants. But then we see an orange-tinted sky and, as a very expensive car comes into view, we wonder just where this story is taking place. Has Mars been terraformed and populated? The disorientation becomes overwhelming as we see twin brothers in immaculate suits exit the car, fall to the ground, and crawl with the peasants toward a jewel-encrusted shrine. When we finally see the object of their devotion we are shocked. Is this the same show I've been watching for two years? Maybe I hit the wrong channel number on my remote control.

The familiar music and the periodic table splash screen tell us that this is, indeed, the opening episode of the third season. For the duration of the commercial break I found myself shocked, unable to process the significance of the opening scene. What a strange, disorienting opener it was!

I have not visited Mexico in over 40 years, so out of curiosity I called up a few recent Youtube videos of the new Basílica de Santa María de Guadalupe. In the course of some 35 minutes of video images taken in the immense plaza surrounding the two Basílicas I saw not a single instance of anyone moving forward on bended knee. Perhaps the custom has been banned, or is no longer practiced. Times change, after all. The Cathedral of Montréal, so important to the history of Canada, is hardly used for worship anymore, but with its lovely blue-lit ceiling has become a tourist attraction. The

Québécois have almost completely abandoned their Christian faith since the opening days of the cultural movement known as the Révolution tranquille, starting in the early 1960s. Perhaps Mexicans have likewise lost interest in traditional Roman Catholicism. I don't know.

La Basílica de Santa María de Guadalupe
(New Basilica; the old Basilica is to the right)
Copyright Padaguan, 2012, CC-SA 3.0

Not able to connect traditional piety to the depiction of peasants crawling toward a shrine, I turned to the color of the opening scene of the third season and other depictions of drug-related activity south of the Mexican border.

The orange color wash used by *Breaking Bad* directors to indicate scenes transpiring in Mexico is much discussed on the Internet. In conjunction with two elements of Mexican culture I had never been exposed to—Santa Muerte and Jesús Malverde—I found the orange-tinted sky not only disorienting, but gravely disturbing. What did this strong, almost harsh manipulation of color mean? My fear was that the unnatural, unpleasant color indicated Mexico itself, with the implication that Mexico meant something evil or unpleasant, inextricably bound to modern fascination with the skeletal 'saint' and a turn-of-the-century Mexican bandit. I made it my aim to unravel the significance of the orange tinting in the scenes shot south of the border.

The truck in which the Salamanca cousins entered the United States crossed into Texas just before it was incinerated, as confirmed by Hank in Episode 3.02. Yet in the final scene of Episode 3.01, when the cousins killed the driver and prepared to burn

161

the evidence of their gruesome murders, the Texas sky was tinted the same orange color that had been applied in the earlier scenes transpiring in Mexico. The orange tint ('anaranjado' in Spanish) didn't symbolize Mexico, then, but something able to cross the border.

I went back to an earlier scene near the border, the DEA stakeout in Episode 2.07, when the head of Tortuga (the DEA informant) appeared on the top of a tortoise in the Texas desert. I saw no orange tinting. Fast forwarding to the fourth season, I took a close look at Episodes 4.10 and 4.11, depicting pivotal events in Mexico. I saw no orange tinting in the laboratory scenes, but the lighting during the scenes around Don Eladio's pool seemed unnatural. I'm no expert in cinematography, but I felt the colors were off, to the point that the scenes were uncomfortable to my eyes, which I take to be the directors' intention.

Analyzing the Mexico-based scenes, some of which were tinted, others that were not, I see but a single feature in common: the presence of one or more members of the Salamanca family or other players in Eladio Vuente's Cuidad Juárez Cartel. Orange tinting, then, means *Cartel*.

La Perversión de la Norma

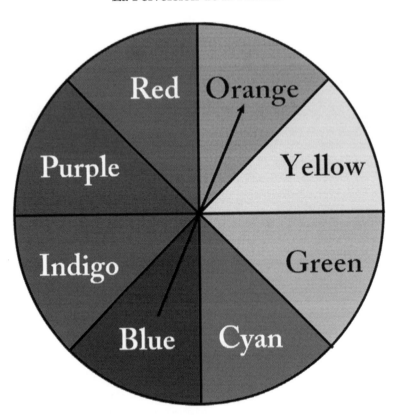

"La Perversión de la Norma"
Pearson Moore, 2013

The orange color wash in Cartel scenes was confusing and disturbing for reasons unrelated to geography or culture, too. We know that orange is Hank's color. In Chapter O, I said, "the dark, somber, almost rust-colored orange preferred by Hank is the color of legitimate, conferred authority." Does this mean that members of the Cartel, tinted orange as they are, enjoy 'legitimate, conferred authority'?

No. First of all, notice that the orange tint is applied to every element of the Cartel scenes, not just to individual players. While a shirt or jacket color implies a personality trait or attribute, a frame-wide color shift implies a condition, emotion, or mood for the entire scene and every participant. But the mood is not one of legitimacy or acceptance. If anything, the orange color and accompanying events seem to indicate coercion, the imposition of nefarious intentions, or the threat of future violence. In fact, we can look at the most important name in the Cartel to understand the meaning of the orange tint.

An Arboreal Salamander (*Aneides lugubris*)
One of over 650 species of salamander
Copyright Bill Bouton, 2011, CC-SA 2.0

Even those fans who don't speak Spanish can probably figure out that the name Salamanca means salamander. But the word carries deeper meaning, especially to South Americans. The word salamander has a cognate of nearly the same spelling in Spanish: Salamandra. Salamandra indicates an ordinary or common salamander. Salamanca, on the other hand, is a flat-headed salamander most often found in South American caves. The indigenous peoples of the area consider the salamanca to be the embodiment of evil spirits, and it is this connotation I believe to have been the writers' and directors' intention in painting the Cartel scenes with an orange palette.

Orange tint represents an inversion, or actually a *perversion*, of the natural order of things. Orange is an 'allowed' color, but it is not a *natural* color. The sky is supposed to be blue, not orange. To obtain an orange color, it is necessary to turn the color wheel on its head, and that is precisely what the directors and color editors did. Orange tint indicates an imposition of human desire, parochial sensibility, and selfish design on the broader world. More importantly, perhaps, it represents the rejection of powers exceeding those of ordinary human beings; Orange tint is the rejection of the Universe.

Hank, in his rust-colored DEA-orange shirts, is not imposing himself on the world, he's merely exercising the human authority conferred on him by the federal government. He's not degrading the overarching blue sky by squeezing it into conformity with orange-based human power. Human authority, as well intentioned as it may be, is nevertheless parochial or limited. Hank is not an agent of objective morality, after all, he's a duly authorized enforcer of human ordinance and statute. As we've already seen many times throughout the series, *Breaking Bad* doesn't care one bit about the laws of the United States of America, it cares only about the inner state of its characters and their relation to each other and the world around them.

When Hank is on an even keel—when his inner state is balanced—he wears orange. When he is exceeding his authority or in a confused state he doesn't wear orange, he wears black, gray, very dark brown, or (in Season Five) red. Check out his barroom brawl in Episode 3.03, for instance. When he challenges the two local potheads to a bit of fisticuffs, he's wearing a dark brown, almost black shirt.

Still recovering from the killing of Tuco Salamanca, Hank splashes water on his face in the bar's rest room. We know he's struggling to gain control of himself not only because of his actions and his facial expressions, but because of the shattered mirror in which we see his broken, fragmented face. Interestingly, he knows he's impaired, and for this reason he leaves his gun in the truck, fearful that in his unbalanced state he would shoot the druggies rather than arrest them. He's more in control than he was in the man cave scene of Episode 2.05, though. Compare his choice of shirts in the two scenes and match them to his actions. The wild pattern shirt of Episode 2.05 and his over-torqueing of the bottle cap both indicate utter lack of control. On the other hand, the conservative stripes (indicating control) and the dark brown color (indicating chaos or confusion) of Hank's shirt in Episode 3.03 indicate a conflicted state somewhere between balanced and unbalanced, reflected in his decision to leave the gun in the truck (control) but to beat the crap out of two inconsequential addicts (lack of control).

Los Símbolos de Mal

The symbolic entanglement of Santa Muerte and Jesús Malverde with Cartel orange demonstrates *Breaking Bad*'s unwillingness to settle for worn expressions of good and evil. Orange is Hank's color; a superficial examination of *Breaking Bad* might lead impatient observers to declare the creators of the series incompetent or unable to present a coherent color symbolism. How can the same color mean both good (Hank) and evil (Cartel)? More careful and respectful analysis, though, reveals the show to be using color at many different levels simultaneously. Orange doesn't mean 'Hank' or even 'good', it means 'human authority'. If that authority is exercised with the intention of fulfilling human objectives, it is legitimate, conferred authority, and we consider it 'good'. On the other hand, if the authority is exercised with the intention of perverting the natural order, essentially trying to force blue to become orange, trying to make the vast Universe conform to parochial schemes and selfish interests, that authority is illegitimate, and we consider it 'evil'.

Notice the nature of that authority is the same in both cases. The only difference is the *objective* of the agents making use of orange-conferred power. From a broader cultural point of view this means that we must consider Hank, Santa Muerte, Jesús Malverde, and any other character, material, or event associated with the color orange to have neutral moral value or authority. The intentions of even a usually good character, like Hank, can lead him to abuse power or authority, as in the barroom brawl or in his decision to take a day off from work so he could cut up his hands with a bottle-capper.

El mundo anaranjado of the Salamancas and the Cartel is yet another indication of the conceptual brilliance of *Breaking Bad* and a source of immense enjoyment as we make our way through Season Three.

"Jesse Pinkman"
Copyright Martin Woutisseth, used with permission

Chapter Mg

Mgmt. of
True Change

"You should be here to learn self-acceptance," the Narcotics Anonymous group leader said. "Self-hatred, guilt—it accomplishes nothing. It just stands in the way."

"Stands in the way of what?"

The group leader stared into Jesse's eyes. "True change."

Everyone in Jesse Pinkman's life was eager to impart to him whatever nuggets of wisdom they possessed. Walter was never short on advice. Even Jane reappeared from the dead, as a flashback in Episode 3.11, to provide Jesse with food for thought resulting from their appreciation of Georgia O'Keeffe's paintings of a door. "Open yourself up and go with the flow—wherever the Universe takes you," Jane instructed.

"Okay, so, the Universe took [O'Keeffe] to a door, and she got all obsessed with it and just had to paint it 20 times until it was perfect?"

No…Nothing's perfect. That door was her home and she loved it."

The bits of advice, thrown at Jesse from multiple quarters, seem contradictory or even nonsensical. Should he seek self-acceptance? True change? Or should he obsess over that which is "his home"?

Breaking Bad, the series, is about Walter White. But the third season belongs to Jesse Pinkman. The convolutions of Jesse's character in this season called for abilities no less formidable than those belonging to Bryan Cranston. Aaron Paul rose to the challenge and won an Emmy for Best Supporting Actor in his tour-de-force performance this season. The third season is my favorite of the five, for many reasons, the most important being the unrelenting focus on one of the most fascinating characters in fiction: Jesse Pinkman.

Vagina Paintings

Jane lured Jesse to the Georgia O'Keeffe museum with the promise of vagina paintings, or so Jesse remembered. "No," Jane corrected him, "I said some of her paintings *looked like* vaginas." No doubt the two of them did get to see several of the famous flower images painted in such a way that O'Keeffe seemed to invite a consideration of vaginal beauty and purpose, but it was the single representative image of a door that took center stage in the introduction to Episode 3.11.

I considered opening this section with the evocative image of Gustave Courbet's 1866 "L'Origine du monde," because I believe it gets to the heart of what Jesse was confronting in the opening scene of Episode 3.11. Why go to all the trouble of bringing back an actress to reprise a role she had completed a full year before—for a scene lasting three minutes and 34 seconds? It had to be done this way because the scene was crucial to the demonstration of Jesse's character.

I'm not exaggerating when I claim the scene was crucial; the outlays of personnel and resources prove the scene's importance. No fewer than five people from the *Breaking Bad* team worked for several weeks to secure approval from the O'Keeffe museum to paint a *replica* of one of her works. They were not allowed to photograph any of the real paintings. When they were done with the shoot, they sent the replica back to the Georgia O'Keeffe Foundation so it could be destroyed. The 'museum' as it appeared in the episode was actually a meticulous recreation of one of the museum's rooms on the *Breaking Bad* Albuquerque sound stage. Five people working for three months on a scene that would last fewer than four minutes? It was *that* important, because without it we would not understand Jesse.

The critical ideas in the scene were identity, movement toward perfection, and acceptance of self.

Those who are familiar with "L'Origine du monde" may have an idea of what I'm driving at here. If you're not squeamish about nudity or eroticism I invite you to google the image. An origin is a starting place, a portal or door, if you will, and this is part of the meaning of Courbet's painting. But an origin is also a determinant of identity. It sets the course one will follow, it is the beginning of a journey.

Courbet depicted a door. We needed to see Jesse contemplating a door, too. We needed to see him standing in front of a door because the tableau planted in our minds the notion of starting point and voyage, of discoveries that would occur or had occurred on the opening of that door. It could have been done with vagina paintings, but making the connection with door as origin and identity would have taken more than a five-minute scene. And the network probably could not have gotten away with showing Courbet's masterpiece. The FCC still has some rules, after all, and they're not afraid of assessing penalties for networks that break those rules. So instead we were treated to the vision of Jesse contemplating a simple door, which had always been the intention anyway.

But what is the greater meaning? What was Jesse supposed to do with that door? Was he to open it? The course he was obliged to follow was not clear. The advice he received had been all over the map: Change yourself [Seek true change].

Don't change yourself [Accept yourself as you are]. Don't worry about yourself, but do re-imagine your world [paint the same door 20 times]. What did all of it mean?

Identity as Portrait

Georgia O'Keeffe
Alfred Stieglitz, 1918

Georgia O'Keeffe's husband, Alfred Stieglitz, was captivated by her expressive sensuality. This unusual collaboration between two visual artists resulted in some of the most striking images caught on camera. Stieglitz was not posing a model to conform to his notion of beauty. Rather, he was capturing on film the purposeful movements of a woman driven by a deep sense of self. The portrait above is my favorite among the hundreds of images the two of them created, but it is unusual, too, in that it does not make reference to O'Keeffe's hands or her nude form.

The hands are important, not only to an appreciation of O'Keeffe, but to our understanding of Jesse Pinkman. I am no art historian, but it seems to me the images of O'Keeffe that most fascinate are those that focus on her hands and the deep meaning she brought to them in Stieglitz's photographs. Her hands are never just 'there', they have a purpose. One might be tempted to assign symbolic value. She was a visual artist, after all, and we might expect that the depiction of her hands was intended as a statement of artistic identity. 'Here are the tools of my trade', essentially. I don't believe that is the significance.

Georgia O'Keeffe
Alfred Stieglitz, 1918

Georgia O'Keeffe
Alfred Stieglitz, 1918

I love the two images above but I don't feel they convey the central idea of the O'Keeffe/Stieglitz collaboration. The hands are essential, but they are only half of the full artistic statement. The most complete statement of the artists' thesis, as I understand it, focused on O'Keeffe's identity not as an artist but as a person. The artistic couple created hundreds of images of O'Keeffe grasping or covering or cupping her breasts, and I believe this series of photographs comes closest to portraying the idea they sought to evoke.

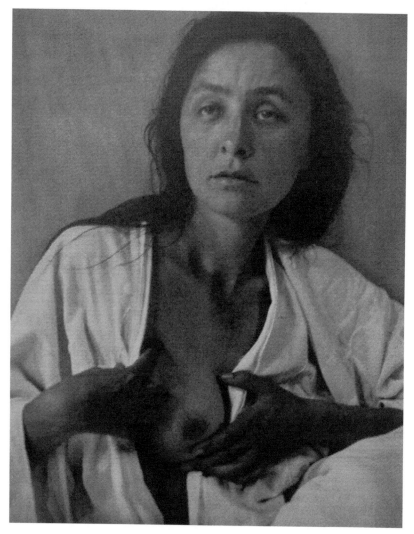

Georgia O'Keeffe
Alfred Stieglitz, 1918

These hands-on-breast images were rendered in all kinds of poses, both clothed and unclothed. I find most of them far less compelling than the simple nudes or the hands-only photographs, but the great number of these, and their at times experimental character leads me to believe the theme of hands-on-breast was enormously important to both artists. The multiplicity of images seems testament to a desire to nail down an idea both of them considered important.

Jane said, "That door was [O'Keeffe's] home and she loved it." Stieglitz and O'Keeffe never achieved the perfect depiction of O'Keeffe's personal identity. This may have been Stieglitz's obsession, but I believe, with Jane, that O'Keeffe eventually came to have a more mature understanding of obsession with hands, doors, and vulvas. "Nothing's perfect," Jane said. She painted the door over and over again because the obsession was "about making the feeling last." Repetition and movement became routes toward the revelation of a thing-as-it-is, the depiction of the full identity of a thing.

We see in many of O'Keeffe's paintings an evocation of the most intimate aspect of the feminine form.

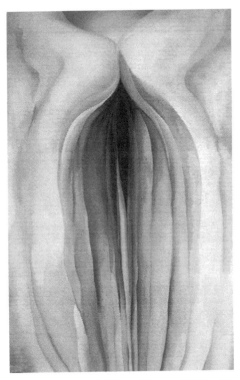

"Gray Lines With Black, Blue and Yellow"
Georgia O'Keeffe, 1922, PD

It seems hard to believe we are only imagining the association. She created an entire series of pelvis paintings, after all, and thousands of art critics over the decades have commented on the obvious similarities between many of her flower paintings and the human vulva. Paintings such as her "Slightly Open Clam Shell" seem almost pornographic in their evocation of sexuality. So she must have been associating flowers with female genitalia, right?

No. O'Keeffe was assaulted from all sides during her life, especially by feminists, who wished to apply their particular interpretations to her work. But she stated repeatedly, in unambiguous language, that the paintings had nothing to do with human body parts. As Marina Galperina noted in 2011, "They are just flowers. Biologically, the centers of flowers are androgynous, not feminine, alright? These flowers were not painted in praise of labia, conversely, these ravenous views are tributes to the sensual forces and ecstasy of nature itself." (Marina Galperina, www.flavorwire.com/231148/ accessed on 8 December 2013)

Jane's interpretation of O'Keeffe's painting of the door takes on greater significance in light of the artist's own statement about the meaning of her works. As with Stieglitz's portraits, the intention is not to create a symbolic representation of something else, but to portray something as-it-is, in its full identity. Stieglitz's portraits are to be understood as sensual, not sexual, the portrayals of a person, not a subject or an object. This is the reason for the critical importance of the hands. O'Keeffe was not a lump of clay, she was co-participant/co-creator in the drama we experience as a photographic portrait.

In seeing 'vagina flowers' we make O'Keeffe's work less than it was intended to be. So sure are we that only human beings can exude a sensual nature that we attempt to stuff her paintings into our own constructs regarding texture and form and identity. O'Keeffe's insistence that flowers and all of nature partake of a unique and vibrant sensuality is beyond our *willingness* to comprehend. That is unfortunate, because if we cannot accept the paintings on the artist's terms, we surrender the ability to see the artist's obsession for what it truly is.

What are the feelings we should try to sustain? Which elements in life are worth obsessing over? This is the central question of Episode 3.11, and it is the central question in Jesse's life.

Home

Episode 3.11 was titled 'Abiquiú', a reference to the village where O'Keeffe made her home from 1949 until her death in 1986. The idea of 'home' permeates the episode, beginning with the door image and Jane's thought that the door was O'Keeffe's home. The episode looks at Walter's strange relationship with his home in which he is a visitor, and it serves up Hank's strong feelings about what home was— and what it could and could not be. Home was not a place for a 'cripple' like him and not a place for hospital beds. Marie's answer to Hank's protests was to throw down a unique challenge: If she could coax him into an erection in less than a minute he would go home. She won the challenge, of course, but the greater implication was that Hank was not a cripple in the way that most defined his virility. Therefore he was not violating any of his self-imposed rules by returning home.

But the most important development of the 'home' theme occurred in Jesse's storyline. He obsessed over a lipstick-stained cigarette butt in an ashtray. Jane was his 'Origine du monde', his door, his home. She was worthy of his obsession, just as O'Keeffe was worthy of Stieglitz's obsession. She was neither subject nor object, but a person-in-herself. The exciting aspect of this was that there were no 'Rules of the Universe' saying this was how it had to be. Walter, we know, thought of Jesse as a son, but treated him as an object, as a slave to do his bidding. Jesse did not objectify Jane.

That critical difference in the way he approached his lover is central to Jesse's identity as Pink-Man: Innocent Man.

An obstetrician considers the vagina and apprehends the birth canal—the starting point, Courbet's 'Origine du monde'. A lover ponders the vagina and understands an entrance. In both cases, the observer sees a door. But what do we perceive if we are not observer, but owner? What do we sense if the door belongs to us? What do we understand about the nature of that door if it is not an origin of movement but a source of stability?

We learn from Jane Margolis and from Georgia O'Keeffe that a door is first of all neither a starting point nor a final destination, but a *home*. A door is a place, a condition or state of being. We can, if we insist, look on O'Keeffe's flower paintings as carrying sexual connotation, but we are much better served if we see them as conveying natural sensuality. If we assign sexual value to the paintings, we need to understand the original intention was sensual, not sexual. In the same way, the essence of the door as stable resting place brings new meaning to our superficial understanding of the door as entrance or exit or mere portal to be traversed in the course of a journey.

A Place-In-Itself

When I travel from Toronto to Ottawa I get on the 401 and follow it about 370 kilometers to the 416 exit, I take Highway 416 until I run into 417, then I follow that road all the way to my final destination, the Canadian capital, Ottawa. I suppose there's nothing wrong with thinking of the trip in this manner, but it's not the only way of considering the route. I could have said, and thought in my mind, that I would move away from Toronto toward Pickering, Belleville, and Brockville and at Ogdensburg I would turn north and pass by the entrance to Rideau River Provincial Park and the turnoff to Ben Franklin Park just before coming up to the Ottawa River, where I would turn east and head into Carlington before finally stopping at Parliament Hill in Ottawa.

It might seem as if the two ways of thinking about the route are more or less the same, but they're actually quite different. In the first example, the highway is a generic portal—a door-as-obstacle—but in the second example, the highway is important only to the extent that it serves as a means of navigation to points of interest along the way that are places-in-themselves, with their own unique identities and histories. In the first example, there is no mention of towns and provincial parks because they are irrelevant to the task of getting from Point A to Point B. But in the second example, the towns and parks along the way carry as much significance as starting point or ending point. The final goal is achieved in both cases, but the second mindset provides a far richer thought environment. When I stop along the way at a truck stop I'm just emptying my bladder and refilling my coffee mug at Timmie's. But when I chance upon Lytle Park I talk with parents watching their kids play soccer and I get a feel for neighborhoods in the southwestern part of Ottawa. Both stops take about the same amount of time, but the first stop does nothing more than satisfy basic bodily requirements while the second stop nourishes mind and soul, too.

When Jesse looks at O'Keeffe's door he's thinking, 'Why paint something as ordinary and boring as a door?' He's missing out on the rich experience of contemplating an entity not as object but as a thing-in-itself, as something possessing its own value and history independent of Jesse's stake in the entity.

Objectification

In Jesse's first talk with Badger and Skinny Pete at the Narcotics Anonymous meeting he was upset that his two assistants hadn't made any inroads selling blue meth to the drug addicts.

"Look, it's not so easy trying to sell to these people. They're here trying to better themselves," Badger complained.

"Yeah," Pete said, "there's like positivity and stuff goin' on here."

"Selling to these people," Badger said, grimacing, "it's like shooting a baby in the face, it's not natural."

"Jesse, it's not so easy like you think," Pete added.

"I'll *show* you exactly how *easy* it is," Jesse said.

That is, Jesse was convinced he could show his friends that the people at the meeting were nothing more than objects to serve as recipients of illegal drugs and providers of hard cash. After all, they weren't people with their own value and history—they weren't innocent babies or people otherwise worthy of respect—they were junkies, nothing more. And with that declaration of intent, Jesse set his sights on Andrea.

For a while Andrea was nothing more than Jesse's current problem, the next obstacle to vanquish and subdue. As he unbuttoned Andrea's blouse he told her he could get 'some of the blue stuff'—and then Andrea's mother came in with Andrea's young son, Brock, disgusted with Jesse and his ilk who were 'sin vergüenza' (without scruples or shame). In fact, this had been Jesse's boast to Badger and Pete: that he could be shameless and aggressive and insensitive to others in pressing them to buy his illicit product.

Something changed in Jesse as soon as Brock walked through the door. He was shocked. It's not that he'd never seen a six-year-old boy, but the thought had never crossed his mind that Andrea was not just a junkie with breasts, she was a daughter and a mother. Soon Jesse learned she was a sister, too, whose grade school-age brother had been turned into a drug dealer. Illegal drugs had affected her personally, to the core. They had ruined the lives of people she loved and taken away the innocence of children.

The next time they made out, we witnessed one of the key moments of Season Three.

Andrea: So…
Jesse: What?
Andrea: I thought maybe, if you're holding, we can do something.
Jesse: What?
Andrea: You know—that blue stuff you were talking about? Maybe you

had a line on some.

Jesse: Wait. Whoa. What? I thought you said the kid is coming home.

Andrea: Yeah. In a few hours.

Jesse: And you seriously want to get high?

Andrea: I don't know what you're getting so pissed about. You're the one who brought it up the other day.

Jesse: Yeah, that was *before* I found out you got a kid. What kind of mother are you?

Whether he understood it or not, Jesse just proved Jane's thesis about O'Keeffe's door, and at the same time outdid both his dead girlfriend and the great artist. Stieglitz and O'Keeffe never came up with the definitive visual statement of O'Keeffe's identity, but here, in this moment, we have the essential, authentic statement of Jesse's being: Jesse is a man who genuinely cares about children—more than he cares about his love interest or even himself. Jesse is that man who understands children as individuals of infinite value.

Jesse doesn't obsess about doors or vaginas. He obsesses about children, about innocents who deserve the love and care of parents and adults.

The point of Episode 3.11's Georgia O'Keeffe touchstone was not to demonstrate the extent to which Jesse had surrendered his own morality. The real significance was that he was more authentic and more human than anyone around him—more authentic even than artists who had been concentrating every faculty on the depiction of deep humanity—and yet, despite his inability to compromise when it came to nurturing and protecting innocents, he nevertheless succumbed to the allure of illicit drugs. He never surrendered anything, as we saw when Andrea asked Jesse for the blue meth. The important message is that even an innocent man—even a Pink-man—can find himself involved in pursuits that jeopardize fundamental aspects of human integrity.

'True Change', if we trust in the door metaphor, is not so much a voyage as an acceptance of self or a rediscovery of fundamental principles. Jesse is who he is. No one could take away his deep obsession with the welfare of children. 'True Change', for Jesse, means ordering his life and its many voyages according to that unchanging, immutable truth. We will learn before the end of the series whether he is successful in bringing that full sense of reality to his life choices.

$\boxed{\begin{array}{l} ^{13} \\ \text{Al} \end{array}}$ Cubil

de la Mosca

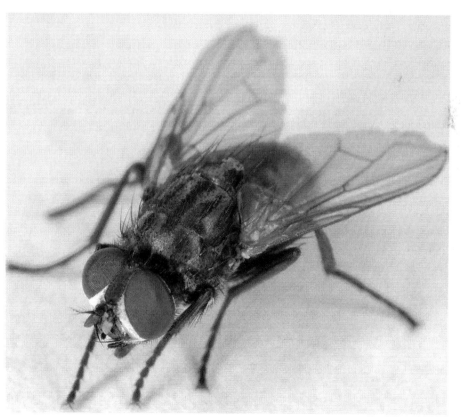

Common Fly
USDA, 2007, PD

Episode 3.10, "Fly," makes just about everyone's Top Five list of best *Breaking Bad* episodes. The episode is heavy on symbolism, dialog, and heartfelt emotion from the two lead characters. There is much to enjoy about this episode and both fans and critics have raised dozens of fascinating topics for our consideration. For me, the most important outcome of the episode was the elevation of the importance of Jane's death with a simultaneous expansion of her death's meaning in Walter's life, in ways I believe will surprise most people reading these pages. In fact, I think Walter's obsession over the fly reveals more humanity than we have seen up to this point in the series, and the brief 24-hour passage in his life demonstrates that his redemption is well within reach.

Color symbolism takes a back seat to other visual and thematic developments, but we will see at least one of the colors, bright reddish orange, developed into a powerful new symbol over the course of Seasons Four and Five. "Fly" lays the groundwork for the symbolic association, and ties the color directly to yellow, as we will see in Chapter Si.

Unsettling Vigilance

Walter began his Groundhog-esque day at 6:00 a.m., not to the confident sound of Sonny and Cher's "I Got You Babe," but to the unsettling reassurance of Skyler's "Mockingbird." He had spent four hours staring at the silent red light of the smoke detector on the ceiling over his head.

It is tempting to assign color-based significance to the big red light we saw at the beginning of the episode, but I don't think any such connections are useful. When I saw the large round light, the first association that came to mind was the red eye of the HAL 9000 in Stanley Kubrick's "2001: A Space Odyssey." On comparing the two images, I'm convinced the similarity was intentional. For one thing, the smoke detector light was not a uniform red, but contained a brighter inner yellow light, just as the HAL 9000 had. The blinking light of the smoke detector, then, was not a simple notification that the detector was working, it was the unsettling presence of an inhuman intelligence, monitoring Walter's every move—or perhaps his every thought. Worse, this strange intelligence was standing over Walter, an indication that it was in some sense superior to Walter, its invariant, regular blinking a sign of its constancy and immunity to the whims and wiles of human prerogative.

Sam Catlin, the writer of Episode 3.10, never seemed attached to the show's rich color schemes. His artistry was tapped for bottle episodes, such as Season Two's "4 Days Out," where the sparse atmosphere and the lack of distractions were used to focus attention on the development of main characters. If we seek symbolic associations, we would normally understand that Catlin's objective was not to sustain or embellish the grand themes of the show, but to concentrate on specific character traits. In 3.10, Catlin will surprise us.

The Perfect Moment

"I've lived too long," Walter said, regret evident not only in tone of voice but in every contortion of his anguished face. Obviously the fly was not a physical 'contaminant'. It was a living reminder or pesky symbol of whatever event or present condition in Walter's life was bringing grief to his thoughts and pain to his soul. But what was the cause of such deep angst?

He had missed 'the perfect moment'. In light of his statement that "I've lived too long," the perfect moment would seem to be the moment of death. If we couple that thought with the spiritual torment he was experiencing, the full significance of 'the perfect moment' is probably the moment in which he could die in peace, without regret.

He mentioned three events as candidates for 'the perfect moment': the 'fugue state', the birth of Holly, and the lung surgery. But he dismissed each one in turn. He didn't give any rationale for attaching significance to Holly's birth or the surgery, but any parent would live and die for children, so the birth of a baby girl carries significance all by itself, no explanation needed.

More interesting are the other two events he enumerated: the fugue state and the surgery. In response to the fugue state possibility he mumbled, "No, I didn't have enough money." This was perfectly credible since we have heard Walter claim many times that he went into illicit drug manufacture to earn money for his family before he died. The implication of having lived past 'the perfect moment' is that now, well into his first three months in the superlab, he had more than enough or too much money. But could having too much money serve as the primary source of deep regret? It doesn't seem likely.

The perfect moment was "definitely before the surgery." Why he should have chosen to die before the surgery I consider the most revealing statement during this period of unguarded expression of thoughts. If he wished to demonstrate his victory or fighting spirit, it seems to me he would have chosen to die *after* the surgery, to prove that he could have or would have beaten the cancer. 'The perfect moment', then, had nothing to do with personal strength, resolve, or inner ability, it was about something else entirely. He was no Hercules, off to complete the Twelve Labors before he could rest in peace. But if he did not have to survive the surgery in order to die in peace, why did the surgery have any bearing on his peace of mind? I believe this is the biggest question of the episode, and its lack of resolution points to a major theme of the series.

We should have known early in the episode the true nature of Walter's discomfort. We received a strong clue when Jesse spent 24 seconds contemplating Jane's last cigarette in the car ashtray. Even in the chaos and horror of the attack on Hank, Jane's death has never been far from the center of the two lead characters' thoughts. When Walter said, "Ah, I know the moment: It was the night Jane died," there was no surprise. Jane's death was Walter's greatest—perhaps single—regret. The fly was not a contaminant in the meth lab. It was a contaminant in Walter's soul. The fly was not the symbol of regret or angst, but the physical manifestation of conscience. The fly was the sign that Walter White still had a heart.

"It's all contaminated," Walter said, superficially in response to Jesse's acquiescence to Walter's fixation on the fly, but actually a surrender to the tumult in his soul. 'It's all contaminated' meant his inner self was compromised or contaminated. That this was Walter's final response to the corrosion of his soul meant he was giving in to it, that he accepted its mastery over him. The vigilant red eye of the first scene had won the battle for Walter's true self. The contamination was not partial, but total ('all'), and therefore could not be relieved in any way. Of course, it is precisely the penitent who bows her head and knows herself unworthy who is ready to receive forgiveness. When a person recognizes and regrets her complicity in evil, and confesses it as Walter has done here, that person is eligible for pardon.

Does Walter's admission of guilt and recognition of blame mean he will be forgiven? We might tentatively conclude that the only thing standing in Walter's way was his less than complete disclosure to Jesse. If only he had confessed to witnessing Jane's death and deciding not to intervene, we tell ourselves, Walter would have redeemed himself and the show would have ended.

The argument seems reasonable, but I don't accept it. Much more is going on in this episode, and it revolves around Walter's belief that he should have died before the cancer surgery.

The Universe

The revelation of the source of Walter's anxiety was not the element that made "Fly" a great episode. A lesser television series would have ended the episode here. It would have made an unexpectedly good episode of a procedural drama like *Law and Order* or *Grey's Anatomy* or *CSI*. But *Breaking Bad* is not *Grey's Anatomy*. Thank goodness! It is infinitely more nuanced and layered, and it is the depth of *Breaking Bad* that propelled the episode into a consideration of more than one man's guilt or anguish.

Of all the moments that might have been 'perfect' it is tempting to believe that Jane's death stood alone in Walter's mind. It did not. Recall that irrespective of any other consideration, the 'perfect moment' absolutely had to occur before the lung surgery. Why? What was the connection between Jane's death and Walter's life-saving surgery? We could spend hours or days trying to find the common link, but such efforts would provide nothing more than tenuous connections. The key to understanding the true nature of Walter's guilt is this recognition: There is no common ground between Jane's death and Walter's contention that he should have died before undergoing surgery.

Walter had two criteria for the 'perfect moment'. He meditated on the second reason when he spoke of his strange meeting with Donald Margolis:

> The universe is random. It's not inevitable, it's simple chaos. It's...it's subatomic particles in endless, aimless collision—that's what science teaches us. But what is this saying? What is it telling us when on the very night that this man's daughter dies, it's me who's having a drink with him? How can that be random?

Indeed. The blinking red eye over Walter's bed was the Universe's declaration that it was not random, that in fact it was highly ordered, that guilt was neither sentimental emotion nor disembodied association. Guilt is consequent to disorder and evil. It is the Universe telling the anguished party that evil acts will receive their due.

"It's all contaminated," Walter says in final submission. But he is acquiescing to only one cause: Jane's death. He accepts blame for her asphyxiation, but *he does not recant from his stubborn claim of randomness.*

Here is the nexus of that maleficence we know as Heisenberg: uncertainty. The full measure of his crime is found in his unfounded, stupid, self-serving notion of the Universe as meaningless and random. It is the claim Heisenberg must retain and defend, even to the point of nervously and preposterously telling hundreds of high school students that Wayfarer 515 was only the 50th worst air disaster in history. If he never gives up his identity as Heisenberg, it will be because he never surrenders his conviction that the Universe is always uncertain, that it never had and never will have meaning.

[For my fellow physical scientists out there, I'm referencing the Heisenberg Uncertainty Principle as a symbolic phrase unconnected to its technical definition as the inability to simultaneously determine both position and momentum, or energy and trajectory, or the implication that the act of observation affects system behavior. I'm pretty sure Vince Gilligan and crew did not have technical definitions or limitation in mind when they created Heisenberg, and I'm equally sure they intended Heisenberg as an allusion to the idea of uncertainty or randomness in all of its *non-technical, non-scientific* magnificence. Don't get too literal with this stuff or you'll never enjoy the show!]

One of the great artistic achievements of the episode was the ironic use of the fly—normally a symbol of uncontrolled randomness—as a sign of the Universe's order and control. Walter's guilt was the inevitable outcome of the unvarying structure of the Universe. Thus, the fly (Walter's angst) was a symbol of universal order and cohesion.

At the level of plot and character development, the episode achieves the strange, superficially contradictory objectives of both promoting the importance of Jane's death and subsuming it to Heisenberg's uncertainty. Walter White is a man wounded by the knowledge that he has caused harm, and in that respect he could, at any moment, receive full pardon for his many sins. But Heisenberg, proud in his ability to rise above the inscrutable madness and chaos of the world, is under the Universe's watchful eye. The Universe, patient and calm, ordered and collected, awaits the proper moment. Heisenberg's uncertainty or no, the Universe *is* inevitable, it *is* rich with meaning—and it will win.

"Gustavo Fring"
Copyright Martin Woutisseth, used with permission

Chapter Si

Signum Sapientiae

"Vitruvian Man," Leonardo Da Vinci, circa 1490

"Man is the measure of all things," the great Sophist Protagoras said. "Of things that are, that they are, of things that are not, that they are not." There are no gods. There are no determinants of the truth or falsehood or value or significance of any event or proposition beyond the judgment rendered by the faculties of human mind and human voice. Wisdom is found not in submission to others, but in assertion of self. In the end, the strong, not the meek, shall inherit the Earth.

Protagoras of Abdera
Greek Sophist, (circa 490 B.C. to 420 B.C.)
Jusepe de Ribera, 1637

Science, in Heisenberg's diseased mind, is the careful application of syllogism to uncovering the principles that have set in motion the random and uncertain universe. Because it is logical, it is the primary tool in the arsenal of the self-assured person. He who wields science with greatest clarity and precision will be strongest in the end. People of lesser intellect and technical skill must inevitably lose. Only one person can become the Measure of All Things, and Heisenberg is sure he is on his way to achieving that distinction.

Man is the measure of all things. If I say it is so, it is so. You can argue with me if you will, but know this: Truth or untruth, worth or insignificance, are determined by the words that come from the lips of the one who best manipulates truth and logic. The ancient art of sophistic or eristic is often understood as having firm basis in the art of persuasion. But 'If I say it is so, it is so' can also be understood as a logic-based assertion. If I truly am the measure of all things, I not only have the power to persuade you of the truth of my proposition, but the concept itself is perfectly in accord with logic and science. In fact, if I am the measure of all things, logic and science must bow to my greatness and obey my strictures.

We see Sophist philosophy in Heisenberg from the very first. "Respect the chemistry," he says, but the underlying command is to acknowledge and pay homage to Walter's superior intellect. The symbolic representation of sophistry is found in the preeminence of a single color in Seasons Three and Four: Yellow.

Wisdom

"Wisdom," Robert Louis Reed, 1896

Wisdom is the knowledge of how best to apply logic. We understand a person as wise when she is able to consistently invoke the laws of reason to devise compelling solutions to difficult problems.

The most difficult, often almost intractable, problem in the *Breaking Bad* Universe, in the eyes of those who follow Protagoras, is randomness. Wisdom works cautiously because sober consideration requires careful calculation of the effects of a multiplicity of variables on the outcome of an event. Thus, the mark of a wise practitioner of science and logic is *caution*.

Those of us not tuned into Heisenberg's 'superior' understanding of the Universe might consider a state of caution to be a condition of fear, a sense of foreboding around possible negative outcomes. But that's not the way Heisenberg experiences caution. He understands caution as a heightened sense of *awareness of multiple options*. Because his is a superior intellect, he will automatically choose the best option. Caution, then, becomes a badge of honor, an assertion of superiority, an ability to see things that other miss.

Yellow represents the fundamental spiritual disposition of the man who for 20+ years has run the methamphetamine business in New Mexico: Gustavo Fring. In almost every one of his scenes he wears a yellow shirt. So what is his fundamental disposition?

"I was told that the man I would be meeting with is very careful. A cautious man. I believe we're alike in that way."

These were the first words Walter uttered when he was sure Gus was the man Saul had told him about. (Episode 2.11) Thus, 'being careful' and 'a cautious man' were, in Walter's mind, the single most important qualities associated with Gus Fring.

Yellow is not a projection of fear. It is the confident assertion of rational superiority. It is the proclamation of mastery over the random, chaotic, uncertain tendencies of the universe. Gus wore yellow in the domain over which he exercised mastery: Los Pollos Hermanos. Walter, the 'maestro', the master of all things chemical, wore yellow in the environment where he was unsurpassed: the laboratory.

This is why, contrary to every practice in the pharmaceutical industry, Walter and Jesse wore yellow splash suits in their subterranean superlab. *Breaking Bad*, so careful to adhere to every convention of present-day pharmaceutical practice, down to the purple and blue nitrile gloves that I myself wear in the lab, consciously decided to violate industry norms and put the two lead characters in obnoxiously bright yellow Hazmat splash suits. I exercised license in similar manner in designing the cover for this book. I wore a yellow nitrile glove (not a latex glove, like the kind sold in supermarkets), not only to contrast with the blue meth (actually rock candy) in my hand, but to symbolize the lesser of two main colors in the *Breaking Bad* Universe: Yellow.

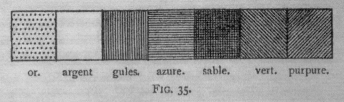

76   A COMPLETE GUIDE TO HERALDRY

maintained itself in use unaltered until the present day, and these are shown in Fig. 35, only that later, hatchings have been invented for brown, grey, &c.; which, however, seems rather a superfluous enriching." None of these later creations, by the way, have ever been used in this country. For the sake of completeness, however, let them be mentioned (see Fig. 36): *a*, brown; *b*, blood-red; *c*, earth-colour; *d*, iron-grey; *e*, water-colour; *f*, flesh-colour; *g*, ashen-grey; *h*, orange;

or.   argent   gules.   azure.   sable.   vert.   purpure.

FIG. 35.

and *i*, colour of nature. In English armory "tenné" is represented by a combination of horizontal (as azure) lines with diagonal lines from sinister to dexter (as purpure), and sanguine or murrey by a combination of diagonal lines from dexter to sinister (as vert), and from sinister to dexter (as purpure).

Color Rules in Heraldry
From *A Complete Guide to Heraldry*, p. 76
Arthur C. Fox-Davies, Edinburgh, 1909

You will read on the Internet and in various other analyses of *Breaking Bad* the same tired ideas: Red is danger, Yellow is caution, Green is money, yada, yada, yada.

No.

The producers didn't wrap Walter and Jesse in yellow because it meant 'Caution' in the sense of fear or foreboding. *Breaking Bad* is full of yellows and oranges and reds. We could see danger and caution at every turn, but these are not the only themes in *Breaking Bad*. In fact, these pedestrian concepts are *peripheral* to the main ideas of Randomness versus Meaning, Self-Deception, Karma as the natural endpoint to spiritual crime, and Guilt versus Pride. The writers zipped Walter and Jesse into yellow suits, against every industry expectation, because the artistic significance of the color far outweighed the technical significance. They didn't go to these lengths simply to create yet another sign of danger or fear.

With Yellow as the embodiment and primary sign of intellectual mastery, the producers brought yet another level of meaning to what was already the most profound series on television.

Paradoxically, the confident assessment of potential and risk is the final evolution of caution in the self-assured master's worldview. He who becomes the Measure of All Things exists on a thin, carefully balanced knife edge between indecision and arrogance. If push comes to shove, though, he will always err on the side of conceit, since in his mind he has evaluated every parameter and taken every contingency into consideration. We will see this mindset play out in the most audacious possible way at the end of Episode 5.01. I will return to this pivotal scene later in the book.

Yellow is confidence based in caution. It is, after Blue, the most symbolically rich color in the *Breaking Bad* Universe.

"Marie Schrader"
Copyright Martin Woutisseth, used with permission

Chapter P

Purple

Purple is a forbidden color. The truth of this is not immediately apparent, but by the time we reach Episode 4.03, "Open House," we have a good sense of the color's deeper meaning. The forbidden nature of the color does not derive of any arbitrary imposition of authoritative fiat. Rather, the color is forbidden because it cannot serve as a character trait. When people such as Marie Schrader attempt to appropriate the color (and its associated personal qualities) to their own use, the consequences are unpleasant for everyone involved, but especially for the person arrogating the color to her personality.

Taking a close look at Marie and her favorite color will tell us much about the structure of the *Breaking Bad* Universe, and Walter White in particular. Just as Marie appropriated forbidden purple for the illegal acquisition of goods, Walter appropriated forbidden blue for the illegal acquisition of money. In analyzing Marie's behavior we will see attitudes and activities shared with her brother-in-law and we will gain an appreciation for the illicit, forbidden nature of these two 'higher' colors.

Royal Purple

6,6'-dibromoindigo, also called Tyrian Purple or Royal Purple

189

The dye historically known as 'Royal Purple' was derived from a species of sea snail, *Bolinus brandaris*. Common to the western Mediterranean, this mollusk excretes a colorless but poisonous milky substance to protect eggs or at times of physical stress, such as during an attack. With exposure to air, the excretion oxidizes to the characteristic brilliant blue-purple color caused by the dibrominated indigo dye Tyrian Purple.

The naturally-obtained colorant was the most expensive dye in antiquity, costing more than its weight in silver. A single gram of the crude dye could be obtained only by grinding more than ten thousand snails; a complete purple-dyed cape and toga ensemble might require the destruction of over a million snails. Such was the value of the dye that it came to have immense cultural significance. Byzantine law, for instance, forbade anyone other than members of the royal family from wearing garments dyed with Tyrian Purple. This distinctive purple color, which did not fade but actually grew brilliant in sunlight, became so closely associated with royalty that the word itself evolved into a synonym for the ruling family. The emperor's children were said to be *porphyrogenitos*—'born in purple', meaning born to rule.

Empress Marie

Empress Theodora, Unknown artist, circa 550 A.D.
The Empress is vested in Royal Purple

We don't have a clear rationale for Marie's kleptomania. Based on selected scenes, our first thought might be that, like the Mediterranean snail, she 'secreted' her royal purple essence as a response to stress. For instance, she stole the shoes apparently as punishment for the store clerk's arrogance (Episode 1.03), and her day of thievery at open houses across Albuquerque (Episode 4.03) could be understood as a response to Hank's lack of gratitude for her attention to his needs. He chastised her for the smallest thing, even shouting at her because she purchased Fritos rather than Cheetos and complained that the Fantasy Football encyclopedia was useless since the season hadn't started yet. When her husband was nitpicking even the nice things she did, who could blame her for going out and stealing a few items of interest?

But the hypothesis of kleptomania as response to stress doesn't fit when we consider the example of Holly's tiara. (Episode 1.07) Empress Marie, without children of her own, was not responding to a shopkeeper's arrogance here, she was requisitioning to her niece's use a beautiful symbol of her standing as royal princess.

We might try to argue that Marie was putting her imperial stamp on the world. Such a hypothesis might explain her theft of the Puerto Rico spoon from the open house homeowner's wall-mounted display. The spoon didn't fit the others in the collection, as she noted when she spoke with the real estate agent. "Puerto Rico is technically a territory," Marie said, correcting the agent when she informed Marie that the spoons were from all 50 states. "You know," Marie said, laughing, "maybe they were thinking 'Some day'."

This behavioral rationale might explain the tiara (it rightfully belonged to a princess, not to a jewelry store owner) and even the shoes (Marie needed them, and she was Empress, after all), but it could not possibly explain the item Hank puzzled over when Marie left to get his Cheetos: The glazed ceramic figure of a boy riding a pig.

How Much Pig Does a Man Need?

Boy on Saddled Pig
Unknown photographer, circa 1900
From the menagerie of Sir Anthony Wingfield, Bedfordshire, England

The figurine Marie stole from the first open house was a Hummel depicting a young chimney sweep riding on a pig. The boy's whimsical avocation explained the ladder he carried in one hand and the chimney sweeping tools he carried in the other. The idea of boys saddling and riding a pig is common enough that I was able to dig up a turn-of-the-century German post card depicting a chimney sweep going about atop a hog.

Pig riding was a not-uncommon pastime in the 19th century. Charles Lyell, on a trip to Cincinnati in 1842, noted

It is a favorite amusement of the boys to ride upon the pigs, and we were shown one sagacious old hog, who was in the habit of lying down as soon as a boy came in sight.
(Charles Lyell, *Travels in North America*, 1856, vol. 2, p. 61)

Chimney Sweep Riding a Pig
Unknown artist, circa 1900

An 1819 law banning loose hogs in New York City was inspired at least in part by young boys' frequent sport of riding around on them. (Hendrik Hartog, "Pigs and Positivism," *Wisconsin Law Review* 899 (1985), 905-906)

That favorite activity of young children, getting a 'piggy-back ride' from adults or older children, apparently began with short rides on real pigs.

Saddled Pig, Unknown Artist, *The Nursery Rhymes of England*, 1842

The sow came in with the saddle,
The little pig rock'd the cradle,
The dish jump'd over the table,
To see the pot with the ladle.
The broom behind the butt
Call'd the dish-clout a nasty slut:
Odds-bobs, says the gridiron, can't you agree?
I'm the head constable, – come along with me.
(*The Nursery Rhymes of England*, 1842)

You don't have to search long or hard to find boys and girls of all kinds riding pigs.

Girl Riding Pig, Unknown Artist, circa 1905

Those with an interest in the truly bizarre can even find turn-of-the-century French post cards capturing adventurous young women, naked as the day they were born, riding about on porcine steeds.

Nowhere is the act of hog riding depicted as serious or edifying or virtuous. The act is universally considered silly, frivolous, and childish. It may be in good fun, but it is nothing more than that, and has neither purpose nor benefit.

For some reason, laying claim to the porcelain figure of a boy riding a pig carried such importance that Marie was willing to risk arrest in order to steal it from the open house. But if the item had no value, if it depicted a childish activity certainly unbecoming a purple-clad Empress, what was the purpose of the little knick-knack, and why did Marie need to take it?

If Marie Had a Heart

I believe the answer can be found in the unearthly strains of Fever Ray's chilling song, "If I Had a Heart." When the realtor at the second open house was done vacuuming, she stopped to look at the spoons display, frowning in disgust when she saw that the Puerto Rico spoon was missing. Playing in the background and growing ever louder were the opening notes of "If I Had a Heart." Without any change in music, the scene switched to Jesse in a go-cart, red-eyed and angry to the point of screaming.

He pulled into his driveway, opened the door to his house, and calmly walked through his living room where his 'friends' were frantically scratching each other while having sex, fighting, dancing, running around, all of it with frenetic energy lacking purpose or goal. When the scene switched again, we were back to Marie at the third open house. This time, rather than 'Charlotte Blattner' who didn't want children, she was 'Mimi' with a young daughter, Lucy, who suffered from endocarditis.

Why the ridiculous names and the intricate backstories? The name Marie chose at the first open house was 'Tori Costner'. The name was not coincidental. Just five episodes prior, Saul Goodman told Walter, "If you're committed enough, you can make any story work. I once told a woman I was Kevin Costner, and it worked because I believed it." (Episode 3.11)

"Saul Goodman's Office"
Copyright Martin Woutisseth, used with permission

The implication is that Marie believed she was 'Tori Costner'. She was telling a story she already believed herself with the goal of convincing others of her identity.

"You're a thief," the real estate agent said.

"Excuse me?" Marie said through clenched teeth.

"And a liar, making up stories about yourself. What's wrong with you?"

"No, what's the matter with *you*, lady? You better just back off, okay. My husband is a DEA agent."

"Oh, I thought he was an astronaut, or an illustrator—you better get your crazy lies straight."

Of course, in Marie's mind she was all of those people—Tori, Charlotte, Mimi, Marie—all of them, simultaneously. It made as much sense as the boy riding on the pig, or Jesse's mindless rage at the go-cart arena, or the frenzied, pointless scratching and fighting and yelling in Jesse's living room. It was acquisitive anger, the chaos of pure affluenza, the result of time to waste, money to burn, and thrills to find. The psychosomatic high Marie experienced after having stolen a useless object was no less intense than the drug junkie's buzz or the sensual overload of biting and screaming and punching at Jesse's den of meaninglessness. All of it was aimed at acquiring, experiencing, riding the blissful rush of rollercoaster terror through every high and low of illicit sensation.

If only she had a heart, as the song title pleads. Marie's constant need to stimulate herself deadened her to others and her relationship with loved ones. She could not really love because every aspect of her being was oriented toward fulfilling the desire for stimulation. You can never get what you want, I told my children when they were young. Whenever a wish is granted or a toy is obtained, there's always another wish, another toy just out of reach, and so on and so forth, regardless of the trinkets and truffles filling closets and purse. A man can never mark out all the land he wants, but all the land a man needs is enough to hold his lifeless form when he no longer has breath to articulate desires and dreams.

A child always wants more, but parents can say 'No'. An Empress always wants more, but nobody can say 'No'. There is never a 'perfect moment' for Walter to die, because there is always more wealth to be acquired. But to assert a right to wear purple—to claim the right to acquire whatever one wishes—is impermissible in a Karma-driven universe. There are no omnipotent children in any known reality and, Marie's personal sensibilities notwithstanding, there is no room for an always-lusting Empress in the *Breaking Bad* Universe. Marie's Karma arrived in the form of Albuquerque Police Officer Tim Roberts, who sat at her side while she wept, recognizing that her life was out of control.

Noblesse Oblique

This life of ours—it can overwhelm. You are a wealthy man now.
And one must learn to be rich. To be poor, anyone can manage.

Gustavo's words of wisdom for Walter in Episode 3.11 addressed the ever-expanding desire for more and more and more. There was no 'Noblesse oblige'—the French Renaissance idea that wealth requires one to accept social responsibilities. There were no responsibilities in Gustavo's world other than duty toward self and superiors. "Don't make the same mistake twice," he told Walter. The take-home message was that as long as Walter didn't do anything to disrespect or impede or harm his boss, he could enjoy all the benefits of unending wealth. Gustavo's nobility was oriented ever upward—in the *sens oblique* as the French would say. His example of deep appreciation of rich culture—fine wine, rare spices, a sensual meal, warm conversation, lively yet restrained music—showed Walter that the studiously rich man could indeed wear purple—or blue.

It was one of the great manipulations of the series. The idea that Gustavo achieved such wealth that he lived in a culturally-charged, worry-free bubble of blissful prosperity was a finely-tuned lie gauged to garner Walter's respect, envy, and industry.

Breaking Bad never addressed the notion of adapting to or dealing with wealth. Gustavo's projection of the balanced, cultured man was an elaborate hoax. There was no such man, and there never was. Perhaps someone who is groomed for wealth, someone who could 'learn to be rich', could wear purple. Perhaps a Queen Elizabeth or a King Juan Carlos of Spain could legitimately wear purple, but the series did not explore this possibility. The question is outside the purview of the show's thesis. *Noblesse oblique* is not nobility at all, it is pure selfishness, but most of all, it ignores the inescapable and essential truth that all of us—even the most wealthy among us—are connected and inextricably linked to and embedded in the world.

    Noblesse oblige is the only legitimate response to the boon of economic prosperity, not so much because a rich person 'owes' a poor person, but because rich and poor alike are dependent upon and subject to the whims of whatever powers hold the Universe together. A rich person cannot separate herself from the greater world. There are no self-created islands where the wealthy or powerful can claim immunity from the slings and arrows. *Noblesse oblige* is the recognition of personal dependency, the acknowledgement that autonomy is a dangerous fiction created by weak minds seeking respite from the ordinary demands of life.

Forbidden and Disordered

"Chaos"
Lorenzo Lotto and Giovan Francesco Capoferri, circa 1540

Purple is the symbol of detached affluence. In the *Breaking Bad* Universe, statements of aloof independence are not just foolish, they are deadly, leading to the chaos of Jesse's frantic, never-ending living room party and Marie's need to pilfer items having value only to those from whom she steals. Incredibly, as if throwing down a gauntlet, *Breaking Bad* forces us to confront a single character who never suffered any consequences for comfortably and calmly wearing the most powerful, most forbidden color of the series:

How on Earth was Skyler Lambert White able to wear blue?

"Skyler White"
Copyright Martin Woutisseth, used with Permission

Chapter S

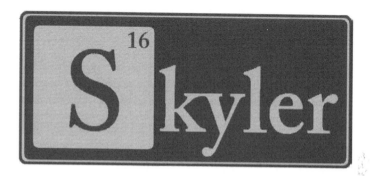

Without Skyler White I would not have watched *Breaking Bad*. It's not that the other characters were boring, or that the acting was anything less than spectacular. The problem is that I am extraordinarily choosey, and not in a way that makes any sense. I watch only three television shows at a time, and one of those is always *Survivor*. I've never missed an episode. Most other television series aren't able to hold my attention. *Homeland* is well acted but poorly written. *Boardwalk Empire* is all glitz and historical interest with no real drama. They fail where *Breaking Bad* succeeds because they lack a Skyler.

Skyler is the foremost example of the fact that there are few 'supporting' characters in *Breaking Bad*. She is every bit the main character that Walter is, and more, because she possesses moral fortitude. She brings vitality to the show because every one of Walter's moves affects her. Thanks to her personal strength, Walter more often than not is forced to change plans or take into account variables he could otherwise ignore. Imagine the lead character from your favorite procedural drama or sitcom. If ever he wishes to do something, he does it. There is no thought of the possible effect on a spouse. There is no examination of the spouse's feelings. There are no arguments. There may or may not be drama, but that drama is focused on the plot, not on character interaction.

Breaking Bad is not procedural drama. It has interest in neither the legal system nor traditional morality. The focus is on the decay of Walter White. The genius of Vince Gilligan was in realizing that in order to understand Walter's descent we had to experience his connections to other people and the way he abused, seduced, enlisted, or degraded them.

Skyler White is no Martha Kent. Martha, the nice little old lady, the widowed surrogate mother to Clark Kent, aka Superman, is never more than a figurehead. If you don't like Martha Kent then you don't like motherhood or baseball and apple pie, either. There's something wrong with you. Skyler, on the other hand, has ambitions and goals. She gives herself to her children, has sacrificed for an unappreciative and largely incapable husband, and has persevered in every good intention despite broken promises and mortgaged dreams. She has real vices, none of them attractive. She consciously smoked cigarettes while pregnant, she flirted shamelessly with Mr. Beneke's son, Ted—and finally had an affair with him in Season Three.

Each aspect of Skyler's character not only carries immediate relevance, but I consider the multi-layered facets of her personality crucial to Walter's story. At various times during her journey she was paragon of virtue, symbol of complicity, fearless mother, evil sidekick, hapless victim. She was never weak, though. Even when she made bad choices, she did so only after examining every possibility. Her deliberation and care brought authenticity and pathos to our examination of her life, and our disgust at Walter's decay into evil.

How Much House Does a Man Need?

"Shack"
Nat Edwards, 2013, PD

Skyler set the rules in the White household, even to the point of instituting unilateral, non-negotiable quality downgrades for Walter's 50th birthday breakfast. He would still receive the birthday bacon shaped into his age in years, but now, at 50 years of age, Walter had to watch his cholesterol and the rule maker—Skyler—ordained that he would eat veggie bacon from now on. Husbands all over the world were groaning at this ego-corroding scene. But she completely smashed any sense of pride Walter may have been clinging to with these instructions about his after hours job at the car wash:

"I don't want 'em dicking you around tonight. You get paid 'til five, you work 'til five, no later."

We've already taken a close look at the birthday bacon scene, but Season Three gave us important background information that we would do well to incorporate into our understanding of Skyler and her husband. If our first impression had been that

Walter was a suffering, hen-pecked husband enduring the abuse of a domineering shrew, Season Three showed us just how wrong our initial assessment was. There was nothing stereotypical in the White family. In fact, Skyler understood early in her marriage that Walter was unstable and unpredictable.

Walter had once been a hot-shot entrepreneur, the co-founder of an up-and-coming company, Gray Matter Technologies. For reasons probably unknown to Skyler, he suddenly sold his share in the company. By the time he met Skyler he was working at a company near Los Alamos, and when he and Skyler, pregnant with Junior, looked at their future home in Albuquerque, Walter was working at Sandia National Laboratories. (Episode 3.13)

Even those unfamiliar with the corporate world will understand that working for an established organization is different in every way from being the founder of a start-up company. Salary is normally fixed in the corporate and government environments, especially for scientists. If you meet expectations you get your five percent pay increase every year, maybe a bonus in the low thousands if you do something spectacular, but that's about it. I have never worked at a government-run laboratory like Sandia, but I have to imagine the potential for bonuses is far less than in the private sector. Institutional work, though, especially for the government, provides job security—a quality lacking in start-ups, 95 percent of which will fail. But the founder of a successful start-up could expect to become wealthy beyond the dreams of avarice, if I'm allowed to quote Dr. McCoy quoting *The Life of Samuel Johnson*. It is that high risk, high reward environment that Walter gave up well before he met Skyler.

By surrendering his entrepreneurial dreams and settling for the staid security of government work, Walter was accepting a low but steady paycheck and turning his back on potential rewards in the tens of millions of dollars. It's a major change in mindset, an aspect of Walter's personality that Skyler would have wondered about, even if Walter was blind to his evolving perspective.

A most revealing conversation occurred in Episode 3.13, when the young Walter and Skyler toured the empty house:

Walter: "We'll need a spare room for a study so I could work at home and you could write…Nah, I don't think this is going to be enough…I just think we need to set our sights high is all, higher than here."
Skyler: "Walt, this is a good neighborhood. It's got a good elementary and supposedly a very good high school…for our price range, this is as good as it gets."
Walter: "Well then let's stretch our price range…Truly. I mean, why buy a starter house when we'll have to move up in a year or two…C'mon. Why be cautious? We've got nowhere to go but up."

As we know, 14 years later Walter had to work a second job just to pay the mortgage on his 'starter house'. Skyler's caution was not only justified, it was necessary.

There is nothing unusual about an adventurous young man, unconcerned about his future, gambling on a high-risk venture but then, when his wife or girlfriend becomes pregnant, deciding to settle down and orient his life around stability and security. The disconcerting aspect of this flashback scene is that at the core of Walter's being he had not decided to embrace and act on a stable and secure lifestyle. "Why be cautious?" he asked.

It's important to recognize that Walter's rhetorical question was not just the result of hubris. He always had immediate access to tanker trucks full of arrogant pride and we had no need to see yet another instance of his egoism setting up his family for suffering and failure. The reason the flashback tableau struck us as dissonant was Walter's inability to act and speak consistently. His words, and presumably his thoughts, were all about 'nowhere to go but up', but his actions showed him to be progressively moving away from high-risk vocations, from start-up to corporate to government and finally to the most secure environment of all: the state-run public high school.

Here's the question Skyler, in the state of hyper-awareness driven by pregnancy, would have been asking:

> Is Walt leaving risk behind out of choice or by necessity? Is he preparing for responsible fatherhood or he is being pushed out of environments in which he is unwelcome or incapable?

'Why be cautious?' was the question that echoed across the years, forming the uncomfortable background for all of Skyler's thoughts. Walter's ideal was high risk and potentially high benefit, but he so compromised his risk-leaning faculties that he ended up working a second job to support his apparently enormous fear of losing. But how could he simultaneously idealize and flee from risk?

Skyler must have recognized intuitively that Walter didn't *choose* a low-risk career: he was forced into it by powers active in the entrepreneurial world. He didn't lack intelligence or inventiveness. He lacked grayness—the ability to compromise. He lacked an attitude of respect toward others and their ideas, not only to his own personal detriment, but to the failure of initiatives that would have succeeded if Mr. 'Respect the Chemistry' (Do it my way or get out of the way) had not been in charge. Most of all, he lacked those tools most frequently used by any father: Common sense, humility, and respect for his spouse.

It was the fact that Walter White was no father that prompted Skyler's initial apprehension and questions and fueled her need to act as the common-sense stable foundation for the White family. Far from being a 'shrew', Skyler was an uncommonly gifted mother willing to give up her dreams when she realized her marriage partner was less than advertised.

How Green Was My Face Mask

Episode 2.01 is perhaps most memorable for the avocado face mask rape scene. In the episodes leading up to Season Two, only one character had been wearing green: Walter White. At the end of the first season, Skyler was firmly ensconced in blue blouses and dresses. Her appearance in green was jolting at two levels: physical and symbolic. The contours of a woman's face are naturally attractive; to cover them in smelly goo or mud transforms her appearance into something almost comically unattractive. But the greater shock was symbolic. We had a sense, from Walter's preference for increasingly darker greens over the course of Season One, that green symbolized greed or money, or the association I favor: unfulfilled desire. The implication of the pivotal face mask scene was that Skyler was greedy, or harbored an unfulfilled desire of some kind. But what 'unfulfilled desire' could this well-balanced woman possibly have yearned for?

I believe the answer begins with wild sex in Walter's Aztek in Episode 1.07.

"Where did that come from?" Skyler asked. "Why was it so damn good?"
"Because it was illegal," Walter responded.

They had sex in public, in their car but parked in a public school parking lot. We might have understood Walter's enjoyment of illicit sex as reflecting the thrill of producing illegal methamphetamine for profit. But the greater significance for Skyler is that Walter's desire for sex was not fueled by his attraction for her. If in response to her inquiry Walter had said, "Because I get hard just thinking about you," or, "You're the sexiest woman I've ever met," we would not have seen Skyler wearing green for the first time in the very next episode. With their 'illegal' sex, Walter planted the idea in Skyler's mind that motivations other than their relationship were behind Walter's personal thoughts and behavior. Something or someone besides Skyler was most important to Walter. In Episode 2.01, with his attempted rape, Walter proved to Skyler that something important was weighing on his mind.

Her first thought was that fear of cancer and death was driving Walter's behavior. "I know you're scared," she said, "but you can't take it out on me."

Skyler was thinking, trying to make sense of Walter's emotions and actions. Those who dismiss the depth of Skyler's character and her importance to the series are at a disadvantage, especially in this episode, for it is in the course of seemingly innocent events that we gain rare insight into her true nature.

Skyler didn't ever stop thinking. Walter's thirst for 'illegal' sex and his attempt at rape were unlike him. On top of that, he was disappearing for hours or days at a time, he had quit the car wash, and he was acting strangely and mysteriously. Skyler was not passive, she didn't accept things without inquiring or even investigating (e.g., when she confronted Jesse for selling marijuana to Walter), and she always sought to get to the bottom of things that affected her life. With Walter going through so many drastic changes, her senses were on high alert.

This is the context in which we must interpret her superficially 'innocent' examination of old photographs toward the middle of the episode. Maybe it was just a filler scene, the Skyler haters say. The director had 35 seconds to fill and decided to show Skyler looking at old photos, a bit of innocent nostalgia just before Hank knocked on the window to get the scene going again.

But this was no bit of innocence. There are no coincidences or 'fillers' in modern television, hemmed in as it is by 20 minutes of commercials for every hour of programming. Writers and directors have to make every second count. In this case, making it count entailed connecting the green face mask not with innocent nostalgia, but with unfulfilled desire.

We saw the photograph of Skyler and Ted for barely a split second. If you blinked during this brief passage you would have missed it. If, with the Skyler haters and everyone else who gives short shrift to the complexity of great drama like *Breaking Bad*, we dismiss the scene, or *don't* attribute it to Skyler's search for post-face mask meaning, we soon forget Ted's face. 'Just an old family friend or acquaintance', we tell ourselves, and then move on to Hank tapping on the window. But the Rule of Economy, as we novelists know it, means there can be no wasted or meaningless moments.

That photograph of Skyler and Ted Beneke in Episode 2.01 was one of the most amazing bits of foreshadowing. We didn't see Ted again until six weeks later, in Episode 2.07, when Skyler applied for a job at Beneke Fabricators. By then we understood she was not so much trying to land a job as she was attempting to rekindle an old flame. Skyler White considered Ted Beneke her unfulfilled desire—he was the reason she wore a green face mask in Episode 2.01.

Cheating

It is without question the most famous birthday salutation in history. On Saturday, May 19, 1962, sex symbol Marilyn Monroe, the most famous woman in the world at the time, serenaded the most famous man in the world, President John F. Kennedy, with the sexiest, sultriest version of 'Happy Birthday' anyone had ever heard. It became the perfect statement of the attraction that Skyler White and Ted Beneke had felt during their several years of working together. (Episode 2.11)

There was nothing tentative or artificial in the breathy cadences of Marilyn Monroe's birthday song. Everyone in the room felt the deep sensuality of her voice. There was no mistaking her attraction for the young president. These two most famous people appeared together several times backstage but only one photograph of the two standing together remains. The Secret Service, exercising authority that today would be unthinkable, confiscated every potentially incriminating photograph showing the President anywhere near the woman. One photo slipped through their fingers.

Marilyn Monroe and President John F. Kennedy
Flanked by Attorney General Robert F. Kennedy and historian Arthur Schlesinger Jr.
The Krim Residence, New York City, 19 May, 1962
Official White House photograph by Cecil Stoughton, PD

The President's protectors did their work well. Over 50 years later there is no unimpeachable proof that John Kennedy had an affair with Marilyn Monroe. Letters purporting to be from Marilyn have been unearthed. Photographs have appeared. But any relationship they might have shared is an open question that history may never resolve.

The important aspect of the historical parallel was the authenticity of sexual tension and emotion. Both Skyler and Ted had felt it for years. As strong as the feelings were, though, they never yielded to them. There was cheating, but not on their marriage partners. Ted began cheating as soon as he inherited his father's business, hiding income from the 'Keller Account' and six other clients. His company owed the federal government hundreds of thousands of dollars in corporate income tax. (Episode 2.11)

Skyler: What are you thinking?
Ted:　I'm thinking…about saving the company. I'm thinking about people's jobs, about their mortgages…
Skyler: It doesn't mean you have to break the law.
Ted:　Yes, it does. Skyler, it's right there in the books. Business is terrible, the bank is on my back, the IRS is grinding me down to a nub…
Skyler: Ted, people go to prison for this.
…
Ted:　Sky, don't report this.
Skyler: I'm not going to turn you in, Ted. But I can't be a part of it.

Skyler knew Ted was illegally concealing income. But because she didn't consciously help him in his concealment schemes, she was innocent, wasn't she? She was free of guilt, right?

Wrong.

Skyler hadn't consciously helped Walter in his drug manufacturing and distribution schemes, either. She knew exactly as much about his illegal activities as she knew about Ted's criminal behavior: In both cases, she knew about the money. Legally, though, not reporting her knowledge of illegality made her as guilty as Ted and Walter. As her lawyer said in Episode 3.05, "You are an accomplice after the fact. You are culpable. You, your children—you could lose everything you own, do you understand?"

The day after Skyler announced she was leaving Beneke Fabricators, never to return, she pulled into the parking lot, entered through the main doors, and quietly resumed her place as Ted Beneke's Director of Accounting. Ted was surprised. Skyler herself seemed surprised. But if we were surprised we should not have been. Her actions made more sense than anyone else's, for she obeyed the rules of the Universe.

The Curve of Binding Emotion

Skyler couldn't report Ted's criminal activity. It's not that she lacked knowledge or proof. She had found fudged records and altered photocopies and she understood the accounting principles demonstrating Ted's guilt. Her decision to remain silent about his schemes had nothing to do with legality and everything to do with empathy for a person she cared about—and more. When she returned to work after saying she wouldn't participate in Ted's schemes, her actions were not based on anything as flimsy as mere sympathy. She *had* to return because she was emotionally connected to Ted. It's the full significance of that emotional tether that *Breaking Bad* explored over five years.

At the end of Season Two she demanded that Walter leave. She recited a grand litany of Walter's lies, a cascade of deception that virtually required his removal from the house and from her children's lives. It seemed clear as day that any reasonable outside observer would side with Skyler's lawyer. "There is nothing to discuss here, Skyler." He had to go, or she had to go. There was no middle ground, no conceivable reason to allow him to stay. In Episode 3.03, when Walter again refused to leave the house, Skyler brought in the police, threatening to tell them about his criminal deeds.

"Do what you have to do, Skyler. This family is everything to me. Without it, I have nothing to lose."

Walter went back to calmly grading papers at the dining room table while Skyler waited for the police to arrive. She must have envisioned them handcuffing him, throwing him in a squad car, and instructing him never to return. It was her house, after all, wasn't it?

"Did he strike you?" the police officer asked.

"No."

"Has he ever hit you?"

"No."

"You're divorced then?"

"Well, working on it, ah…right now we're separated."

"Legally separated?"

"Well, there's not a court order, if that's what you mean…I changed the locks! Isn't that breaking and entering?"

"Whose name is on the title to the house?"

"Both of us, it's ah…it's jointly owned."

"We can't arrest a man for breaking into his own house."

The police officer continued his inquiry, desperately seeking any legal justification for removing Walter from the house but coming up with nothing. But recall *Breaking Bad* is not about legalities. The real reason Walter could not leave, and Skyler would never again truly have the heart to ask him to go, is that he was the children's father. When, during the police interrogation, Holly began to fuss, Walter immediately broke off, took Holly in his arms, and gently calmed her. Both of the police officers and Skyler herself realized there was no reason for Walter to leave.

The officer threw out one last possibility: If Walter had done anything illegal, even if she only thought he might have done something, they could remove him from the house. But she didn't give Ted to the police—how could she give up her own husband? She wouldn't, as she revealed two episodes later.

"And *you* say, 'Tell him the truth'," Skyler said, ranting as she spoke with her therapist—er, her lawyer, I mean. "Tell him about his father. But I can't—ever. How could I?" (Episode 3.05)

Skyler had to balance two facts in her mind:

1.   Walter was a criminal.
2.   Walter was her children's father.

If there is a moral dilemma in *Breaking Bad*, this is it. Walter's depravity existed in its own special sphere of morality, but the ethics of Walter's cohorts could be boiled down to the simple two-edged truth of his negative and positive attributes. Skyler made the decision point clear.

Her children needed a father, and they *had* a father, as Walter demonstrated in Episode 3.03 by sharing a grilled cheese sandwich with Junior and rocking Holly while he fed her from the baby bottle. If they ever found out their father was a criminal they would be robbed of what they needed as children. Walter the Criminal was of no use to anyone. Walter the Father, on the other hand, was raising a family. In the end, how could anyone fault Skyler for investing emotion in a relationship with the father of her children?

Skyler had another relationship, too. As she said, "This man that I'm seeing, you know, as wrong as I know it is, as much as I know I'm probably doing it just to make Walt leave me…" (Episode 3.05) There was no 'probably' about it, though. Her family came first. The casual observer would conclude she was merely giving into the temptation she'd felt all these years, and enjoying the sweet revenge of being able to tell Walter over a glass of white wine, "I fucked Ted." (Episode 3.03) But as with virtually everything she did in the early part of Season Three, her relationship with the tax cheat had nothing to do with sexual fulfillment or revenge but was instead oriented toward her children's welfare. If she made Walter angry enough, or jealous enough, he would leave and she'd never have to divulge his criminality. Her children could believe their father was perfect.

It was family, again, that caused her to finally leave Ted. While Skyler dried off after her post-coital shower, Ted asked if she wanted to "grab a quick bite," but she said she had to get home. And an hour later, there they sat, Skyler, Walter, and Junior, enjoying family time around the dinner table. When Holly fussed, Skyler invited Walter. "You want to take her?" she asked. She would never again have sex with Ted. She had made up her mind about something far more important than a momentary fling.

Skyler's question to Walter was a declaration of intent. The next day, wearing a white undershirt, she came upon Walter's duffel stuffed with cash. She picked up a stack of hundreds. Later, in the lawyer's office, she wore GREEN. Unfulfilled desire. It's no wonder that both we and the lawyer understood Skyler's mental gyrations as an activity more suited to the therapist's couch than the lawyer's office. "Let me just say that I'm half as qualified and twice the price of a therapist," the divorce lawyer said, exasperated with Skyler's verbal and emotional prevarications. "There is nothing to discuss here, Skyler."

I will not lay out a full defense of Skyler. In the end, I believe those who see her as "Mrs. Heisenberg" can provide an argument no less convincing than anything her defenders could devise. But when she picked up that stack of money and we next saw her wearing a green shirt, I think it's too easy to assign her complicity in Walter's crime as an indication of monetary greed. I don't see her as greedy, and it is for this reason that I never understood the color green to indicate the species of greed that most people associate with the color. I believe Skyler expressed the only truth she knew, and she said it right there in the lawyer's office:

"I'm just saying, you know, we have a history. He's the father of my children."

Believe as you will regarding Skyler White and her motivations. I believe she remained true to her family. She wore green in the second half of Season Three because *her unfulfilled desire was to share completely in Walter's life.* In the moment that she picked up that stack of hundred dollar bills she realized she had never been completely in his life. There had been Gretchen and teaching and a thousand other thoughts, but also such a deep desire to provide for his family that he was willing to circumvent the law to accomplish that most laudable of goals. Skyler wore green because she wanted to get to know her husband. *That* was Skyler White's unfulfilled desire.

Chapter Cl

Cleaning

"The Salamanca Cousins"
Copyright Martin Woutisseth, used with permission

There is a kind of rhythmic periodicity to the *Breaking Bad* Universe, obeyed by players large and small, whether law-abiding or criminal. Certain things are simply not done because they disturb the harmony inherent in a well-ordered world. Walter's ignorance of this fact, his idea that a new player could simply project a 'blowfish' aura, nearly got him killed in Season Two and again in Season Three.

There are rules. There are hard-and-fast expectations, so invariant in quality that deviations are not tolerated. Heisenberg's execution of the Cartel's local distributor, Tuco Salamanca, might have been attributed to innocence or ignorance, the honest transgression of a drug trade neophyte. But he coupled the bloody execution of the Salamanca family's favorite son with blatant trespass into Cartel territory, sending out his minions to expand profit margins at the expense of the long-established administrators of Albuquerque's methamphetamine business. The Cartel wasn't going to be intimidated or even mildly impressed by a 'blowfish'.

Sangre por sangre. It was the necessary and accepted rule of behavior in the drug world. Those who so disrespected the norms of comportment that they executed fellow businesspeople became subject to the ancient law of retribution, unchanged since the Hammurabi Code of 1772 B.C. An eye for an eye, a tooth for a tooth, or as the Cartel put it, Sangre por sangre.

Walter's salvation came in two parts: the reasoned argument of his new boss, Gustavo, and the convenient fact that it had been Hank Schrader, not Walter White, who had delivered the lethal bullet into Tuco's body. Hank would suffer the cost in blood, not Walter. The Salamanca cousins would travel all the way from Mexico, using a gleaming silver axe to clean up the mess Heisenberg made.

We will see several 'clean-up' operations in the final three seasons of *Breaking Bad*, some of them grislier than anything previously presented on television. We can apply our knowledge of color symbolism to gain deeper understanding of the full meaning attached to the bloody business of cleaning the messes left by struggles for control and power.

Five Shades of Gray

When *Breaking Bad* depicts grim, determined players on a mission, the color of choice has almost always been black. In Chapter C, I wrote that black was the color of 'decisive commitment' of people 'on a mission'. Could any mission have borne greater importance than the Salamanca cousins' task of eliminating the man who had spilled Salamanca blood? Yet the Cousins wore shiny gray silk suits, not black. More than that, the color choice, the smooth texture, and the sheen of the fabric all seemed intentional and important in themselves. Why were these two assassins, dispatched to perform critical Cartel business, vested in boring gray rather that the darker, more serious color of 'decisive commitment'?

Leonel and Marco Salamanca did not lack any intention of immediate, decisive engagement. They were clearly people on a mission. Our first instinct, three seasons into a show whose color symbolism begins to make sense to us, is to puzzle over the suit color. But serious intent can be portrayed in many ways. Hank—naturally bald— was always serious about putting away drug dealers. When Walter wished to show his serious, 'bad ass' side, he chose to shave his head. Fans of the series have long understood baldness as an indication of seriousness, and this message of grim purpose was communicated in simple, clear terms by the brothers' shaved heads. They didn't need to wear black to convey the idea of grave intent.

Gray Necktie
"Oriental or small knot"
Copyright Keith S. Brown, 2007, CC-SA 2.5

But why did they need to wear gray? My first thought revolved around practicalities. For a good portion of my pharmaceutical career I was issued a gray lab coat, not the standard white. My projects have always required a mix of laboratory experiments and pilot- and production-scale work. In the early years, a good chunk of my time was spent preparing and cleaning equipment, but even as a principal scientist I had to be ready to literally get my hands dirty if the situation could benefit from my direct involvement. The smallest bit of dirt and grime are immediately visible on a white lab coat but might go undetected on a gray covering. The Salamanca twins constituted a kind of 'wet team' and they were bound to get dirty during the course of their duties. Wearing gray suits made practical sense.

We gain an appreciation of the brothers' personal trajectory by examining their histories. We learned important biographical information in the opening scene of

Episode 3.07 ("One Minute"), all of which has bearing on the twins' attire and its symbolic importance.

A young Don Hector (Tio Hector, Tuco's wheelchair-bound uncle) watched the two brothers, then children, while they played. He took a phone call. Someone in the Cartel, possibly Don Eladio or his predecessor, was inquiring about 'the chicken man' (Gustavo Fring), detested among Cartel members because he was Chilean, not Mexican. Don Hector's words are critical to our understanding of the Cousins:

"Nunca confíes a un sudaca—sucia, sucia gente."

"Tio Hector"
Copyright Martin Woutisseth 2011, used with permission

In English: "Never trust Southern Trash—dirty, dirty people." It's hard to bring the full flavor of Don Hector's insulting words into English. 'Sudaca' means

'South American', but it's a derogatory word. Respectful Spanish uses the equivalent for 'South American': *Sudamericano*. Chile is culturally very different from Mexico. Don Hector chose to indicate his distrust of and distaste for the Chilean Gustavo Fring by using a strongly negative word to describe him: *Sudaca*.

The insult is fascinating to me as a linguist. While the word was used as a noun (**un** sudaca), it has more of the flavor of an adjective. Grammatically, the word sudaca is genderless; a South American man is called *un sudaca* and a South American woman is called *una sudaca*. The word carries a slight insult just in the fact that it is genderless and in its feminine sound. I imagine, for example, the Spanish language version of Skinny Pete—Flaco Pedro—being referred to not as Flaco Pedro but simply as 'Flaca'. The correspondence is not perfect, since the adjective 'Flaco' has a gender in Spanish. There is insult, too, in the fact that sudaca sounds like an adjective, not like a noun. A Mexican is a *mexicano*, an American is an *americano* (though a person from the United States is a *norteamericano* or an *estadounidense*—or more likely a *gringo*—a word that use to have derogatory connotations but is now almost universally applied in common conversation in Mexico) and a respected South American is a *sudamericano*. Note that almost all of these nationalities end in –ano. This is by no means a rule. A Frenchman is a *francés*, a Canadian is a *canadiense*, and so on. But the word *sudaca*, to Latin ears, just doesn't sound like a nationality. It's an insult, pure and simple, and that is the intent.

Don Hector's position that South Americans are 'sucia, sucia gente' forms the backdrop for the foundational event we see next. The twins have been playing and now they're fighting, Marco taunting Leonel. He complains to his uncle.

Leonel: He broke my toy!
Don Hector: He was just having fun. You'll get over it.
Leonel: No! I hate him! I wish he were dead!

Don Hector proceeded to give Leonel what he wanted. He asked Marco to get him a cold beer in the ice bucket at his side. When the boy knelt down to grab the bottle, Don Hector pushed his head under water and kept him there, apparently to drown him.

"No! No!" Leonel shouted, trying to free his brother from his uncle's deadly grasp. After a minute or so, confident the boys had learned their lesson, Don Hector released Marco. Standing over them, gazing on them with stern eyes, he delivered his admonishment with deep, gravely voice: "La familia es todo," he said.

We are to understand from this never-to-be-forgotten lesson that there is an important difference between la familia Salamanca and people like Gustavo Fring. Gustavo is a 'dirty' Chilean but the Salamanca family is in every way clean. They are clean because they don't fight with each other over petty, stupid things. They keep in mind that they are brothers. Before all else and above all else, they are family. There is an order to their universe, with everything in its place, and the foremost truth of their universe is the inviolable, immaculate nature of family. When the Cousins are sent out on family business, then, everything about them is clean and orderly. Their faces and heads are perfectly shaved, their suits are cleanly tailored, their hands and fingernails are manicured, and their appearance is crisp and business-like. When a threat is posed to the family's interests, it is something disordered, unclean, and must be dealt with by the shaven-head 'Mr. Clean' lookalikes.

The importance of family means that even personal interests are secondary. A spirit of teamwork pervades every thought in la familia Salamanca. There is no prideful white, no obsessive black. The twins wear gray because that is the color of teamwork, of *esprit de corps*. It is the color Walter rejected. He will never give himself to the Cartel. Though he works for Gus Fring, he spends nearly every waking moment fixated on schemes to put himself over and above his boss. Walter will always wear white. The twins, on the other hand, are the very definition of team players, and for that reason alone they vest themselves in the color that means collaboration and synergistic strength. Walter understands gray as compromise, weakness, surrender of self to an ungrateful, unappreciative entity. To Leonel and Marco, though, familial cooperation is the single greatest weapon in an organization's arsenal. Cooperation means strength, it means coordinated action against any enemy. It is the aspect of the Cartel's structure that has allowed it to endure several decades, even in the face of constant attacks from government, police, other cartels, other *countries*, and bit players like Heisenberg.

The Wetsuit

U. S. Navy SEALs
U. S. Department of Defense, 2008, PD

We first saw the orange splash suits in Episode 3.10, "Fly." The suits seemed innocent enough. Two minutes into Episode 10, Walter and Jesse were in the orange coveralls, cleaning the reaction vessels with soap and water and the biggest scrub brushes you'll find anywhere.

Laboratory apparel of this kind is waterproof and often solvent-proof, constructed in such a way that it protects the wearer from liquid hazards likely to be encountered during use. Splash suits are worn in some types of Hazmat (Hazardous materials) responses and also in routine cleaning operations. In Episode 3.10 we learned the suits were designated for cleaning and for no other operations. Day-to-day manufacturing operations were performed in the bright yellow Hazmat splash suits.

Why orange? The color is unusual for the laboratory and it again conjures thoughts of danger, of threats hidden at every turn. I believe the association to perils unknown is both real and intentional, however, as with yellow, I believe the connection is secondary to the greater symbolic meaning.

By the end of Season Three, when we first saw the orange clean-up suits, we had a fairly well-established association of orange with the idea of 'legitimate, conferred authority'. (see Chapter O) If you're struggling to see the routine scrubbing of pharmaceutical production equipment as the end result of 'conferred authority', you have never worked in the most highly regulated industry in the world, where literally everything you are *authorized* to do is written up as an SOP which must be followed to the letter without slightest deviation. But after watching the critical Episodes 3.10, 4.01, and 5.08 several times, I believe the connection between neon orange and 'conferred authority' is by means of contrast, not example.

Hank Schrader, the man who 'owns' the color orange, does not wear fluorescent orange. Even his Schraderbräu shirt is a bright but natural orange color. The brewmaster's shirt proclaims giddy excitement and happiness with the world, but this is not Hank's natural emotional state. He is subdued and cautious yet aggressive, committed, and determined, with the full power of the United States government standing behind him, and the color representing this conferred and determined authority is not happy orange or neon orange but dark, almost brown or rust orange. In fact, Hank's color is in all senses natural, stable, *grounded*. We orient our thoughts in the proper direction when we consider DEA Orange to be an *earthy* orange color.

There is nothing earthy about the unnatural fluorescent reddish orange of the laboratory splash suits of Episodes 3.10 and 4.01, and certainly nothing natural about the neon orange jumpsuits of Episode 5.08. The colors are glaring and artificial. There's nothing conferred about this color. This is a color seized, representing power assumed, stolen, or claimed. When Gustavo slit Victor's throat in Episode 4.01, he did so only after he had calmly and methodically donned the fluorescent orange wetsuit.

'Wetwork' is a euphemism, rendered in *Breaking Bad* as the visual symbolism of the orange laboratory splash suit. Real 'wet teams' among the elite Special Forces branches of Western militaries are more likely to wear a sniper's ghillie suit or ordinary tactical suits, but the choice of garments is governed by the wet team's ultimate goal, which is precision execution or assassination. 'Wetwork' refers to the fact that the mission objective is the spilling of blood.

In the *Breaking Bad* context, wetwork is associated with the notion of 1. cleaning up a mess 2. for the purpose of maintaining or expanding power. This is why, symbolically, the 'wetsuit' had to be a garment used in actual cleaning operations. The color had to be some variant of orange to establish contrast between unnatural, stolen power (neon or fluorescent) and natural, conferred power (rust or dark orange). Fluorescent orange is its own authority. It is the corrective tactical statement that the wearer is the 'Measure of all things' (Chapter Si).

Season Four began with wetwork. Gustavo had to surgically execute his first lieutenant, Victor, because he had brazenly walked into the crime scene following Jesse's murder of Gale Boetticher. Worse, when Mike asked Victor if people had seen him at Gale's apartment, he answered, "Yeah. So what?" He was exuding cocky arrogance and only exacerbated the sense that he was dangerous and out of control when he started a new batch of product. "We ain't missin' no cook," Victor said, expressing his opinion that Gustavo could proceed with the execution of Walter and Jesse since Victor was capable of synthesizing the drug himself. He almost forgot the aluminum catalyst, remembering the critical step at the very last minute. But as Walter noted in his brilliant speech, a million other things could go wrong.

> Catalytic hydrogenation: Is it protic or aprotic? Because I forget. And if our reduction is not stereospecific then how can our product be enantiomerically pure? I mean, it's 1-phenyl-1-hydroxy-2-methylaminopropane—containing, of course, chiral centers at carbons number one and two on the propane chain—then reduction to methamphetamine eliminates which chiral centers again? 'Cause I forgot.

Walter was worried, but he needn't have been. Gustavo was intent on expanding his empire. He had Don Juan (Juan Bolsa, second or third in command of the Juárez Cartel) assassinated (Episode 3.08), and now he was moving to expand his meth empire throughout the Southwest, at Cartel expense. His long-term leverage came from the superiority of Walter's product. Thus, taking a chance on Victor and the high potential for mistakes and low product purity was never an option. Victor's arrogance, combined with the fact that he had been seen inspecting the site of Gale's murder, constituted a threat to Gustavo's security and power. It was a mess begging to be cleaned up.

And so the orange wetsuit. Slitting Victor's throat in Walter's presence allowed Gustavo to accomplish every one of his ambitions, including the most important objective: putting sheer terror into Walter and Jesse. Make product, or you're dead. Do what I say, or you're dead. The message was clear, profound, and unforgettable.

Trajectories Royal and Red

Success, in the mind of those reckless and proud, wraps itself in royal purple or regal blue. But purple haughtiness, founded on self-made white, will never find true success, which is cooperative gray founded on sturdy orange.

Real success grows organically. It is the natural outcome of the forces of nature and the laws of physics. If we really, truly 'respect the chemistry', it means we understand success as something connected to the trajectory of the Universe, not to our personal whims or ambitions. Success is the prosperity that evolves out of humble submission to the harmonies of the Universe.

False success seeks strength in domination over others. It is the assertion of self, the proclamation that Man Is The Measure Of All Things, the attitude that there are no gods, there is no natural law, there is no Universe to which I must scrape and bow. There is only me and my superior intellect.

Victor had to die because he asserted his own feeble abilities over the unstoppable power of the Universe. In the same way, I reveal no spoilers when I say both Gustavo and Walter will die before this series is over. Every color and symbol and law of the Universe tells us so. There is, after all, a rhythmic periodicity to the world they inhabit, creating a relentless harmony not even the highest intellect can defy.

"Mike Ehrmantraut"
Copyright Martin Woutisseth, used with permission

Chapter Ar

Architecture
of Virtue

The Four Cardinal Virtues: Justice, Prudence, Fortitude, and Temperance
Dirc van Delf, circa 1402
From the Henry Walters Manuscript W.171

So devoted was Walter White to his family's welfare that he repeatedly put his life on the line. Is this not virtue? In what respect could an honest person say Walter White did not cultivate the highest degree of personal integrity? We witnessed in Episode 3.12 a moving display of courage, unanticipated because its outcome was the correction of a grave injustice involving a child Walter didn't even know. Has television drama ever portrayed a more virtuous, selfless act?

We all have a sense of honor and justice. Walter's decision to bring violent end to two men who killed an 11-year-old child was shocking and disturbing but in a greater sense satisfying, for in his courageous act he became an agent of righteous karma. No one should be able to murder a child, especially not for personal financial gain. Few would disagree with the proposition that there is a special place in Hell for evil scum such as the two drug dealers who killed a fifth grader, young Tomás Cantillo.

Our evaluation of the situation should have been easy. In a lesser television series, Episode 3.12 would have been the season finale: a crisp, clean exposition of good triumphing over evil and a satisfying conclusion to a year of mayhem. But the 12th episode was not the last word. The final two episodes of Season Three were among the most thought provoking of the series because we were forced to consider virtue, morality, and hierarchies of value in ways we never have before. We thought we understood virtue. Season Three showed us we were wrong, that personal integrity and values guiding human behavior are far more complicated and interesting than we ever knew.

Virtuous Balloons

The final episode of Season Three contains one of the most brilliant sequences in the series. Mike Ehrmantraut brought his favorite granddaughter, Kaylee, a big bunch of metallic balloons. Seeing that the back seat of grandpa's car was full of the same balloons, she asked the obvious question.

Kaylee: What about the rest?
Mike: The rest are for me.
Kaylee: No, they're not. You're too old for balloons.
Mike: You're never too old for balloons. Give me a hug.

In the very next frame we saw the unflappable Mike standing outside the chemical warehouse, metallic balloons in hand. When he released them they floated to the power lines overhead, shorting them out and cutting off electricity to the warehouse.

"You're never too old for balloons." It is such brilliant statement, lifting the balloons from mere symbols of ambiguous morality to a veritable metaphor and deep commentary on human virtue. Mike was "never too old." He was a child at heart, and children were first in his thoughts. We sensed in every minute spent with Kaylee Mike's delight in her innocence and a determination to ensure she was surrounded by love.

"You're never too old"; you're never too old to act like a child. That was the obvious logical rejoinder to Kaylee's syllogistic dismissal of her grandfather's interest in balloons. He couldn't actually enjoy balloons because only children liked them. Papa

(Kaylee's affectionate name for her grandfather) was way too old for balloons. But no, Papa said, I'm just as much a child as you are, Kaylee. I still like balloons. It made sense. His warmth was genuine, as we had seen already in the way he doted on her and took pleasure in her childish enjoyment of life. He was like Santa Claus, but even more devoted to children. I know I'm not the only viewer who believed Mike Ehrmantraut was not too old to indulge himself with a few balloons, just for fun.

The next scene showed us that Papa was so far from innocence that he made James Bond look like an incompetent and unstudied fool. The balloons became the unconventional first weapon in his calm, confident assault on the warehouse. We have to call it an assault, yet his tranquil self-assurance and slow, steady gait were astounding, showing him to possess an audacity solidly grounded in wisdom so rare he could outsmart the baddest of bad guys. He took out the first two Cartel goons with a single bullet; the next three rounds were merely insurance.

Then there was the green shoe: the unusual, wrap-top high-heeled shoe attached to the receptionist's foot. Mike took several seconds to gently untie the green ribbons. It was an action we would normally associate with foreplay—a lover's touch, the deliberate unwrapping of a woman, the intimacy of fingers caressing naked flesh— but Mike was focused on solemn mission, not on sexual merriment.

The shoe brought forth the next goon, calmly dispatched with another three bullets from Mike's gun. Kinda wasteful, but he made up for it just down the hall, when he saw Duane Chow sitting at his desk, hands up in the universal gesture of surrender. But Chow was one of Gustavo's guys, the owner of Golden Moth Chemical; why would he fear Mike? Mike figured it out, leading to one of the most amazing, audacious spy-stuff sequences demonstrating Mike's unbelievable mastery of lethal situations and ending with a single bullet fired with deadly precision through drywall and then through the final goon's skull.

Ruthless killer or doting grandfather? He was both, of course, but we find ourselves asking which bunch of balloons truly defined the man. That they are the same balloons suggests the possibility that Mike Ehrmantraut is a study in the half-empty/half-full glass. Maybe he is the person we believe him to be, regardless of the templates we feel justified in applying to his life. Or perhaps he is a mirror into our own souls, our own ideas of the well-ordered life, or our own concept of the ideal society.

I find Mike level-headed, never rash, always deliberative and prudent in his decisions. The word 'courage' doesn't come to mind when I think of him. Even in Episode 4.04, when he waited inside the ice-cold refrigerated Los Pollos truck, the gunshots outside didn't cause trepidation in his mind, only disappointment. He frowned and shook his head in disgust, as if to say, "Damn Cartel guys again." He waited until the two men outside emptied hundreds of rounds into the truck, stopped, and opened the doors to inspect their work. It was only then that he calmly put three rounds into the henchmen, killing them instantly. Even the wound to his ear caused more annoyance than anything else, demonstrated in the way he rolled his eyes as the opening splash and theme music began. Most of us, I suppose, would be traumatized for years to come if we had to endure the sheer terror of sitting in the dark, unable to see anything, while two men intent on killing us stood outside with machine guns, shooting armor-piercing rounds above and below and all around. For Mike it was just another day at the office. If the Cartel guys hadn't been so predictable in their irritating stupidity it would have been a boring day for this man who had seen everything.

"Los Pollos Hermanos"
Copyright Martin Woutisseth, used with permission

Full Measures

Mike's 'Half Measures' speech (Episode 3.12) revealed his core philosophy. The lesson he tried to impart to Walter was that sometimes a warning or a threat was not enough. Sometimes the only reasonable response was a 'full measure': The transgressor had to be killed. But that bit of acquired wisdom was not his core ideology.

The most interesting part of this long, fascinating speech was the central personal philosophy written between the vocalized words. Not a day passed that did not include a number of events Mike found disappointing or annoying or beneath his dignity. He just let them go. But the case of the unrepentant, abusive boyfriend was different. "There was this one guy—this one piece of shit—that I will never forget: Gordy. He looked like Bo Svenson."

Gordy never threatened Mike. He never made threats against Mike's family. In Mike's story Gordy had a name, but his girlfriend was just another nameless, abused woman. She was important only because she was the victim. Gordy was important because he was the anomaly. He, not his girlfriend, required correction, and that was the reason he bore a name. His girlfriend's life would proceed as it should as soon as the noxious effect of Gordy's abuse was removed. It was that corrective action that was most important to Mike. The other annoyances of life could continue, but the *injustice* of Gordy's abuse had to stop.

It was during that speech that I finally realized why I liked Mike so much. He was an exemplar of the four cardinal virtues: prudence, fortitude, temperance, and the most important of the four: justice.

Mike's 'full measure' was not murder. The full measure for Mike was *justice*. Injustice was an unacceptable anomaly for Mike Ehrmantraut. If it was in his power to correct an unjust situation, he felt compelled to do so.

Heisenberg Virtues

We saw at the end of Episode 3.12 a side of Walter White I would never have predicted. The two drug dealers who had killed Tomás Cantillo were about to make a quick end of Jesse Pinkman. But out of nowhere the puke-colored Aztek appeared, mowing down the two bad guys. Walter jumped out of the car and put a bullet through the head of the second druggie, the one still moving. He stood still for a second just to make sure both guys were dead, then looked up at Jesse and said, "Run."

We knew of some of Walter's virtues before this scene. He had devotion, for instance: to his family, to Skyler. Resourcefulness, too. But here he demonstrated courage. Perhaps not on the battlefield, but there are many forms of courage.

But these virtues—devotion, resourcefulness, courage—aren't on any list. (Well, there is *one* list—a few moviegoers have figured it out already, I know.) The virtue we find heading the list of cardinal virtues is justice. The two drug dealers had just murdered an 11-year-old boy—for fun and profit. Walter used his beat-up old car to deliver a strong dose of long-overdue justice to the two bad guys, becoming an agent of the Universe's karma to make things right again in Albuquerque.

It was strange, this unforeseeable eruption of a sense of justice in the heart of Heisenberg. It was surprising enough that he had a heart at all, but here he was risking his life to correct a grave injustice.

The ancients tell us that one who practices a single virtue perfectly will practice all virtues perfectly. If Walter was just, then, we would expect to find that he also cultivated temperance, fortitude, and prudence. Yet Episode 3.13, the season finale, begins with a young Walter White telling Skyler they had to look at much bigger houses. "Why buy a starter house? Why be cautious?" Walter was anything but cautious. That is, Walter lacked prudence. But we've seen over three seasons that Walter also definitely lacked temperance and fortitude. Whence his sudden interest in justice?

The Calculus of Affinity

Early in Episode 3.12 Jesse demanded the ricin so he could kill the dealers who forced Tomás to murder Combo. "They used him like a puppet," Jesse said, barely able to control his anger. Recruiting and turning the 'hearts and minds' of children was part of their *modus operandi*, a distinguishing feature of their scrambled system of ethics. "The whole entire world would be better off," Jesse said, if he used ricin to execute them.

Jesse: It was a good plan back when it was Tuco and it's a good plan now.
Walter: Tuco wanted to murder us. These guys don't…

223

Jesse: Combo was *us*, man. He was one of us. Does that mean nothing?

Walter analyzed every part of Jesse's plan, dismissed the rationale for his desire to off the men, and berated him for not taking the initiative months before. "Murder is not part of your 12-step program," Walter said. But he delivered the final and most serious objection to Jesse's plan with these words: "This is not some amends that you have to make. What you are talking about here is *pointless*."

This was Walter's response to Jesse's rhetorical question regarding the value of Combo's life. In Walter's book, Combo was not 'one of us'. He was just another pawn, not worth 'some amends' or even their time.

"This achieves *nothing*. It accomplishes *nothing*," Walter said.

Walter had no feelings for Combo. In Walter's playbook, murder was justified only if it achieved or accomplished some greater value. He made no allowance for justice, ethics, responsibility, or any other quality inhabiting the pantheon of virtues.

Casual viewers of *Breaking Bad* may feel the murder of Tomás later in the episode so overwhelmed Walter's acquired tendencies toward cold logic that he acted on the boy's behalf in spite of himself. We will experience events in Season Four that will cast doubt on this assessment, but we need to keep in mind that Walter's mental and emotional states were constantly evolving. If our analysis of his motivations is truly satisfying, it will draw on Walter's tendencies and behaviors at the time of the incident.

Based on his state of mind and his well-articulated order of priorities during Seasons Two and Three, I believe Walter might have shaken his head and grumbled for a few seconds at the news that Gustavo had ordered the killing of a child, but after that bit of deference to human sensibility he would have returned to whatever schemes occupied his thoughts. The murder would not have weighed on his mind or affected his plans. It was not the murder itself but the knowledge of Jesse's sure response that focused Walter's logical faculties. Jesse was his partner, but more than that: Jesse was the only person Walter could mold and carve into a reflection of himself.

Even so, the stakes were high. The objects of Jesse's righteous fury were Gustavo's men. In the calculus of affinity, Jesse may have been more Walter's child than even Junior, but I don't think Jesse alone would have warranted the risk Walter incurred by slamming his car into the child killers. He needed some other incentive.

Royal Prerogative

Gustavo was the boss of a drug empire that spanned the entire Southwestern United States. He had it within his power to reduce Walter to unrecognizable blood and bones whenever he wished. Walter considered the situation and requested a meeting in the desert, just the two of them. Flanked by Mike and Victor, Heisenberg and Gustavo faced each other in one of the most iconic images of the show.

Gustavo: Has your condition worsened?

...

Walter: I'm quite well, thank you.

Gustavo: No. Clearly you're not. No rational person would do as you have done. Explain yourself.
Walter: My partner was about to get himself shot. I intervened.
Gustavo: Some worthless junkie? For him you intervened?...
Walter: That's right...he was angry because those two dealers of yours had just murdered an 11-year-old boy.
Gustavo: I heard about it. He should have let me take care of them.
Walter: Maybe.

Walter made a show of not understanding Gustavo's query concerning his health. He knew to expect confrontation, though. More important was the single word he uttered after Gustavo asserted the privilege of any boss. "He should have let me take care of them."

A subordinate does not question a ruler's prerogative. Walter did not enter into the discussion as a subordinate, though. The placement of the two men of nearly identical height, facing each other with nearly identical body posture and facial expression, framed by the camera to create a sense of balance and harmony, was done to form in our minds a single idea: Equality. With that solitary word—Maybe—Walter was claiming the right of assessment. He boldly declared his personal prerogative to weigh and judge Gustavo's actions.

In any corporation I've been a part of, questioning a superior's authority in this manner is called insubordination. The incident is documented and the offender is subject to virtually any punishment up to and including termination of employment. In Walter's case, the range of penalties included his death and the murder of his immediate family. He knew that. He'd known for the better part of a year. He carefully weighed the risks and decided to proceed with this bald, dangerous act of intellectual treachery.

Heisenberg's Full Measure

The final episode of Season Three was called "Full Measure." If the action had centered around Mike, the theme and final outcome of the episode would have been the re-establishment of justice. But Mike's involvement was peripheral. The nexus of concern was the battle between Heisenberg and Gustavo.

Gus Fring seemed to have the upper hand in the first minutes of the episode, but Heisenberg challenged him in the desert confrontation, tying his continued service to the right to exercise personal discretion. It was a bold move, but Gustavo was forced to accede in light of Walter's unique laboratory skills. Walter knew Gus would move immediately to groom Gale as his replacement. He miscalculated, though, figuring he had at least a few days to put his own plan in place.

The 'full measure' involved the death of a nearly innocent man: Gale Boetticher. Justice had nothing to do with Walter's instructions to murder him. His death did not indicate the possession of prudence, fortitude, or temperance. But surely the 'full measure' was based on some strongly-held virtue?

"You wrote to me once, listing the four chief virtues." The young man, denied the high office he thought to be his right, addressed his father. "Wisdom, justice, fortitude, and temperance. As I read the list I knew I had none of them." In this respect he was not much different from any other man lacking virtue. It is difficult to attain to perfection, after all. But the next words he spoke might have come out of the mouth of Walter White:

> But I have other virtues, Father. Ambition: That can be a virtue
> when it drives us to excel. Resourcefulness. Courage; perhaps
> not on the battlefield, but there are many forms of courage.
> Devotion: To my family, to you.
> [Gladiator, Dreamworks/Universal, 2000]

Heisenberg's full measure was identical to Commodus' defining quality. The virtue that most accurately represented the power-hungry son of Marcus Aurelius was pure, unbridled Ambition. This was the energy driving Walter's calculating mind, his willingness to risk all, even the family to which he claimed perfect devotion. But devotion, resourcefulness, and courage—the lesser elements in Heisenberg's tool kit—were all in service of the virtue that would obtain for him the final objective of his quest: to become Emperor.

Chapter K

K¹⁹oyaanisqatsi

Train Wreck at Montparnasse Station
Levy and Sons, 1895

In virtually every episode of *Breaking Bad* we see faster-than-realtime passages. These hyperactive animations usually chronicle a scene transition, often the movement from night to dawn and into full daylight, a period of many hours condensed into eight or fifteen seconds. Every now and then we are treated to a scene rendered at four or ten times normal speed. The decision to offer a segment in this manner is an artistic one. The implication is that the passage contains more information than simply the rapid sequence of images on our television screen.

The cinematic technique borrowed by *Breaking Bad* is not new. In fact, it had its best expression in a 1982 film born in Albuquerque. The movie was called *Koyaanisqatsi*, a word from the Hopi language which means "life of moral corruption and turmoil" or "life out of balance." Delivered without narrative or context and with Hopi chants and frantic synthesizer music as the only accompaniment, the movie depicts a world so engulfed in manic energy that rapid-fire movement becomes its own reference; there is no reality outside the mania. Some of the most memorable, even haunting images from the film compress hours of nighttime traffic along busy streets into a few minutes or seconds of screen time.

"End of the Tunnel"
Copyright Tim Krech, Berlin, Germany, 2006, CC-SA 2.0

The director, Godfrey Reggio, said *Koyaanisqatsi* has "never been about the effect *of* technology, *of* industry *on* people. It's been that everyone: politics, education, things of the financial structure, the nation-state structure, language, the culture, religion, all of that exists within the host of technology. So it's not...that we *use* technology, we *live* technology."

If we think the Albuquerque-born imagery and techniques of *Koyaanisqatsi* are being used intentionally in *Breaking Bad*, and I believe they are, we have to decide the extent to which those techniques influence our understanding of characters and plot.

To me, the absolutely fascinating aspect of this is that *Breaking Bad* is not social commentary. I explained this point in detail in the introduction to *Breaking Blue* because I think understanding Vince Gilligan's position on social structures is essential to a full appreciation of Walter and company. On the other hand, it seems clear to me that *Koyaanisqatsi* is one of the most potent visual social commentaries ever created, virtually demanding a response from viewers. If this is true, and if it is also true that the creators of *Breaking Bad* are intentionally using *Koyaanisqatsi*-inspired imagery to add **essential** artistic detail to the plotline, what do these scenes and scene transitions mean?

I think of *Koyaanisqatsi* as a depiction of technology out of control, to the point that it becomes the primary force, the contours of which define our lives. I think for Vince Gilligan there is another yet greater force. Every once in a while a character will have an epiphany, or something will occur for which a character can identify no cause. Probably the most memorable instance of this was in the pivotal Season Three episode, "Fly" (3.10):

> My God, the universe is random, it's not inevitable, it's simple chaos. It's subatomic particles in endless, aimless collision. That's what science teaches us, but what does this say? What is it telling us that the very night that this man's daughter dies, it's me who is having a drink with him? I mean, how could that be random?

Many fans of *Breaking Bad*—Bryan Cranston among them—point to Episode 2.12 ("Phoenix"), as Walter White's turning point from a man who might be redeemed into a demon beyond the possibility of salvation. It was in the last minutes of that episode, after all, that Walter watched Jane Margolis choke on her own vomit and made a conscious decision not to save her life.

I think a case can be made that Walter's moment of no return actually occurred months later, in Episode 3.10, when he came close to abandoning his long-held idea that "the universe is random… it's simple chaos." The Universe sent Donald Margolis to that bar as the agent of Walter White's redemption. How else to explain such an unlikely, virtually impossible alignment of the two individuals weighing most heavily on Jane Margolis' last gasps of life?

But by the end of the episode, after weighing the evidence, Walter decided, naw, the universe really *is* random. That decision to reject the inherent order and meaning of the universe, I think, could be seen as the crime for which the *Breaking Bad* universe offers no forgiveness.

Simply put, I believe a purpose-driven universe in which human life has meaning is at the core of Vince Gilligan's vision of the world of *Breaking Bad*. The frantic *Koyaanisqatsi* madness of Walter White's world is a temporary overlay, a deviation from normalcy that will be corrected soon enough, in a way that will visit a full measure of retribution upon Walter White.

~~~~~

Up to this point I have been examining motifs, images, and themes in some depth. For the next few chapters, though, I'm going to adopt a new tack. I will make brief statements, or even merely pose a question, and then quickly move on to the next idea or inquiry. I may not develop the concept at all, or I may offer a brief defense or supporting ideas from the series. Sprinkled throughout this *Koyaanisqatsi*-like environment I will offer the occasional longer essay. The connection between the Learn'd Astronomer and Hank and Walter, and their two colors—orange and blue—will receive a full analytical discourse, for instance. But other questions—the true nature of Jesse Pinkman, as an example—will receive the hit-and-run treatment.

I have three reasons for doing this, one practical and the other two a bit more high-minded. First, in a utilitarian sense, the longer this book is, the more it will cost. This is not so true of the ebook version, but publishers pay printers by the page for paperbacks and hard cover editions; the cost of printing a 400-page paperback is invariably almost exactly twice as much as the cost of a 200-page book. But publishers can't charge the public twice as much—free markets don't work that way! Inukshuk Press, my publisher, was happy with *LOST Identity*, but balked at even accepting my sci-fi epic, *Deneb*. *LOST Identity*, at just over 200 pages, earned Inukshuk a far higher profit than *Deneb*, which weighs in at a massive 552 pages. Shorter books keep the publisher happy, and keep costs lower, too, for readers.

I could just offer the book without the additional unanswered questions. This is certainly a possibility. I have made such a decision in previous work. In my *Lost* writings, for instance, I have consciously addressed fewer than a hundred or so of the 500+ questions that fans and scholars have identified. I could have offered a kind of *Koyaanisqatsi* list of questions, but I decided not to do so, for reasons peculiar to the *Lost* universe. First, anyone with deep interest in the series' concepts can find tens of thousands of *Lost* lists online. Second, and more importantly, *Lost* is multi-layered science fiction. It's *dense*, mythology-based, and therefore inherently hard to understand. Posing hit-and-run questions would just frustrate people. *Breaking Bad* has a more traditional narrative. The questions posed have every bit as much substance and depth as those posed by *Lost*, but the narrative framework is easier for most of us to understand.

So, presenting the themes and concepts for thought and discussion is preferable to not listing them at all, simply out of concern over book length. But there may be another, more powerful advantage to the rapid-fire presentation. A change in the pacing of concepts sometimes triggers new connections in our minds. If I read the exposition of a single theme, with all its documented support spread out along six pages, I gain an appreciation of that theme. But if I confront 24 ideas in those same six pages, I may have a brainstorm or sudden intuition about the deeper meaning or consequences of three or four of those concepts, tripling or quadrupling the rate at which I come to an understanding of the show.

So, put on your yellow splash suits, get out a big bowl of crystal blue rock candy, and let's begin our frenzied sprint.

Ca cophony of Connections

The Labyrinth
Lake Erie Arboretum at Frontier Park, 2006, PD

"Albuquerque gets 330 days of sunshine" every year, or so said the radio DJ as Skyler made her way in Albuquerque traffic. I know AMC was enticed to Albuquerque with some hefty tax incentives. In fact, Vince Gilligan originally placed the action in Riverside, California, close to the center of the movie and television industry in the southern part of the state. He had to rewrite the pilot for Albuquerque. AMC's decision was probably one of the best things that happened to the series.

As the *New York Times* noted, "Vince Gilligan now considers Albuquerque a character of [the show]." (Emily Brennan, *New York Times*, August 6, 2013) The beauty of the Albuquerque sky became critical to the plot. "All the wonderful…geographical elements we put to good use in the show," he said. "…you … perceive the immense size of the sky," he said. "[It goes] on forever some days."

The sky is the first attribute of New Mexico that Gilligan noted in his NYT interview and has certainly played a major role in several *Breaking Bad* episodes. Skyler, of course, began the series with a mostly sky-blue wardrobe. The vast blue sky is central to *Breaking Bad*'s color-based symbolism.

I believe the *simplicity* of New Mexico landscapes, as well as their high color contrast, became a factor of great significance to the show. I will return to this discussion before the end of the fourth period.

~~~~~

What is the meaning of the color pink? Is it primarily a mixture of red (youthful anger, danger, or simple anger) and white (pride or purity)? How can we reconcile such an idea with Holly's frequent appearance in pink garments? Does the name Pinkman indicate a pink different from Holly's, or is it the same? Is Jesse in some sense innocent? Does pink mean innocence about to die, or innocence slaughtered or ignored, or innocence lost? Do we need a completely different paradigm to explain Jesse's surname?

~~~~~

"Whoa there, Pearson!" some of you are saying. "You're over-analyzing this! I saw that sequence in 'Gliding Over All' (Episode 5.08) where you said they were all wearing 'fluorescent orange'. Well, I counted, and there were five in orange, two in yellow, and two in khaki. I say you're over-simplifying. You're bending things to fit your way of looking at *Breaking Bad*. You're making stuff up that doesn't fit what's really happening on the show."

This is a legitimate point of view. I offer no apology. However, this book already contains sufficient support for any reader interested in offering a spirited defense of my contention that color is used heavily by the writers and directors of *Breaking Bad* to convey symbolic meaning. I leave the question for each reader to decide.

~~~~~

The floor of the superlab is painted deep blood red. In Season Five we will see an important floor having the same color. In Season Four the sheets of Jesse's bed were bloody red. What is the significance of these colors? Are the objects related? For those who believe the colors lack significance, please inquire of your friends in the pharmaceutical industry about the number of blood red production floors they've seen.

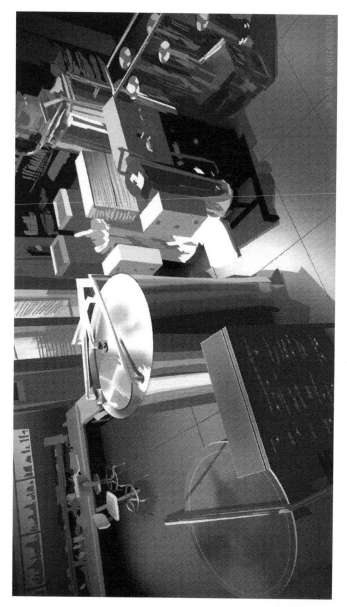

"The Superlab"
Copyright Martin Woutisseth, used with permission

~~~~~

Skyler often comes up with creative, non-violent schemes to address problems others assert can only be solved by brute force. In Season Four we saw her connect soap going down the kitchen drain to a trumped up drama around supposed ground water pollution caused by Bogdan Wolynetz's car wash. (Episode 4.03) She devised a convincing show for the IRS when it came to inspect Ted Beneke's out-of-whack books, saving him hundreds of thousands of dollars in tax penalties and a possible prison sentence. (Episode 4.09) She feigned an asthma-like medical condition to gain entry into Walter's apartment (Episode 4.01), similar to her pregnancy-related fakery in the jewelry store in Season One. We've seen several other bits of scheming and acting over the last four seasons.

Beyond satisfying the immediate goal of obtaining something she wants or needs, is there any rhyme or reason or connection between these actions and her identity as a person?

~~~~~

Okay, so what about those red shoes? In Episode 4.01, Walter replaced his blood-soaked clothing with a generic Kenny Rogers shirt, Dickies pants, and red tennis shoes. Those were no ordinary shoes, though, and the director made sure we got an extreme close-up of the red PF Flyers when Walter exited his car.

"Wizard of Oz," you say. Yes, the shoes could be a reference to Dorothy's red sequin-covered slippers in "The Wizard of Oz," but I doubt it, for two reasons. First, Dorothy received those shoes from the freshly-killed Wicked Witch of the East, who was crushed by her house when it landed in Munchkin Land. They acted as protection from the Wicked Witch of the West. I find no witch correlates in the series. Also, no one gave Walter the shoes; he bought them.

The close-up shot just about took my breath away, because I've seen those same shoes before. Same brand, same color, and—I will argue—similar circumstances.

I saw the identical shoes in *Lost*, Episode 3.08, "Flashes Before Your Eyes." Desmond Hume was chatting with the 'Time Cop', Eloise Hawking, when a gentleman dressed in a business suit and red PF Flyers appeared briefly. A moment later, he lay under a mound of construction rubble, the only part of him visible being the lower part of his legs and his pristine red tennis shoes.

The *Lost* scene was obviously a reference to "The Wizard of Oz," but the significance, as we learned from Desmond's conversation with the strangely wise woman, was that Eloise Hawking knew the man with red shoes was going to die. "But you could have saved him," Desmond argued, nearly shouting at her. No, she said, shaking her head. He would have died, if not that day then the next. He would have slipped in the shower or been run over by a bus. The universe has a way of 'course correcting', she said. The death of the red-shoed man was inevitable. It was his destiny.

Jesse wore a red shirt when he shot Gale. Walter's red PF Flyers, I believe, were a reference to *Lost*. They symbolized either Walter's death or his nature as a murderer. More importantly, the shoes symbolized *inevitable* death or murder. There are no time loops in the *Breaking Bad* Universe, but there are strong etiological connections between behavior and consequence. The red shoes were an instance of reinforcing that idea using imagery from a television show brimming with themes around inevitable destiny.

Chapter Ga

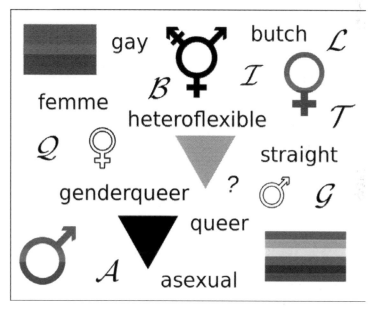

Ga llimaufry

"Sexuality Confusion"
Copyright Adela Mae, 2006, CC-SA 1.0 Generic

The contrast between Walter's discomfort and bumbling in the criminal underworld and the well-worn, *dans-sa-peau*, folksy kind of ease exuded by his contacts, such as the gun dealer, is fascinating to watch. The supreme example of the experienced, practical, no-nonsense bad guy is, of course, Mike Ehrmantraut.

~~~~~

Walter often hits his head on furniture or some other obstruction as he's rising from the floor or from a confined space, but sometimes from a high perch, too (as in

235

Episode 3.10). This heavily-used motif connects directly to an important personality trait.

~~~~~

"Okay, I give up," the frustrated reader says. "What the hell is Gallimaufry? I looked it up. It's not even in my dictionary!"

~~~~~

Flowers are a shared Marie/Hank motif. I didn't realize this until my third viewing of the series. I usually have an opinion or theory or can otherwise form an argument around a motif or theme, but in this case I have to admit I'm coming up without a convincing idea that explains the Schrader family fascination with bouquets of flowers. It seems like something worthy of investigation.

~~~~~

Reverse of the 2010 Sacagawea Dollar Coin
Featuring Iroquois imagery, including the Five Arrows, a symbol of Confederacy strength
U.S. Mint, 2010, PD

So now Jesse has a purpose in life, thanks to Gustavo. He knew Jesse felt hopeless, saw no value in life. Gus gave him hope, a reason to live. "I got like two jobs now." He's an important man, doing important things—like guarding Mike Ehrmantraut. (Episode 4.05) What a thoughtful man Gus is.

That's not what was going on at all. Gustavo couldn't have cared less about Jesse, the 'worthless junkie'. His only value was the strength he brought to Walter. He demonstrated that strength already, in allowing Walter's will to be expressed in two places at once. (Episode 3.13) Gustavo wasn't acting with Jesse's welfare in mind. His strategy was cold and calculating: Divide and conquer. If he could pull Jesse out of Walter's sphere of influence, he could win the grand chess game that formed the entire plot of Season Four.

~~~~~

Gustavo Fring, he of the eternal yellow shirt, lives in a yellow house. Of course. A sensible, well-thought-out yellow brick house.

~~~~~

"This is not a rock, Marie. This is a *mineral,* for like the tenth time."

I haven't done a formal count, but I know Hank corrects the uninformed at least seven times during the course of Season Four. They're minerals, dammit. And they are *central* to the imagery of *Breaking Bad.* I will have much more to say about this before the end of Period Four.

~~~~~

The Eye

The Eye of Horus
Louvre Museum, Egypt, circa 600 B.C.
Photograph by Marie-Lan Nguyen, 2005, PD

We see the pink teddy bear's severed eyeball several times during Seasons Three and Four. A book could be written on the symbolic significance of the eye. Notice the way Skyler looks at the eyeball in Episode 4.01, the way she dismisses it after brief confusion. It's a meaningless knick-knack to her. Compare this with Walter's passionate interest in the object. In Episode 3.01, for example, he looked closely at the eye after finding it in the backyard pool and decided to keep it. I have to imagine Skyler, or anyone else for that matter, would have discarded the eyeball without a second thought.

For Walter, the eye had enough significance that he decided to pack it in his suitcase (Episode 3.02) and keep it in a readily accessible drawer in his apartment (Episode 4.01). Here's what Vince Gilligan said about this immensely important symbol:

> The teddy bear eyeball that Walt found in his swimming pool is symbolic. It's very, very symbolic. However, I'm not sure I can tell you with 100% certainty of what the symbolism is, what it represents...On the face of it, when we were coming up with that eye as an image, it probably represented some form of the eye of the universe, the eye of god, the eye of morality, I suppose judging Walter White...And so symbolism like the eyeball, I'm not sure what it means to me completely but I'm always interested in hearing what it means to viewers of the show. I guess if you're going to hold my feet to the fire, what it means to me is the eye of God on Walt. If not necessarily judging him, nonetheless watching him, keeping tabs on him. And then the question: If that is what the symbolism stands for, then why does Walt keep that eye? Why does he keep it in his drawer versus discarding it?

"Uncle Sam"
James Montgomery Flagg, 1916

I could, and probably should, write a long chapter on this symbol. If I did, I would connect the image to the Eye of Horus, the strong accusatory presence of the teddy bear, and ideas and images connecting conscience, guilt, behavior, responsibility, destiny, karma, and the nature of the *Breaking Bad* Universe. I would weave in the intentional facial parallel between the teddy bear and Gustavo in "Face Off" (Episode 4.13) and the other internal references, such as the fly, the red light of the smoke alarm in Walter's apartment, and so on.

As you see from the above list of interconnected ideas, I do not exaggerate when I claim a book could be written on that eyeball. Many fans of the series have written extensively on the symbol. I could certainly put my stamp on the idea, too, but the thrust of this volume is color symbolism, and I have intentionally slighted many of the other obvious symbols in this short treatment.

So, I will provide no analysis. I will state simply that I believe with many others that the teddy bear's eyeball is proclaiming, with the full force of the Universe, *J'accuse.* The Universe sees what Walter has done, and will not allow him to forget.

I should say, just because I have yet to see anyone else mention it, that the fact that Walter is moved by the eyeball, and feels all manner of discomfort and angst, indicates he has somehow maintained a connection with an elementary sense of right and wrong. The eyeball, above all else, is a sign that Walter has a conscience. As long as he looks at that eyeball and draws meaning from it, I believe the intention is to say, symbolically, that Walter may yet be redeemed.

Chapter Ge

Ge·eks
32
Nazis &
Zombies

Zombies
"Night of the Living Dead," 1968, PD

Badger, Skinny Pete, and a host of invited and uninvited guests at Jesse's season-long open house/drug fest/sex orgy spent a good portion of time discussing the many fascinating intricacies and technical aspects of zombies, and especially Nazi zombies. What is the deeper significance? I think one of Jesse's anonymous guests summed it up best near the end of Episode 4.03:

> No one's really paying attention to where these things are, I mean there's gotta be thousands of them all over the world. I don't know: Boats coming right for us and phoning inside an ice cream truck, driving up to San Francisco…and I'm not even that scared of burning up in cannibalism. The thing's that—the thing that worries me is, is getting trampled or shoved up against a chain link fence because if you really think about it, if you're up against a chain link fence, and you've got a lot, I mean a lot of people trying to escape, pushin' hard enough forward, that's not a joke: You're going to get squeezed right through the chain links, like Play-Doh or some kind of soft meat…Uh, and this is inevitable, okay? And there's nothing you or me or anyone can do about it. And if the fence posts are stuck deep, really deep and this and that, way down inside the ground, then that's definitely happening to you.

The poet laureate continued his speech for another several minutes, every word no less profound than the one before it.

Okay, I'm being facetious here. The anonymous philosopher made no sense, and that is the final point of Jesse's party. It was an exercise in pure nihilism, reflecting Jesse's hopeless surrender to forces beyond his control. His girlfriend drowned on her own vomit, dead because of drugs. Jesse's new girlfriend was a drug addict, her baby brother a murderer and himself executed by other drug dealers. Jesse, a drug dealer and manufacturer, found himself lecturing Andrea about her wretched lifestyle when his life choices had lately been far worse than hers. And on top of all this, the most powerful man in the Southwestern United States was going to murder him at a time and place of his choosing.

But there is a profound connection between Jesse's party and Gale's impassioned recitation of "The Learn'd Astronomer." The Nazi zombie exchange between Badger and Skinny Pete in Episode 4.02 is their second longest dialog in the series, after the Star Trek pie eating contest (Episode 5.09) and begins to establish the connection. But the clincher is the Radiation Speech in Episode 4.04. We'll take a close look at the speech in Chapter Se.

~~~~~

"Hey! I just realized this is Chapter 32," an angry reader says. "That didn't seem right, so I went back and checked Chapter Ga. It was marked 31, but then the chapter before it, Chapter Ca, was marked 20. WTF? This is too confusing, man. Where did the missing ten chapters go, anyway?"

~~~~~

Nazis

Sergeant Schultz, Colonel Hogan, and Colonel Klink
Hogan's Heroes, Publicity Photo, 1968, PD

Season Four featured a lot of talk about Nazis, and especially Nazi zombies. As Badger told the clueless Skinny Pete, "Nazi zombies don't wanna eat ya just 'cause they're craving the protein. They do it 'cause, they do it 'cause they hate Americans, man. Talibans. They're the Talibans of the zombie world."

Badger reduced the 20th century's most infamous cultural malignancy to a set of video game cartoon characters, but he was adhering to a well-trod path of entertainers who have taken a serious subject and found ways to laugh at it. Even during the war, comedians and radio personalities were taking humorous swipes at the Nazis. Lighthearted as it was, back in those days the humor bore an authenticity it simply cannot have today.

Much of the cast and crew of the celebrated World War II sitcom *Hogan's Heroes* had personally suffered under Nazi tyranny. Werner Klemperer, who played Colonel Klink, fled Germany in 1935, in fear of his life. John Banner, who played Sergeant "I know nothingk" Schultz, managed to escape in 1938, but most of his immediate and extended family died in concentration camps. And so with many other cast members. Robert Clary, the affable French Corporal LeBeau in Colonel Hogan's gang, spent *three years* in Nazi concentration camps, from early 1942 until he was finally liberated on April 11, 1945. He spoke freely about his experience, even penning an autobiography titled *From the Holocaust to Hogan's Heroes: the Autobiography of Robert Clary*, published in 2001.

Robert Clary (Corporal LeBeau on *Hogan's Heroes*)
Publicity Photo, William Morris Agency, 1953, PD

I never met Robert Clary. But I knew men like him. Most of us Boomers were the daughters or sons of World War II veterans. If not, we learned some of our first lessons in life from grade school and high school teachers who had served on the front lines in Europe and in the Pacific. These were not beaten or defeated men, but individuals who had learned so much that they were able to rise above the horrors they had experienced in their teens or early 20s. They approached life with gusto and good cheer, and it showed in almost everything they did. If only my generation had learned more from this Greatest Generation. Hell No We Won't Go was as close as we came to any kind of patriotic spirit, and personal responsibility amounted to knowing how to use a roach clip so you didn't burn your fingers when you took the last few puffs. There's authenticity here, too. Our parents were tested on the beaches of Normandy. We were tested on the mud fields of Woodstock.

We're going to experience a lot more Nazi-related stuff in Season Five. After the jokes of Season Four, we will see a very serious side of Swastika-bedecked skinheads during Heisenberg's final days. I should make an admission here: If you're wondering how the swastikas on Sergeant Schultz's and Colonel Klink's uniforms disappeared, you can blame me for their removal. I have carefully removed or altered the swastikas in every photograph in which they appear. Don't look for historical accuracy here! Many people find swastikas offensive. They are illegal in much of Europe. I don't like them either, so out they went.

~~~~~

Gallimaufry:

1.   A hodgepodge; jumble; confused medley.
2.   A ragout or hash.
[Webster's New Universal Unabridged Dictionary, 2001]

~~~~~

Hank Schrader is to John Locke as Walter White is to [fill in the blank]

Walter White is to Donald Draper as Skyler White is to [fill in the blank]

Hank Schrader is to Steven Gomez as Han Solo is to [fill in the blank]

You might have to google this one:

Walter White is to Anna Gunn as Mark Craig is to [fill in the blank]

~~~~~

No chapters are missing. As I explained in the introduction, the chapters are organized according to the periodic table of the elements.

I removed the *transition elements* from my version of the *Breaking Bad* periodic table. The transition elements begin with Scandium (Atomic Symbol Sc), Atomic Number 21, occurring in the regular periodic table just to the right of Calcium. The transition elements are sometimes called the 'D-Block' elements because they have partially filled d orbitals. I removed these metallic elements to simplify the table and to reduce its size. If I had included these elements and devoted a chapter to each one, this book would have contained more than 70 chapters!

~~~~~

The correct answers:

The Man in Black
Peggy Olson
Chewbacca
Bonnie Bartlett

If you answered Thomas Hobbes for the first one, you read too many books and you don't watch enough television! If you answered Betty Draper to the second one, I'd accept it, but Peggy Olson is better. The idea of 'learning from a master deceiver' supersedes 'being married to an obnoxious womanizing/drug dealing husband'. Chewbacca was an easy one, but it makes up for the final correlation, which was obscure. The wife of Dr. Mark Craig in *St. Elsewhere* was Mrs. Ellen Craig, played by actress Bonnie Bartlett. Interestingly, Bonnie Bartlett is the wife of William Daniels, who played Dr. Mark Craig.

Why the Man in Black? Why not Jack Shephard? Because Jack Shephard learned from the Science v. Faith debate; the Man in Black did not. If you don't know what I'm talking about, don't sweat it. This is the Koyaanisqatsi/Gallimaufry part of the book. Not everything's gonna make sense.

The
Learn'd
Astronomer

Walt Whitman, circa 1854

Walt Whitman is where the rubber meets the road. He is the foundation of *Breaking Bad*. He is the thesis, the point from which all symbols and images and colors flow. The next three chapters—As, Se, and Br—are the heart of this volume. They express the central idea of *Breaking Bad*.

I don't honestly know whether the notion of Whitman's foundational importance is generally accepted. I do know that I have searched—scoured!—the Internet, seeking any blogger or author who has been able to reconcile such crucial elements as Hank's obsession with minerals. Most bloggers, as far as I can tell, label Hank's hobby a 'missed opportunity' to develop a complete metaphor. The thread is labeled a 'dead end', a vaguely interesting preoccupation that ended with an inglorious and ignoble fizzle in the writers' room. O, bloggers! How wrong you are. How very wrong you are. You've missed the whole point of the series.

Walt Whitman didn't sneak up on us, making his only significant appearance during Hank's 'info dump' moment on the toilet in Walter's bathroom. (Episode 5.08) He occupied center stage from the very beginning, though we didn't recognize him until Gale Boetticher introduced the man, who before then had been content to occupy the background, in deep shadow. Gale recited his favorite poem, from the collection of thoughts Walt Whitman called *Leaves of Grass*. The poem he recited was "The Learn'd Astronomer." From that moment in Episode 3.08 until the fall of Ozymandias late in Season Five, Walt Whitman never relinquished the spotlight.

The Learn'd Astronomer

William Herschel, Astronomer
Lemuel Francis Abbott, 1785

It is a beautiful, insightful, mind-bending poem. Built on a wordsmith's crucial sleight of hand, "The Learn'd Astronomer" is an appropriate central touchstone for a television series that demands thorough and careful thought about symbols, metaphors, and images, but most of all, places before us the essential concepts of relation and connection. "The Learn'd Astronomer" is about the most important connection in Vince Gilligan's fictional world: the relationship between the individual and the Universe.

We know "The Learn'd Astronomer" is the most important poem in the series. Television dramas are allotted so little time to tell their stories. A one-hour television show is really 45 minutes long—sometimes less than 42 minutes is all the director has. So we are given bits and pieces: truncated scenes, a bit of dialog here, a quickly displayed image there, a short montage or a close-up shot to reveal the character's anguish or joy, then it's off to the next commercial. We rarely see the full sweep of an action from beginning to end. Rarer still is the unhurried recitation of a story or anecdote from literature. We know "The Learn'd Astronomer" is important because we heard it recited *twice*.

Here is the full poem:

When I heard the learn'd astronomer;
When the proofs, the figures, were ranged in columns before me;
When I was shown the charts and the diagrams,
to add, divide, and measure them;
When I, sitting, heard the astronomer,
where he lectured with much applause in the lecture-room,
How soon, unaccountable, I became tired and sick;
Till rising and gliding out, I wander'd off by myself,
In the mystical moist night-air, and from time to time,
Look'd up in perfect silence at the stars.

Gale respected Walter White's professional and technical magnificence. In fact, he felt himself in awe of this man who could achieve an impossibly high final product purity from such a difficult multi-step synthesis. Gale was sure that Walter was possessed of such quiet and sure technical prowess that his skill exceeded the normal bounds of human ability. Walter was rare, extraordinary in every sense, and Gale was humbled in the presence of the master's greatness. He could think of no greater compliment to Walter than the dedication he made in his laboratory notebook:

To W. W. My star, my perfect silence.
[Episode 4.04]

Gale worshipped Walter. We have the uneasy feeling that the sentiment was misplaced, and not just the emotional component, but the rigorously scientific aspect of his respect. Certainly Walter's mastery of difficult technical matters was to be respected, but we would appropriately defer to the very human inclination to *applaud* Walter's genius, just as we read in the poem: "He lectured with much applause." That applause is the crux of the problem for Walt Whitman, and it is the outward sign of an incorrect, incomplete order of values in Gale's mind.

Gale was inclined toward this type of inner obeisance, at one point even saying to Gustavo, "I doff my proverbial cap to you, sir!" The book dedication demonstrates his complete understanding of the deep meaning of the poem he quoted, but he misunderstood Walter's place in the poem. Walter was not the perfect silence. He was the Learn'd Astronomer, worthy of much applause.

The Lecture-Room

Lecture at the Rochester Institute of Technology
Anonymous photographer, 1982, PD

"Where are the stars?" you ask, examining the illustration I chose for this section. "He's an astronomer. He'll have pictures of stars." [Shaking your head: disgusted, disappointed.] "That Pearson and his meaningless illustrations."

Go back to Whitman's poem. Find the part of it that says the astronomer ever mentioned stars. I'll make it easy for you; if *Breaking Bad* can recite it twice, so can I! Here are the first four lines of the poem:

When I heard the learn'd astronomer;
When the proofs, the figures, were ranged in columns before me;
When I was shown the charts and the diagrams,
      to add, divide, and measure them;
When I, sitting, heard the astronomer,
      where he lectured with much applause in the lecture-room…

So then, where are the stars you were worried about?

It's quite an amazing poem, from just about any point of view you'd like to take. Whitman's stuff is usually free verse, but a good reader might apply a stiff meter, a kind of punctuated staccato, to good effect. The reader's intention would be the goal of demonstrating an emotional disconnect. Something is amiss. Something momentous.

There is something very, very wrong with this scene. Notice that although the place is called a lecture-room, and there is 'much applause', only two people are mentioned as being present: the narrator and the learn'd astronomer. *We* did not hear the learn'd astronomer. *I* heard him. The learn'd astronomer did not present his proofs and figures to anyone except me: "When *I* was shown the charts and the diagrams," the narrator said, ignoring anyone else, for *they had no function* at all in this tableau until it came time to acknowledge whatever it was the learn'd astronomer was doing. It was only when someone or perhaps a gaggle of people or maybe an audience of thousands gave 'much applause' that we learned anyone else was there, and it was only after that we learned all this was taking place in a lecture-room.

The audience members, who they are, the number of people present, why they came—none of these things matter. It is important only that they gave 'much applause' for the 'proofs, the figures', 'the charts and the diagrams'.

We know they are not students. Students don't applaud a professor. We know they're not fellow astronomers; the narrator was invited, but he was no astronomer. This was a general lecture intended for a public audience of perhaps mildly interested people. What the people received for their two bits or two dollars or whatever it was they paid to hear the learn'd astronomer was something unexpected but in no way disappointing. There were no planets or stars. There were no glorious descriptions of strange and fascinating celestial phenomena. There were only mind-numbing charts and graphs and columns of figures and long proofs of who-knows-what. None of it could be connected in any obvious or discernible fashion to any stellar or astronomic phenomena that anyone in the lecture hall understood.

It didn't matter to the audience. They loved the presentation. Not because it had anything to do with astronomy, for no one saw any relation to the moon and stars in the scientific gibberish he was spewing in front of them. They loved it, though, because the lecture demonstrated the learn'd astronomer's rare intellectual prowess.

Only one person was disappointed in the lecture. In fact, the presentation so disturbed him that "soon, unaccountable, [he] became tired and sick." So he left the lecture-room and ***glided*** outdoors, to the "mystical moist night-air," there to look on and appreciate and wonder "in perfect silence" at the glory of the stars. It was there, at the end of the poem, that the stars were finally mentioned. It was the narrator, not the learn'd astronomer, who loved the stars.

The narrator was not really looking for stars, or even for a learn'd astronomer who could describe the stars to him in new and compelling ways. He sought something deeper. He sought a *connection* to something. It was the only thing on the narrator's mind—so much so, in fact, that he ignored everyone else in the room. Something 'mystical' had to happen this night, and he sensed it revolved around *this* lecture.

You may wonder what all this has to do with *Breaking Bad*. Friend, fellow fan of the show: This poem has everything to do with *Breaking Bad*. It is the show's beating heart. In order to convince you of that, though, we need to help Marie open a bunch of boxes just delivered by the UPS guy. We have to make sure they're not damaged.

"Rocks?" you say. You and Marie look at each other, sharing a moment of stupefied disbelief.

No, not rocks. For like the tenth time, they're minerals. Hank's mineral collection holds the key to understand *Breaking Bad*.

Se lenium

Chalcanthite and Gypsum Minerals
Copyright Didier Descouens, 2009, CC Att. 3.0 Unported

Hank doesn't need to tell us what minerals are. Most of us take a multivitamin every day after breakfast, so we know all about minerals. The multivitamin I use conveniently breaks out the vitamins in one column and the minerals in the other. The very first mineral listed is selenium, a potent antioxidant used to boost the body's natural defenses against disease. The manufacturer claims each tablet contains 100 mcg (micrograms) of the mineral. We hear about 'vitamins and minerals' all the time.

Unfortunately, the word we casually throw around when discussing human nutrition has nothing to do with Hank's understanding of the term. In fact, Hank would tell us that selenium is a metal or an element, not a mineral. If we wish to understand Hank's mineral collection, we need to begin with definitions.

Minerals

Amethyst
A quartz mineral
Copyright Didier Descouens, 2013, CC-SA 3.0

mineral (min′ər əl, min′rəl), *n*. **1**. any of a class of substances occurring in nature, usually comprising inorganic substances, as quartz or feldspar, of definite chemical composition and usually of definite crystal structure...
[Webster's New Universal Unabridged Dictionary, 2001]

We need to draw three important elements from this definition. First of all, the minerals Hank is interested in are crystalline. Because that's Hank's focus, we will disregard any natural material not presenting as crystals. This includes Marie's 'rocks', an overly generic, non-descriptive word that doesn't tell us anything useful.

Second, minerals occur naturally. When you're out hiking or camping you can find minerals just about anywhere. If local law permits, you can even 'hunt' minerals, taking the best ones home with you. [Harvesting rocks, minerals, or other artefacts is sometimes forbidden in parks, forests, or nature preserves. It's always best to check with local authorities before filling your backpack—and having to pay a fine!]

Finally, anyone can appreciate and collect minerals. You don't need to be a scientist to enjoy them. I held onto my mineral collection until well after I had graduated college. In some fit of downsizing upon my return from Peace Corps service in West Africa, I gave them all away to an interested friend. Every now and then I find myself missing them and feeling guilty; most of the minerals were gifts from my grandparents, who had collected them on their travels all over the world.

I was an amateur geologist for a time, but I must confess I was less interested in the science and more interested in just gazing on my collection. It was a thing of beauty. In that simple appreciation I shared something with Walt Whitman, but there was far more to the famous poet's enjoyment of the stars than my infatuation with crystalline stone.

The Learn'd Mineralogist

Early in my pharmaceutical career I played host to a tour group. These were high school students interested in learning more about careers in science. I had never taken on a tour all by myself, so I was nervous when the appointed hour drew near. I felt a bit of relief when the door to my lab opened and my boss entered, inquiring about the latest batch of experiments. He had designed an ingenious apparatus to study temperatures of mixing and I was using it to scope out the range of thermal responses from various vendors' raw materials. It was actually pretty interesting stuff. And it was a closely-guarded industrial secret.

Just as I was in the middle of alerting my boss to an unexpected dividend from my work, my fingers literally on the apparatus, the high school kids walked in. I knew already that my boss hated tours. He was all about results, hard numbers, hard facts, moving projects along. Public relations could be handled by administration people. He was a scientist, not a circus performer.

After my five-minute spiel, one of the kids asked what we were doing. I was not a little shocked when my boss turned to the young man and told him, using every bit of technical jargon he could throw at the kid, exactly what we were doing.

I don't remember if my jaw fell open, but that would have been an appropriate response. Our work was an industrial secret. It would never be patented because the process was too simple, too easy to copy, and streamlined studies of the type we were doing in such a way that we had a tremendous advantage over competitors. Here was my supervisor, handing out hard-won industrial secrets to a high school student. Workers in industry have been sent to prison for less.

I couldn't believe the audacity. When the kids had left, I asked him about it. He shrugged his shoulders. "They didn't understand what I said. It got them out of here faster."

He was right. By lacing his explanation with terminology these young adults had never been exposed to, he ensured their sudden disinterest in our work. They moved on because we had done nothing to engage them. My boss: the Learn'd R&D Chemist.

In Episode 4.04 we were treated to a close-up view of one of Hank's favorite minerals, rhodonite, a pretty pink crystalline form of manganese. Little did Hank know, he would be faced with a world-class mineralogist invading his bedroom.

Hank: Now that one right there, that's rhodonite, it's manganese inosilicate.
Junior: Cool. What makes it be all pink like that?
Hank: Well, that's the manganese part, okay? It oxidizes, you know, like rust.
Walter: Exactly. Manganese can have an oxidation state of between minus three and plus seven, which takes it through a range of colors: purple, green, blue, but its most stable state is plus two, which is usually pale pink...So...
Hank: Exactly. Whatever the hell *he* said. [He took back the mineral from Junior] Anyway , you, ah... you get the idea.
Walter: Yeah, it's interesting. Interesting stuff. Really.

What started as two guys looking at some beautiful crystals was ruined by a lesson in geochemistry that neither Hank nor Junior had requested. The situation went from happy and calm to nervous and tense—all because a Learn'd Mineralogist had destroyed the 'mystical moist night air' in Hank's dark bedroom.

Why? What was the characteristic of Walter's words that destroyed the wonder-charged atmosphere permeating the space around Hank's viewing lamp?

We don't have to go far to find out. In that very same episode, not 17 minutes later, we heard again from Jesse's anonymous poet laureate, this time on the subject of radiation poisoning:

> I'm not even kidding, because if you really think about it, you can't even see it, so how can you know just how bad radio frequencies and microwaves and cell phones and stuff are getting you? I mean, you could be strolling through security at the airport on the way to visit your grandma or whatever, and then you get waved through a full-body [unintelligible] scanner, and the next day you could be dead or dying, at least dying from all the radiation that they say is safe, but there's no way it can be because it has to do with your concentrated dose, okay? Enough to penetrate your clothes so the accumulated amount could *definitely* be dangerous to susceptible individuals, especially if you're from a rural area, and the ozone layer's already thin because of the *cow* farts...

The anonymous homeless man's passionate speech was laced with pseudo-scientific nonsense and misplaced concerns and worries about things he could not possibly understand. Yet it all sounded so much like Walter's geochemistry discourse. The common thread is hard to discern. The spaced-out junkie in Jesse's trashed living room had no idea what he was talking about. Walter, on the other hand, knew exactly what he was saying, and could back up every one of his words with findings and theories and well-accepted facts—those proofs and figures and charts and diagrams that Walt Whitman railed against in his famous poem.

Natural Blue

I believe the common thread is contrast with the natural state. Regardless of Walter's vaunted state of erudition and the homeless man's utter lack of even the most basic scientific knowledge, both discourses focused on that which is man-made. The number of electrons in a hybridized orbital may have relevance to a theoretical chemist, but such knowledge brings nothing to anyone's appreciation of a pretty pink crystal.

Those who were paying attention in the early part of Season Four already knew all this. The scientific mumbo-jumbo of Episode Four was just confirmation of the lessons learned two episodes before. In Episode Two, Hank was in bed, awake. He used his grabber to pick up the most important mineral in his collection. We know it was the most important mineral because its value warranted his attention even at such an odd hour.

Marie: Can't you sleep?
Hank: Actually, Marie, yes, this is me sleeping. What's it look like?
Marie: It looks like you're looking at a rock at…2:24 in the morning.
Hank: This is not a rock. This is a mineral, for like the *tenth* time.
Marie: Okay. Got it.
Hank: Blue corundum, to be precise.
Marie: Blue corundum. Well, it's very pretty.

Hank said it again, just before Marie lowered her side of the bed: "***Blue corundum.***" He emphasized each word. We didn't hear any other mineral name repeated three times, nor will we. Only one other blue crystalline material is mentioned more frequently on the show—and it isn't a mineral, it's a poisonous, mind-altering drug.

Corundum is a crystalline form of aluminum oxide. It has one of the highest hardnesses in the mineral kingdom, 9.0 on the Mohs hardness scale. It's nearly as hard as diamond. The gem quality variants of the mineral are known to all of us: They're called sapphire. The type of mineral Hank was handling at 2:24 in the morning could be referred to as blue sapphire. It often has a pale blue color very similar to the pale blue crystalline methamphetamine coming out of the superlab.

Man-made crystal blue meth versus nature-made crystal blue corundum.

"So what," some readers are saying. It's just a little tidbit, an isolated fact, a disconnected piece of nothing the writers threw in just for fun. It has no greater significance. Could be. I'm always ready to entertain counter-arguments. But there's a mighty impressive supporting conceptual architecture to overcome here.

Episode 3.07:

"I swear to God, Marie, I think the universe is trying to tell me something. And I'm finally ready to listen."

In those precious hours before he was shot, Hank understood something important was happening. He was ready to listen to the Universe. A few weeks later, in Season Four, without rhyme or reason, he began ordering minerals. Lots and lots of minerals. He didn't purchase the rocks because he was listening to himself. He surrendered to an urge that came from outside his being. The Universe was the starting point for his urge to study natural crystalline material. The minerals were the outward sign that Hank was *listening*. He was in tune with the 'mystical moist night-air', and 'from time to time, look'd up' from his bed in 'perfect silence' at the crystals.

Crystals: The *Breaking Bad* version of Walt Whitman's star.

Hank, not W.W., is the 'perfect silence', the 'star' that Walt Whitman described in his poem. Here, then, is the guiding star for all of *Breaking Bad*:

> **The marvelous, magical essence that Walt Whitman sought in "The Learn'd Astronomer" was connection with nature.**

Vince Gilligan merely replaced Walt Whitman's 'Nature' with the equivalent *Breaking Bad* term: Universe.

Walter has been confronted with far greater servings of nature's unforgiving fury than Hank ever felt. Yet he refused to listen.

Episode 3.10:

"The universe is random. It's not inevitable. It's simple chaos. It's subatomic particles in endless, aimless collision. That's what science teaches us, but what is this saying? What is it telling us, when on the very night that this man's daughter dies, it's me who's having a drink with him? How can that be random?"

The Universe is random, uncertain in every respect. That is to say, the Universe adheres to the Heisenberg Uncertainty Principle. This is Heisenberg's thesis, but in Episode 3.10 he was temporarily troubled by the incongruity of the idea. The assertion of random uncertainty made no sense when fate or destiny or some other force able to overcome randomness and uncertainty sent Jane's father to sit with him on the night she died.

Nevertheless, even with the frightful, fear-inducing power of the well-ordered, **certain**, non-random Universe proving itself to him, Walter chose to believe in randomness and uncertainty. He chose what is man-made over that which the Universe created. He chose the homeless poet laureate's mindless stupidities over the unstoppable forces of nature.

In 1967 Vicky Leandros told us, "L'amour est bleu."
In 2001 Vince Gilligan told us, "La vie est bleu."

And that life—the fullest measure of that life—is found in the joyous appreciation of a rock: a pretty blue crystalline mineral that reveals the ineffable beauty of the Universe and gives lie to Heisenberg's cheap, perverse imitation.

Ad Astra
("To the Stars")
Akseli Gallen-Kallela, 1907

Br[35] eaking Blue

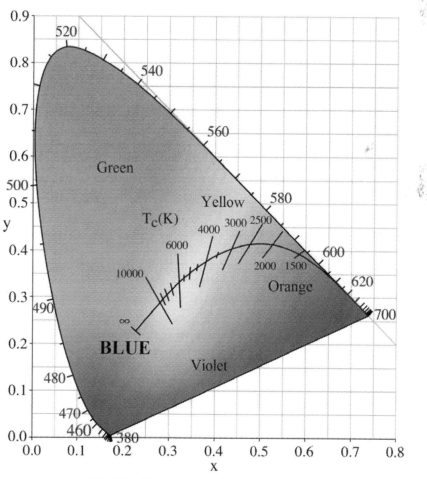

The Planckian Locus of Color Temperature
CIE xy 1931 Reference

The highest temperature achievable by a practical black body radiator is 20,000 Kelvin. To give you some idea of how high that temperature is, the air in the average room is around 295 Kelvin (or 295 K). The surface of the sun is a relatively constant 5800 K. It might seem as though 20,000 K—a temperature over three times higher than the sun's exterior—is so high as to fall outside normal human experience. But remember this temperature corresponds to what physicists call a 'black body'. A black body is a physical entity that absorbs all the radiation that hits it. That energy has to go somewhere, and according to the laws of physics, a perfect black body emits light back out to the world. The wavelength (the color of light) emitted by the black body depends on only one factor: the temperature. It happens that 20,000 K, the highest temperature a practical black body can reach, corresponds to a wavelength of light we're all familiar with. Look up, into the cloudless afternoon sky. The light you see above you has a color temperature of 20,000 K. Sky blue. Skyler blue. The loveliest color. The color that defines *Breaking Bad*.

Color Perfection

The hottest part of a flame is always blue. The highest possible black body emission color is blue. By the laws of physics and the dictates of nature there is no color higher than blue. Not even the surface of the sun can come close to matching the awesome spectral and visual energy of a blue flame or the brilliance and ineffable wonder of a deep blue sky. *Blue is the perfect color.* Artists honor humankind's innate sense of amazement in the majesty and splendor of nature when they reserve to this color the highest symbolic and cultural significance.

Blue is the color to which we surrender all arguments, to which there are no logical rejoinders or equivalents. "I lost myself in her deep blue eyes," we say, indicating an emotional state unrivaled in effect. "Off we go!" the Air Force pilots sing, "Into the wild *blue* yonder! Climbing high, into the sun!" It is there, in the wild, deep blue, that I can "dance the skies on laughter-silvered wings," and climb, "up, up the long, delirious, burning *blue*," to tread "the untrespassed sanctity of space"—this place of blue perfection—there to "put out my hand, and touch the face of God."

"High Flight" is one of the most powerful poems ever written. It helped define American and Canadian culture for half a century. Readers of a certain age will remember these awe-inspiring verses from their local TV station 'sign off', back in the days before 24-hour television. As a young boy I sometimes stayed up late just so I could see the Air Force pilot in his F-104 Starfighter and spend two minutes listening to the magical cadences of John Gillespie Magee Jr's classic poem.

In *Breaking Bad* we saw perfection in the deep, silent blue of the New Mexico sky. Whenever we confronted meaningful events, momentous decisions, or tension-inducing confrontations, we were ushered to the desert, there to experience drama played out against the two-tone, ever-silent honesty of rust-colored rock and endless blue sky. We found perfection here, for there was no other place on earth that so thoroughly reduced conflict to its primordial elements.

The touchstone for the notion of perfection was Heisenberg's crystal blue methamphetamine. No one, not even a highly trained master's-level chemist such as Gale Boetticher, could approach Heisenberg's 99+ percent pure product.

Purity Assay, Liquid Oxygen
Angela Virnig, U.S. Navy, 2003, PD

"It really is quite good," Gale said, pointing to the teenth bag of blue meth. "The purity, of course, I'm speaking of—speaking in strictly chemical terms. And I can't, as of yet, account for the blue color. But…if that is our competition, we have our work cut out for us…so to speak."

Gustavo: You don't have any competition, Gale. Not as far as I'm concerned. After all, how pure can pure be?"
Gale: It can be pretty darn pure. Mr. Fring, I can guarantee you a purity of 96 percent. I'm proud of that figure. It's a hard-earned figure—96. However, this other product is 99—maybe even a touch beyond that…That last three percent—it may not sound like a lot, but it is. It's tremendous. It's a tremendous…gulf.

Even before he met Walter White, Gale stood in awe of his rare abilities. As a scientist specializing in purification, I was pleased to see this heartfelt homage to the formidable challenges of separations science.

Separations is a highly specialized area requiring expertise rarely found among synthetic chemists. Gale was a typical synthetic chemist, the kind of fellow I've worked with for over 30 years. If his mindset was anything like that of the chemists on my teams, his solution to any purification challenge was probably crystallization or a silica column. These are perfectly good technologies—if you're working in 1953. I made my mark in the pharmaceutical world with radically new and efficient crystallization methods, but it's in cutting-edge chromatography where I've been most useful to my sisters and brothers in synthesis. I rarely recommend anything as blunt-force in effect as a silica column.

If my synthetic colleagues typically understand almost nothing about separations, my skill in synthesis ranks far below even most bachelor's-level scientists. My first assignment in research was the synthetic preparation of precursor for a photochemical rearrangement. I spent the entire summer churning out dimers and other garbage entirely useless to my superiors. Needless to say, I did not pursue a career in synthesis.

It is unusual bordering impossible to find a scientist skilled in both synthesis (putting things together) and separations (pulling things apart). Walter White was the rare jack-of-all sub-disciplines who was just as nimble with synthetic reducing agent as he was with separations solvent. Gale understood the unique, god-like skill possessed by Walter White. In his mind, Walter was an unobtainable perfection.

Purity

Even if we despise Heisenberg, I suspect most of us harbor a fascination or even an admiration for his keen intelligence and raw cognitive power. We see his intellectual prowess manifest in intricate, well-thought-out plans and in his ability to fabricate seemingly unimpeachable lies, but we have a sense that these skills are not unusual, one-off abilities. Heisenberg exudes a confidence strongly grounded in broad technical expertise; he doesn't generally boast or make unfounded claims. His greatest strength derives of his proven ability to turn nebulous theory into concrete material. Nowhere do we see this play out with such spectacular results as in the purity of his blue methamphetamine.

The last three percent that Gale marveled over is indeed difficult to achieve. At such high purities one must specify not only the instrumental method but every detail of the guiding SOP (standard operating procedure) when making the purity claim. An NDA (New Drug Application) will typically include half a dozen or more instrumental determinations of purity, including methods such as HPLC, LC/MS, FTIR, DSC, and good old-fashioned elemental analysis, still the 'gold standard' for most drugs other than proteins and biologics.

I always get a chuckle from scenes like the gas chromatograph assay in Episode 4.10. Before the next commercial break, the machine told Jesse and the Mexican chemists that the purity of his product was 96.2 percent. They can perform in a matter of seconds something that would take a professional chromatographer like me a few hours to complete. It's not just the assay, of course, it's the system suitability, standards checks, impurity characterization, baseline fingerprint, trials runs, and so on. But I suppose none of that would really make compelling television drama…

One of the important messages of Episodes 4.01 and 4.10 is that the perception of product purity was important. The 99+ percent purity of Walter's meth impressed Gale to the point that he became philosophical about it. The Juárez drug cartel spared no expense in obtaining higher purity for their product by stealing away one of Gustavo's cooks (Jesse).

But actual purity carried even more importance. I imagine most viewers would not disagree with an assertion that Walter's product, at 99+ percent pure, had more value than Jesse's 96 percent material, which in turn had greater value than the Mexicans' 90 percent concoction.

I bring a lot of industry knowledge to our consideration of purity. I have written four industrial texts on the subject of separations: two on analytical HPLC, one on a technique called preparative HPLC, and a short text on general separations theory. I've created software that allows rapid scaling from analytical or small-scale preparative work to large-scale chromatography. I could take this discussion in a lot of different directions; I could easily write hundreds of pages on the concept of purity as applied to *Breaking Bad*. But I'm going to concentrate on a single, non-technical aspect of the idea because I believe this will do the most to bring a new dimension to the discussion.

Most of you have heard of the 80/20 Rule. The rule certainly applies to separations science, just as it does to virtually any process one can invent or maintain. Just for fun, let's take a look at the kind of work I do for a living, and let's consider it from the point of view of time and resources.

Imagine you're sitting in your office in front of the computer, sipping on the first cup of morning Joe. Your boss comes in, drops a sprig of pine on your desk. You pick it up. Ah, no, it's not pine: It's yew. You inhale its distinctive scent, examine the needles for a few seconds. You look up at your supervisor.

"*Taxus?*"

Your boss nods.

"Looks like *Taxus canadensis*," you say. (It's a guess.)

Your supervisor chuckles. "You shoulda been a taxonomist."

So apparently it was a *good* guess. You try not to smile too much.

"We need all the 7-xylosyltaxol you can squeeze out of this."

"What's the target purity?"

"We need three products: 80 percent for the Spanish market—"

"Oh, yeah, they're treating natural products the same as fermentation now, aren't they."

Your boss nods. "Wish the FDA would follow Europe's lead."

"We can always dream."

"Yeah." He snorts. "We need some 95 percent for synthesis precursor and 99-point-oh for final drug product."

"Timeline?"

"It's gotta be done yesterday."

"Of course."

You've already brought up your New Project spreadsheet and begun filling in some of the pertinent information specific to Canadian Yew trees and your target molecule, 7-xylosyltaxol. In less than ten minutes you email your boss with these numbers:

7-Xylosyltaxol Project

Delivery Timeline, 1.0 Kg Lots

Purity	Delivery
80 %	3 weeks
95 %	15 weeks
99.0 %	10 months

Laypeople looking at the above table might be asking, "How can it take five times longer to deliver 95 percent product than it does to make 80 percent material? That's only a difference of 15 percent. The 95 percent should take less than four weeks, not 15!"

Pharmaceutical executives all over the country are nodding their heads right about now, in full agreement with the lay assessment. (Not because they actually believe it, but because even executives are allowed to dream.) Unfortunately, it really will take four or five times as long—possibly longer—to deliver that 95 percent product. It requires exponentially more time because the difficulty is exponentially greater. The impurities that don't peel away in the first round of purification are more tenacious, structurally more similar to the target compound, so the separations scheme used to obtain the material must employ more creative or more time-consuming techniques. Obtaining the 99 percent product is almost an order of magnitude more difficult than the 95 percent material.

If you're still having trouble understanding, look at it this way: The 80 percent product contains *four times* more impurity than the 95 percent material. The 95 percent crystals contain five times as much impurity as the 99 percent drug-grade final product. You can be four or five times more lax in your purification of the 80 percent material and still achieve specifications; that ability to be careless allows you to go faster.

The estimate of ten months for the 99 percent product is probably a low-ball guess. The groundwork has to be laid for making accurate purity determinations. These assays become more difficult as the purity increases. Basically, it's hard to distinguish 98.8 % product from 99.3 %, but with an absolute threshold of 99.0 %, you need to be sure, and that level of certainty just plain takes time. Once you've figured out all the impurities and know their responses and peculiarities in the way they affect the assay, then the purity assays are no more complicated or time consuming than any other test. But a big part of R&D is getting the analytical figured out, and the purity assays are among the most difficult to work out.

Perfection

"The Image of the Supreme Soul As a Point of Light"
Copyright Tamasin Ramsey, 2009, CC-SA 3.0

That's a lot more detail than Vince Gilligan and his team went into, I'm sure. But I'm convinced they considered something akin to the 80/20 Rule when they repeatedly told us about Walter's 99 percent pure product. The thing is, as good as Walter's stuff is, *it's not perfect*.

Imagine your boss came in and asked for 99.7% pure 7-xylosyltaxol. He wants a kilogram. How long will that take? Years. Even after five years, you might not be absolutely sure of your purity. Walter's meth—let's say 99.2 percent pure—is still *years* away from being 99.7 or 99.8 percent pure. He'll never achieve 100.0 percent purity, of course. There is no such animal in the scientific universe. Perfection does not exist there. Except…

Except *Breaking Bad* is not limited to the scientific universe. When Hank hears the Universe telling him something, when he hears and acts on instructions to collect minerals or arrest bad guys or make love to his wife or buy her a bouquet of flowers, he's not hearing the scientific universe. He's hearing the perfection of a blue sky. I hear the blue sky in Lloyd Stone's 1934 poem "This Is My Song," set to Jean Sibelius' powerful hymn "Finlandia." You can find excellent renditions of the hymn on Youtube.

Walter might be able to achieve 99.7 percent purity after many years of relentless struggle. He'll never obtain the purity of a blue sky. Blue—real, honest-to-goodness, perfect blue—belongs only to the Universe. For Walter to think he can appropriate it to himself, to claim perfection, is laughable. Hank's blue corundum is

263

perfect. Blue sapphires are perfect. The blue sky is perfect. Walter's blue methamphetamine is a pretender's claim, a pretentious boast, a crude perversion.

Skyler Blue

"The Mother"
Anchise Picchi, 1989, PD
[The mother is wearing a deep blue dress.]

If Walter is not perfect and is not allowed to wear blue, how could Skyler possibly be allowed to vest herself in the color? By the beginning of Season Four she was collaborating with Walter in the meth business. Yet her very name invokes visions of blue sky, and she started the series wearing blue almost to the exclusion of any other color.

True enough. But Skyler had a special exemption, reflected in her physical-hormonal-parental state in Season One. We haven't seen her in a predominantly blue outfit since the last episodes of Season Two. We won't see her in flagrant blue again until certain important scenes in Season Five.

Just as Hank is allowed to wear the rust orange of the perfect New Mexico desert, Skyler was allowed to wear the deep blue of the perfect New Mexico sky. Hank listens to the Universe, but he's humble. He doesn't reach for blue. When he's in the presence of blue, as in the deep blue elevator at the downtown federal building where he works, he bows his head. He trembles. He falls apart. But he's allowed to wear rust-orange, the humble color of the perfect rust-colored earth, because he listens to the Universe.

Skyler was allowed to wear blue because as an expectant mother, ready to give birth at any moment, she was definitely tuned into the Universe. That green face mask in Episode 2.01, the emblem of her desire for illicit sex (as in the back seat of Walter's car in the school parking lot at the end of Season One) or the illicit whatevers that Walter was throwing at her, was the first sign that her personality was changing. A third of the way into the second season she gave up blue entirely. It was only toward the end of the season, when concern for her children outweighed every other matter in her conscious mind, that she briefly returned to the purity of blue. By the second half of Season Three she was firmly into the gimme-gimme-gimme state of mind reflected in her all-green wardrobe. During Season Four she's been mostly the Woman On A Mission, coming up with all manner of schemes and pushing forward with them over others' objections, so she has been wearing black—the color of determined mission. She wore black in her battles with Bogdan Wolynetz and Ted Beneke. Both men lost. Bogdan was cheated out of hundreds of thousands of dollars for his car wash, and Ted ended up in the hospital with a life-threatening spinal injury. But the Woman In Black got her way both times. No longer the mother, Skyler White has become the schemer.

Whether we wish to acknowledge it or not, a kind of perfection exists in the state of motherhood. There is an uncommon and profound beauty in the image of a mother and child that is simply found nowhere else in human society or art. Skyler and her blue blouses and dresses in Season One fit perfectly with her position as an expectant mother. Well, maybe she didn't fit in so very well at the Schwartz's all-beige birthday party! (Episode 1.05)

"How pure can pure be?"

"Madonna of the Streets"
Roberto Ferruzzi, 1897

Roberto Ferruzzi was a little-known Italian artist in the late 19th century. He scraped by as he could, painting portraits and landscapes. Sometime in the 1890s he saw an 11-year-old girl, Angelina Cian, carrying her baby brother, a little boy named

Giovanni. Something about the tableau struck him as magical. He asked the girl to pose for him, and she consented. The painting he created became one of the most celebrated and reproduced artistic creations of the turn of the century. Ferruzzi's intention extended no further than the depiction of a sister carrying her baby brother. But the truth that he captured in his painting was not that of a sibling relationship, nor even of mere motherhood. Perhaps if he had not vested the girl in blue he could have exercised artistic prerogative over his painting. Maybe if he had made the girl's facial expression different in some way he could have prevented the enormous wave of unintended religious sentiment generated by his masterpiece. We will never know, because the painting was instantly recognized as a depiction of the Virgin Mary carrying the Christ Child. The painting has come to be known as "Madonna of the Streets."

I have read a dozen tellings of the story of this painting, each one a little different. We may never know the title Ferruzzi gave his painting. We cannot know the truth he saw in this perfect work of his hand.

One thing we can know with absolute certainty, though: The little girl Roberto Ferruzzi found walking the streets of Venice was most emphatically allowed to wear blue.

Krönung des neuen Königs

Napoleon Bonaparte crowning himself Emperor
Detail from "The Coronation of Napoleon"
Jacques-Louis David, 1807

"I won."

The statement was simple, but more than that, it was definitive. To say "I won" is to claim that the contest is over, that the one who has struggled ceaselessly without rest can now go on to enjoy the fruits of victory, the sweet reward of one who was tested and found equal to every task.

We know an entire season remains, but we find ourselves wondering just what obstacles stand in the way of any venture Heisenberg might wish to take on. Gustavo decimated the Cartel. The only remaining member of the Salamanca family now exists as a million bit of human flesh splattered across the walls of a private room in Casa Tranquila. Gus himself lost the 'face off', and not even the Pollos Hermanos mourn him. The entire Southwest, all the way to Phoenix, anyway, is open to any distribution system Heisenberg wants to put into place, and no one on either side of the border can stop him.

Isn't the story over?

How Much Green Does a Man Need?

Lev Tolstoy
Mikhail Nesterov, 1907

Breaking Bad is touted as the study of the transformation of Mr. Chips into Scarface. But I've always thought of the show as an exploration of Lev Tolstoy's question to his fictional character Pakhom from the famous 1886 short story, "How Much Land Does a Man Need?" It was clear to me at some point in Season Three that this show would not end until Vince Gilligan and Company answered the question in precisely the same way Tolstoy did 130 years ago. The story ends when Heisenberg is stuffed into a coffin and lowered into six feet of earth, for in the end that is all the land a man needs.

The series is a character study. Heisenberg is presented with a problem and he makes a choice about the route he will follow to solve it. Usually that choice involves some tradeoff around a moral or ethical principle, or his willingness to sacrifice others or their needs for his immediate urges or long-term schemes.

The show specifically focuses on methamphetamine. It could never have been about robbing banks or stealing works of art. Banks are insured, people who collect artwork are fabulously rich. There is no stake, nothing for anyone to lose. If Walter White became just another Jesse James his story would not have had impact because it would have lacked the devastating effects on ordinary people. Heisenberg is causing everyone around him emotional suffering, spiritual turmoil, mental anguish, physical injury, and painful death. He knows all this, and every moment of that horror and terror is part of the ground he must tread and the landscape he must create as he measures out the kingdom he desires.

"Midas' Daughter Turned to Gold"
Walter Crane, 1893

We know the story is not over. In some ways, the tale has only just begun. What will Heisenberg do, now that he essentially has carte blanche? Certainly he is the newly-crowned King Midas, and those who have read the ancient Greek story appreciate the full ramifications of a Midas touch. The king cannot eat because every bit of food he touches turns to gold. He cannot ever again touch a loved one, because if he does, that person becomes an immobilized golden statue. He dies a wretched, lonely man, because the lust for wealth has transformed him into a person who places no value on the real, most enduring riches of human life. Instead, he forces everything in his sphere of influence to conform itself to his intemperate will.

We have many more indications that the show is not over. From our immersion in the color symbolism of the series we know that Walter still wants something. He was wearing deep green in the last seconds of the final episode of Season Four, indicating some kind of unfulfilled desire.

The program can be understood as an allegory of virtue (or the descent from virtue), and we can see Heisenberg's present state as not yet having achieved the full depravity required of him in this morality play. But that is the overview. The devil is in the details, as they say, and there are plenty of important loose ends that need to be tied off before the series is artistically complete. One of the most interesting of these details is a recurring instance of Chekhov's Gun. That little vial of ricin keeps coming up, in almost every episode now, but it has yet to be used in an irreversible way. Devices like this are called Chekhov's Gun. Here is the original statement of this dramatic principle, in the master storyteller's own words (translated from Russian):

> If you say in the first chapter that there is a rifle hanging on the wall, in the second or third chapter it absolutely must go off. If it's not going to be fired, it shouldn't be hanging there.

Anton Chekhov
Iosef Braz, 1898

Chekhov's Gun is actually part of a broader principle called economy, but we don't have to go deep into literary theory to understand the basic idea. That vial of ricin is going to be used, and it will be a critical part of Heisenberg's endgame.

Again in overview mode, we know the complete story has not been told. The sin of Heisenberg is not drug manufacture and distribution *per se*. His sin is the destruction of human connections. We have seen a few important instances of this in early seasons, but the final season will deliver the complete definition of the man. The way he goes about giving over loved ones to the wolves and hyenas will show us who he really wished to become.

Mourning and Weeping in this Valley of Lilies

Lily of the Valley, Plant Parts
Franz Eugen Köhler, 1897

Walter could have used the ricin on Brock. He knew all about LD_{50} levels and body weight and how to calculate a lethal dose. He could have taken a fraction of the amount of ricin necessary to kill a child of Brock's weight, the kid would have lived, and Jesse would still have been brought back into the fold. There are at least two reasons this didn't happen.

First, from the standpoint of the penultimate act of a five-act play, the use of ricin would have unnecessarily complicated the story. As the Albuquerque police detectives noted when they interrogated Jesse, the FBI tends to take an active interest in any use of terrorist-related toxins such as ricin. I have no doubt Heisenberg could have dealt with the poking around this would have involved, but it would have required that he spend time addressing the issue, and that was a problem from a storytelling point of view. The penultimate act is a time to start bringing things together for the final showdown. It's generally not a good time to introduce problems of the kind that have already been addressed.

More importantly, lily of the valley was metaphorically perfect, especially in the greater symbolic context of the show. *Breaking Bad* is all about the contrast between artificial, self-created Heisenberg and the natural, Universe-created world of pure blue sky and rust-orange earth. Lily of the valley is a creature of that natural world. When we saw the potted plant from a distance in the final shot of Season Four, it was just a nice bit of greenery that someone had added to the Whites' back yard. It was an innocent, perfect part of the natural world, brought in to create a more inviting environment for anyone spending time with the Whites. It was only as the camera came close enough for us to read the words on the flower tab that we understood what the potted plant really was.

Walter has already arrogated blue to his persona, making it part of his signature product. He has transformed perfect, pure sky blue into a symbol of evil and death.

271

People in the *Breaking Bad* Universe are not allowed to wear blue, let alone twist the color into something as perverted as a substance whose only purpose is to turn people into slaves who rob and kill, strictly for the benefit of the one selling the drug. Seen in the harsh light of *Breaking Bad's* central theme, blue meth is the ultimate Fuck-You to the Universe.

The application of lily of the valley to the suffering and death of children was a propagation of the central theme. Lily of the valley is a thing of beauty, but it is to be appreciated on terms the Universe dictates. Walter appropriated that beauty to his own sick use, again twisting an exquisite and natural element into something ugly and wicked. He used beautiful perfection to force suffering on a person innocent and young.

I will confess that foreknowledge of this event was one of the facts that drove my analysis of Walter's motivations at the end of Season Three. I have been trying in this companion book to tailor my commentary to the events of a particular season, unlike my *Lost* companion, *LOST Humanity*, in which I consciously used several types of disorienting techniques to explain *Lost's* story as I understood it. *Breaking Bad* is a very different kind of story. One of the important themes is the slow conversion of Walter into Heisenberg. Just as I tried to honor *Lost's* nonlinearity by explaining it in an intentionally disorienting manner, I felt I had to do my best to honor Walter's moral journey by not injecting knowledge of future events into early decisions. But I had trouble framing my understanding of Walter's Season Three indifference toward children without subtle interference from my knowledge of this season's events. End of confession.

Ricin would have been not nearly as satisfying a poison from an artistic point of view. Vince Gilligan's team *consciously* chose Lily of the valley. It took them quite a while to figure it out—I'm willing to say that here, knowing full well that someone on the writing staff will read this.

How many of us would have thought of lily of the valley as a poison? Common poisons are arsenic, cyanide, strychnine, belladonna, botulinum, and hemlock. The writers must have looked at some or all of these, and lots of others, too. By Season Four they were conscious of the natural/artificial knife point they had created—that bit of philosophical, artistic intuition formed the basis for Hank's obsession with crystalline minerals. But it seems to me unlikely they would have lighted upon lily of the valley as the perfect poison without considerable wrestling with the idea and how it would fit into the larger symbolic topography of the show. They would have considered arsenic and cyanide, but these were too much like ricin, all of which required human intervention: someone had to purify the poison. Hemlock was out of the question thanks to that famous death in 399 B.C.

I imagine Vince Gilligan rising from his chair at some point in the protracted discussion, anxious to reach a decision so they could move on to the next bullet point on the season outline. "What are we really looking for here, people? What does the poison *need* to do?"

Someone—one of the junior writers—had put together a long list of potential poisons. Another person on the staff looked at the jumble of photos of all different sizes and resolutions.

"What's that?" she said, pointing to the photo of a green plant with white flowers. "It's beautiful."

The beauty was the key, I'm convinced. They brought the photo to Gilligan, or he saw it, momentarily flashed on their shared presentation screen. "Yeah, it's mildly poisonous," one of the writers would have said as Gilligan looked on, weighing options. At that point it would have taken just a few seconds. Someone or a few people were talking, but Gilligan was silent.

"That's the one," he said. "It's perfect."

Indeed.

Ricin was probably the original agent, at least in some of the writers' minds or in their fiercely defended arguments. Others were less enthusiastic. Gilligan would have been non-committal or in the skeptics' camp. "We can't just keep on kicking the ricin can down the road," one of them would have said. "This is the perfect time and place to use it." Enough of the team was skeptical or didn't like the idea that a larger discussion arose, precipitating a request to put together a list of poisons—or maybe the junior writer earned brownie points by doing it before anyone asked. Oh, I would have so much enjoyed being in the writers' room that day!

The end result was the ideal (natural, Universe-created) poison—but then Chekhov's vial of ricin got kicked down the road again, too—all the way to Season Five.

Ay, There's the

Hand Waving
Copyright Pearson Moore 2012

Why did Mendeleev have to use the symbol Rb for rubidium? Ruthenium is Ru, but no one uses it or cares about it. He could have just exchanged the symbols. I would have had an easier time making up chapter headings.

I could have inserted a real word in the chapter title. "DistuRbing Images" would have done the trick. I decided to go with "Ay, There's the Rb" to make a point about the purpose of this book, and also to say a bit about what this book is not. In the end, the discussion in this chapter will focus on the heart of our consideration of *Breaking Bad*.

If you think about the title of the chapter, glance at the image below it, and factor in the caption ("Hand Waving") you probably have some sense of the direction I will be going. "Hand waving" in the technical realm I inhabit can mean "building an argument on insufficient evidence" or "acting authoritatively without merit" and so on, but the meaning I intended to convey with the caption was "forcing adherence to theory after the fact." That is, it can be argued that I have created a theoretical framework for *Breaking Bad* that does not fit the conceptual or symbolic topography of the show. Where I lacked information or understanding, I "waved my hands": I filled the holes in the structure with stuff I made up or drew from my own experience. Sometimes, theory doesn't fit well, as with the conceit of using elements from the periodic table to fashion chapter titles.

All of that is true, but there is far more to our shared exploration of *Breaking Bad* than the generation of theories and attempts to force the elements of Vince Gilligan's artistic creation into the narrow confines of our limited understanding. For even though it is certainly true that my insight into the series is hampered by deficits in comprehension—and yours is, too—the very fact of our ignorance is in some respects useful, and may actually serve to magnify our appreciation of the bits and pieces we managed to apprehend.

In the end, our speculations and attempts to fit an artistic work into a conceptual framework are not only a matter of momentary diversion. As interesting and entertaining as our contemplation of *Breaking Bad* may be, the fact that we are doing it—that hundreds of thousands around the world are engaged in the process—indicates the value that might be found in bringing our voices to the discussion.

Expert

I am not an expert in anything, unless you count chromatography or purification process design and related sub-disciplines, in which I have somehow succeeded in convincing others that I know what I'm talking about (I can be very, very good at hand waving!). I have no training in any field remotely similar to film theory or literary analysis. When you read my interpretations of a scene or character, then, you are gleaning the uneducated musings of someone interested but not necessarily qualified to provide authoritative guidance on understanding or appreciation.

So why should you pay attention? Even though I have no formal training in analysis, I maintain professional interest in the written word. I have been employed as a technical scientific writer for more than three decades. I have created scientific style guides. In my leisure time, just for fun, I write novels. I am the son of a journalist, the grandson of a printer, the great grandson of a literary critic (it had to be in there somewhere!).

But the most important qualification by far is that you and I share a deep interest in *Breaking Bad*. My hope is that I bring to the table concerns and emphases and ways of looking at characters and events that resonate with your own enjoyment of the series.

Relevance

Does it matter?

I have presented ideas on themes, symbols, and motifs. But what if I'm wrong? What if a more erudite or better educated observer would offer insights and commentary more in keeping with the film and literary traditions to which *Breaking Bad* might be assigned by experts in the field?

First, I don't believe there is any such thing as 'being wrong' about the meaning of an artwork or portions of the work. Imagine you have invited Vince Gilligan to a party at your home. You ask him about *Breaking Bad* and he agrees to give you honest answers.

"What about the colors?" you ask.

"White means good, black means bad," Gilligan says.

"Really?"

"Yeah. And red means danger, yellow means caution, green means money. It was never more complicated than that."

"Wow. Say, have you seen Pearson Moore's book about—"

"Oh, yeah." Gilligan chuckles. "Boy, he messed everything up. Doesn't have a clue."

So, do you move on to your next guest, vowing to throw this book in the trash when the party is over?

I hope not. The fact is, even though Vince Gilligan was the creator and primary writer, he created the show for **us**. Your opinion of the show, what it means, how it relates to other productions, the way it highlights themes from your own reading or appreciation of movies is up to you to decide. My opinion of the series, my interpretation of motifs and symbols and images is every bit as relevant and 'correct' as Vince Gilligan's or yours.

Recall Roberto Ferruzzi's painting of Angelina Cian holding her baby brother Giovanni. He could insist all day that he painted a common girl in the streets of Venice. That was all he intended to do and 'girl carrying younger brother' constituted the full meaning—symbolic or otherwise—of the painting. In fact, he might say, you are completely wrong in assigning any meaning other than the one he intended. It doesn't matter what Ferruzzi thinks, though, whether he likes it or not. Millions of people around the world look at the painting and think "Oh, the Madonna and Child." Not only that: Master's theses have been written on the painting. Entire church communities have adopted the painting as depicting Mary and her Son. Learned authorities have weighed in on the subject. Ferruzzi has arrayed against him a formidable army of experts and authorities and devout religious who claim this painting clearly represents the Virgin Mary carrying the Christ child.

Think of the hundreds of thousands of visitors to the Georgia O'Keeffe museum in New Mexico, eager to see the 'vagina paintings'. Hundreds of learned experts in art history and painting theory agree: O'Keeffe was painting stylized images of the human vulva. It matters not a bit that O'Keeffe swore until her last breath that the paintings had nothing to do with human anatomy.

In the same way, Vince Gilligan can go on CNN right now and tell the world that Pearson Moore is completely wrong when he says blue in *Breaking Bad* represents the Universe. "It's just a pretty color," Gilligan tells Anderson Cooper. "Pearson Moore doesn't know what he's talking about." Even then, I will continue to insist that blue is *Breaking Bad*'s symbolic reference to the quiet karma of the unbending Universe.

But does it matter?

Lost Thought University Edition, copyright 2012

If our discussion has meaning for you and me, I'm satisfied that it 'matters'. You may seek more, and there's nothing wrong with that.

Two years ago, a bunch of *Lost* bloggers collaborated with a handful of university professors on a book called *Lost Thought*, a collection of essays on the television series. Since then, *Lost Thought* has been used in university courses on religion, film theory, theater, and literature. My own attempt to interpret *Lost*, *LOST Humanity*, has become required reading in several college courses. Evidently, then, even non-academics (like me!) can add to larger, ongoing discussions regarding the significance of a television program. I cannot know whether a similar outcome awaits *Breaking Blue*, but the potential exists.

The bottom line, for me, is that your opinion of the show matters as much or more than Vince Gilligan's, Bryan Cranston's, or Melissa Bernstein's. We didn't create the show, but it's ours to discuss and enjoy.

The Chewing Gum Wrapper

Sometimes our own limitations allow us to squeeze more meaning out of a work of art than we could if we possessed all the formal education available in the field. As Lex Luthor said back in 1978, "Some people can read *War and Peace* and come away thinking it's a simple adventure story. Others can read the ingredients on a chewing gum wrapper and unlock the secrets of the universe." ("Superman," 1978) Or as William Blake put it in 1803, in "Auguries of Innocence":

> To see a world in a grain of sand
> And a heaven in a wild flower,
> Hold infinity in the palm of your hand,
> And eternity in an hour.

We don't need advanced learning to appreciate the meaning of *Breaking Bad* or other great television series in our lives, in our understanding of human life. The low-level technician who entered the ingredients on the chewing gum wrapper had no more advanced training than anyone else. Any meaning we attach to the ingredients comes out of our own imagination, or understanding, or intuition, not from the technician. In *Breaking Bad*, Vince Gilligan and his stable of writers and several hundred actors, musicians, makeup artists, lighting engineers, and artists in two dozen other fields came together to communicate to us something they considered important and worthy of our time. They created a work far more complex than a chewing gum wrapper, more intricate than *War and Peace*. If we apply ourselves, we can recover from this show truly magnificent gems of human significance.

Authority

Imagine you are an executive at AMC. You've just given Vince Gilligan the green light to proceed with a full screenplay from the treatment he showed you for a series about a drug dealer.

"But," you tell him, "I need to be there with you, every minute."

Gilligan agrees. For the next six years you see every keystroke Vince Gilligan makes on his computer. You're there for every meeting in the writers' room. You know exactly when it was decided Walter would strangle Krazy-8. You heard the writers argue over the season finale five times. You kept accurate notes. You can tell anyone, to the minute, exactly when the smoke detector light made its appearance in the script for Episode 3.10. You can speak with authority regarding the order of events, the way writers and directors and cameramen and actors related with each other. You know how much sugar each makeup artist took in his coffee and which of the gals in lighting was never satisfied with a shot.

The one thing you cannot address authoritatively is the *meaning* of *Breaking Bad*. You can wager an opinion. You can even write a book, like this one. But you cannot speak with authority. As we've already discussed, there's an important sense in which Vince Gilligan himself cannot spell out the meaning of *Breaking Bad*. He can tell us what his *intention* was in a particular scene or over the course of the series. He cannot assign the final significance of his creation. If no one on the writing staff can offer the definitive interpretation of the show, I certainly cannot. And neither can you.

The Fifth and Final Period

The format for the final period (Season Five) is slightly different from the previous four. As with the Koyaanisqatsi series of fourth period, I offer brief observations on disparate themes in a couple of chapters. I face the issue of German motifs in Chapter In ("Inhalt Deutsch," meaning 'German Content'), taking on one of the more uncomfortable aspects of *Breaking Bad*. Finally, the last four chapters are devoted to a thematic and color-driven analysis of the final episodes of the series. This will be a no-holds-barred discussion of important themes and motifs using the full color palette of the *Breaking Bad* Universe. This is going to be a bumpy, manic, thrilling ride. Hold onto your pork pie hats!

Redirect

Di Sr epute

The Keystone Cops
Mack Sennett, Keystone Film Company, circa 1918

"What about a magnet?"

But Jesse's words went unheeded. Heisenberg, who had only hours before crowned himself Emperor ("I won"), had a plan to deliver an 'incendiary device' to the Albuquerque Police Department's evidence room. Why should an emperor listen to an uneducated failure of a street dealer? Did Jesse have a master's degree in chemistry? Did Jesse understand science? Was it Jesse who killed the biggest drug kingpin in the Southwestern United States?

Heisenberg didn't have to listen to anyone. After all, as he told Skyler in Episode 4.06, "I *am* the danger. I am the one who knocks."

The scene in which Jesse, Heisenberg, and Mike discussed the destruction of Gustavo's laptop computer was full of delicious, ironic juxtapositions and inversions. The most magical of these, and the one I believe gave the most complete sense of the meaning of Heisenberg, was Jesse's intuitive sense that magnets provided a logical resolution to the problem of remote destruction of a device. The kid who a year ago pointed to a volumetric flask and called it a 'beaker', who regularly exclaimed, "Yeah, science!" as if by doing so would gain insight into its mechanisms, was now using science and reason to solve a real-world problem—and showing more sense in the matter than his boss, the Emperor.

Everyone held Jesse in disrepute, thought him incapable, but he showed intuition and elegance of thought in the opening moments of Season Five. On the other hand, the man who was at the top of his game had ample reason to doubt his ability to maintain that lofty position. His blindness to shortcomings and dearth of intuition prevented him from seeing the instability inherent in his ascension to empire. Heisenberg's downfall was foreshadowed in the entire sequence. The first two episodes of the fifth season constituted a summons to redirect our thoughts, to call others into disrepute for reasons we have not yet considered.

Freedom

The 52nd birthday breakfast at Denny's was sad in so many ways. Only Skyler could form the bacon into the numerals representing his age. But here he was, without Skyler, the wedding band missing from his finger, having to perform the task on his own. Skyler was deceased, estranged, divorced, in jail, or running his drug empire for all we knew. There was no way to tell from the flashforward where she was, or her condition, but we knew she was not with Walter. The implication was not a mere physical rupture, but a spiritual sunderance.

Breakfast was the most frequently depicted meal in *Breaking Bad*, invariably taking place around the dining room table in the White residence. It was the meal that introduced us to Walter and his family in the first minutes of the pilot episode. Breakfast was *Breaking Bad*'s symbol of stability, continuity, and family. The ultimate sign of familial unity was Walter's birthday breakfast, with the bacon ritual figuring as the central motif. That Skyler was not present to perform her sacred duty changed the entire tenor of the family relationship. Regardless of what has happened to Skyler, we are to understand that some kind of chasm now existed between Heisenberg and his wife.

"Free is good," the waitress said, "even if I was like rich. Free is always good."

She was trying to talk Heisenberg into a free breakfast meal. The lonely man relented, but we saw again an unhappy, disconcerting irony. The waitress, in her poverty, had far more freedom than Heisenberg in all his great wealth. He was traveling incognito, a slave to disguises. We think of money as granting freedom and happiness, but this broken man had not a single emotional attribute we would associate with a condition of spiritual or financial liberation.

The defining character of Heisenberg's freedom was his ability to impose his presence, to force others to tremble at his magnificence, and that capability shone bright in his name. "Say my name," he will command Declan in Episode 5.07. His name, of course, was no longer Walter White at that point. But even in the first episode of the final season, we knew something was wrong when the great and celebrated Heisenberg was skulking around using his wife's maiden name. Heisenberg meant fear for everyone else, but it signified freedom for Walter. The flashforward scene showed us that every aspect of freedom Heisenberg had ever enjoyed was now stripped away, leaving a broken, sad, enslaved man.

'Live Free or Die': So the proud and free residents of New Hampshire have been saying since the Revolutionary War. Heisenberg was not free. He was barely living.

Keystone DEA

"I had him out to my house," George Merkert said. "Fourth of July, cooked out in the backyard…Fring brought sea bass…The whole night we were laughing, telling stories, drinking wine…and he's somebody else completely. Right in front of me. Right under my nose."

The DEA and the Albuquerque police at times seemed to have agreed on a competition aimed at determining which squad was more incompetent. The DEA under ASAC Merkert coddled up to Gustavo. The APD was no better. When Heisenberg magnetized the evidence room the police came running out, doing their best Keystone Cops impression.

But by the end of the episode it was the police officers who had the last laugh when they uncovered Gustavo's secret Cayman accounts, complete with access codes. And now, thanks to Hank's 'outstanding police work', Fring's drug empire was unraveling and even executives in far-off Germany were electrocuting themselves in rest rooms. Hank was the disgraced DEA agent who lost his cool over a common street dealer, now he was the hero who knew all along that Gustavo Fring was a meth kingpin.

Things were starting to look good for the police on all fronts, but we're privy to information they lacked. The George Merkert/Gustavo Fring 'under-my-nose' relationship, as bad as it was, could not compare to the Hank Schrader/Walter White 'under-my-nose' *family* relationship. Hank sees through a glass, darkly, but soon enough he will see face to face. Some of you recognize the reference. 'Through a glass, darkly' is a legitimate way of looking at the orange-tinted desert confrontation scene, too, when Mike pulled out his gun, intending to shoot Walter dead. I'll return to this idea of child versus adult and vague reflection versus clear vision in a later chapter.

Inversion and Perfection

We saw plenty of upside down relationships in the first two episodes. The unbridled absurdity and irony of Skyler White scaring the crap out of Ted Beneke was at first amusing, but then sad. With his head painfully wired in place so as to prevent movement, his physical rigidity was not as confining as the stifling danger he felt in seeing Skyler. Only a few months before she had been the one scared of not landing a job. Now Ted was scared—not for his job, but for his life. This woman could scratch up $622,000 like it was nothing. She had armies of nasty guys to break into people's homes to do her dirty work for her—guys who no doubt were handy with knives and guns. For Ted, Skyler was the danger. She was the one who knocked.

But there's danger in service of a rational goal, and there's danger that is its own being and end. I believe that was the final inversion we saw in the first two episodes. Walter always had an objective to strive for. Everything was on the line. But then he told Skyler, "I won." It was a turning point.

Consider Heisenberg's actions when he had scooped the last bits of his bomb-making debris into plastic bags. He was wearing the 'I want something' dark green shirt in which he had succeeded in killing Gustavo. But with Fring dead and the evidence in trash bags, he went into the bedroom and changed from a dark green shirt to a dark blue shirt—and poured himself a double shot of brandy. The blue shirt and the brandy were one and the same action: a celebration of victory. The inversion was from the green condition of wanting something to the blue condition of *owning* it. He was there. He had arrived. He could sit back now and enjoy the majestic feel of his empire.

The fact that Albuquerque police had managed to get their hands on an incriminating computer hardly even fazed him. It was just another annoying little problem that would succumb to the dictates of his superior intellect. When the deed was done, he had no fears.

Mike: You left the truck behind.
Heisenberg: So what.
Mike: So what? So what if they find prints? What if they trace it back to the wrecking yard?
Heisenberg: They won't. There's no prints. I made sure of that. There's no paperwork on the truck, the magnet, or the batteries. Untraceable salvage, all of it. I made sure of that, too.
Mike: You got all the answers. So you tell me, Answer Man, did all that even work just now?
Heisenberg: Yes, it worked.
Mike: I'm supposed to take that on faith? Yeah? Why? How do we know?
Heisenberg: Because I say so.

Mike posed the question that became the verbal form of Heisenberg's celebratory blue shirt: "I'm supposed to take that on faith?"

Notice Heisenberg didn't repeat his mantra, "Respect the chemistry." He didn't say, "No, Mike, don't accept what I say on faith. Let's look at the logical progression of this"—and then go on to prove that the magnet worked. This wasn't about science anymore, if it ever had been. This was about a man so sure of himself that even science itself had to bow to his perfect will. Everyone had to accept his word *on faith*. Science was turned on its head.

I've seen the series three times now. I believe this post-magnet conversation in Mike's getaway car was the supreme moment of Heisenberg's dark career. Yet this brief twinkling of perfection was built upon a constant flow of short-sighted mistakes and gaping imperfections. That they had to go to such lengths over the computer was due to his unaccountable amnesia regarding the surveillance that had been a thorn in his side every day in the superlab. If someone who wished to kill me had recorded my every move for several hours every day I don't think I would have forgotten about the recordings. When the time came to devise a solution to the problem he created, it was Jesse, not Heisenberg, whose lucid, logical mind provided the answer.

The first two episodes of Season Five proved the only perfection Heisenberg possessed was an unfailing demonstration of hubris, an unfounded but unshakable conviction that he was the Answer Man, to whom all must genuflect. We can almost hear him utter the words: Look on my works, ye mighty, and despair. We will hear those words again before the end of the season.

We began the second episode in a language we're not accustomed to hearing on *Breaking Bad*. This was not our first experience of German culture during the series, but surely Herr Schuler's glassy-eyed enjoyment of his final meal on earth, including 'Franch' and 'Cajun Kick-Ass' dips, has to rank as one of the most unforgettable. We will see a lot of German names and themes in the final season. I'm going to address these themes in the next chapter.

Chapter In

In halt
49
Deutsch

German Imperial Coat of Arms, 1848
Copyright Trajan 117, 2010, CC 1.0 Generic

"So, how many Krauts we got?" Hank asked.

"Well, enough to invade Poland." Gomez responded.

The exchange was good for a laugh or two, but then the following scene, in which the executives of Madrigal Elektromotoren GmbH were depicted in menacing black suits and the DEA agents opposing them were shown in soft browns, made me uneasy. By the time we got to Episode 5.08, Heisenberg was actively collaborating with a gang of Neo-Nazis led by Jack Welker. But more unsettling for me were the conceptual bridges—either real or imagined—that connected those who invaded Poland in 1939 with the black-clad German executives in 2013. The biggest question on my mind after uncertainties around Heisenberg's demise was simple: Was *Breaking Bad* conflating Germans and Nazis?

My conclusion is that there was no conflation. There was an *appearance* of accidental or attempted equation of Germans and Nazis, but as I will discuss here, I believe this somewhat clumsy failing of the show relates to an aborted plotline and the real need to push the envelope to the outer limits of good taste. The primary plotline, after all, was about the conversion of a good-natured man into the darkest of demons.

In this chapter I intend to explore the supporting rationale for my conclusion that the show maintained clear distinction between Germans and Nazis. I will also share some personal thoughts on my conception of the difference between German identity and the perverse movement that coalesced around Adolf Hitler in the late 1920s and led to his ascension to the Chancellorship in 1933. The discussion at times will be heavy. Some readers may wish to skip over this chapter.

Chilean Mystery

Josef Mengele, Nazi SS Officer
Unknown photographer, Argentine ID Photo, 1956

I sought the origin of the surname Fring in archives of Latino, Spanish, Mexican, Chilean, and Argentine tax registries, church records, and census data. Nada. The very substantial Florida Cancer Registry, listing over 12,540 Latino surnames, did not include Fring, Fringa, Fringo, or any other derivative of the name. On the other hand, I found the relatively common German surname *Frings* listed in several sources. Gustav, of course, is among the most Teutonic of German names, leading to the conclusion that the chief antagonist of Seasons Three and Four, Gustavo Fring, had substantial German ancestry and that his real name was Gustav Frings.

In Episode 4.08 we learned Gustavo emigrated from Chile to Mexico in 1986 and began living in the United States on an entry visa in 1989. Hank's team investigated Gustavo but found not a single record of his life prior to the three years he spent in Mexico. He was a Chilean national with nebulous ties to the Augusto Pinochet government of the 1980s. Gustavo, attempting to explain the identification difficulties, said Pinochet was "guilty of a great many sins: first and foremost were his human rights abuses, but it was also notoriously unreliable about keeping records."

'Los sudacas', as Don Hector would call them, were 'sucia, sucia gente' in the minds of the Salamanca family, and one of the qualities that made Chileans 'dirty' certainly had to be their willingness to associate with the likes of Josef Mengele and other monsters and demons from the ranks of Nazi Germany.

One of the most notorious Nazi hangouts in South America was Villa Baviera in the Maule Region of Chile. Founded in 1961 by Paul Schäfer [no relation to musician Paul Shaffer], a child molester and former Nazi from West Germany, Villa Baviera was a large compound surrounded by a barbed wire fence. Its occupants were secretive, but Simon Wiesenthal and others presented strong evidence that Josef Mengele and other high-ranking Nazi war criminals had at least visited and may actually have taken up residence at the compound.

This Nazi refuge was a veritable fortress. Guarded by machine guns, automatic rifles, rocket launchers, and even a battle-ready tank, locals knew to steer clear of the facility. General Pinochet used this ultra-secure location as a torture center. Many of the Germans were enthusiastic participants in Pinochet's terror. During investigations in 1991, the Chilean government found that "a certain number of people apprehended by the DINA were really taken to Colonia Dignidad [Villa Baviera], held prisoner there and…some of them were subjected to torture…besides DINA agents, some of the residents there were involved in these actions."

We don't know that Gustavo Fring's backstory connects with Villa Baviera. The tantalizing evidence of a dark connection to the Pinochet regime was offered, but it was never developed. Gustavo was young enough that he could have been an early resident in Villa Baviera. He could even have been born there. If so, he would have been tortured and sexually abused. According to a confession published in April 2006 in *El Mercurio*, Paul Schäfer sexually abused children at the compound over a period of more than 40 years. On 24 May 2006, Schäfer was convicted of sexually abusing 25 children. He was three years into a 20-year sentence when he died in prison in 2010.

This is one of the most horrific stories ever to come out of Chile. If I were writing a television series like *Breaking Bad* and I had the opportunity to fit in something like this, I would certainly try to do so. Whether or not the *Breaking Bad* team intended to connect Gustavo to the infamous Chilean torture compound, the intimation of dark Pinochet connections suffices for well-founded speculation that whatever Gustavo was doing in Chile, it probably wasn't good. The possibility that Gustavo was tortured and abused as a child could have put a radically different spin on the series, and would have acted as a strong counterbalance to any thought of conflating German and Nazi motifs. In the pantheon of evil, sexual abuse of children must outweigh in gravitas any vague ideological or genealogical connection to Nazis or Nazism.

The Chilean Pinochet backstory indicates the likelihood that the original intention was to connect the Nazi motif with associated evils, such as child abuse. With a limited commitment to just five seasons (or six, depending on how you look at the gargantuan 13-month interlude between Episodes 5.08 and 5.09), my guess is that the writers decided they had to eliminate extraneous plot threads to concentrate on the outcome for major characters.

Some Internet bloggers have speculated that the German/Nazi conflation was getting too heated for network executives and they told the writers to knock it off. However, this speculation posits even more assumptions than my line of reasoning, including the possibility that there was real or accidental conflation, a notion which I reject based on close study, such as the Fring analysis above.

Uncertainty

Werner Heisenberg circa 1933
Bundesarchiv, 2008, CC-SA 3.0 Germany

Until Season Five, the Heisenberg motif was tied to a single idea in my mind: a non-scientific understanding of the Heisenberg Uncertainty Principle. I was pretty sure someone like Vince Gilligan, untrained in physical science, would not invoke heavily technical tropes to deliver dramatic symbolism. His bachelor's degree is in film production, not theoretical physics. He never had to work out the wavefunction for the hydrogen atom, as I did. If anyone tells you they actually *enjoyed* second semester physical chemistry, leave immediately: You know that person has deep psychological problems!

It didn't cross my mind that Heisenberg's Nazi connections might come up in conversation, but they surely did in the final season, when many fans contacted me via email. There was even a telephone conversation, and I found myself scurrying to old textbooks and Internet resources to obtain the answers. I knew Werner Heisenberg had worked for the Nazis. I vaguely recalled he had connections to nuclear energy research in the 1930s. What I discovered was that he was no mere participant in Nazi atomic research—he was one of the leaders of the program, and possibly spearheaded the effort. The German Nuclear Energy Project was initiated in 1939, with Heisenberg and a handful of top scientists at the helm. By the summer of 1942, Heisenberg was brought before Albert Speer to report on the possibility of developing a nuclear weapon. He worked tirelessly for the next two years, laying the theoretical groundwork for the construction of a nuclear bomb, but his resources were thin and he produced little in the way of practical knowledge. Beginning in 1943 he repeatedly had to move himself and his family as the Allies were beginning to bomb the larger German cities.

Images and Meaning

Adolf Hitler at a Nazi Rally, 1928
Presse Illustrationen Hoffmann, Berlin, 1928
Seized by United States Army, 1945
Declared U.S. Property, 1951, now in PD

You might think images of Adolf Hitler, ubiquitous as they are, would be easy to put into a book. In fact, obtaining rights to reprint a photograph of the Nazi dictator is among the most challenging enterprises faced by an essayist like me. I don't like paying for images (I've had to pay up to $900 for a single image; a collection of 34 images last year cost me $3550), so I use public domain artwork and photographs whenever I can. Most images of Hitler are owned by the German government, and they're quite fussy about rights. Understandably so. Misunderstanding of German connections to Nazism can cause grave harm to innocent people. It is the potential for that type of misunderstanding that prompts this somewhat lengthy essay.

Two of my uncles fought in Europe in World War II. Another was a Navy Seabee in the Pacific Theater from 1943 to 1945. First-hand accounts of Nazi atrocities were part of my upbringing from earliest childhood. My grandfather's hometown of Trondheim, Norway, was seized by the Nazis. A distant relative of mine became a saboteur and apparently succeeded in killing a few of the Nazi parasites. Both sides of my family bore a robust hatred of Nazis, and the strong rationale for fighting them was imparted to me as a sacred trust.

It was in this context, then, that I was handed the assignment of entertaining a German expert in herbal medicine in 1996. I was on the 'lunch team' that month, which usually encompassed only those scientists interviewing for positions in our department, but it happened that I was working on a couple of the herbals that the German consultant was helping us with, so I landed the job of taking him out to lunch. One of my superiors, 'Bob', didn't normally volunteer for the time-consuming task of entertaining visitors, but he asked to join us, and the director agreed.

It was a mistake.

'Bob' was possibly the most disagreeable person in our department. The fireworks began as soon as the consultant got comfortable in the passenger seat of my car, with Bob in back.

"My family's from Poland," Bob said.

"It's a pretty country," the German consultant said. "I've skied there."

"The Germans invaded Poland."

If Bob had extended family in Poland in 1939, I can't imagine things went very well for them. He didn't bring that up, but he did launch into an extended harangue for the next several minutes on all things German. I did as best I could to jump in and redirect the conversation, but Bob wouldn't have it. After a few minutes of unrestrained attacks, the German had enough.

"The Americans killed my father in 1945," he said.

Those words sufficed to close Bob's mouth for a few seconds.

The only thing that saved the lunch was the fact that I pulled into a parking space at the restaurant and physically separated the consultant from my intemperate co-worker. The next hour was a horrendous series of verbal jousts in which I verbally batted down anything Bob had to say and tried to make the outing tolerable for my company's guest. Needless to say, I dropped Bob back at the lab and took the consultant directly to the airport. It was the last time he spoke with anyone at our company.

I reported the incident immediately, of course. But evidence indicates no one at the company ever spoke with Bob about his unacceptable behavior. What could they have said? If, as seems likely, his family suffered or died as a result of the invasion of Poland in 1939, how could anyone tell him not to harbor ill will toward Germans?

Before my co-worker's relentless attacks began, I had found the German fellow affable, engaging, and pleasant to talk with on any number of subjects. He often visited Colorado (where I was working at the time) for skiing and enjoyed hiking with his family back in Germany. He was no racist. He was no Nazi. He was just a well-read, interesting man who had acquired expertise in herbal medicine. He was a baby when the Nazis invaded Poland, barely a kindergartener when Allied bombers turned his country into a barren moonscape. If he was 'guilty' of anything it was an excess of patience in putting up with the impolite, downright abusive taunts of my co-worker.

Why dredge up the horrors of war in a companion book to a bit of entertainment created by a cable television network? The problem I am addressing is the potential for the numerous German motifs of *Breaking Bad* to engender unintended disrespect toward Germans. My task in this book, as I see it, is to explain my understanding of *Breaking Bad*'s themes and images, and their meaning. My personal experience indicates innocent people can be harmed by even well-intentioned statements. My Internet research reveals fans and critics are discussing the subject of the dozens of German reference in the series. In light of these facts, I've taken on the challenge of addressing this issue in a matter-of-fact way, drawing on my own experience and feelings on the matter.

German Motifs in *Breaking Bad*

"Decadence"
[*Breaking Bad*, pre-Great War, Jugend-style]
Ernst Stern, circa 1910

I've put together in the following table just a few of the German names and references from the five seasons of *Breaking Bad*.

Methamphetamine is a German invention? Ja, natürlich. Back in the 1970s when I was earning my bachelor's degree in chemistry, a year of German language training was part of the degree requirements. Virtually every major advance in chemistry during the 19th century and into the 1920s was made by German chemists. So, German became my fourth language (after English, Spanish, and Russian).

I point out the historical fact of Germany's primacy in physical sciences because I believe Herr Schuler's final meal scene was intended as a playful manipulation of the common stereotype of Germans as highly educated, technically oriented, efficient, precise, and somewhat rigid. This stereotype dates to the 19th century, during the period of Germany's scientific and technical ascendancy.

The stereotype is largely positive, and even Germans picked up on appreciation for sturdy technical know-how.

German Motifs in *Breaking Bad*		
Names	Identification	Meaning
Walter	Protagonist	'Army ruler'
Heisenberg	Protagonist alter ego	German physicist
Skyler **Lambert**	Skyler's maiden name	'Bright Land'
Hank **Schrader**	Walter's brother-in-law	'Tailor', Cutter, Shoemaker
Marie Schrader	Skyler's sister	'Bitter' 'Tailor'
Schraderbräu	Hank's home brew	Schrader's Brew
Löwenbräu	Hank sang ad lyrics	'Lion's Brew'
Elliott **Schwartz**	Walter's former partner	'Black'
Gretchen Schwartz	Walter's former lover	'Pearl' 'Black'
Gustavo Fring	**Gustav Frings**	'Staff of God' 'Severe'
Mike **Ehrmantraut**	Gustavo's hitman	'Man of honor'
Gale **Boetticher**	Gale Böttcher	'Cooper', Barrel maker
Ted **Beneke**	Skyler's lover	'Brave bear'
George **Merkert**	Hank's boss	'Watchman', Lookout
Dan **Wachsberger**	Mike's lawyer	Wax mountain dweller
Ricky **Hitler**	Jesse's name for Todd	Nazi dictator
Madrigal Elektromotoren GmbH		German conglomerate
Themes and Images		
Methamphetamine	German invention, 1887 Given to German soldiers, 1937-1945	
Heisenberg	Protagonist alter ego	German physicist
Kafkaesque	Franz Kafka Ep. 3.09	
Nazi Germany	Ep. 4.12	
Nazi zombies	Ep. 4.02	
Neo-Nazis	Jack's gang Ep. 5.08-16	
Swastikas	Ep. 2.07, 5.08-5.16	
Major Tom	German pop song by Peter Schilling Gale sang this song. Ep. 4.04	
Gustav Gun	Immense WWII German rail-mounted cannon Ep. 1.07	
German speakers	Madrigal employees, corporate lawyer, Ep. 5.02 Lydia Rodarte-Quayle, Ep. 5.04	

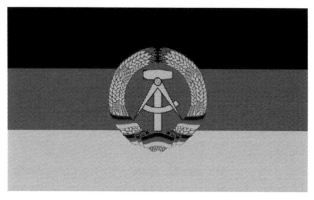

Flag of East Germany, 1959-1990
Deutsche Demokratische Republik

The focal point of the East German flag, for instance, was the Soviet-influenced coat of arms, at the center of which was a compass, intended to symbolize intellectual prowess. The hammer was taken from the Soviet hammer and sickle, and the wheat surrounding the central icons represented agricultural abundance.

The idea, then, is that technical information is highly valued by Germans, and especially by Germans in positions of authority. With that in mind, let's look at the German food scientist's report to Herr Schuler as he is trying each of the sauces in turn:

> Honey mustard. This is our sweeter formulation, for the American Midwest. While we've upped its Brix number by 14 percent, we in fact use 2.2 percent less honey…Smoky Mesquite BBQ with three percent more smoke flavor…

Anyone who has had to report to senior executives knows that you do not lace your presentation with technical details, and you *never* include any discussion of percentages. This scene took place in Germany, though, and the repeated articulation of meaningless numbers was part of the sharp contrast between ultra-technical, fully-engaged food scientists and the zoned-out, in-another-world appearance of the Madrigal executive. This scene would have been not nearly as funny in France or Scotland or Bolivia. The reason it works so well in Germany, and that it had many of us not only amused but laughing out loud, is that we expected the German executive to be intensely interested in the numbers. "Three percent." the Vizepräsident frowned. "Please explain. I was told we would achieve 3.017 percent. Why are we below projection by 0.017 percent?"

The surprised/disappointed/shocked expression on the German food scientist's face was there in part because Herr Schuler should not only have been engaged, he should have wanted and actually needed to hear every last technical detail. Because, you know, he was German, and that's the way Germans think, nicht wahr?

I believe we see something of this juxtaposition of expectation and practice in Hank's late Season Five behavior as well, but I want to postpone that discussion until the final essays of this book.

Bad Guys Wear Black

I believe it is the pre-World War II stereotypes of Germans that *Breaking Bad* imaged throughout the series, and especially in Season Five. The depiction of Madrigal executives dressed uniformly in black, I submit, was intended as a symbolic depiction of humorless, angst-ridden, German über-severity. The first image that popped into my mind was the black leotard-clad Dieter (Mike Myers) from his parody of pop German culture, *Sprockets*, which became an ongoing skit from 1989 to 1997 on *Saturday Night Live*. Putting the Madrigal executives in black suits resonated with my understanding that black, as used in *Breaking Bad*, means *mission* and does not necessarily include any symbolic reference to dark deeds.

The Madrigal team, then, was on a mission to redeem the integrity of its name, going back to the current CEO's grandfather, who founded the company. That was my reading of the black suits, though I thought there was probably also an intention to make a vague visual reference to the brand of über-seriousness parodied in the Mike Myers sketches.

But many bloggers have already seized upon the black-clad Germans as an indication of nefarious deeds. I suppose we might forgive their natural conclusion that the black suits meant Madrigal was intent on industrial domination, no matter the cost, and they actually conspired with U.S.-based Neo-Nazis. Lydia, of course, was a Madrigal employee, and she was actively in collusion with Jack and his gang, so she was the link that could be rationalized to prove corporate-wide guilt.

The connections are weak, but they're strong enough to serve as the foundation for some ill-directed character assassination. "All Germans are really Nazis at heart," some might decide based on the Lydia connection and the decision to create symbolic contrast in Episode 5.02 by vesting the Madrigal staff in serious, evil-looking black suits.

I cannot prove there was no intention to depict Madrigal as immersed in a conspiracy led by a Neo-Nazi gang. The best I can do is to offer my thoughts on the matter, and to discuss what I believe to have been Vince Gilligan's rationale for leaving the Madrigal plot thread hanging.

The *Jugendstil* Revolution

Alphonse Mucha was a Czech painter in the vanguard of a revolutionary movement that swept Europe beginning in the late 1880s. Called Art nouveau in most of Europe, the artistic style still goes by the name *Jugendstil* in Germany.

The central premise of Jugendstil was that art is everything, and everything should be art. Jugendstil was to unite high-minded visionary art with practical, everyday devices. The idea was not new. Archeologists have found intricately-carved atlatls (spear throwing devices) dated to 17,000 B.C. But Jugendstil was an intentional, prophylactic philosophical response to two earlier movements.

"Spring"
Alphonse Mucha, 1900

Academic art of the mid-19th century was said to be artificial and too removed from nature. The Art nouveau reaction was to incorporate stylized, natural lines, like the 'whiplash', visible in the woman's hair and in the curved flowers of her bouquet in Mucha's painting above.

Artistic fashions come and go, though, and I find reading these debates both pointless and boring. The real revolution, in my mind, was the insistence of Jugendstil proponents that life could no longer be mundane. It could not become ugly, ungainly, or sterile, which was the direction the Industrial Revolution seemed to be headed. Jugendstil was a direct assault on mass-produced ugliness. Even something as utilitarian as a bicycle had to be beautiful.

Cycles Perfecta Ad
Alphonse Mucha, circa 1900
[Notice the whiplashed hair engulfing the painting]

The leading voice for the revolutionary, in-your-face Jugendstil was *Jugend* (Youth) magazine, which began publication with the intention of spearheading the Art nouveau movement in Germany. It is the pervasive influence of this single magazine that transformed European thought on the meaning of Art nouveau, and the reason that the German brand of Art nouveau will forever be known as Jugendstil.

Jugend magazine cover, 1896, No. 22

The fact that Jugendstil was intended to transform all of society was a breathtaking concept. The movement achieved its objectives, so that even today, well-accepted social practices such as naturism (nudism), 'back to nature' groups, and certain political and artistic movements still very much alive and stirring controversy have their origin in the revolution this magazine sparked.

All revolutions have as their final objective the conversion of hearts and minds, and the free-thinking, natural orientation of Jugendstil eventually came face to face with the narrow-thinking, evil orientation of a later movement.

"Die Kugelläuferin"
Fidus (Hugo Reinhold Höppener)
Jugend magazine, 1896 No. 13, page 296
[Notice the woman's long, flowing whiplashed hair]

This illustration by Fidus, one of the most frequent contributors to *Jugend*, features a nude woman riding a speckled ball. Called "Die Kugelläuferin" (The Ball Runner), I understand the woman to represent beauty and the ball to symbolize the world. Thus, 'beauty makes the world go around', which was the central tenet of Jugendstil.

The story of Fidus illustrates perfectly the philosophical clash that occurred in Germany after World War I. Fidus and artists like him were willing to push society to its limits in order to achieve the positive transformation they sought. Hugo Höppener earned the nickname 'Fidus' (which also became his professional artistic name) when in 1886 he was arrested for public nudity. He served a jail term in place of his friend, Karl Wilhelm Diefenbach, best known as the founder of the German Naturism (nudism) movement, an element of German culture that came to be widely practiced in the 1920s and 1930s and is still popular today.

"Du sollst nicht töten"
[Thou Shalt Not Kill]
Karl Wilhelm Diefenbach, 1903

Hugo Höppener's new nickname was no small matter for him, indicated by the proud signature 'Fidus' (Faithful) on every one of his drawings and illustrations after 1886. That Diefenbach's followers called Hugo 'Faithful' was a badge of honor, meaning that Fidus was faithful to the many philosophical dispositions that accompanied Jugendstil: naturism, nudism, pacifism, vegetarianism (depicted as a supreme virtue in Diefenbach's famous "Du sollst nicht töten" (above)), and—the most dangerous one—socialism.

Fidus lived in Diefenbach's commune in Munich for a while but in 1892 he started his own commune near Berlin. He was, for that time, a radical free thinker, even contributing to the gay magazine *Der Eigene.*

If the illustration appeared in *Jugend* between 1895 and 1915 and it depicted nude women or men, chances are it was created by Fidus. He became the most famed illustrator in Germany. His work was praised, studied, and the best magazines sought his drawings.

Fidus' interests turned to German folklore and mythology, and he brought the same enthusiasm and no-holds-barred nudity to his depictions of Teutonic knights and damsels in distress and other mainstays of German mythology.

Mythological Illustration
Fidus, *Jugend* magazine, 1897 No. 18

While Fidus was busy creating art in his commune in 1920s Berlin, an untalented landscape painter, Adolf Hitler, was sitting in a prison cell, dreaming of a Germany cleansed of anyone other than pure-blooded Aryans. The economic hardships and political and social turmoil following Germany's defeat in World War I provided fertile ground for Hitler's hate-filled agenda.

Among Hitler's Brownshirts were some of the best propagandists the world has ever known. One of their first targets in the hearts and minds campaign was any institution related to German traditions, history, folklore, and mythology. The socialist-leaning nudism movement was co-opted by the Nazis, who encouraged nudism but enjoined socialists and Jews from attending nudist resorts. Virtually all Protestant churches, and many Catholic parishes, were infiltrated, to the point that swastikas began appearing on altars and the interior walls of Christian churches throughout the country. Few stood up to the Nazis. A celebrated example of defiance was the Lutheran Saint, Dietrich Bonhoeffer.

Fidus by then stood out as one of the foremost artistic interpreters of German mythological tradition, a prime target of the Nazis' campaign of indoctrinating the public in the great virtues of Nazi thought. They were either unaware of or willing to overlook his socialist inclinations. He was accepted into the Nazi Party in 1932. The Nazis were never enthusiastic about his participation or membership, though. In 1937 the Nazis seized his artistic works and banned their sale.

Suppressed by the Nazis, his work was virtually forgotten until the late 1960s. But societies change, old values are rediscovered; many of Fidus' illustrations are on permanent display at the Museum Für Moderne Kunst in Berlin. His 1905 work 'Am Grossen Gitter', depicting the *culturally*-based separation of society into rich and poor, is considered prescient.

Notice it's the rich kids who are naked (symbolically poor), while the excluded boy wears a primitive skirt. The rich children look at the boy with contempt, not because he's poor (he has clothing, they do not), but because he's primitive and therefore beneath them since they are perfect little Aryan children.

"Am Grossen Gitter"
Fidus, *Jugend*, 1905

It was the open-mindedness toward people of different cultural backgrounds, ethnicities, and races that got Fidus and Jugendstil artists like him into trouble with the Nazi authorities. Jugendstil wanted to free society from the shackles of artificiality, cultural triumphalism, and racism. The movement aligned itself with concurrent artistic expressions, such as Orientalism, which actually began developing a few years before, in the 1860s. But by the early 20th century both movements were feeding off each other both artistically and philosophically.

"Two Nautch Girls," Edwin Lord Weeks, circa 1915

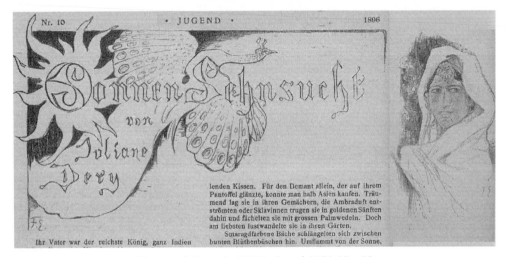

"Sonnen Sehnsuche," F.E., *Jugend*, 1896, No. 10

Orientalist paintings such as Edwin Lord Weeks' "Two Nautch Girls" and stories like "Sonnen Sehnsuche" ("Sun's Longing"; a story about an Indian Princess in the 10th issue of *Jugend* in 1896) would have been unthinkable to the Nazis because they depicted the beauty of brown-skinned women. Indians, North Africans, Gypsies, and Black people could not be beautiful because they were not German.

Any artistic work that portrayed racial equality, such as Nicaise de Keyser's "The Orient and the Occident" was confiscated, banned, or destroyed.

"The Orient and the Occident"
Nicaise de Keyser, 1854

I do not argue that the natural German inclination is toward free-thinking socialist nudism. But the opposite extreme, narrow-minded fascist racism, was far less mainstream in German thought. There were German racists before World War II. Anti-Semitism was a recurring theme throughout Germany for hundreds of years. But the bulk of evidence from every conceivable cultural and social quarter during the 19th and early 20th centuries indicates Germans were for the most part well educated and were cultivating diverse interests outside their own traditions. The phenomenal success

303

of *Jugend* and magazines like it, I believe, must be taken as proof of German humanity, cultural sophistication, and open-mindedness.

I visited München in 2006. I used my limited German only once (English works just fine in Deutschland), during a breakfast in which two fellows from the eastern part of the country joined me at my table. We spent the morning conversing in a mish-mash of German, Russian, and English, which was much fun. I enjoyed every minute of the week I spent at the analytical chemistry conference, speaking with German chemists and conference presenters and ordinary people. The only less-than-positive experience occurred on the train back to the airport. For some reason the fellow seated next to me thought I was Canadian, not American. I was not surprised; I've been adopting Canadian mannerisms for more than a decade. I don't know if he assumed I didn't speak German or if he just wanted to be exceptionally rude, but he turned to his girlfriend and said, "I hate Canadians. They're dirty people." He pulled the words from Don Hector's mouth. I guess Gus Fring and I have something in common!

The Loose Thread

With so much potential for misinterpretation of German themes in *Breaking Bad*, why did Vince Gilligan leave the Madrigal thread still hanging at the end of the series? Why didn't he depict the Madrigal CEO as leading the SWAT team to arrest or kill Walter White, who had profaned German integrity by adopting the name of a celebrated German scientist as his personal icon of mayhem and murder? Why was there no attempt to restore justice and honor?

We are going to see a far more heartbreaking instance of justice ignored late in the season. Having seen the entire series and the perfectly-honed artistic message this masterpiece delivered, I believe Vince Gilligan *could not* depict Madrigal as innocent, even though it almost certainly was. If he had taken pains to show innocence, or had depicted the rooting out of a few bad apples, he would have harmed the artistic integrity of *Breaking Bad*. It may seem there is an unnecessarily twisted form of logic at play here, but I believe the artistic rationale will become clear after viewing and analyzing the two most important installments in the *Breaking Bad* saga: Episodes 5.13 and 5.14. The former, "To'hajiilee," is my favorite episode in the series. The latter, "Ozymandias," is considered by many the finest 60 minutes of television so far this decade.

Chapter Sn

Spider

En Sn are

Mexican Redknee Tarantula (*Brachypelma auratum*)
George Chernilevsky, 2009, PD

We're scared of them, even when we know they're not poisonous. When we see them, we recoil. Our hearts race, a jolt of fright passes through us. A split second passes, and the fear withdraws. We stand immobile, transfixed at the sight of this silent, uninvited, fear-inducing visitor in our home.

Spiders are fearsome creatures. We know they're insect hunters, but they are equal-opportunity distributors of venom, whether deadly or not. Our fear derives not so much from their potential for harm but more from their ability to stalk us silently, surreptitiously, using stealth and cunning to achieve mastery over a much larger and more powerful foe. We fear them, but perhaps more than that we despise them—for being able to outwit us, surprise us, and invade us where we live. They are unpleasant reminders that we are never safe, even when we construct great mansions and store up immense wealth. No one is safe from spiders—not even an Emperor.

Two Blue

"'Spider ensnare'. What the hell is that supposed to mean? Didn't Pearson learn anything in English class? You can't say 'spider ensnare'. You can say 'The spider ensnared' or 'Someone ensnared the spider'. But you can't say 'Spider ensnare'."

I could defend myself by claiming use of imperative: "Spider ensnare!" That's perfectly good English, but I did not intend to indicate anyone is commanding a spider to do anything. My intention is to push two ideas into close proximity with each other. I didn't want to convey the idea that 14-year-old Drew Sharp had captured or ensnared a spider, but neither did I wish to narrow the construct to a discussion of the spider's ensnarement of any of the characters. The spider is obviously another instance of Chekhov's Gun, but it is a symbolic gun, and it's a mighty powerful weapon. The spider represents Todd, but the image carries far more weight than that. Within a few episodes anyone paying attention to the television screen will recognize the character to come under attack by the symbolic spider, but even that potent relationship will not fully define the allegorical situation focused on arachnid symbolism.

In the same way, I've headed this section 'Two Blue' not 'Two Blues'. Much is occurring in the backyard scene in which Skyler slowly descends into the brightly lit swimming pool. (Episode 5.04) Skyler is being pulled by two opposing forces. One of those forces is stronger than the other. Both of them are blue.

Skyler's slow, silent dip in the pool is a stand-out moment in the series. Everything came to a head for Skyler in Episode 5.04. For the first time in *years* we see her wearing her signature blue, but not a blue blouse. This is one of those scenes the writers and directors and actors and even the lighting technicians haggled over and worked on for many weeks because everything had to flow seamlessly and apparently effortlessly into the calm waters of the Whites' backyard pool. The casual observer isn't aware of it, but every element of the scene was chosen so as to focus our complete attention on the glowing blue water.

In Episode 5.04 Skyler has come to her senses. She is alert enough to recognize that Walter is not defined by a relationship to her. He is not defined by any of the qualities or concerns or relationships that one normally considers to characterize a human being.

The bedroom scenes in Season Five are so horrible, so disgusting they become exquisite. It's almost impossible to watch Skyler, curled up away from Walter's side of the bed, being degraded—I don't abuse the language if I say she is being *raped*—by the touch of Walter's hand on her shoulder. Walter's touch is a violation far more disgusting, inhuman, and repulsive than anything I've ever witnessed in cinema, and I've seen some nasty stuff. But I've never seen pornography as degrading as the bedroom scenes of the fifth season. The scenes are not pornographic, of course, but they stir sentiments and evoke ideas far more potent than anything a pornographer can elicit.

Walter is not a human being anymore. Not as we understand the concept of woman and man. This truth is conveyed neither with images nor with dialog, but with six musical notes in Episode 5.06. That brief, almost throw-away scene was the turning point for me in Walter's evolution. I realized there was nothing left to redeem because nothing human remained.

Skyler reached her epiphany regarding Walter's true nature before I did. Her emotional epiphany occurred in her office at the car wash, when Marie told her she couldn't smoke. (Episode 5.03) She didn't shout 'SHUT UP' into Marie's face four dozen times because she hated her sister. She hated her life. She hated the fact that there was no way out. But worse than that, she realized in a way she could not put into words that something was terribly wrong. It wasn't just that she was helpless. The whole world was out of kilter somehow.

The significance of the 'SHUT UP' scene was that something fundamental to her relationship with the world had changed in a frightening and irreversible way. Her psyche understood something she could not yet process in a conscious, logical manner, so the truth of it came out as incessant screaming. The screams were her subconscious self trying to warn her and the world around her that something unthinkably evil was going on.

The trigger for the 'SHUT UP' outburst was Walter's unilateral decision to move back into the house at the beginning of Episode 5.03. He didn't ask Skyler's permission, he just did it. She couldn't stop him. But what was worse, her input no longer carried any significance. She wasn't a person anymore, not to Walter. She was more akin to a wrench Walter might use in the laboratory to work on a piece of equipment. Skyler was just an object or a tool. She was one of the things Walter manipulated—twisted this way or that—to get things the way he needed them.

Skyler didn't understand, but we did, that the man violating her bedroom was not named Walter. He called himself Heisenberg, and that's as good a name as any. Demon or Lucifer or Eichmann would probably have fit better, though. Heisenberg was the entity that by sheer force of will wrapped itself in the most potent symbol of unopposable power: Blue.

Skyler had been under the sway of Blue once before in her life, and in fact, she still was. She wore blue underwear, as we know. Walter wore white underwear, symbolizing pride. Skyler wore blue, symbolizing her submission to and representation of the silent, ineffable power of the Universe. Heisenberg, he of blue meth and dark navy blue shirts, was trying to wrest Skyler from the clutches of the Universe.

Heisenberg's claim on Blue was false. The Universe, like the calm waters of the Whites' backyard pool, simply IS. There is no DO THIS or DO THAT frenetic movement about the Universe in *Breaking Bad*. It just IS. It's there, like the constant blue sky, like the gentle undulations of the glowing blue swimming pool. Heisenberg, on the other hand, had to be moving, scheming, synthesizing, destroying and killing all the time because it was harder to swat down a moving object. The consumption and frantic use of enormous quantities of energy were the only ways Heisenberg could survive, because the very structure of the Universe was folding in on top of him. That's the full significance of the spider.

The blue was calming, attractive, compelling. It called to Skyler. Superficially we could say she was scheming, no less than Heisenberg. She had a plan in place to show Hank and Marie that she had become mentally unstable. If Heisenberg could violate her house, her bedroom, and her body, if he could invade the family like a creeping black poisonous fluid, she could find a way to protect her children. Pretending that she was drowning herself would serve as proof of her mental instability, and that would force Hank and Marie to take her children into their protective care.

But there was no pretending in this scene.

"Is that what your pool stunt was about? Trying to protect my children from me?"

"Not just you. There's blood on my hands, too."

That is, she was guilty because her actions had caused Ted to end up in the hospital with a serious, nearly life-threatening spinal injury. So we could attribute her immersion in the pool to a psychological need to cleanse herself. The water could be understood as a kind of baptismal font.

We could certainly interpret the scene that way. Skyler was asking the Universe to forgive her, or she simply sought cleansing in its perfect waters. I understand the imagery, but I don't believe that was the full intention. The intention is not in the direction of Christian imagery, of that I am certain. Vince Gilligan was brought up Roman Catholic, but *Breaking Bad* has shied away from religious symbolism—though I think some interesting Christian imagery may have worked its way into the final episodes—and into Episode 5.06.

Baptism is a violent process, as anyone who has studied the theology of it can tell you. The swimming pool, on the other hand, was intentionally depicted as calm, warm, and inviting. Skyler was definitely not experiencing baptism, and I don't believe she sought cleansing, even though that was the gist of her conversation in response to Walter's inquiry about the significance of her 'pool stunt'.

The blue pool was nothing more than a reference to the Universe. It's always there, waiting. By calmly walking into the pool Skyler was not making amends or seeking redemption or asking to be cleansed of evils or sins, she was simply returning to the Mother's arms, or the Father's care, or the Universe's embrace. She wore blue underwear, symbolizing her grounding in the power of the Universe. The writers could have depicted her stripping down to bra and panties but they decided instead to put her in a sky-blue skirt and a pure white blouse. The skirt represented her fundamental grounding in the Universe, the blouse represented her attraction toward Heisenberg (who wore blue on the outside but white on the inside), and the pool was the supreme, irresistible power of the Universe. The blue skirt indicated she was governed by the Universe, the white blouse said she was being pulled toward Heisenberg, but her decision to immerse herself in the pool was the definitive statement that Heisenberg no longer exercised spiritual control over her life.

Skyler placed herself in the hands of the Universe.

Time

"An Allegory of Time Unveiling Truth"
Jean-François de Troy, 1733

From the timeless waters of the blue pool we were brought to the time-conscious bedside of Heisenberg, who has chosen to measure his life by the ticking of an expensive chronograph. But this was no ordinary timepiece. Its features were disorienting because it was marking time in a way we're not used to experiencing.

The watch was analog, so it had hour and minute hands, but it also had a separate face to mark off seconds. In fact, the mechanism is properly called a chronograph because it measured time in different ways, and accorded different levels of importance to each timekeeping function.

One of my most prized possessions is a gift I received from my son just a few weeks ago. It was a complete surprise, being that it was a 'Hobbit' gift. My son gave me a very expensive official U. S. Marine Corps chronograph on October 18, 2013. I call it a 'Hobbit' gift because October 18 was the day he graduated from Marine Corps boot camp and earned the Eagle, Globe and Anchor (the Marine Corps insignia). He became a Marine that day, and he decided to honor me with a gift full of symbolic and emotional meaning. It's the kind of thing to make a father cry, because the significance is so much greater than anything contained within the shining quartz and steel and the inner mechanism. He valued some unspoken aspect of my 20-year effort to raise a son. He placed value on a crucial aspect of our relationship, but he did it in such a way as to indicate his graduation from boyhood into manhood. He turned a day I thought would be for him into one that had meaning and purpose for everyone in his family. I was not the only one to receive memorable gifts—he caught his mother and his girlfriend off guard, too. Probably we should not have been surprised. He was not only graduating into manhood, but into an organization that has meaning and value and purpose not just for him and his new brothers, but for an entire country. He was constantly aware of that truth, and he showed it in his generosity.

The chronograph was a gift from Jesse. There must be significance in that fact, but we need to understand the Jesse-Heisenberg connection in terms of the only close-up view we are going to have of the gift. There is much more to the watch than Jesse's appreciation of Heisenberg's tutelage and fatherly care.

I don't believe the decision to display the small seconds face of the chronograph was accidental. I'm guessing that 99 percent of us are used to seeing a second hand approach the 12 on an analog watch, not the 60-second position. The disorientation didn't stop with the watch face, though. The fast ticking of the watch created its own uncomfortable tension.

"I bought it for myself," Heisenberg said in Episode 5.05. The surface-level reason for what seemed like a lie was that he didn't want Hank to ask who gave him the watch. The easier dishonesty was to deflect the inquiry entirely. But his words could also be understood as a personal investiture in the timepiece, and that makes sense from a symbolic point of view. The 60-second face and the three-ticks-per-second tempo both pointed to a kind of mad, frantic dash toward High Noon. Walter chose to accept the hyper-fast ticker as the sign post of his life. It wasn't really a gift from Jesse. It was more like a reminder from the Universe, but the Universe, as we see in the unmoved blue sky and the calm blue pool, is timeless, unhurried, always waiting. The rushing madness of the wristwatch is the antithesis of patience and permanence.

The watch symbolizes the always-moving, unsettled, undisciplined life Heisenberg has chosen for himself. He said "I bought it for myself" because in a sense he did. He chose to floor the accelerator, close his eyes, and see what would happen. (Episode 3.09) His life is an accident waiting to explode into a horrible splattered mess because he bought it for himself. At some point, the watch reminds us, Heisenberg is going to drive his speeding car right into the unmoved brick wall that is the Universe.

Kato's Spider

If you were around in the 1960s you saw Van Williams, probably on a weekly basis. 'Van who?' you ask? He was the lead character in one of the most popular television series of the time. I would guess fewer than one in five thousand could tell you who he was or what he did, but probably 99 out of a hundred know the actor who played his television sidekick: Bruce Lee.

Usually the fellow stuck playing second fiddle receives no acclaim or recognition, and something like that happened in Season Five of *Breaking Bad*. We think of Heisenberg as being Batman to Jesse's Robin, but in fact, by the time we reach Episode Five of the final season, Heisenberg is already off his game—he's become the Green Hornet to Jesse's Kato. Heisenberg has the big guns, but Jesse has all the moves and all the brains.

It was Jesse who figured out how to destroy the evidence on Gustavo's impounded laptop computer. It was Jesse in Episode 5.05 who put together the foolproof plan to steal a thousand gallons of methylamine from a train without anyone finding out about it.

The Green Hornet, 1966 Publicity Still, PD

"You guys thought of everything," Todd said to Heisenberg in his golly-gee voice. Actually, Heisenberg thought of nothing, but he accepted Todd's worshipful praise anyway. Perhaps if Heisenberg *had* thought of everything, or even one little thing, they might have had a contingency in place for the unexpected appearance of a teenage boy on a motorcycle.

Todd was the boy next door. He had the clean-scrubbed, all-American face that said innocence and charm. Don't think Matt Damon's Jason Bourne, think Ron Howard's Opie Taylor.

The Andy Griffith Show
Andy Griffith with Ron Howard as Opie Taylor
CBC Television, 1961 Publicity Still, PD

Todd wasn't like Jesse, caught up in the dangerous business of synthesizing and selling illicit drugs. He worked for a pest control company. He was just an ordinary, completely innocent guy helping out a couple of people who needed a third pair of hands on a project, wasn't he? He certainly wasn't like Heisenberg, the embodiment of evil. In fact, he had a big heart. Isn't that why he warned Heisenberg about the nanny cam in the house they had just tented? (Episode 5.03)

If Skyler's epiphany occurred when Heisenberg's evil-slimed hand touched her shoulder in bed, Jesse's took place at the moment an innocent child was slain for three men's greed. Heisenberg pulled out all the stops in Episode 5.07, all but falling to his knees to beg Jesse to stay, but the death of Drew Sharp was the point of no return. Children had always been sacred to Jesse, off-limits to any of Heisenberg's schemes. Now that a child was dead, Jesse would leave and never come back. He even gave up his share of the methylamine money. It was dirty money, after all.

Jesse wasn't clean. He remained pink, which we might consider a symbol of innocence, but we might also think of the color as half-white; Jesse was poisoned by pride but not quite to the extent that Heisenberg was.

Probably few of us were surprised by Jesse's decision to pull out. He was emotionally and spiritually attached to children and could not abide the thought of harming them. Jesse was not the one who surprised. Heisenberg remained true to character.

The person who caught us off guard, coming out of the shadows as if from between floorboards, crawling on our skin before we even knew he was there, was Todd. Fresh-scrubbed Todd, the innocent boy, should have been devastated by the death of a child at his own hands. Instead, he just shrugged it off. "Shit happens, huh?"

The death of an innocent boy was just a minor inconvenience during the 'mission'. He had more emotional attachment to the spider in the jar than to a human life he had casually wasted. This was a new level of evil, a villainy so depraved it lacked any connection to humanity.

So there's the spider. The innocent newbie playing third fiddle turns out to be the most menacing figure in Heisenberg's world. The meth emperor is losing his touch, the brains of the operation has decided to quit, and now the new guy, the one who seems innocent, incapable, and innocuous, is the one who has the most venomous sting. There's a new Kato in town, boys, and this one's more powerful than Heisenberg and Jesse put together.

Song of Songs

"I'm in the empire business," Heisenberg told Jesse over a glass of brandy. The standard visual symbol of the emperor is purple robes, but Heisenberg was not that kind of emperor. He wore a rich royal *blue* shirt during the 'empire' speech.

"Is a meth empire really something to be proud of?" Jesse asked.

Damn straight. And this Emperor wore the color that indicated his dominion over everything. Even his signature product was blue.

"Christus et Ecclesia"
Brother Thomas, Eberbach Monastery, circa 1175 A.D.

If there was any question regarding Heisenberg's symbolic extension of his middle finger toward the powers of the Universe, that question was answered 18 minutes into Episode 5.06. Jesse saw the news report about Drew Sharp's disappearance. Walter consoled him in his usual fashion: In *a year or a year and a half* they would have plenty of time for soul searching. They would just buckle down until then because, you know, that's what normal, well-adjusted, non-psychopathic people do. They put their emotions and ethics and morals on hold for a year or a few years or for the rest of their lives or whatever. Because there's methylamine to turn into methamphetamine to turn into gold, and what's more important, anyway? An ordinary human life or extraordinary, unimaginable wealth? It was such a ludicrous statement, this 'Let's put our soul searching on hold for a year and a half' business. But Jesse was probably too upset even to know what Heisenberg was saying.

Jesse didn't understand what happened next—not unless he was in the practice of attending church on a regular basis. I wish I could have shared in his ignorance. Heisenberg didn't whistle very well. The notes were a little off. But it was close enough for me to figure it out.

Christians tend to look at the Hebrew Bible as a kind of precursor to what they consider the real meat and potatoes, which is the Christian Scriptures and the story of the birth, life, death, and resurrection of Jesus of Nazareth. For those of us who believe, Jesus is not just teacher and prophet, but fully the Son of God. When we look at the Hebrew Bible, then, we more often than not refer to it as the 'Old Testament' and we like to see the history and stories and figures of speech contained in its pages as a kind of allegory for the life of Jesus, and therefore as a voluminous explanation of our relationship to God.

The Hebrew book called the 'Song of Songs', or sometimes the 'Song of Solomon', is superficially a back-and-forth poem between two lovers, but the allegorical Christian understanding is that the man in the poem represents Jesus and the woman represents the Christian church. One of the figures of speech used in the poem is 'Lily of the Valley', found at Chapter Two, Verse One: "I am a Rose of Sharon, a lily of the valley." Christians don't take the poem at face value. Both 'Rose of Sharon' and 'Lily of the Valley' are understood to refer to Jesus the Christ, the Son of God.

About 1870, a musician by the name of William Charles Fry set 'Lily of the Valley' to music, creating one of the most beloved Christian hymns. This was the hymn Heisenberg whistled after he told Jesse how upset he was about Drew Sharp's death.

If Heisenberg had merely been whistling 'Row, row, row your boat' or some other generic cheery tune we might have been sickened enough, but he deliberately chose as his happy-time melody a song referencing his poisoning of a little boy, the child that Jesse cared about most. But going from bad to worse to unthinkable, this little ditty was a hymn of praise to the Christian God.

The only cinematic parallel I can think of that comes close to this level of blasphemy is the so-called 'crucifix scene' from the 1973 film 'The Exorcist', which was really blasphemy and sacrilege all rolled into one. I call it the 'crucifix scene' because there's really no other way to describe it without using language and images that many people would consider too repugnant for print. If you've seen the movie—even if you saw it 40 years ago—you will never forget the crucifix scene, so you know what I'm talking about. If you haven't seen the film, I will advise that it is strong stuff, and often difficult to watch. Don't say I didn't warn you!

Regan (Linda Blair's character in 'The Exorcist') was possessed by the Devil. Father Merrin had every hope of saving the girl because it was a simple matter of expelling the demon. Well, not so simple, but the girl's salvation didn't depend on any decision she had to make. Heisenberg has not been possessed by demons. He has decided, all by himself, to *become* a demon. Mike and Jesse left him; murderers and scoundrels they may have been, but they couldn't stand one more minute of Heisenberg's evil presence. The only people in this world who could tolerate him were Nazis like Todd.

With the whistled notes of 'Lily of the Valley' I lost the ability to imagine Heisenberg's redemption. I think that was probably the writers' intention in placing this hymn where they did. They knew it would be the final straw for a lot of people. Others will find their point of no return in Episode 5.08. Maybe most people were done with Walter way back in Episode 2.12 (Jane's death). But by the end of Episode 5.08, I have to believe at least nine of ten viewers will not care what happens to Walter White—as long as whatever it is involves his gruesome death. And the rest of us will probably just want him to disappear.

"The Lily of the Valley"
William Fry, circa 1870, printed 1904, PD

Chapter Sb

Αχιλλεύς ἀντίμονος

(Achilles, Never Alone)

"Achilles Triumphant"
Franz Matsch, 1892

If you are novelist, playwright, or film director, you felt your breath taken away during Episode 5.13. The rough edges melted into smoothness, every character arc found completion, and the entire weight of six years of story fit perfectly into the tense silence of calm sky and patient earth. If you are, like me, connected to the world of cinema and television only by means of the flat screen in your living room, the experience was almost surreal in the way it evoked emotion and recognition of events from seasons long past. Like "Two Cathedrals" (*The West Wing*, Episode 2.22; Season Two finale), "The City on the Edge of Forever" (*Star Trek* TOS, Episode 1.28), and "Made in America" (*The Sopranos*, Episode 6.21; series finale), "To'hajiilee," the 13th episode of the final season was a flawless creation of storytelling depth and cinematic brilliance.

This episode completed the grand, torturous circle we began riding—rollercoaster fashion—six years ago. We returned to the series origin, where Walter and Jesse had their first cook. It is amid the quiet stones and the constant sky that untamed men from uncivilized places arrived to discover their character, test their mettle, and assert their authentic selves. Every player in tonight's showdown sought and proved his true identity, as calm sky and patient earth demand.

The strange perfection of this episode is found in the deliberate and opposing assertions of ten angry and fearful men. All of the questions have been answered. The story is incomplete only because it is tragedy. Mr. Chips became Scarface—Walter became Heisenberg; we await only the knowledge of the manner in which calm sky and patient earth will repay Heisenberg for hubris, greed, and inhumanity. "To'hajiilee" was a rare gem and solid proof of *Breaking Bad*'s standing as drama that will endure the ages.

Perfect Circle

In the pilot episode Walter began a video confession but then thought better of it. He pointed his gun at the approaching sirens, at himself, and finally at the ground. Killing a police officer, committing suicide, or accidentally discharging the pistol while he figured out the safety mechanism were equally valid outcomes in his frazzled, confused state. In Episode 5.13 he was not confused. He calmly surrendered his weapon and took slow, deliberate steps to comply precisely with Hank's commands. He knew exactly what he had to do.

More importantly, and in striking contrast with his confusion in the pilot episode, he knew who he was. In the first few minutes of the series he could no longer call himself Walter White (though he attempted to do so in the video confession) because he was becoming Heisenberg. That soul-wrenching transition, and not the approaching emergency vehicles, was the nexus of his Season One confusion. On this afternoon in the bright New Mexico sun he was calm and dignified, no longer in a green shell half-covering his white underwear, he was vested in a white shell half-covering his blue shirt. He had long ago assumed the name Heisenberg but now he understood and accepted his final identity as fallen lord. Ozymandias is an appropriate name, and it is the one Vince Gilligan applied in the following episode.

The story of high school teacher become drug lord become fallen king ended where it began and closed Walter White's story arc. His character arc would be complete if he lacked connections to others, but his links to major characters were intentionally made richer and stronger than those of possibly any other lead character in modern television; simply demonstrating his fall is insufficient to the completion of the story. The details of Ozymandias' descent into oblivion constitute the core lesson of this morality play.

We have seen time and again in *Breaking Bad* that events of greatest moment occur far from the city, on rust soil under blue sky. Poetically, and within the rubrics of storytelling, the highest level of continuity and significance is achieved by plotting a circle that returns to its origin for the final battle and denouement. Sometimes the poetic terrain of the final conflict is conceptual. So, for instance, *Deneb* begins with the death of an innocent man and ends with the death of an innocent woman.

Partial view of "The Battle of Dabtik Havtan"
Illustration by Chris Rallis, commissioned for *Deneb*

Circularity in the story events of *Deneb* gains emotional and poetic impact through the development of conceptual opposition between those who were once allies and friends. The circle is conceptually closed by the simultaneous completion of story arcs in four inter-connected timelines spanning 45,000 years. The completion of the circle, then, is made possible by ironic role reversals among the major characters.

"To'hajiilee" concentrated on Hank, presenting a reversal of character that acted as the perfect culmination of his story. We often saw him working alone, or contrary to his superiors' wishes. In this pivotal episode Hank was not alone, and thus the title of this chapter. Sb: Ἀχιλλεὺς ἀντίμονος, transliterated Sb: Akhilleus antimonos, is the only chapter in this book not to incorporate the chemical element into a word. There is irony here, because Sb—Antimony—was an element the ancients could not separate from other metals. Tin, for instance, is a mixture of antimony and lead. To reinforce the ironic nature of the episode I kept Sb by itself, but the subtitle reflects the nature of antimony, the heroic truth of Achilles, and the foundational aspect of Hank's character: Achilles Never Alone.

Similar ironic events occurred in the other major character arcs. Jesse was always on the wrong side of the law. Less than two years ago he received a pummeling from Hank's fist; now he was collaborating with Hank to corner a bad guy. Heisenberg always managed to outsmart even the most diabolically intelligent opponent. Tonight his DEA brother-in-law and the business partner he lambasted for incompetence bested him with the fake photo of buried money. As Vince Gilligan said, "Heisenberg has been out-Heisenberged for the first time in history."

That role reversal is yet another indication of the completion of the circle, given form and substance and physical meaning by the coming together of forces at the geographic origin of the series, in the desert of the To'hajiilee Navajo Reservation.

To'hajiilee is a Navajo word meaning 'to bring up water from a natural well'. That we have never seen water in these desert scenes may or may not have been intentional on the part of writers and directors, but to my mind the unseen water works well as a physical sign of the Unseen, Unmoved Judge always present at these desert gatherings. I think it's the **human process** of bringing up water and the identity of the place as a **natural** well that carry the symbolic importance of To'hajiilee. In Vince Gilligan's karma-directed Universe we see *human processes* that either conform to or deviate from the *natural* expectations of the Universe. Karma—the expectation-become-result of the unseen, unmoved *Breaking Bad* judge—is always pronounced and delivered on orange desert under blue sky.

Walter's story arc is complete. Hank's story arc, too, has reached its natural endpoint, as I will discuss later in this essay. My guess is that most viewers, even if they didn't have full, conscious awareness of this idea came away from "To'hajiilee" feeling a kind of completeness, a satisfaction with events they may not have been able to pinpoint. I believe the completion of the circle was the necessary goal of tonight's episode.

A few commentators expressed the feeling that the episode fell short of perfection by not showing the end of the gun battle. I disagree with that assessment, for reasons I intend to outline in this essay. I have never been shy in pointing out the imperfections of *Breaking Bad*. I've made fun of the purple-hued excesses of Marie, where I think the writers have gone a bit overboard in their visual humor. In online essays I took a swipe at Hank's character early in Season Five, saying I was going to ask the commanding general of Fort Pendleton to invite Hank to Marine Corps basic training.

Achilles' Honor

"The Rage of Achilles"
Giovanni Battista Tiepolo, 1757

Achilles was never at his best when he was angry. Pallas Athena was always having to straighten him out during his tantrums, bringing him back to the path of honor and glory. Achilles is the finest representative of honor in the *Iliad*, and he is therefore the ideal of Greek manhood and civility. But honor was never a given for this greatest of Greek heroes. He constantly struggled with it, as he struggled with Agamemnon and with the Trojans. The *Iliad* can be understood as a discourse on the crucial concept of honor, with Achilles and Agamemnon acting as advocates for extreme interpretations of the idea. It seems to me the Achillean interpretation comes out ahead, but the conflict between warrior and king I don't think was meant to be winner-take-all. Agamemnon's position on honor had to be acknowledged, too, and understood as an important minority contributor to Greek thought. Agamemnon is certainly no hero, as his early death in the *Odyssey* indicates. But important aspects of his position influenced much of the *Iliad*. If the king's ideas on honor carried no weight they would have been dismissed and discussed no more, but they were not dismissed.

There are so many parallels between Hank and Achilles. Hank was never in his superiors' favor, he often went off and did things that detracted from his basic sense of duty and commitment, and he spent most of the second half of Season Five allowing his rage and thirst for vengeance to pull him far away from the path of honor. The destructive nature of his diffuse anger was on full display in his color choices after the 'info dump' on Walter's toilet in Episode 5.08. In the very next episode, we saw Hank in a blood red shirt pick up his garage door remote, stare at Heisenberg with unreserved wrath, and clobber him with a well-landed punch to the face. He felt good, we felt good, but that angry red shirt and his righteous fist didn't accomplish anything useful.

Hank spent the next four episodes vesting himself in every color of the *Breaking Bad* rainbow, including Marie Schrader™ purple, but never orange. Not a few times, I found myself yelling at the television screen: *For the sake of everything decent, put on an* **orange** *shirt, Hank!* Orange, of course, is my shorthand for Hank's status as the appointed representative of human justice and *honor*. But in the course of those long four episodes he never listened to my pleas.

The Immortality of Achilles

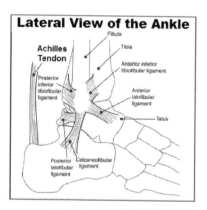

"The Human Ankle"
U.S. government illustration modified by Pearson Moore 2014

Achilles, hero of the *Iliad* and the greatest warrior who ever drew breath, lives forever.

I suppose such a statement would not create much controversy, especially among those who've read the *Iliad*, but others may be scratching their heads. "Wait a minute, Pearson. Didn't Achilles die from an arrow wound to the ankle? Isn't this where the expression 'Achilles' Heel' comes from?" But even those who've read the classics may feel a bit uncomfortable with the assertion that Achilles lives forever. "The Iliad is a record of humankind's struggle with mortality," we might hear them saying. "That Achilles' death is not portrayed in the *Iliad* is beside the point," they might contend. "All heroes, even Achilles, must die."

Precisely. When I say 'Achilles lives forever', I mean his struggles during the Trojan War—with other Achaeans, with the Trojans, with the gods, with himself—render him an unforgettable ideal of virtue. A thousand generations from now our grandchildren's grandchildren's most distant descendants will read Homer and find in

Achilles a superlative model of our shared humanity. I don't mean that he is literally immortal.

Now, the fascinating thing about the *Iliad* is that the story focuses on Achilles but it never mentions his death. Paris' shot to Achilles' vulnerable ankle is a later accretion to the story of the Trojan War, first appearing several centuries after the Golden Age of Athens. But even then, the death of Achilles didn't really tell us anything about Achilles *per se*. It confirmed and entrenched the Greek idea of human mortality; Achilles, after all, is not the only human being with a prominent weakness at the ankle: All of us have an Achilles' Heel. The only other take-home lesson from Achilles' death was that Paris was a real jerk, lacking in all the Greek virtues but especially deficient in honor. Achilles' death told us nothing more about him as a human being, and it is for that reason that his death was rightfully left unportrayed in the *Iliad*.

The meaninglessness of Achilles' death is one of the reasons that I consider Episode 5.13 a rare example of the perfect installment of a serialized television drama. The biggest question on most of our minds at the end of the episode could be expressed in three simple words: Did Hank die? The answer: It doesn't matter. Hank Schrader, like Achilles, lives forever.

Orange Crush

Just as Achilles' death is a later, unnecessary addition to his story, the outcome of the gun battle is immaterial to Hank's character arc. The biggest question at the end of Episode 5.12 was, as I put it, "Is Hank going to stop wearing Marie Schrader™ purple and become the man he's supposed to be?" The answer was a resounding YES.

All season long I lamented Hank's inability to regain his moral equilibrium in the battle to bring Heisenberg to justice. Hank's vacillations, his personal vendetta against Walter, and his dreams of personal glory were all interfering with his ability to act in a manner conducive to bringing Heisenberg down. All of that changed in this episode.

For the entire 46 minutes—and for the first time this season—Gomez backed Hank and stood at his side. He began by giving Hank a firm warning. "I'm going to tell you this up front, Hank. This guy decides that he wants to lawyer-up, I don't care if you are my boss: I'm going to put a stop to this." It was a fair warning, and it put Hank on notice that Gomez understood the plan to be outside the purview of the DEA. "He won't lawyer-up," Hank said. And he was right.

Gomez's warning and Huell's interrogation were the last scenes containing even a trace of conflict between the ASAC and his first lieutenant. They were also the last scenes in which the two DEA men did not coordinate their attire.

During their last meeting in the Purple Palace (the smothered-in-purple Schrader home) both of them wore almost the same shade of green. Crucially, at the showdown they were both vested in black jackets and DEA rust-orange shirts. Gomez never left Hank's side, physically or figuratively. They stood together, as one.

"Hank Schrader's Home"
aka The Purple Palace
Copyright Martin Woutisseth, used with permission

The upshot of dressing the men as if they were twins is not only demonstration of their single-mindedness, but symbolic visual representation of Hank's adherence to the rules of the *Breaking Bad* Universe. As Steven Michael Quezada noted during the *Talking Bad* discussion following the television broadcast, "The cool thing about Gomez, he's the only character on *Breaking Bad* that never broke bad." Gomez's moral purity was essential to the episode and to Hank's character arc. For several episodes I prayed that Hank would find himself, stop wearing every weird color under the sun, and return to his color, which is natural, desert-rust orange. It finally happened, and with such poetic perfection as I could not have imagined. Let's hear it for DEA orange!

The characters of *Breaking Bad* do not fulfill personal destiny in a vacuum. That Hank has rediscovered his moral center would have proven an interesting but largely uneventful footnote to the drama if he had not used his new-found virtue to dethrone Heisenberg. That is precisely what he did, and there is no going back, as we will see.

The Emperor Dethroned

"Do not come," Walter said. It was his last command as Emperor Heisenberg. He could have instructed Uncle Jack to bring extra firepower, to prepare for battle with the DEA. He called off the Nazis neither as a tactical maneuver nor out of fear of later reprisals. As we learned during the gunfight, Walter stepped down from the throne of his own accord as a way of protecting Hank and his immediate family. He was not taking a temporary leave of absence or an imperial sabbatical. He knew the game was over. There is no more Heisenberg, except as a graffitied taunt on the inner wall of a federally-repossessed drug house.

"Emperor Napoleon Defeated at Fontainebleu"
Paul Hippolyte Delaroche, 1845

Regardless of the outcome of the shootout in the desert, we know Walter will survive not as Heisenberg, but as Ozymandias, and we know he suffered the fall of his own choice, rather than becoming the cause of Hank's death.

I am not sure of the complete significance of Walter's choice. Probably we can say that at this moment in time, at least, Walter retained some small morsel of humanity. He wished for a connection to other human beings, even if only to his family. His Season Five 'confession' wrongfully accused Hank, but perhaps he thought of the tactic as nothing more than a warning—part of his counsel to 'tread lightly'—not understanding that it was the axe that severed forever the familial bond between Skyler and Marie and Hank and himself.

Authenticity

Walter's posture during the surrender scene was provocative and fascinating, with undertones obvious to anyone who attends liturgical churches on a regular basis.

Priest, Arms Outstretched During Celebration of the Mass
Fr. Jose Bautistarojas, USS John C. Stennis
Lex Wenberg, U. S. Navy, 2011, PD

The decision to put Walter in a traditional priestly posture may have been written into the script or it may have been a little 'extra' thrown in by the director, Michelle MacLaren. I know practically nothing about her, but I do know, from several interviews, that Vince Gilligan grew up as a practicing Roman Catholic and has since become agnostic in his beliefs. If Gilligan added posture instructions to the scene, the undertone could not have been accidental.

Another explanation is that Gilligan was drawing not from liturgical rubric but from the way the Roman Catholic Mass was ritualized by parishioners of the time. The arms-outstretched posture was often adopted by Roman Catholic parishioners during recitation of the Lord's Prayer in the late 1970s and 1980s, when Vince Gilligan would have been attending Mass. The posture is still used today, though the practice has fallen out of favor since the liturgical reforms of the last twelve years. The stance indicates not only openness to the Deity, but communicates the idea of humble submission, penitence, and contrition.

I believe it's that very personal experience of the Mass that the writers or the director chose to inject into this scene. I believe the intention was to convey the idea that Walter was coming forward as his true self, not as Heisenberg, not as High School teacher Mr. Walter White, but simply as Walter, the now defeated man. What we saw in this scene, I believe, was the authentic Walter White, stripped of every grain of artifice or falsehood.

I don't think he's consciously seeking forgiveness. But perhaps in outstretched arms, in hands subtly turned, in fingers reaching out as if in hopes of grasping something precious, some suppressed aspect of Walter's inner self—perhaps the part of him that insisted on Hank's safety above Walter's personal gain—is yearning to find expression in his thoughts, in his words, in what he could do, in what he might now refuse or fail to do. Maybe the posture represents a kind of subliminal, pre-penitential *Confiteor*, as it were.

I believe we are to understand through Walter's outstretched arms that he carries within himself the potential to beg forgiveness. Whether any such forgiveness is possible in the *Breaking Bad* Universe is another matter entirely. My own thinking is that Heisenberg's fall to desert sand and wind is inevitable, that the karma-driven world of *Breaking Bad* offers no quarter to the likes of Walter White, and that his miserable descent to become the Ozymandias who once was is as certain as the coming end of the series.

Chapter Te

Temple

of the

Will

Ramses II, Luxor, Egypt
"Ozymandias Statue"
Copyright Steve F. E. Cameron, 2005-2006, CC-SA 1.0 Generic

If a man without a soul falls in the desert, will anyone hear?

Walter White fell in the New Mexico desert in Episode 5.14. But this was not the fall that took our breath away, that left us stunned and without words. Probably we knew already the fate of this story's greatest hero. As Uncle Jack said, "Sorry, Man. There's no scenario where this guy lives."

We didn't hear the fall of Walter White. We didn't see it, we didn't acknowledge or understand it, so consuming and utterly unthinkable was the murder of Assistant Special Agent in Charge Henry R. "Hank" Schrader.

But it was Walter's fall that caused Hank's assassination, that destroyed Jesse, that severed every bond he used to have with his wife, his son, and his daughter. "I am Ozymandias, King of Kings! Look on my works, ye mighty, and despair." Ozymandias, of course, is a grand fiction, a self-deception to which all tyrants succumb. Twenty-three years ago we saw the statues of Lenin fall to the ground. Sixty-nine years ago, amidst the bombed out ruins of Berlin, the statues of Hitler came tumbling down. Tonight a man with stone-cold heart fell in the desert, and we did not hear.

Sociopathic Professionals

Review the Shootout and take a good look at the face of Todd Alquist. He shows practically no emotion. "Yeah, but, Pearson, Todd is played by this new, inexperienced actor: Jesse Plemons. He's just not a good actor yet, that's all." No, that's not it. Plemons is quite a talented actor. In fact, as I write, he is auditioning for the lead in Star Wars VII. Take a look at the other Nazis in the shootout scene. What do you see?

We expect gunfights to be emotional, so the passionless nature of the shootout is disorienting. But cold, systematic killing is nothing new to Uncle Jack and his fellow sociopaths. Recall the scene from Episode 5.10 when Jack took a puff on his cigarette just before putting a bullet in Declan's head.

Tonight, when Jack stood behind Jesse and pointed a gun to his head, he looked over at Walter and asked, "Good to go?" He might as well have been asking about the placement of a potted plant—though such an inquiry likely would have carried greater emotional content than the matter-of-fact request to blow Jesse's brains out.

The emotional sterility of the shootout and aftermath is not the only disorienting aspect of the scene. We saw Kenny pump several dozen rounds in the general direction of Hank and Gomez. Then Hank stood up and got off a dozen rounds. All the while machine guns, rifles, and handguns were pointed at Hank, getting off round after round. He just kept on firing, as if alone on the shooting range, not a care in the world. What was up with that?

Several commentators on Episode 5.13 thought the inordinate length of the gunfight—without a single casualty—was a mistake on the part of director and editors. Some counted the gun battle a major flaw in an otherwise well-executed episode. They rushed it in editing, showed too many bullet dings, prolonged the shootout to ramp up suspense, and so on.

No. Sorry. The scene was not rushed in editing, nor was it artificially prolonged. It depicted exactly what it had to show, which was the true identity of Jack and his goons and their true relation to Walter.

If we didn't have the mechanical rat-a-tat-tat of pistols, machine guns, rifles, and handguns in this scene, if the scene didn't call upon a half dozen other important visual clues, we could simply shrug our shoulders and say, "They're neo-Nazis. Sociopaths. They don't show emotion when they're killing because they're heartless white supremacists. It's kind of like they're just doing their job. They're professionals."

But accompanying the passionless expressions of these hired thugs we have the mechanical action of several hundred bullets fired one after another. There are a lot of other things going on, but we don't even need to discuss those to figure out what's really taking place in the gun battle scene.

Jack is not Walter's hired gun. It seemed like he was. When Walter called Todd and said, "I think I might have another job for your uncle," Todd said, "Oh, okay…which jail, how many targets?" It was like Todd was taking Walter's breakfast order. It was just another routine request for mercenary work, and Jack was Walter's man for the job. Jack had done this before, after all, and we had no reason to believe he wouldn't do it again. So Walter's request to kill Jesse fit perfectly into Jack's position as hired assassin. When Walter called Jack from the desert, the goons didn't waste any time. While Jack spoke they were putting on bulletproof vests, grabbing rifles and checking cartridges. They were ready to jump at Walter's command, as they always had been.

Seconds later, when Walter told Jack to stand down, we had no reason to believe Jack would disobey. Jack's only connection to Walter was weak. Lydia wanted blue meth, which Jack was willing to supply. "We'll just throw in some food coloring." Problem solved. Even if the solution was not to Lydia's liking, it didn't really matter to Jack.

So why did Jack disobey? If he wasn't a slave to Lydia's desire for blue product of higher percentage quality, why did he act on his own initiative to come out to the desert even after Walter told him to stand down?

The reason that our calculations don't add up is that they can't. If we assume that Jack was demonstrating extraordinary care about the wellbeing of Walter, or immediately thought Walter's coordinates indicated the X on a treasure map, we're left feeling cheated. We feel there must be more to it. In fact, there was more to this than Jack's sudden ability to think for himself. He wasn't acting on his own at all.

Jack was an agent.

He put a bullet in Hank's head, but Hank cannot die, as we discussed in Chapter 5b. The most significant result of Jack's appearance at To'hajiilee was not Hank's death but Heisenberg's fall. Jack was not sent on this mission to act as Heisenberg's mercenary. He didn't go out there intent on murdering anyone who stood in Heisenberg's path to world domination. Jack wasn't sent out there to punish Hank for not having his priorities straight. Killing Hank was the only way to bring about Heisenberg's fall, so that's what happened.

It was Heisenberg's fall that caused Jack's appearance, which is counter-intuitive because any such connection violates the rules of cause and effect. But that's okay in this instance, because Jack's boss—the entity for which he was agent—was not Walter, but the most important entity in *Breaking Bad*: Jack was the agent of the Universe.

I'm just throwing out the idea. But it's more than an idea. Jack was the gruesome agent of the *Breaking Bad* Universe.

The Fall of Ozymandias

Walter had to fall just so: Eyes squinted shut, mouth open. I would not be surprised to learn that Vince Gilligan himself was present for the execution of this scene, because it was essential that Walter not fall as a human being, but as a statue.

I met a traveller from an antique land
Who said: `Two vast and trunkless legs of stone
Stand in the desert. Near them, on the sand,
Half sunk, a shattered visage lies, whose frown,
And wrinkled lip, and sneer of cold command,
Tell that its sculptor well those passions read
Which yet survive, stamped on these lifeless things,
The hand that mocked them and the heart that fed.

And on the pedestal these words appear:
"My name is Ozymandias, king of kings:
Look on my works, ye Mighty, and despair!"

Nothing beside remains. Round the decay
Of that colossal wreck, boundless and bare
The lone and level sands stretch far away.'

["Ozymandias," Percy Bysshe Shelley, 1818]

Yes, the sculptor well those passions read, and we see them, stamped on this lifeless, soulless thing—on this colossal wreck that used to be a man. We know of many instances of Ozymandias, the King of Kings who thought himself mightier than mighty.

My Name is Agamemnon, King of Kings

The two statues below depict Agamemnon, King of Mycenae (Greece) in the 12th century B.C. Since these two enormous statues stand not in Greece but in Thebes, Egypt, you may wonder how I can make such a strange statement. Well, I have it on good authority. We can be certain of the statues' identity because when Alexander the

Great conquered Egypt in 332 B.C. he told us whom the statues commemorated. In fact, to this day they're called the Colossi of Memnon.

The Colossi of Memnon
Copyright Roweromaniak 2007, CC-SA 2.5

They were constructed around 1300 B.C., right about the time that Agamemnon ruled in Mycenae. The most careful modern dating techniques have confirmed the statues' age. So Alexander the Great *had* to be correct in his assignment of the statues' identity. Right?

It probably never occurred to Alexander or his men that 12th century Egyptian masons would not have spent 15 years constructing beautifully carved statues in tribute to figures from Greek mythology. In fact, the statues were commissioned in memory of Amenhotep III, Pharaoh of Egypt from 1391 to 1353 B.C., the ninth pharaoh of the 18th dynasty.

We can probably forgive Alexander his cultural hubris. Many in modern times are so ignorant of other cultures and histories and so enamored of their own that they make blunders no less sweeping and ludicrous than Alexander's. I feel the awful truth of this, having made a fool of myself on several occasions.

But the larger issue, and the one that relates to *Breaking Bad*, is the fact that *Alexander was ignorant of his own culture.* You see, Homer didn't uphold King Agamemnon as a paragon of virtue. If anyone had said, in response to Homer's nearly month-long recitation of his tale of the Trojan War, "Hey, I'm going to erect a statue in memory of Agamemnon," Homer may well have shed tears at the unbelievable stupidity of his listeners. "Agamemnon was King of the Mycenaeans," Homer might have said, "but he was the worst tyrant we have ever suffered." It was the kind of stupidity and arrogance that Alexander showed in Egypt that Homer had fought valiantly to prevent when he strung together several tales of the Trojan War into the epic poem known as *Iliad*.

Homer understood well the human tendency to accept and even celebrate the foibles of others, especially if those others enjoy positions of power, wealth, or social standing. So he began the *Iliad* with the striking image of a lowly soldier, Achilles, reading the riot act to the exalted king, Agamemnon:

Then looking darkly at [Agamemnon] Achilleus of the swift feet spoke:
'O wrapped in shamelessness, with your mind forever on profit,
How shall any one of the Achaians readily obey you?'

By the beginning of *Odyssey*, Agamemnon had been murdered (*Odyssey*, Book 3) but Achilles, as we've already discussed, lived forever. Agamemnon was assassinated, at least in part, for dragging the Greek world into a war against the Trojans—all to satisfy his own lust for power and to allow his brother to save face over having lost beautiful Helen to the Trojans.

The revolutionary idea of the *Iliad* is that everyone in society is called to a life of virtue and honor. When a leader strays into dishonor, it is up to us—even the least powerful among us—to stand up to that leader and correct him. In Homer's view there really are no 'lowly' citizens, for everyone who lives honorably is as worthy of poem and song as the most exalted king.

The flip side of the *Iliad* is the seductive power of lust for personal wealth and glory—'shamelessness' and a 'mind forever on profit', as Achilles put it. Achilles, not Agamemnon, represented the Greek ideal of honor. Achilles is the perfection of Greece.

My Name is Heisenberg, King of Kings

Walter: I'm the Cook. I'm the man who killed Gus Fring.
Declan: That's bullshit. The cartel got Fring.
Walter: You sure?
Declan: [No response]
Walter: That's right. Now: Say my name.
Declan: You're Heisenberg.
Walter: You're goddam right.

—Episode 5.07, "Say My Name"

Flagrant dishonor committed by those of wealth or authority is not something we can ignore or consider outside our sphere of consciousness. We cannot relegate the acts of dishonorable women and men to the periphery of our awareness because their putrid thoughts contaminate our lives. When Walter White goes down he takes dozens of people down with him. Because he is a nexus of wealth, power, and influence, he corrupts as surely as Agamemnon and Hitler and Pol Pot. *Breaking Bad* is not an episode of *Law and Order*, where there's just one bad guy and everyone else is untainted and perfect in every way, smelling of lilacs and roses. No, *Breaking Bad* took great pains

332

to show the myriad of Walter White's intimate connections and now we see the day of reckoning affects everyone around him.

Why did Hank feel the urge to gloat, to take precious seconds to express to Walter his glee in surpassing him? Why did he call Marie to brag? Why didn't he contact the Navajo Tribal Police first?

Why was Skyler seduced by 80 million dollars? Why didn't she report Walter to the police?

Why did Jesse succumb to dreams of luxury and wealth? Why didn't he do what he knew to be right?

We could ask the same types of questions of everyone who has fallen under Heisenberg's spell. The answer is the same for each inquiry. Those closest to Heisenberg saw in him someone to be bested, emulated, or adored. Heisenberg is not an independent entity, he affects and brings into his unholy web everyone around him. As Homer feared of those under Agamemnon's sway, Heisenberg corrupted everyone with whom he came into contact.

My Name is ASAC Schrader

He is no king, but he is without question the noblest of warriors. His name will outlive Walter's. If Hank's statue should fall, it will be repaired, restored to its place of honor.

We won't experience the catharsis of ASAC Hank Schrader's funeral. We can imagine the aftermath, though, when Marie's widowhood is confirmed, when Hank Schrader becomes a hero celebrated in death. Some, like George Merkert, might shake their heads and silently wonder how Hank could have allowed a notorious murderer and drug kingpin to operate—right under his nose. "For now we see through a glass, darkly; but then face to face: now I know in part; but then shall I know even as also I am known." (1 Cor. 13:12) Paul of Tarsus speaks of the difference between childish lack of knowledge and the full measure of awareness and maturity.

We think less of people for their inability to perceive the faults of others. Hank didn't understand Walter's fabrications as the lies they were. Even when he did finally unmask the Heisenberg monster hiding in the form of Walter White, Hank sought to bring him down on his own. Scared of losing his job (as George Merkert had, for not seeing the evil 'right under his nose'), he should have feared Heisenberg's power. Hank's job was not on the line. His life and Marie's life were. He should have known that—or so we tell ourselves. Hank saw and behaved as a child, seeing the world through a glass, darkly. Maybe, we say at the end of the series, Hank had to die. He fell short.

I don't think that is the final message on Hank Schrader's life and death. Hank was allowed to wear rust orange, the color of the New Mexico desert and one of the two natural colors of *Breaking Bad*. He didn't reach for endless blue, he had his feet anchored on solid ground all the time. He was not perfect, but there is not a woman or man among us who has not made some of the same mistakes Hank did. Walter transgressed the most fundamental laws of the *Breaking Bad* Universe. That led to the Universe's use of deadly force to put an end to Heisenberg's reign, which unfortunately meant the death of a good man. There was no karmic retribution for Hank's imperfections. Hank could have been in every way perfect—he still would have died so that Heisenberg could fall.

Heisenberg offered Jack 80 million dollars in exchange for the life of Marie's husband.

Jack: What do you think, Fed? Would you take that deal?
Walt: It's *Hank*. His name is Hank.
Jack: How about it, Hank? Should I let you go?
Hank: My name is ASAC Schrader. And you can go fuck yourself.

Heisenberg thought 80 million dollars was enough, that it was something for which Jack would accept any risk. More importantly, it was such a vast amount of money that it surpassed the value of a man's dignity and human worth. Hank would beg, Heisenberg knew. Hank was no 'Fed', after all. He was just a man, like any of us. These were Heisenberg's thoughts, anyway, in the final seconds before he fell.

Achilles is the perfection of Greece. Jack referred to Hank as 'Fed'—agent of the Federal Government of the United States of America. "No, you have that wrong," Walter said. "He's not 'Fed', he's family first. He's Hank." He's just like any of us.

But Walter was the one who had it all wrong. Hank was not his brother-in-law first. Jack knew Hank better than anyone else: He *is* Fed. He is the federal agent any of us would like to believe we'd have the courage to be. He's no ordinary man, but he is the man any of us could be. He and Steve Gomez were the only characters at the end of the series who had the right to wear a natural color. They were the only characters entitled to represent the Universe.

Hank was not perfect. Like Achilles, he struggled with virtue and vice, honor and disgrace. He flirted with taking that which was not his—in days of inner conflict and turmoil, symbolized in his appropriation of Marie's purple and violet shirts. But he died perfectly, heroically, vested in orange, an exemplar not only of the DEA, but of all of us. In his death, Hank Schrader is the perfection of America.

My Name is Skyler Heisenberg

This is visual poetry of such breathtaking majesty we could spend hours contemplating the meaning of the five simple elements perfectly arranged in the chilling tableau below. Was there a viewer anywhere in the world who at this moment in the episode was not shouting, "Pick up the phone, Skyler! Call the police!"

This scene will be known as Skyler's Choice in film theory texts. But the significance of the scene extends far beyond the question of Knife or Phone.

The knife here is not a symbol of power, it is a symbol of personal vanity. It is the physical expression of the Heisenberg ideal of mastering a situation without assistance.

Skyler's Choice
Pearson Moore 2014

The phone is a symbol of surrender of self to a greater good. It is the instrument of surrender of personal vanity. It is the instrument of personal salvation.

In drawing the knife from the block, Skyler was asserting her belief that she could control the situation herself. It's hard to tell in the melee that followed, but Junior implored first his mother and then his father to "Stop it!" By shouting the same command to both parents he was proclaiming his understanding that each of them had succumbed to evil. It was finally Junior, the only non-Heisenberg in the house, who took the responsible action of calling the police.

Just a year ago, Skyler would not have seen the knives. She would have seen only the telephone. More than likely, Mrs. Heisenberg tonight didn't see the telephone, so deep was the poisoning of her soul by the monster with whom she shared a house.

Analysis of Skyler's Choice
Pearson Moore 2014

Old Skyler in the portrait on the wall and New Skyler walking toward the Choice define an apposition of life (thin blue circles) and death (thick red circles) reflected in the parallel but reverse juxtaposition of knives (death) and fruit (life). From our perspective as observers we see Knife v. Phone as a Choice. But from within the context of Sky Blue (Old) Skyler, there are no knives on the countertop, there's only a telephone, because the knives are off-limits—'forbidden fruit', if you will. If Old Skyler knew a murderer was in her house she would not even think of the knives, she would grab the phone.

From within the context of White (New, infused with Heisenberg pride) Skyler, there is no telephone on the countertop, there are only knives, and the best one is the deadliest one. The phone is as useless to her in the present emergency as the bowl of fruit.

The Lone and Level Sands

How could it have come to this? How could Heisenberg have severed every connection to the family for which he was willing to sacrifice the last dollar of his ill-gotten wealth? The answer is difficult to understand, but we saw the truth of it play out in the life of Walter's adopted son, Jesse.

The answer is simple and very sad: Walter White never had a family.

Many commentators have noted the seemingly strange fact that Walter gave Jesse far more attention and 'love' than he showed his biological son. That Walter thought of Jesse as his son was clear as early as the first episodes of Season One. The strangeness of his adoption came to light in Episode 4.10. Junior, speaking of his new car, said, "It drives great." Walter, on the edge of sleep, replied, "That's good, Jesse."

But Jesse was Walter's surrogate son only as long as he blindly carried out Walter's will. As soon as he demonstrated the ability to think on his own, Walter rejected him utterly, calling Uncle Jack to order Jesse's murder.

Walter was, indeed, closer to Jesse than he was to his biological son. So estranged was he from his own daughter that she didn't recognize him as her father. "Mama," she cried at the rest room changing station. In Holly, Walter thought he had the one person in the world who could never betray him. But her calls for "Mama" were the most powerful indicators of the extremity of Walter's fall. He has no brother-in-law, no sister-in-law, no wife, no son. At one time or another he created false connections to all of them, but he never even bothered to create connections with his biological daughter. By the end of the episode he had lost every connection he ever had.

Pathos

He stands on the outside looking in, isolated from the world of human beings. He wishes he could enter, but his nature forbids it. He is in every sense hideous to us. Walter is Frankenstein's monster, playing with the little girl by the lake, hoping for some connection to humanity, but finding none.

There was deep pathos in the second to last scene of Episode 5.14. Walter used every fiber of his intellect to design the perfect alibi for Skyler. He knew the police were standing right next to her, listening and recording. So he parodied a Skyler that never was, a Skyler who rejected Heisenberg at every turn, a Skyler who was completely innocent. "What the hell do you know about [my illegal work] anyway? Nothing! I built this. Me. Me alone. Nobody else." But the last bit was ingenious. Walter knew his crimes were so great that the entire weight of United States law enforcement would be mobilized against him. But a greater enemy remained: Uncle Jack. So Walter added this critical line to his recorded message: "Toe the line. Or you will end up like Hank." The intention was to divert DEA and FBI attention away from Uncle Jack so that the neo-Nazi goons would not seek out and murder Skyler.

There is some small part of Walter that shares in our humanity. Even on the run, when he could have been felled by FBI or Nazi bullets coming at him from any direction, he tried to keep his family out of harm's way. I don't know that I've ever read in a novel or witnessed on film such a twisted, profound, utterly compelling portrait of a self-made Frankenstein's Monster. We wish to reach out to the compassionate, loving part of him, but he has so utterly divorced himself from everything human that his redemption is impossible.

Gazing on the colossal wreck that was once a man, we see with sad eyes the lone and level sands that stretch far away. Somehow, wrapped as he is in shamelessness, we look on Ozymandias, and we mourn.

Chapter I

Blood, Meth & Tears

"Vanitas"
Pieter Claesz, 1630

We knew Lydia would get the ricin.

Almost every commentator in the blogosphere predicted it. Many of us, like me, who didn't offer an opinion, knew the truth of it in our bones. Lydia would get the ricin, the Nazis would die in the bloodiest way we could imagine.

Predictable, rote, mechanical. It was a final episode in three acts that seemed more epilogue than dénouement, a logically requisite extrapolation of events to a natural conclusion. If we sought catharsis we received only a sliver of our objective, in Todd's death by asphyxiation at Jesse's hands. If we sought retribution for the dozens of lives Heisenberg destroyed we were served up an entire hour that played out according to Walter's plan. The drama ended on Walter's terms. It was a below-average final statement from an otherwise superlative series.

I know other commentators weighed in with similar statements. "'Ozymandias' was the true ending," they're saying, if not in so many words then they screamed it between the lines. "Felina" was a predictable disappointment, but that's okay, because we have so many great episodes before it.

That's not what I see in this episode. In fact, what I found was one of the most unpredictable episodes in the series, beginning with Walter's theft of a car and his unthinkable trip to the Schwartz compound in Santa Fe. If we consider only the mechanics of this final 55 minutes of *Breaking Bad* we are justified in considering it below average. But *Breaking Bad* has never been about mechanical superficialities. The ricin and the M60 machine gun were artistic devices whose role was not to eliminate this or that character, but to point to a theme or thesis. If we're going to appreciate the rich meaning of *Breaking Bad*, we need to orient our thoughts not toward the mechanics, but toward those themes. Our final objective is not catharsis or a feeling that justice has been served. Rather, our goal is the elucidation of the underlying thesis and its meaning to our own lives. In this respect, "Felina" surprised, caught us off guard, and articulated a full thesis statement that both delights and repulses.

We knew Lydia would get the ricin. Sure. But we didn't know Walter White. We learned his true nature from a Western love song set in El Paso. Felina was not a woman, not Skyler, Gretchen, or Marie. Felina was a child: the noxious, poisonous blue-colored offspring who was Walter White's true love. We knew it all along. But "Felina" surprised us nevertheless, showing us just how deep that love ran. The implications are personal and unsettling, constituting a human statement we wish to dismiss but would do well to consider. *Breaking Bad* is all about Baby Blue.

Agency

"Just get me home. I'll do the rest."

The episode started with a bang. The turn of events was unprecedented and should have alerted us to the strangeness of scenes to follow. We've witnessed a character turn his eyes to the heavens to utter a plea only once before in this series. Earlier this season (Episode 5.12) we saw Jesse in Walter's house, gasoline can in hand, Hank's Glock 22 pointed at his chest. Jesse turned his eyes upward, beyond the ceiling, in earnest appeal to the powers of the Universe.

"He can't keep getting away with this!"

Jesse's plea went unanswered. In fact, Walter *did* keep getting away with it, despite Hank's best efforts to stop him. Far from hearing and acting on Jesse's appeal for karmic justice, the Universe instead gave Jesse to the neo-Nazis, allowed him to suffer unending months of physical and psychological torment and forced him to watch as his closest friend was shot in the back of the head. Hank, the person best equipped to stop Walter from getting away with it, was unceremoniously executed in the desert.

The Universe, we've learned over the last five years, has its own timeline, and it's not much interested in the degree to which a particular player must suffer. That Walter thought the Powers That Be were interested in his welfare or his plans should have irritated us. But the event that occurred next should have horrified us.

Walter sat in a car not his own, his eyes lifted upward in supplication. He brought his hands forward and up, still appealing to powers greater than his. When he flipped the sun visor, his prayer was answered, immediately and directly empowering him with the means to get home.

Why was Walter's prayer answered so quickly and easily when other prayers have been ignored for years?

Team Walter must have been cheering at this point, and they would continue cheering throughout the episode. All of Walter's initiatives, no matter how small, were perfectly executed and completed, fulfilling Walter's mission in every particular.

Team Walter's victory dance must have put a damper on the small bits of vindication felt by Team Karma. "Okay, he got to leave nine million dollars to his kids. So what? He died in the end." The words ring hollow because Walter's victories became the unrelenting tidal wave that brushed aside all opposition and brought closure to every hanging thread in the story.

I have to believe that Walter's unprecedented success in the final episode was the factor that caused so many commentators to find the episode mediocre, in some sense distasteful or not in keeping with the spirit of the series. From a superficial point of view, Walter 'went out on his own terms'. But the metallic implement in Walter's outstretched hand is the key to our deeper understanding. That key fell from the sky, created entirely out of the unstoppable will of the Universe.

Manna From Heaven
Unknown Artist, circa 1300

It was, almost literally, manna from heaven.

Walter held the key to our understanding of the final episode, and that understanding is simple yet profound, because if we turn the key in the ignition we can see with new eyes the intended significance of every event that followed. Walter is not the conquering hero. He is not Heisenberg reborn. In fact, he occupies a position new to him. He is not master, but servant. He is a slave to forces greater than his own—forces that determine outcomes of their choosing.

The key to our understanding is this: Walter White became the agent of the Universe.

True Colors

Gretchen wore Walter's first color: White. Her choice of clothing should seem symbolically paradoxical. But Walter's fashion statement—the khaki-gray coat—ought to seem metaphorically out of bounds.

In terms of the rubrics of suspenseful storytelling, Walter had to enter the Schwartz house quietly, purposefully, and without apprehension of any kind. This feeds into suspense, for we know Walter could kill Elliott and Gretchen without remorse and without hesitation. He's been doing it for years, after all. But the symbolic statements in this scene scream louder than even the suspense.

Walter entered the den of those committed to destroying his name. They tried to take away the White name by diluting it into Gray Matter Technologies. Walter refused. After all, the pinnacle of his power was achieved when he could force a drug kingpin to utter his name. "Say my name!" he commanded Declan, the most powerful drug distributor in Phoenix. He left Gretchen decades ago, gave her up to Elliott, because he could never surrender the White name.

This meeting of white-clad Gretchen and gray-clad Walter is the supreme irony, rendered astounding and virtually unthinkable by the bizarre turn of events that occurred around a table piled high with nine million dollars of drug money.

Decades ago these three people could not agree on anything. Gretchen held that humans had a soul, Walter just laughed. Gretchen and Elliott wore gray and insisted on Walter's conformity. Walter refused to give up the white shirt of pride for the gray shirt of collaboration, so he left his girlfriend and sold his share in the company.

When Gretchen and Walter shook hands—at gray-clad Walter's insistence—the irony carried greater meaning than anything we have so far witnessed in this series. The woman who had insisted on gray all of her life now vested herself in white and agreed to collaboration with a man who had rigorously refused to give up white—and was now dressed entirely in gray.

If you think the implication is that Walter surrendered, recall please the last seconds of the episode, when Walter touched the stainless steel shell of the reaction vessel as if caressing a child's face.

Walter was surrendering nothing in this scene. He was calm and collected not only because this served the purposes of suspense-laden storytelling, but because in this scene he was not white-loving Heisenberg but rather gray-loving Universe. He was a dark angel, the agent (slave, servant) of the Universe.

Walter did not surrender but this was because he was already beaten. We saw his fall from power two episodes ago.

A beaten man does not surrender. A prisoner of war does not say, "Okay, I give up." That man is already conquered; any expression of will or volition is meaningless. A beaten man can only die or serve other interests. His will—his desires and agenda—is immaterial because it is the Universe that now decides his fate. The Universe's decision was to use Walter to serve greater interests. Keys rained down from heaven because Walter is no longer master but servant.

We saw true colors in the final episode. Walter could no longer wear white or blue or purple. These colors are forbidden because of the deeper meaning they hold. He is left with gray (service to the Universe) or green (unfulfilled desire, sometimes called 'greed'). Gretchen is allowed to wear white because her deepest self is about service (gray), and she can take pride (wear white clothing) in that truth.

Woodworking

Those lacking intimate familiarity with laboratory research may not understand the comparison of Jesse's perfect wooden box with his blue methamphetamine. The juxtaposition of a flashback scene in which he worked on the box with the present reality in which he pulled on a dog chain was a visual announcement of his long-held conviction that the epitome of science was found not in formulas and equations, but in symmetry and beauty. "You're an artist, Mr. White," was his way of bestowing on Walter the ultimate compliment for his crystal meth prowess.

I have 35 years of experience in chemical process R&D, most of it in the pharmaceutical industry. While I cannot speak with authority on what science or technical research is or is not, I think 35 years have at least earned me the right to articulate an opinion about science that must be considered valid and meaningful, if not necessarily 'correct' or 'essential'.

While industrial scientific research is founded on scientific principles and commercial expectations of efficiency, we cannot think of R&D projects as nothing more than a periodic table harnessed to the 80/20 Rule. The successful industrial scientist must be well-versed in technical theory, and she damn sure has to design her work on the basis of corporate time constraints, but above all, she needs to cultivate a certain attitude about her work. That attitude probably finds its most meaningful expression in the language of art. There is an underlying simplicity, harmony, and symmetry to the world. To the extent that such clarity and beauty is reflected in experimental design, the scientist faithfully elucidates the true structure of the universe. Only artists are capable of achieving such vision, especially in the mundane and often confusing and contradictory details of laboratory research.

Walter and Jesse were both self-centered criminals, but they were both artists, too.

Walter did not appear in the woodworking flashback, or in the laboratory scene following the close of the daydream. Jesse was the only one present. The invocation of Jesse's most beloved memory as an artist served several purposes, the most obvious being his sense of helplessness; the only way he could assure Brock's survival was through faithful delivery of superior baby-blue methamphetamine.

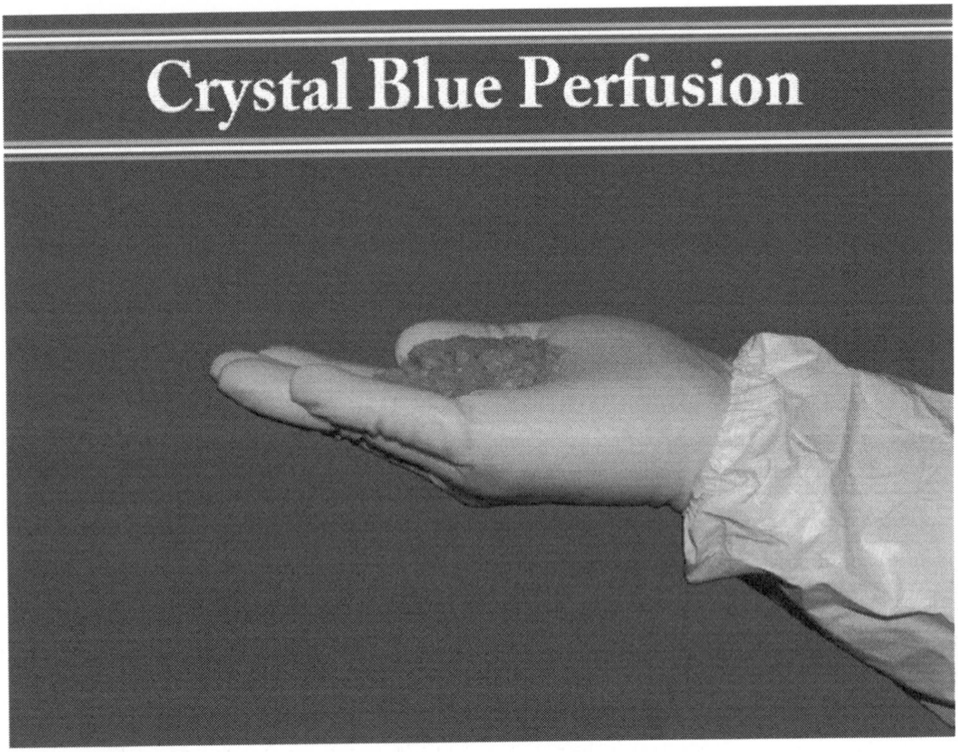

Crystal Blue Perfusion

"Crystal Blue Perfusion"
Copyright 2012 Pearson Moore
Created for *Breaking Blue*

But Walter's absence from the scenes and the emphasis on Jesse's interpretation of his laboratory work as art points to a truth that brings greater meaning to his situation. For Jesse the highest expression of science was the creation of a product that was simple and beautiful. Purity had less meaning to him than the fact that high purity meant 'glass grade'—a high grade recognizable by its existence as perfectly symmetric, beautiful crystals. Walter, on the other hand, couldn't care less about crystallinity. For Walter it was not beauty but purity that was the driving factor. "Respect the chemistry," we've heard him say nearly a dozen times. Recall that in Walter's world there was no soul, only chemistry. 'Respect the chemistry' meant many things, but we must count among those things Walter's contention that there was no art, only chemistry.

I don't know that Vince Gilligan and company were trying to say in this bittersweet sequence that Jesse was more of a scientist than Walter. Certainly there is no question of Jesse's standing as the more capable artist. The last reported purity of his product was 96 percent. He was approaching Walter's level of purity not because he understood chemical principles but because he deferred to artistic precepts.

The tragedy of Jesse's enslavement was magnified by the fact that he was being forced to create and deliver pearls for swine. Art is created through a surrender of that which is most personal. "Do not throw your pearls in front of pigs, or they may trample them and then turn on you and tear you to pieces." (Mt. 7:6) Jesse's enslavement was more horrible than any such confinement of Walter would have been. Walter would never have delivered pearls—the most precious parts of his soul—because he had no concept of soul or art or human worth as something inviolate. Jesse, on the other hand, delivered his very soul to the swine who trampled his art and turned on him and tore him to pieces.

Yeah, Science!

"Newton"
William Blake, 1795

Walter White may not have been an artist, but when it came to logic-based engineering of gadgets, he could outmacgyver the best of 'em. Not even James Bond's Q could hold a candle—or M60 machine gun—to Walter White. But none of it mattered, since Walter's technical prowess and creativity never worked perfectly—until this episode.

Breaking Bad has taken pains to drive home the message that actions based entirely on scientific principles are inadequate to the successful fielding of real human problems. Even if Walter figured out a way to steal 1000 gallons of methylamine from a train without having to injure or kill anyone, a boy on a motorcycle would show up and foil his perfectly executed plan. Even if he could vanquish the impregnable steel door to a chemical warehouse, creating showers of burning thermite more spectacular than fireworks, DEA agents could laugh at his stupidity in hefting the methylamine barrel rather than rolling it.

We had our first lesson regarding the undisputed primacy of Murphy's Law in the pilot episode, when Emilio Koyama died after inhaling Walter's phosphine gas but

Krazy-8 suffered only facial and throat burns. "Yeah, but, Pearson, you're forgetting about 'Face Off'. Walter engineered a bomb to kill Gustavo Fring and it worked! This disproves your statement that Walter's contraptions 'never worked perfectly'. The bomb *did* work perfectly." Actually, if you go back to the final scene in Hector Salamanca's room and listen closely you'll hear not fewer than 40 dings of Tio Hector's bell before the bomb finally exploded. Gus was killed not because of Walter's faulty contraption, but because Hector Salamanca's hatred of Gus was so great he never stopped trying to make it work. With respect, I stand by my statement.

The foolishness of placing one's faith in science has been a constant refrain through the six seasons of *Breaking Bad*. It's not for nothing that whenever Walter came up with a science-based solution to intractable problems, high school dropout Jesse Pinkman would exclaim, "Yeah! Science!"—a proclamation of technical superiority that carried about as much validity as Jesse's confident assertion that a long-necked glass container was properly called a 'volumetric beaker' (Episode 1.05, Jesse showing off his new-found scientific expertise to his friend, Badger). He at least correctly identified the 'volumetric' part of it.

The invincibility of science is an attractive idea to grade school children, high school dropouts, and socially inept science nerds like Walter White. To the rest of us, and to *Breaking Bad*, the assertion of science as the answer to all problems is meant to be a laughable proposition.

After so many failures of Walter's homemade machines, why did his pop-up auto-fire machine gun work perfectly—the very first time he tried it?

We could pose other questions, all carrying the same value, all requiring the same response: Why is water wet? Why does the sun rise in the east? Why did keys fall from heaven as soon as Walter made his request?

The answer to all four of the above questions is the same: Because the Universe so ordained.

A Critique of Pure Mechanics

That Walter was agent in this episode, not master, should not cause any of us to infer that Vince Gilligan created a mechanistic universe. If he had done so, we might expect that Walter White, with his exemplary understanding of cause and effect, would have been able to rise to any challenge. But just as the logic of Mr. Spock was insufficient to the solution of any problem on Star Trek, Walter's widgets and wonders were more likely to create problems than solve them.

The Universe of *Breaking Bad*, as far as I can tell, is not a rigidly pre-determined environment. But there are laws. If you jump up into the air you should expect that gravity will pull you back down to the ground. You're not going to go floating off into the stratosphere. If you violate the laws of Karma you should expect retribution. You're not going to 'keep getting away with it' as Jesse said.

In Star Trek neither Mr. Spock (pure intellect) nor Dr. McCoy (pure heart) fit perfectly into the galaxy. Only Captain Kirk (pure soul, the complete human being) could take on any challenge and succeed. In the same way, the purely scientific approach of Walter White was doomed to fail in the *Breaking Bad* Universe. It was only when Walter showed humanity that he could succeed.

The Universe did not ordain that Jesse Pinkman would survive the 'Say hello to my little friend' moment inside the Nazi clubhouse. Walter decided that, and the Universe allowed him to do so, because it was the human thing to do.

Baby Blue

"I did it for me. I liked it. I was good at it. And…I was…really…I was alive." Walter showed his true colors throughout the episode, but especially in the heartbreaking meeting with Skyler in the kitchen after Marie's call. He had the honesty and presence of mind not to apologize or seek forgiveness. He knew he was far beyond redemption.

He came to us as Walter White, wearing only white underwear, denoting undignified pride in himself, and a green shirt, denoting unattained desire or greed. Cancer was the catalyst that activated long-dormant seeds of envy, anger, and pride. The synthesis of crystalline methamphetamine was not something he did 'for the good of the family' nearly as much as it was an assertion of self, a proclamation that Walter could 'do something better than anyone in the world'.

He loved Baby Blue because it obeyed the rules of science. It never complained, talked back, or tried to make Walter less than he was simply out of spite. Baby Blue was the proof of his superior intellect. No one else in Walter White's world found the dictates of logic and mathematics sufficient to a satisfying life. Only Walter and his one true love, 99.1% pure methamphetamine—the work of his hands, the creation of his mind—found in the cold world of pure logic a place of contentment because it reflected Walter's greatness.

But his celebration of self meant a devaluation of others, to the point that murder became a useful means of attaining important goals. It was important to instill fear, essential to be able to say, "I'm the one who knocks," because fear meant respect, and respect meant a proper appreciation of his name and all of the great achievements that name stood for. "Say my name!" was the most important command he ever issued to an underling.

By allowing Walter to retain shards of his humanity, as flawed and beyond redemption as he was, the writers held Walter as an example and a warning. All of us carry inside ourselves dormant seeds of greed, hatred, and pride. When a difficult set of circumstances coalesces in our lives we have the choice to act selfishly or selflessly. Any one of us can become Walter White.

The Death of Walter Shephard

During the final fight of the series he sacrificed himself, sustaining a lethal wound to the lower right abdomen. The wound bled so much it soaked both his shirt and his slacks. The only real friend he had left him. His mission completed, he returned to the place where it all began. As he made his way down a narrow passageway, he seemed to be retracing steps he had walked earlier, pausing every now and then in nostalgic wonder to examine things that had been important many seasons earlier. No longer able to support himself, he fell to the ground. But as he looked up he realized he was not alone. The one who had loved him all along was at his side. As the camera pulled away we saw him looking upward, happy even in death, surrounded by the place he had known so well.

We could certainly apply this description to the scene of Walter's death. Walter sacrificed himself for Jesse, who left him to die alone, the lethal abdominal wound bleeding over shirt and slacks. He walked through the forest of laboratory apparatus and equipment, fell to the ground, and died with Baby Blue—his blue meth—the one who always loved him—right at his side.

In fact, though, the death scene was written not for Walter White, but for Jack Shephard of Lost (2004-2010, ABC Television). He suffered a lethal wound in exactly the same part of the abdomen as Walter. Just like Walter, he died in a place of his choosing, a place where he found comfort.

From the moment Walter entered the laboratory the visual parallels to the death of Jack Shephard occurred one after another in rapid succession. I don't imagine we will have to wait too long for the first Youtube side-by-side comparison of Walter's final walk through the laboratory and Jack's final walk through the jungle back to his place in the bamboo. [I wrote this on September 30, 2013. Exactly one month later, on October 30, Tjimi Cole posted the side-by-side. I was surprised by the match of detail—like the police officers showing up around Walter at the same instant that Jack saw the Ajira plane fly away. You can see the video match-up at Youtube.]

I have read two commentaries that compared Walter's death to the final scene of carnage in the 1976 classic "Taxi Driver." I watched the film again today. I made valiant efforts to see the parallel. Other than some technical similarities (overhead camera, subdued lighting, choreographed approach of police officers), the scenes shared practically nothing in common. Besides his desire to kill for no apparent reason, Travis Bickle had no mission. He was wounded in the neck and in the arm, not in the lower right abdomen. He didn't die. There are many other reasons to dismiss the strange, half-baked comparisons of Breaking Bad with the ambiguous, postmodernist mess that is "Taxi Driver."

I found Breaking Bad's homage to Lost touching and entirely appropriate. I know I am not alone in considering the two series the best programs ever created for television. They're very different stories, told in distinct ways. While Breaking Bad is told in a conventional manner, it delivers bold, difficult statements about human nature. Lost, on the other hand, unfolds in possibly the most complicated visual and narrative style ever applied to a television series, but it delivers conventional, palatable statements about humanity.

But the two series share much, especially in terms of the depth of artistic detail and symbolism attached to names, characters, colors, scenery, and events. Breaking Bad's meager 30-year backstory cannot compete with Lost's intricate 2000-year history, but Lost's handful of symbolically significant colors cannot be compared to Breaking Bad's grand obsession with color symbolism. There are at least four distinct shades of orange in Breaking Bad, each of them bearing enormous symbolic meaning. The same can be said of blue, yellow, red, white, and the other major hues. Lost has Dharma blue,

Island yellow, and Dogen green and that's about it. Regardless of the story, though, the symbols carry immense thematic value and lift these two cinematic creations far above anything else written for television.

Journey to an Antique Land

Two vast and trunkless legs of stone
Stand in the desert. Near them, on the sand,
Half sunk, a shattered visage lies…

We know the forces that caused the fall of Ozymandias. Mr. Chips became Scarface. The seeds of the grotesque transformation lay dormant, buried deep inside, until circumstance allowed dark seeds to grow. Even this we knew, though, for none of the showrunners hesitated to explain the thesis of the show, even before the pilot aired.

The result was not and could not have been surprising or unanticipated. It's not the thesis, or the result, or the ending that gives the show value. It's the journey itself that brings life and depth and meaning to the core themes and extrapolations from the thesis. I'm beginning my fifth rewatch of *Lost*. At the same time, I'm completing my third rewatch of *Breaking Bad*. In these journeys to antique lands I continue to find fresh ideas, startling connections, and bold assertions about the human condition. The journeys never grow old. If you wish to come with me, be sure to pack a warm jacket and plenty of tea. It's cold and dry in the desert after dark, especially when Jessie destroys the generator. But, ah…don't wear a blue jacket, and definitely never, ever put Stevia in your tea.

Chapter Xe

Final EXegesis

"Genghis Khan"

He committed genocide on a scale the world has not seen before or since. Entire civilizations were wiped out off the face of the earth. He and his loyal followers slaughtered ten percent of the human population of the world, nearly half of the population of Asia. Iran did not recover its pre-Mongol population until 1965, more than 700 years after the invasion. With over 40 percent of Asia's farmers butchered, so much cultivated land became forest again that atmospheric carbon dioxide levels plummeted.

He was arguably the single most destructive force the world has ever seen. Yet in Mongolia, Genghis Khan is celebrated as the greatest leader in history. Historians agree that he and his murderous hordes exterminated 40 million human beings. They see in the Mongol Empire an occupying power that directed the course of Asian history for hundreds of years. But they have yet to identify common ground in their assessment of this most successful of dictators. Is he to be considered more evil than Stalin and Hitler, or was he the positive force that unified Asia in a common bond of human productivity?

We could pose similar questions regarding the evolution and death of Walter White. Was he redeemed in the end, or were his crimes of such magnitude as to preclude pardon?

It seems to me reasonable people can build valid arguments for a wide range of conclusions regarding Walter White's final spiritual status. We should expect disagreement and debate. If scholars cannot agree on Genghis Khan's moral standing, should we have any expectation of finding common ground in our assessment of Walter White? I anticipate three schools of thought regarding the final outcome of Walter's life.

Walter Was Redeemed

Churchill, Roosevelt and Stalin at the Yalta Conference
U.S. Defense Department, 1945, PD

Josef Stalin was the detested Bolshevik dictator of Communist Russia during the 1930s, a murderer of millions, but during World War II President Roosevelt referred to him as 'Uncle Joe', throwing him both military and political support. Winston Churchill bristled at the alliance, saying to embrace him as an ally was to 'shake hands with murder', but embrace him they did, and the Soviet Union ended up fighting harder and sacrificing more to destroy Nazism than all of the other allies combined. Some 21 million Russians lost their lives during World War II, roughly 14 percent of the population. For comparison, the United Kingdom lost 450,000 souls, or less than one percent of its population. American fatalities amounted to 415,000 soldiers, sailors, and airmen, or just over a quarter of one percent of the U.S. population. Probably few Russians consider Josef Stalin in any sense a hero, but when I was studying the language and speaking on a regular basis with Russians, there was no question about the greatest scourge the Russian people had ever faced. Placing flowers at the local memorial to the dead heroes of the Great Patriotic War (as World War II is known in Russia) was the almost universally-practiced ritual of just-married couples in the Soviet Union for many decades.

There are valid reasons to consider that Josef Stalin redeemed himself during the War. Indeed, even though he murdered millions of his own people, many Russians consider him a hero to be emulated and admired. I believe we can apply similar reasoning to conclude that Walter White was redeemed by the end of *Breaking Bad*.

Walter committed hundreds of crimes, killed dozens of people, and was indirectly responsible for hundreds of deaths and the suffering of thousands. But in the final episode he sacrificed his own life so Jesse could live. He made sure both of his children would be taken care of financially for the remainder of their lives. He killed nearly a dozen Nazis, which has to be good in just about anybody's book. John 15:13 says, "Greater love hath no man than this, that a man lay down his life for his friends." Walter laid down his life for Jesse, an act we can easily fit into the most stringent definition of love. He poisoned the noxious blue parasite Lydia, an act many would consider positive.

Most of all, Walter demonstrated deep, heartfelt remorse over the death of his brother-in-law, and bitter regret over the suffering he had caused his family. Even Walter's detractors would have to admit his sorrow was deep, genuine, and enduring. In his darkest days he never surrendered devotion to family, he never considered sacrificing Junior, Marie, Skyler, or Hank for his own selfish gain.

For all of these reasons and more, a solid case can be made that Walter offered more than sufficient penance to gain his redemption.

Walter's Disposition is Ambiguous

None of Walter's actions post-Heisenberg rises to the level of earning him redemption, forgiveness, or salvation. He was not performing penance. He was carrying out the mission he had carved out for himself in the first episodes: to provide for his family after his death. Not even his behavior changed. He threatened and coerced Elliott and Gretchen Schwartz into acting as guardians of his children's fortune, he killed anyone standing in his way, as he always had, and he reverted to his misplaced affection for Jesse, sparing his life at the last moment.

We should not be surprised that when he pushed the gun over to Jesse, the young man didn't even want to waste the time or the spiritual energy to kill his former mentor. "You do it," he said. Walter was not worth Jesse's time. His son wished him dead. Marie wished him dead. If Skyler mourned him, she would have been grieving over the man he once was, not the monster he had become. Walter died alone because no one considered him worthy of time, love, or companionship. If the Universe granted him redemption, it was an extraordinary and unexpected act incommensurate with the depth of his evil.

Walter Died Alone and Dispossessed

"The Bad Rich Man in Hell"
James Tissot, 1890

I did not mourn Walter White. I shed no tears for him. I imagine a majority of us feel Walter's gesture to save Jesse and his final ploy to help his children, as well intentioned as they were, fell short of the penance or act of contrition that would have been required to dig himself out of the spiritual pit he created.

Walter had the opportunity to beg Skyler's forgiveness. The thought didn't cross his mind, and he expressed no sorrow. All of the grief he caused his wife and children, the machinations that led to Hank's death, and the dozens of lives innocent and guilty that he eliminated were just things that had to be done so he could make meth. "I did it for me. I liked it. I was good at it." The lies, the murders, the death of hundreds, the suffering of thousands, the sins and crimes beyond measure or account—all of it to serve Walter's pleasure.

To my mind, there is no difference between Walter and the most sadistic killer. The sadist derives pleasure directly from the act of torturing and butchering his victims. Walter derived pleasure from making a drug that led to suffering, crime, murder, and death. Like a vampire or other deadly parasite, he 'was alive' only because he took others' lives.

His apology to Skyler was not an admission of guilt but a declaration of just cause. He found a vocation at which he excelled and the exercise of his rare proficiency justified murder and mayhem. It may or may not be true that he loved Junior and Holly, and maybe even Skyler. Probably Adolf Hitler truly loved Eva Braun. Perhaps, like Walter, he even sacrificed for a brother-in-law. But Hitler was still a demon, and so was Walter White.

Justice versus Karma

I suppose I will do no harm to our examination of *Breaking Bad* if I confess my desire ever since Season Three to experience Hank's triumph over Heisenberg. We're all fortunate I was not in charge of directing the last four episodes, then. The series was stronger by remaining true to its original charter.

Breaking Bad never set out to portray the kind of justice we are used to seeing on the television screen. This was a series dedicated to the study of one man's descent into criminal depravity, and the negative effects he brought to bear on everyone around him. *Breaking Bad* was far more interested in examining a character's capacities for evil than it was in portraying heroism or virtue.

Every human quality in the series must be seen in its relation to the natural power of the Universe. Hank was a hero, but the only reason we know this is his confession to Marie in Season Three: "I swear to God, Marie, I think the Universe is trying to tell me something." *Hank listened to the Universe.* He began cultivating a nature-oriented mindset, studying his crystalline minerals. It's because he listened, and tried to modify his behavior and do as the Universe commanded, that he was entitled to wear natural rust-orange in the final confrontation with Heisenberg and the Nazis. He died a hero because he was true to everything good and just.

Marie didn't listen very well. She continued wearing Princess Purple. But notice the colors she wore in her final confrontation with Skyler. The neck-to-heel black outfit told all of us she was on the most important mission of her life: She demanded that Skyler tell Junior about Walter's crimes.

Walter didn't listen at all. The Universe virtually bombarded him with messages: the impossibly coincidental meeting with Jane's father on the night of her death, the one-eyed teddy bear, the fly, the teddy bear eyeball, the smoke detector light, and on and on. Walter dismissed every transmission and insisted on his own interpretation of events. It was only after his fall that the Universe finally took him on as agent so he could kill Lydia and the Nazis. The final irony in his capacity as agent was to carry out the Universe's will by bringing about his own death.

The karma in Vince Gilligan's *Breaking Bad* Universe has a sparse quality. Marie didn't extract vengeance for Skyler's sins. Most deaths were painless and fast. Walter suffered physically, but not as much as I was imagining he would. Most of the suffering was psychological and spiritual, brought on by the people themselves, not by any act of the Universe.

Moral orientation vis-à-vis the Universe was the attribute under the *Breaking Bad* microscope. Explorations of Hank's heroism or Madrigal's moral innocence would have detracted from the relentless focus on the single-strand connection to the Universe, and would have weakened the series overall. In the heat of the moment, I didn't care about all that. If *Breaking Bad* wasn't going to allow Hank to bring Heisenberg to justice, I at least wanted the show to give him a decent funeral. If the writers suggested corporate-wide guilt among Madrigal executives, I wanted to see this play out.

On both fronts I was stymied and disappointed. But in imagining scenarios in which there was an emotional funeral or several scenes demonstrating Madrigal's innocence, I see how the full effect of Walter's disengagement with the Universe would have been diluted. Ultimately the integrity of the show was maintained by *not* having a funeral and by leaving open the question of others' complicity or innocence. Unless a character arc required direct interaction with the Universe, there was no need to complete it or demonstrate any kind of disposition relative to innocence or guilt.

Respect the Chemistry

For six years Walter told us to 'Respect the chemistry'. But I think Jesse's position on good science might be the more important bit of advice for us in considering the totality of *Breaking Bad*:

> This is glass grade. I mean...you got crystals in here two inches,
> three inches long. This is pure glass. You're a damn artist! This is
> art, Mr. White!

Breaking Bad is glass grade through and through. I felt privileged over the last six years to spend 1200 hours of my life with the best damn artists—and the best damn chemists—I've ever known: the writers and cast and crew of this most entertaining and thought-provoking of television productions. I doff my proverbial cap to you, artists and chemists all.

Pearson Moore
January 2014

Epilogue

What is the sound of one hand clapping?

As you have gathered from the tone of this book, I consider that any of us trying to make sense of *Breaking Bad* are participants in the drama, not merely viewers or observers. In fact, my strong bias is to believe that no one attempting legitimate understanding of noteworthy drama can simply sit back and allow the story to wash over her. She must be involved, she must participate.

"Crossed Book and Quill"
United States Navy, 2011, PD

In the same way, writing is not an exercise I conduct in a vacuum. As readers of this book, you are participants no less than me, the publisher, Martin Woutisseth, Michael Rainey, or anyone else connected with this work. In fact, your participation in this book is more important than mine. I speak here not of any academic theory of communication, but of very practical matters related to the give-and-take that brings form and substance to the world of writing and publishing. **You** are vital to that enterprise.

This book is independently written and published. I do not work for any writing house or publisher. While this affords me a tremendous degree of freedom in the types of books I can offer you, it also means that my books are not backed by any advertising department.

As you may have guessed, *you* are the advertising department for this book, and for any books I have written. Fortunately, though, you are not obliged to work eight hours a day as part of your participation in this book. In fact, if you commit to nothing more than *four or five minutes of your time*, you **can have an extraordinary impact on this book** and its ability to reach other interested reader-participants.

If you found this book entertaining, useful, or helpful in your enjoyment or understanding of *Breaking Bad*, I would be grateful if you could visit the online retailer where you purchased this book. Go to that retailer's page for this book, *Breaking Blue*, and leave a brief review.

Honest reviews by customers have a greater impact on sales (and therefore book availability) than any other form of advertising, including celebrity endorsements. I would rather receive your honest review than the endorsement of any actor or celebrity associated with *Breaking Bad*, because your review is far more helpful.

Use any criteria you wish to attach a point value (or number of stars or whatever system is used at the retailer). If you wish me to write more books of this type in the future, a 4- or 5-star rating will be most helpful to achieving your goal. But I will be grateful for any honest review.

Reviews are precious to me, and to every independent writer. Your review counts, and counts a lot. I typically sell over 1200 copies of a book before receiving a single review. That means very slow sales, but more importantly, it means that people who might otherwise have enjoyed the book will never get to read it. So, do your part! Help others enjoy this book, and voice your opinion regarding the value of my contribution to our *Breaking Bad* dialog: Leave an honest review of this book.

Thank you so much for considering this request.

<u>Participant Notes</u>

Participant Notes

Printed in Great Britain
by Amazon.co.uk, Ltd.,
Marston Gate.